Windows NT® and HP-UX System Administrator's "How To" Book

Hewlett-Packard Professional Books

Atchison	Object-Oriented Test & Measurement Software Development in C++
Blinn	Portable Shell Programming: An Extensive Collection of Bourne Shell Examples
Blommers	Practical Planning for Network Growth
Caruso	Power Programming in HP OpenView: Developing CMIS Applications
Cook	Building Enterprise Information Architectures
Costa	Planning and Designing High Speed Networks Using 100VG-AnyLAN, Second Edition
Crane	A Simplified Approach to Image Processing: Classical and Modern Techniques
Fernandez	Configuring the Common Desktop Environment
Fristrup	USENET: Netnews for Everyone
Fristrup	The Essential Web Surfer Survival Guide
Grady	Practical Software Metrics for Project Management and Process Improvement
Grosvenor, Ichiro, O'Brien	Mainframe Downsizing to Upsize Your Business: IT-Preneuring
Gunn	A Guide to NetWare® for UNIX®
Helsel	Graphical Programming: A Tutorial for HP VEE
Helsel	Visual Programming with HP VEE, Second Edition
Holman, Lund	Instant JavaScript
Kane	PA-RISC 2.0 Architecture
Knouse	Practical DCE Programming
Lee	The ISDN Consultant: A Stress-Free Guide to High-Speed Communications
Lewis	The Art & Science of Smalltalk
Lund	Integrating UNIX® and PC Network Operating Systems
Madell	Disk and File Management Tasks on HP-UX
Mahoney	High-Mix Low-Volume Manufacturing
Malan, Letsinger, Coleman	Object-Oriented Development at Work: Fusion in the Real World
McFarland	X Windows on the World: Developing Internationalized Software with X, Motif®, and CDE
McMinds/Whitty	Writing Your Own OSF/Motif Widgets
Mikkelsen /Pherigo	Practical Software Configuration Management: The Latenight Developer's Handbook
Norton, DiPasquale	Thread Time: The Multithreaded Programming Guide
Phaal	LAN Traffic Management
Pipkin	Halting the Hacker: A Practical Guide to Computer Security
Poniatowski	The HP-UX System Administrator's "How To" Book
Poniatowski	HP-UX 10.x System Administration "How To" Book
Poniatowski	Learning the HP-UX Operating System
Poniatowski	Windows NT® and HP-UX System Administrator's "How To" Book
Ryan	Distributed Object Technology: Concepts and Applications
Thomas	Cable Television Proof-of-Performance: A Practical Guide to Cable TV Compliance Measurements Using a Spectrum Analyzer
Weygant	Clusters for High Availability: A Primer of HP-UX Solutions
Witte	Electronic Test Instruments
Yawn, Stachnick, Sellars	The Legacy Continues: Using the HP 3000 with HP-UX and Windows NT

WINDOWS NT® AND HP-UX SYSTEM ADMINISTRATOR'S "HOW TO" BOOK

Marty Poniatowski

To join a Prentice Hall PTR Internet
mailing list, point to:

http://www.prenhall.com/mail_lists/

Prentice Hall PTR
Upper Saddle River, NJ 07458
http://www.prenhall.com

Library of Congress Cataloging-in-Publication Data
Poniatowski, Marty.
    Windows NT and HP-UX system administrator's how-to book /
Marty Poniatowski.
      p. cm.
    Includes index.
    ISBN 0-13-861709-0 (pbk. : alk. paper)
    1. Microsoft Windows NT. 2. HP-UX. 3. Operating systems
(Computers)
    QA76.76.O63P655   1997
    005.4'469--dc21   97-9550
                                                CIP

Editorial/production supervision: *Patti Guerrieri*
Cover design director: *Jerry Votta*
Cover designer: *Talar Agasyan*
Manufacturing manager: *Alexis R. Heydt*
Marketing manager: *Miles Williams*
Acquisitions editor: *Karen Gettman*
Editorial assistant: *Barbara Alfieri*
Manager, Hewlett-Packard Press: *Patricia Pekary*

Published by Prentice Hall PTR
Prentice-Hall, Inc.
A Simon & Schuster Company
Upper Saddle River, NJ 07458

The publisher offers discounts on this book when ordered in bulk quantities.
For more information, contact: Corporate Sales Department, Phone: 800-382-3419;
Fax: 201-236-7141; E-mail: corpsales@prenhall.com; or write: Prentice Hall PTR,
Corp. Sales Dept., One Lake Street, Upper Saddle River, NJ 07458.

HP-UX is a Hewlett-Packard registered trademark. Microsoft, Windows NT, and MS/DOS are
registered trademarks of Microsoft Corporation. OS/2 is a registered trademark of International
Business Machines Corporation. FrameMaker is a registered trademark of Adobe Systems
Incorporated. All other products or services mentioned in this book are the trademarks or service
marks of their respective companies or organizations.

Printed in the United States of America
10 9 8 7 6 5 4 3 2

ISBN 0-13-861709-0

Prentice-Hall International (UK) Limited, *London*
Prentice-Hall of Australia Pty. Limited, *Sydney*
Prentice-Hall Canada Inc., *Toronto*
Prentice-Hall Hispanoamericana, S.A., *Mexico*
Prentice-Hall of India Private Limited, *New Delhi*
Prentice-Hall of Japan, Inc., *Tokyo*
Simon & Schuster Asia Pte. Ltd., *Singapore*
Editora Prentice-Hall do Brasil, Ltda., *Rio de Janeiro*

PREFACE   **xvii**

The Book   xvii

The Approach   xix

Examples and Systems   xx

Operating System Releases   xx

Chapters in This Book   xxi

Conventions Used in the Book   xxii

Acknowledgments   xxiv
Dick Watts   xxiv
Charlie Fernandez   xxiv
The Author - Marty Poniatowski   xxv
Reviewers   xxv

CHAPTER 1   **Setting Up Your Windows NT System**   **1**

Introduction   1

Setup Flowchart   2
Confirm Windows NT Support for Your Hardware (F1)   5
Have Background Information Ready (F2)   5
Create Three Setup Floppies (F3)   5

Loading Windows NT   8

Boot System From Installation Floppy (F4)   8

Text Based Portion of Setup (F5)   9
    NTFS and FAT   16

Graphical (Windows NT) Based Portion of Setup   22

Gather Information About System (F6)   22

Install Windows NT Networking (F7)   25
    TCP/IP Networking Background   27
    Internet Protocol (IP) Addressing   31

Finish Setup (F8)   34

Loading Other Software   36

HP Netserver Navigator   39

CHAPTER 2   Setting Up Your HP-UX System   41

Using the Setup Flowchart   44

Assemble Team (F1)   45

Inspect Site and Assemble Hardware (F2)   46

Hardware Configuration   *47*
Software Configuration   *47*
Order Documentation   *48*

Install HP-UX 10.x(F3)   48

Loading HP-UX 10.x Software on Series 700   *49*
Loading HP-UX 10.x Software on Series 800   *59*
Installing Software with Software Distributor-HP-UX   *69*

Build an HP-UX Kernel (F4)   84

Configure Additional Peripherals (F5)   90

All About Device Files   *90*

System Startup and Shutdown (F6)   99

System Shutdown   *104*

CHAPTER 3   **Windows NT File System Layout**   **109**

Windows NT File System Layout   109

NTFS and FAT   110

New Technology File System (NTFS)   *110*
File Allocation Table (FAT) File System   *112*

Using the Windows NT File Systems   114

Starting Windows NT Explorer   115

Viewing Properties with Windows NT Explorer   117

Attributes (under General Area of Properties)   120

Security (under Properties)   121

Permissions (under Security Area of Properties)   123

Auditing (under Security Area of Properties)   127

Chapter 4   The HP-UX File System Layout   133

HP-UX File Types   133

Text Files   134

Data Files   135

Source Code File   135

Executable Files   137

Shell Programs   138

Links   139

Device Files   140

The **file** Command   140

File System Layout   143

CHAPTER 5   Windows NT File System Management   155

Introduction   155

Disk Administration Tasks and Windows NT Disk Administrator   155

Windows NT Disk Management Terms   156

Windows NT Disk Administrator   158

Volume Properties   161

Create a Partition   163

Be Careful with Mark Active   168

Create a Repair Disk   169

CHAPTER 6   HP-UX File System Management   171

Logical Volume Manager Background   171

Viewing File Systems with bdf   187

File System Maintenance with fsck   188

Initialize with mediainit   192

CHAPTER 7   Windows NT System Administration Tools   195

Windows NT Administration   195

True for Any Windows NT System Administration Tool   196

Access to Common Administrative Tools   197

Control Panel   200

MS DOS Console   202

Devices   204

Network   205

Networking Commands   208

Services   212

Printers   214

Tape Devices - An Example of Using Control Panel   215

Administrative Tools (Common)   221

Administrative Wizards   221

Backup   223

Disk Administrator   242

Event Viewer   243

Performance Monitor   248

User Manager for Domains   248

The Registry   261

CHAPTER 8   HP-UX System Administration Manager (SAM)   267

SAM Overview   267

Running and Using SAM as Superuser   269

Running Restricted SAM Builder   274

Accounts for Users and Groups   277

Assigning Users to Groups   280

Adding a User   285

Adding a Group   288

Auditing and Security   289

Audited Events and Audited System Calls   292

Audited Users   294

System Security Policies   294

Backup and Recovery   296

Scheduling a Backup   297

Interactive Backup and Recovery   303

Performing a Restore   305

Disks and File Systems   306

Disk Devices   308

File Systems   310

Logical Volumes   311

Swap   313

Volume Groups   313

Kernel Configuration   313

Configurable Parameters   316

Drivers   317

Dump Devices   318

Subsystems   319

Networking and Communications   321

Bootable Devices   323

Internet Addresses   325

Network Interface Cards   326

Network Services   327

Network File Systems   328

System Access   329

UUCP   331

Peripheral Devices   332

Cards   334

Device List   336

Tape Drives   339

Terminals and Modems   339

Uninterruptable Power Supplies   340

Printers and Plotters   341

Print Requests   342

Printers and Plotters   342

Save/Restore Spooler Configuration   346

Process Management   346

Performance Monitors   348

Process Control   352

Scheduling Cron Jobs 355

Routine Tasks   357

Backup and Recovery   359

Find and Remove Unused Filesets   359

Selective File Removal   360

System Log Files   363

System Shutdown   365

Run SAM on Remote Systems   365

Software Management   366

Copy Software to Local Depot   368

Install Software to Local Host   370

List Software   371

Remove Software   372

Time   372

NFS Diskless Concepts   372

ENWARE X-station Administration (optional)   374

CHAPTER 9   Windows NT Performance Overview   377

Performance Monitor - Charting   377

Performance Monitor - Proactive with Alerts   384

Performance Monitor - Logging   386

CHAPTER 10   HP-UX Performance Overview   389

Where Are Your HP-UX System Resources Going?   389
System Components   391
Commands and Tools for Determining How System Resources Are Being Used   393
Taking Inventory   395

Standard HP-UX Commands   396
I/O and CPU Statistics with iostat   397
Virtual Memory Statistics with vmstat   399
Network Statistics with netstat   401
Network Statistics with landiag and lanadmin   406
Check Processes with ps   407
Show Remote Mounts with showmount   410
Show Swap with swapinfo   412
sar: The System Activity Reporter   414
timex to Analyze a Command   415

HP GlancePlus/UX   415

    Global Screen Description   417

    CPU Detail Screen Description   422

    Memory Detail Screen Description   425

    Disk Detail Screen Description   428

    GlancePlus Summary   431

    What Should I Look For When Using GlancePlus?   431

CHAPTER 11   **Windows NT User Environment**   **435**

The Environment in General   435

Start at the Beginning with *Start*   438

Windows NT Explorer   439

Task Manager   449

CHAPTER 12   **HP-UX Common Desktop Environment**   **455**

Common Desktop Environment   455

Why a Graphical User Interface (GUI)?   456

    The Relationship among X, Motif, and CDE   458

    The X Window System   459

    Motif   459

    CDE   460

X, Motif, and CDE Configuration Files   461

How Configuration Files Play Together   472

Specifying Appearance and Behavior   475

The Sequence of Events When CDE Starts   476

Customizing CDE   477

CDE and Performance   487

Conclusion   492

CHAPTER 13 Windows NT and HP-UX Interoperability - The X Window System

493

Interoperability Topics   493

Why the X Window System?   496

X Window System Background   496

X Server Software   497

CHAPTER 14   Windows NT and HP-UX Interoperability - Networking   505

Why Cover Interoperability?   505

NFS Background   506

Using Windows NT and HP-UX Networking   509

File Transfer Protocol (FTP)   514

Other Connection Topics   521

CHAPTER 15   **Windows NT and HP-UX Interoperability -**

                            Advanced Server 9000   **527**

Windows NT Functionality on HP-UX   527

Installing Advanced Server/9000   530

Sharing a Printer   537

Sharing a File System   540

CHAPTER 16   **Windows NT and HP-UX Interoperability - Posix Utilities   545**

cat   547

chmod   549

cp   551

find   552

grep   553

ls   554

mkdir   558

mv   559

rm   560

touch   561

wc   562

Chapter 17   **Windows NT and HP-UX Interoperability -**

                            SoftBench OpenStudio   **563**

HP SoftBench Openstudio - Client / Server Comes to the Development Environment   563

Four Key Features of SoftBench OpenStudio   564

Manipulating HP-UX Source Code   565

Conclusion   569

INDEX   **571**

PREFACE

The Book

Welcome to *The Windows NT and HP-UX System Administrator's "How To" Book.* This book provides you with the information you need to get started quickly with Microsoft® Windows NT® and Hewlett Packard's HP-UX.

The topics I chose to cover in this book represent the common denominator of tasks that most all system administrators will need to perform. If a task needs to be performed by more than 90 percent of system administrators, there is a strong possibility it is in this book. If, on the other hand, a task needs to performed by less than 50 percent of system administrators, it is unlikely I included it in this book. I want to get you up and running quickly and leave the more obscure and advanced topics to other resources such as the manual sets for these two operating systems.

Most of the topics covered in this book are first covered for Windows NT in a chapter and then covered for HP-UX in a separate chapter. Some topics, such as Windows NT - HP-UX interoperability are covered in chapters dedicated to this topic. I covered many of the topics in separate chapters because you may be a Windows NT expert and wish to see a topic covered for HP-UX, or vice versa. I do not cover a topic first for Windows NT and then for HP-UX because I want you to compare the chapters. One to one comparisons between operating systems is usually dangerous because you begin judging an operating system based on what someone has written. For instance, the topic of system administration tools should not be compared for the two operating systems. HP-UX has the System Administration Manager (SAM) which is an umbrella administration tool in which almost all aspects of system administration can be performed. Windows NT has administration tools in many different areas. These two chapters are, therefore, organized differently

Could I ever cover every aspect of system administration in this book? Could any system administration book ever cover everything you need to know about system administration for any operating system? The answer of course, is no. In fact I often find the longer the book, the less useful information it contains and the more extraneous information it contains. The Windows NT book and HP-UX book I own with the greatest "thud factor" are the two least useful I own on these topics. Since I couldn't possibly cover every aspect of system administration, I will instead cover what I believe are the most important topics. There are guidelines in system administration, but there is too little structure in system administration for me to provide you with an exact list of tasks to perform. No matter how detailed a training course or manual, they always leave out some of the specific tasks you'll need to perform. Instead of getting mired down in excruciating detail, I'll provide the common denominator of information every system administrator needs to know. I'll provide you with all the essential information you need so you'll be able to take on new and unforeseen system administration challenges with a good knowledge base.

You may very well find that you'll need additional resources as your system administration challenges increase. No matter what anyone tells you, there is no one resource that can answer everything you need to know about system administration for these operating systems. Just when you think you know everything there is to know about system administration, you'll be asked to do something you've never dreamed of before. That's why I'm not trying to be all things to all people with this book. I cover what everyone needs to know and leave topics in specific areas to other people. You may need training courses, manuals, other books, or consulting services to complete some projects. In any case, I'll bet that every topic in this book will be worthwhile to know for every system administrator.

I include information from a variety of sources. One of the most common sources is the on line help of Windows NT and the manual pages in HP-UX. The developers of these operating systems did a fine job providing on-line information that is helpful and easy to access. I took advantage of this useful information.

The Approach

To those of you who have read my books in the past you know I like to start at the beginning. This seems to be obvious and make perfect sense, yet I have seen very few operating system books which start at the beginning. Most assume you already have the operating system installed and begin covering system administration procedures.

To me, the beginning is loading the operating system. I don't much care about the background of operating systems; I just want to use them. The installation chapters for both operating systems covered in this book include an installation flowchart. This will help you visualize the topics covered in the chapter. As part of installing an operating system there is background information that you need to know in order to proceed. Although I don't like to diverge too much from the installation process, I will provide this background information where necessary. For instance, in Chapter 1 I cover installing Windows NT. You reach a point in this installation where you must select the type of file system you wish to install. At this point I provide some background into the two selections you have for file system types.

Information sometimes appears in two places. The file system types covered as part of Windows NT installation also appear in the file systems chapter. I do this because I don't want you to have to flip back and forth between chapters. When I perform a process I like to follow the process straight through and not have to flip back and forth between chapters.

The book in general is a blueprint for performing system administration of Windows NT and HP-UX. The blueprint includes the setup flowcharts I earlier mentioned, and many tips and recommendations from my experience working with these operating systems as well as what I have learned from the many knowledgable system administrators with whom I have worked. I recommend you do the same and make liberal use of the on-line information.

Examples and Systems

When I introduce a Windows NT topic, I usually do so on a modest, stan-dalone Window NT system. This is so you can see the process of perform-ing such tasks as configuring a backup from scratch, or setting up the Performance Monitor for the first time.

The same holds true for HP-UX. Many topics are introduced on a small workstation and server system and some topics are covered in a more advanced fashion, such as performance examples, on a real production sys-tem.

I have always taken great care to introduce topics in such a way that you get the information you need to become familiar with the topic and show examples that will allow you to quickly perform the tasks associated with the topic on your system. This doesn't mean you'll be an expert on the topic after reading a chapter and trying it out on your system. It means you will quickly gain some familiarization on the topic and be in a good posi-tion to get started with this topic on your system.

Operating System Releases

The vast majority of examples in this book use Windows NT 4.x and HP-UX 10.x operating system releases. In general, the system administration topics covered are operating system release independent. This means that the tasks you would perform as part of a topic do not vary dramatically from release to release of the operating system.

I use examples liberally throughout this book in order to describe how to perform a task. If you are using different versions of the operating system than I am using in an example, this should not reduce the effectiveness of the example. This is because the fundamental system administration tasks you perform remain the same from release to release of an operating system. Only the "wrapper" of a system administration tool tends to change from release to release, such as specific menu picks, and not the underlying task you are performing.

Chapters in This Book

The Windows NT and HP-UX System Administrator's "How To" Book is comprised of the following chapters:

- Chapter 1: Setting Up Your Windows NT System

- Chapter 2: Setting Up Your HP-UX System

- Chapter 3: Windows NT File System Layout

- Chapter 4: HP-UX File System Layout

- Chapter 5: Windows NT File System Management

- Chapter 6: HP-UX File System Management

- Chapter 7: Windows NT System Administration Tools

- Chapter 8: HP-UX System Administration Manager (SAM)

- Chapter 9: Windows NT Performance Overview

- Chapter 10: HP-UX Performance Overview

- Chapter 11: Windows NT User Environment

- Chapter 12: HP-UX Common Desktop Environment

- Chapter 13: Windows NT and HP-UX Interoperability - X Window System

- Chapter 14: Windows NT and HP-UX Interoperability - Networking

- Chapter 15: Windows NT and HP-UX Interoperability - Advanced Server 9000

- Chapter 16: Windows NT and HP-UX Interoperability - POSIX Utlities

- Chapter 17: Windows NT and HP-UX Interoperability - Software Development with SoftBench OpenStudio

Two chapters that work together and build on one another are Chapters 13 and 14. In Chapter 13 I cover Windows NT and HP-UX interoperability by running an X server program on a Windows NT system which provides graphical access to an HP-UX system. Then, in Chapter 14, I use a networking product on the Windows NT system that provides transparent access to the data on the HP-UX system using Network File System (NFS). Using X Windows you have a graphical means of connecting a Windows NT system to an HP-UX system and using NFS you have a way of easily accessing the data between these two systems. These two technologies, X Windows and NFS, provide the foundation for a variety of other useful interoperability between the two operating systems.

Conventions Used in the Book

I don't use a lot of complex notations in the book. Here are a few simple conventions I've used to make the examples clear and the text easy to follow:

italics   Italics are used primarily to denote menu picks and selections in dialog boxes, and the names of system administration programs. In the *Windows NT Disk Administrator* section of Chapter 5, for instance, you see *Tools - Properties...* which is the *Properties...* pick from the *Tools* menu. In that same chapter you are instructed to use the *Check Now* box in a dialog box. In the HP-UX System Administration Manager (SAM) chapter italics is also used extensively when referring to menu picks and functional areas.

$ and #
       The HP-UX command prompt. Every command issued in the book is preceded by one of these prompts.

bold and " "
       Bold text is the information you would type, such as the command you issue after a prompt or the information you would type when running a script. Sometimes information you would type is also referred to in the text explaining it and the typed information may appear in quotes. Path names are always in bold for both Windows NT and HP-UX.

<---
       When selections have to be made, this indicates the one chosen for the purposes of the example.

Acknowledgments

There were too many people involved in helping me with this book to list them all. I have decided to formally thank those who wrote sections of the book and those who took time to review it. I'm still not sure if it takes more time to write something or review something that has been written to ensure it is correct. Aside from the reviewers and those who wrote sections of the book I must thank my manager John Perwinc. Not only did John put up with my writing this book, but he also encouraged me to write both this book and my previous books. He also sponsored the training I required to gain the knowledge to write this book and supported me in every way possible.

A group that requires special thanks is my family who put up with a workstation on our kitchen table for the year I was writing this book and for putting up with the many late nights I spent at customer sites and HP offices working on the book.

Dick Watts

Dick is a Senior Vice President of Hewlett-Packard Company and General Manager of the Computer Systems Organization (CSO). Dick acted as the executive sponsor of the book. His support was invaluable in helping get the resources necessary to complete this book.

Charlie Fernandez

Charlie has been working in the graphical user interface area for the last ten years, first as a technical writer for HP X Window System documentation, then as a product manager for HP VUE, multimedia, and collaboration, and most recently as the Strategic Planner for desktop, multimedia, and collaboration.

He wrote *Configuring the Common Desktop Environment* published by Prentice Hall. Charlie's book is a practical guide to understanding and working with all CDE files to tailor the CDE desktop to your end-user environment needs. Charlie's book is a requirement if you're going to be doing any work with CDE.

The Author - Marty Poniatowski

Marty has been a Technical Consultant with Hewlett Packard for ten years in the New York area. He has worked with hundreds of Hewlett Packard customers in many industries including on line services, financial and manufacturing.

Marty has been widely published in computer industry trade publications. He has published over 50 articles on various computer-related topics. In addition to this book, he is the author of three other Prentice Hall books: *Learning the HP-UX Operating System* (1996); *The HP-UX 10.x System Administrator's "How To" Book*(1995); and *The HP-UX System Administrator's "How To" Book*(1993).

Marty holds an M.S. in Information Systems from Polytechnic University (Brooklyn, NY), an M.S. in Management Engineering from the University of Bridgeport (Bridgeport, CT), and a B.S. in Electrical Engineering from Roger Williams University (Bristol, RI).

Reviewers

I'm not sure what makes someone agree to review a book. You don't get the glory of a contributing author but it is just as much work. I would like to thank the many people who devoted a substantial amount of time to reviewing this book to ensure I included the topics important to new system administrators and covered those topics accurately.

Special thanks goes to Donna Kelly of Hewlett Packard in Roseville, CA. Donna performed a careful technical review of the entire manuscript. Donna has extensive experience with many operating systems including HP-UX, Windows NT, MPE, and AS/400.

Other reviewers of the manuscript I would like to thank are: Brian Beckwith of Dow Jones & Company; Suneal Verma of Hummingbird Communications; Eric Roseme of Hewlett Packard; Jerry Duggan of Hewlett Packard; and David Fahrland of Hewlett Packard.

CHAPTER 1

Setting Up
Your Windows NT System

Introduction

You are going to have a great time setting up your Windows NT system(s). Installing Windows NT Server and Windows NT Workstation are similar processes and you can use the setup example in this chapter for both types of installations. Installing Windows NT is easy. Most of the installation process involves answering questions about your configuration and what you would like to install. You are asked to make decisions along the way about the way in which you would like your system configured. As long as you understand the questions, you should have no problem proceeding with the installation.

The example installation that I provide in this chapter uses Windows NT 4.x. The installation procedure changes from revision to revision of Windows NT; however, the installation process is similar for different revisions of Windows NT so you can expect your installation process to be similar to that which I show in this chapter.

The installation process is not complex; however, you will have to answer several questions. Therefore, what I have chosen to do is structure this chapter similar to an engineering notebook. I record all of the steps as I perform them, as you would in a notebook, but I don't cover a lot of background because the process of installing Windows NT is not complex.

The Windows NT systems I have worked with are used for a variety of purposes. Some are stand alone systems that interact minimally with other Windows NT, HP-UX, or personal computers. Some are large networks of Windows NT systems that share data and other resources. I have even worked with one production installation that consisted of a distributed Windows NT application on which some modules of the application ran on one Windows NT system and other parts ran on other Windows NT systems.

In all of these installations there is a base level of Windows NT knowledge that is necessary to set up and maintain a successful environment. And this is what I cover in the Windows NT portion of this book - **the common denominator of Windows NT knowledge that applies to all systems**.

Setup Flowchart

To help you understand the tasks you will have to perform I have included a flowchart for setting up Windows NT systems. One of the most intimidating aspects to setting up a new system is that there are so many tasks to perform, it is easy to get lost in the detail. Figure 1-1 helps put in perspective the tasks to be performed and the sequence of performing them. I hope this helps make your setup more manageable.

The installation requires you to know some background information in order to make some of the decisions. What I have done is include the background in the appropriate setup step. This way you're not reading background information for the sake of reading background information. Instead, you're reading background information that applies to a specific setup step. An example of this is providing background information about the file system type you will use for Windows NT. You have two choices and I give you a rundown on both during this step in the installation process. Similarly, TCP/IP may be new to some of you so I include some background in this area at the appropriate time.

Although I can't include every possible step you might need to perform, I have included the steps common to most installations. If a step is irrelevant to your site, you can skip it. Based on the many installations I have performed, I think I have discovered the common denominator of most installations. In any event, you can use the flow diagram in Figure 1-1 as an effective step-by-step approach to getting your system(s) up and running.

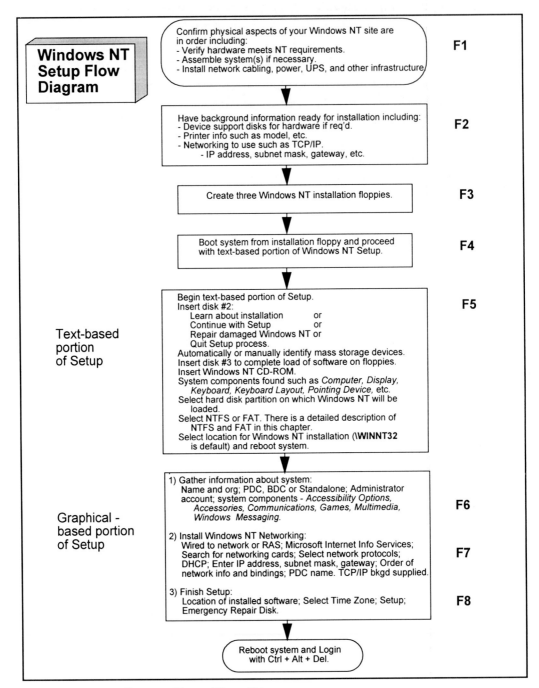

Windows NT Setup Flow Diagram

Confirm physical aspects of your Windows NT site are in order including:
- Verify hardware meets NT requirements.
- Assemble system(s) if necessary.
- Install network cabling, power, UPS, and other infrastructure.

F1

Have background information ready for installation including:
- Device support disks for hardware if req'd.
- Printer info such as model, etc.
- Networking to use such as TCP/IP.
  - IP address, subnet mask, gateway, etc.

F2

Create three Windows NT installation floppies.

F3

Boot system from installation floppy and proceed with text-based portion of Windows NT Setup.

F4

Text-based portion of Setup

Begin text-based portion of Setup.
Insert disk #2:
    Learn about installation   or
    Continue with Setup   or
    Repair damaged Windows NT or
    Quit Setup process.
Automatically or manually identify mass storage devices.
Insert disk #3 to complete load of software on floppies.
Insert Windows NT CD-ROM.
System components found such as *Computer, Display, Keyboard, Keyboard Layout, Pointing Device*, etc.
Select hard disk partition on which Windows NT will be loaded.
Select NTFS or FAT. There is a detailed description of NTFS and FAT in this chapter.
Select location for Windows NT installation (**\WINNT32** is default) and reboot system.

F5

Graphical - based portion of Setup

1) Gather information about system:
    Name and org; PDC, BDC or Standalone; Administrator account; system components - *Accessibility Options, Accessories, Communications, Games, Multimedia, Windows Messaging.*

F6

2) Install Windows NT Networking:
    Wired to network or RAS; Microsoft Internet Info Services; Search for networking cards; Select network protocols; DHCP; Enter IP address, subnet mask, gateway; Order of network info and bindings; PDC name. TCP/IP bkgd supplied.

F7

3) Finish Setup:
    Location of installed software; Select Time Zone; Setup; Emergency Repair Disk.

F8

Reboot system and Login with Ctrl + Alt + Del.

Figure 1-1 System Setup Flow Diagram

Confirm Windows NT Support For Your Hardware (F1)

There are a minimal set of hardware requirements for Windows NT. There are two forms of Windows NT: Windows NT Workstation and Windows NT Server. There are different hardware requirements for each. In addition, you can run Windows NT on an Intel-based computer (one running the X86 instruction set), or a Reduced Instruction Set Computer (RISC). There are different requirements for each of these hardware platforms as well. See that these systems are properly assembled. You also have to consider all aspects of ensuring that your site is prepared to accept the systems for installation.

Have Background Information Ready (F2)

As with any other system installation, you need to perform some background work before you begin the installation. You should have handy device support disks if you think you may be using hardware for which there are no drivers on your Windows NT CD-ROM. If, for instance, you have a new SCSI adapter, you should have a device support disk ready before you begin the installation. If Windows NT identifies a SCSI adapter at the time of installation for which it does not have support, you will be prompted to insert a device support disk.

You also want to have all networking information such as IP address, subnet mask, default gateway, and host name for TCP/IP configuration.

Create Three Setup Floppies (F3)

You produce three Setup floppies that are used to install Windows NT along with the CD-ROM. To produce these floppies with the CD-ROM from the command line, you would issue the following command:

F:\I386\winnt32 /ox

In this example **F:** is the CD-ROM and the **winnt32** program in the **I386** directory is used to create the floppies. Figure 1-2 shows the window you see when you first issue this command.

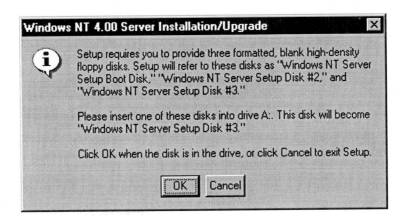

Figure 1-2 Creating Three Windows NT Installation Floppies

winnt32 has several options. You can view these by using the **/?** option to **winnt32**. An area where I have found Windows NT to be strong is in the on-line help. You don't get excruciating detail; you just get a quick explanation for the command and options so you can proceed. Here are some of the basic options to **winnt32**. To see all of the options type **winnt32 /?**.

Winnt32.exe - Installation or upgrade of Windows NT.

Options

/b	Boot files are loaded on the hard disk rather than floppy.
/e: command	Install Windows NT and the run the specified command.
/i: inf_file	The file name of the setup information.
/ox	Create boot floppies as in the example in this chapter.
/s: sourcepath	Specify the location of Windows NT source files.
/r: directory	Install in the additional directory specified.
/t: drive letter	Temporary files are sent to this drive.
/u	Upgrades Windows NT in unattended mode. You could do this in order to upgrade to a new version of Windows NT without installing.
/u: script	Update using a script for user settings rather than taking user settings from existing system.
/x	Don't create boot floppies.

The floppies are produced in reverse order. You are instructed to insert floppy number 3 first, and floppy number 1 last. The first of the three Setup floppies is sometimes called the "Setup Boot Disk". To begin the Windows NT installation you would boot your computer from this floppy.

Using the **/u** option, you could upgrade to a newer version of Windows NT.

Loading Windows NT

In the following example I load Windows NT 4.x on an HP Vectra. I included many of the screens that you would see when loading Windows NT. Even though you may be using a different version of Windows NT, it is useful to see these screens so you get a feel for the process of loading Windows NT, the type of information that is reported to you during the software load, and the type of information that is requested of you.

This example takes place using the three setup floppies I earlier produced and the Windows NT 4.x CD-ROM.

Boot System from Installation Floppy (F4)

After inserting the first of the three floppies, sometimes called the "Setup Boot Disk", and turning on the computer, it booted and quickly made its way to the screen shown in Figure 1-3.

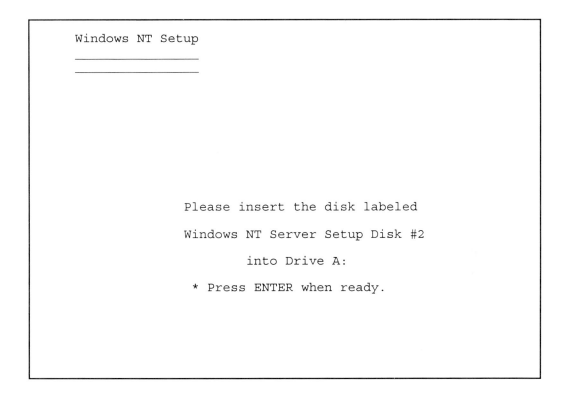

Windows NT Setup

Please insert the disk labeled

Windows NT Server Setup Disk #2

into Drive A:

* Press ENTER when ready.

Figure 1-3 Screen of Windows NT Setup Disk #1 (Setup Boot Disk)

When the Setup Boot Disk completes its work, you insert Windows Setup Boot Disk #2.

Text-Based Portion of Setup (F5)

After inserting disk #2 you see the files loaded in the lower part of the screen. You will see messages about such drivers as SCSI, video, keyboard, and others being loaded. These messages fly by at a rapid rate. Figure 1-4 shows one of the initial messages you see.

```
Windows NT Setup
_____
_____




















Setup is loading files (Windows NT Setup)...
```

Figure 1-4 Messages Fly By with Setup Disk #2

You reach a point in the procedure where Windows NT is giving you options on how to proceed as shown in Figure 1-5.

```
Windows NT Setup
_____
_____


Welcome to Setup.

The Setup program for the Microsoft(R) Windows NT(TM)operating
system version 4.x prepares Windows NT to run on your computer.


  - To learn more about Windows NT Setup before continuing, press F1.

  - To set up Windows NT now, press ENTER.

  - To repair a damaged Windows NT version 4.x installation, press R.

  - To quit Setup without installing Windows NT, press F3.




ENTER=Continue  R=Repair  F1=Help  F3=Exit
```

Figure 1-5 Setup Options

If you select F1 you can read several pages about Windows NT Setup under the heading of Setup Help. I would recommend reading Setup Help the first time you load Windows NT. Among the useful information described in Setup Help is that there is a text-based portion and a Windows NT-based portion of Setup. Setup performs the following tasks in the text-based portion:

• Identifies correct hardware settings for your computer.

• Confirms selection of partitions for your hard disks (we'll get into partitions soon.)

• Confirms file system to be used on disk partition that contains Windows NT (file systems are discussed in detail in this chapter.)

• Confirms directory in which you will store Windows NT files.

• Copies essential Windows NT files to your hard disk.

The text-based portion of Windows NT also selects appropriate settings for you. The items for which settings are selected for you include:

- Mouse

- Printer

- Printer port

- Keyboard and layout

- Network adapter card, IRQ, and base port address

- Computer name and domain (you will have to set these)

We'll now go ahead and proceed with the Windows NT setup by pressing *Enter*.

Setup will next detect mass storage devices automatically if you press *Enter*. If, however, you want to skip the automatic detection of mass storage devices and instead manually select these, you can do so by pressing *S*. If you wish to automatically detect mass storage devices, you are asked to insert Setup Disk #3. There are several device drivers loaded after Setup Disk #3 is inserted and you can watch these fly by at the bottom of the screen. In the case of an HP Vectra I was loading with Windows NT, the messages shown in Figure 1-6 appeared.

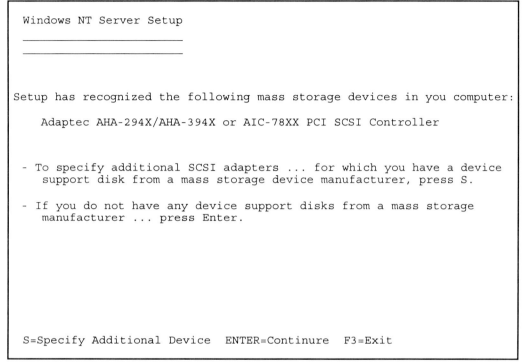

```
Windows NT Server Setup
_____
_____



Setup has recognized the following mass storage devices in you computer:

    Adaptec AHA-294X/AHA-394X or AIC-78XX PCI SCSI Controller


 - To specify additional SCSI adapters ... for which you have a device
   support disk from a mass storage device manufacturer, press S.

 - If you do not have any device support disks from a mass storage
   manufacturer ... press Enter.






 S=Specify Additional Device   ENTER=Continure   F3=Exit
```

Figure 1-6 Windows NT Setup Mass Storage Device Selection

In Figure 1-6 Setup has identified my only mass storage device which is really an Adaptec SCSI controller. The next two messages, which I abbreviated in the figure, give you two different options for proceeding. The first is to insert a disk which contains device support information to specify additional devices or a device that was not found. The second is to proceed with the device(s) automatically detected. In this case I am happy with the controller that was automatically selected and I press *ENTER*.

If indeed you have additional SCSI adapters, press *S* and use the floppy that has on it material to support your SCSI adapters. This represents a break in the installation process whereby you specify additional adapters and then jump right back into the installation process.

After pressing *ENTER*, you again see messages fly by about information that is loaded onto your system such as the NTFS.

Installation of Windows NT 4.x can take place from a number of sources such as the CD-ROM and the network. In this example I will proceed with the installation from CD-ROM because this is the most common way of loading Windows NT at this time.

Figure 1-7 shows the screen instructing you to insert the Windows NT CD-ROM.

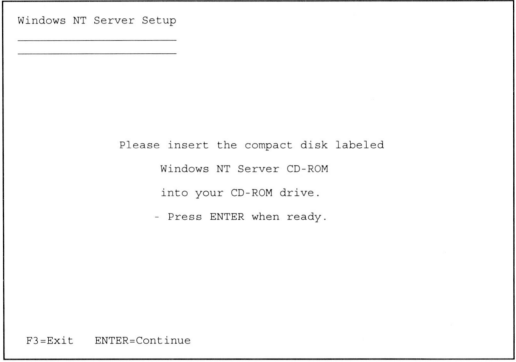

```
Windows NT Server Setup
_____
_____






               Please insert the compact disk labeled

                    Windows NT Server CD-ROM

                   into your CD-ROM drive.

                   - Press ENTER when ready.







  F3=Exit    ENTER=Continue
```

Figure 1-7 Windows NT Setup from CD-ROM

After installing the CD-ROM and proceeding with the installation, an excruciatingly long message appears for you to read related to the Windows NT license agreement. At the end of this message you can either agree or disagree with the licensing agreement.

If indeed you agree you can proceed with the installation and a window appears in which various system-related components are listed. Among the items listed are *Computer, Display, Keyboard, Keyboard Lay-*

out, and *Pointing Device.* You can either accept the items listed or select and change them on an individual basis. I agreed to select the items as they were listed and proceeded with the installation.

You then proceed to specify on what partition you would like to install Windows NT. Figure 1-8 shows a portion of the Windows NT Setup screen for my computer allowing me to select the partition on which I want to install Windows NT.

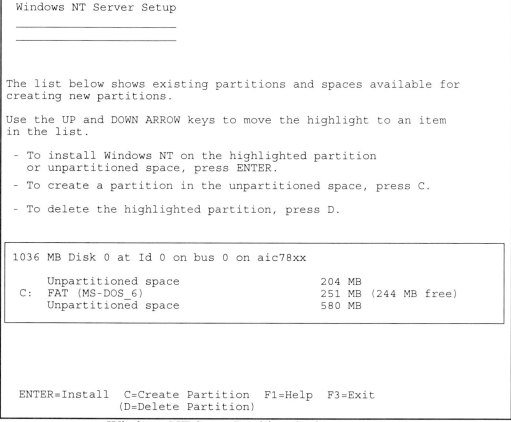

```
Windows NT Server Setup
_____
_____



The list below shows existing partitions and spaces available for
creating new partitions.

Use the UP and DOWN ARROW keys to move the highlight to an item
in the list.

  - To install Windows NT on the highlighted partition
    or unpartitioned space, press ENTER.

  - To create a partition in the unpartitioned space, press C.

  - To delete the highlighted partition, press D.


 ┌──────────────────────────────────────────────────────────────────┐
 │ 1036 MB Disk 0 at Id 0 on bus 0 on aic78xx                         │
 │                                                                    │
 │      Unpartitioned space                    204 MB                 │
 │   C: FAT (MS-DOS_6)                          251 MB  (244 MB free)  │
 │      Unpartitioned space                     580 MB                │
 └──────────────────────────────────────────────────────────────────┘



   ENTER=Install   C=Create Partition   F1=Help   F3=Exit
                   (D=Delete Partition)
```

Figure 1-8 Windows NT Setup Partition Options

In this example there are three choices for partitions on which to install Windows NT.There are two unpartitioned spaces and the partition on which DOS now exists to load Windows NT. In this case I would like to load Windows NT on the 580 MB partition. When an unpartitioned space is highlighted you are given the "Create Partition" option. When a partitioned space is highlighted, you are given the "Delete Partition" option. After having selected that partition, I am asked which of the following file system types I would like to use to format the partition:

- *Format the partition using the FAT file system*

- *Format the partition using the NTFS file system*

There are some trade-offs to consider when deciding whether to use FAT or NTFS. The following is a brief comparison of NTFS versus FAT that also appears in the file system chapter.

NTFS and FAT

New Technology File System (NTFS)

New Technology File System (NTFS) is the best file system to select for running Windows NT on your system. If possible, I recommend using NTFS. The following bullet list describes some of the more important characteristics and features of NTFS:

- **NTFS File Names** can be up to 256 characters. This length includes any extensions you might use in a file name. You can use both upper and lower case in a name, however, file names are not case sensitive. The only reserved characters in NTFS file names that you can't use are the following:

  ? " / \ < > * ! :

- **NTFS is a recoverable file system**. There is a transaction log associated with NTFS that keeps track of directory and file updates.

This means you can redo or undo an operation should your Windows NT system fail.

- **Windows NT security** can be used with NTFS. You can configure various auditing and permissions on files and directories in Windows NT if you use NTFS.

- **NTFS has no undelete utility** as a standard part of the operating system. To those of us with a lot of UNIX experience this is nothing new. If you have had the luxury of an undelete utility in the operating system(s) you have used in the past, then look at not having an undelete utility as adding much needed excitement to your life.

- **NTFS has substantially more file system overhead** than FAT. Along with all of the advantages of NTFS come the requirements for more of pretty much everything. As you work your way up the functional ladder of operating systems, it is a general rule that you will require more resources in general. A low-end, single-user personal computer needs minimal resources and one person to load and use it. A gigantic corporate mainframe may need a fleet of people just to handle security! It is therefore expected that NTFS would require more file system overhead than FAT.

- **NTFS requires large partition sizes**. Don't even play around with small partition sizes when using NTFS. Although 50 MBytes is the minimum file system size normally associated with Windows NT, you should have more than 100 MBytes of file system for NTFS if you are going to use the system for application, file, or print purposes. This should not be a problem when you consider the typical configurations of today's systems. Even the "toy" system I used in the installation example had a 1 GByte hard disk drive.

- **NTFS has a large partition capacity**. Since I just spent some time talking about the minimum end of an NTFS partition size, I may as well cover the maximum size. An NTFS partition can be as large as 2^{64} bytes in Windows NT. This, of course, is outrageously large. Although today's systems are not going to have a partition of this size, it is possible that future systems may require a large partition size and it is admirable that Windows NT possesses such great head room for the future.

- **NTFS has a large file size**. The maximum file size for NTFS in Windows NT is also 2^{64} bytes.

- **No NTFS formatted floppies**. It is not now possible to have an NTFS formatted floppy disk. Along with all of the advantages of NTFS at the high end come some minor drawbacks at the low end. There is just too much overhead in NTFS to allow you to have an NTFS formatted floppy disk. This, however, is a small price to pay for all of the advantages of NTFS at the high end.

- **NTFS attempts to store files in contiguous space**. All things being equal, it would typically take longer to access a file if it is located in an uncontiguous area rather than in a contiguous area of the disk. If NTFS is able to store files in a contiguous area, you will see a performance advantage as a result of this feature.

- **NTFS is only accessed through Windows NT**. You can use NTFS with Windows NT, but it is not now accessible through other operating systems.

File Allocation Table (FAT) File System

Although I recommend using NTFS if possible on your Windows NT system, millions of people have successfully used FAT for many years with most MS-DOS® computers. FAT can also be used for Windows NT and OS/2®. If you would like to boot your computer with both MS-DOS and Windows NT, then you will need a FAT partition. NTFS is more robust than FAT, but you may not need any of the additional features of NTFS. The following bullet list describes some of the more important characteristics and features of FAT:

- **FAT File Names** can take on two different forms in Windows NT. The standard MS-DOS FAT name can be used which is eight characters, a dot which acts as a delimiter, and then a three-character extension. **autoexec.bat** is a file name with eight characters, the dot delimiter, and a three-character extension. In this case the name must start with a letter or number. There are no spaces permitted in the name. Names are not case sensitive and case is not preserved in the file name. The following names are reserved:

NUL, PRN, LPT1 - LPT3, COM - COM4, AUX, CON

In addition, the following characters are reserved:

? " / \ ^ , = * ! : ; [ ]

- **Alternatively, you can use Long File Names (LFN)** with FAT under Windows NT. In this case you can have a name with 255 characters, which includes the full path, but excludes the extension. This is a big advantage over the eight-character name. In addition you have the flexibility of using spaces and multiple extensions with period delimiters in the name. Names are not case sensitive but do preserve case.

- **Windows NT security** cannot be used with FAT.

- **FAT has no undelete utility** when running under Windows NT. It may, however, be possible to use an MS-DOS FAT partition to undelete a file on a Windows NT FAT partition. I would not count on this and instead do everything possible to prevent files from being mistakenly deleted.

- **FAT uses very little file system overhead.**

- **FAT does not require partition sizes as large as NTFS**. If you will be using your Windows NT system to run a demanding application or for file and print services, you will still want to have a healthy size partition.

- **FAT also has a large partition capacity**. A FAT partition under Windows NT can be as large as 2^{32} bytes. This is also a large partition size.

- **FAT has a large file size**. The maximum file size in Windows NT using FAT is also 2^{32} bytes.

- **FAT formatted floppies are supported**.

- **FAT can be accessed through Windows NT, MS-DOS, and OS/2.**

Table1-1 compares some of the features of FAT and NTFS.

TABLE 1-1   Some important FAT and NTFS characteristics

Characteristic	NTFS	FAT
File name and directory length:	255 characters	8 characters plus 3-character extension (w/o LFN)
		255 characters (with LFN)
Preserve case in file name?	yes	no
File name case sensitive?	no	no
Reserved file and directory name characters:	? " / \ < > * ! :	? " / \ ^ , = * ! : ; [ ]
Is it possible to format a floppy in this file system?	No NTFS formatted floppies.	No problem with FAT formatted floppies.
Associated operating system(s):	Windows NT	Windows NT, MS-DOS, OS/2
Security Features?	yes	no
Partition Size	2^{64}	2^{32}
File Size	2^{64}	2^{32}

Let's now return to the setup. My strong preference is to use NTFS and after having selected NTFS, a Setup window appears giving your status showing the percentage complete of the formatting process.

After formatting the partition as NTFS, which took only a few minutes, I was asked the location in which I wanted Windows NT installed as shown in Figure 1-9.

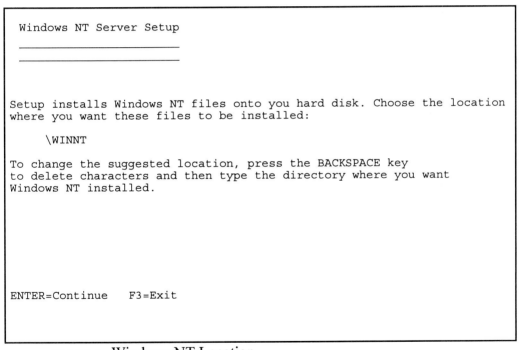

```
Windows NT Server Setup
_____

_____


Setup installs Windows NT files onto you hard disk. Choose the location
where you want these files to be installed:

    \WINNT

To change the suggested location, press the BACKSPACE key
to delete characters and then type the directory where you want
Windows NT installed.




ENTER=Continue    F3=Exit
```

Figure 1-9 Windows NT Location

I like the location **\WINNT** so I selected this. You are then asked if you wish to perform an "exhaustive secondary examination" of the hard disk or skip it. I skipped the examination and proceeded directly to the point where files were copied to the hard disk.

Copying files from the CD-ROM to disk takes only a few minutes and at its conclusion a window appears informing you that this portion of the installation process is complete and you press ENTER to reboot the computer.

When your computer reboots, you will see the option to boot using Windows NT 4.x and you can move on to the next phase of the installation process.

Graphical (Windows NT) Based Portion of Setup

After the system boot, the Setup proceeds in Windows NT mode instead of text mode. The Windows NT CD-ROM is used in this part of the installation.

The first window that appears in Windows NT informs you that the following three Setup steps will be performed:

- Gather information about your system.
- Install Windows NT networking.
- Finish Setup.

Gather Information About System (F6)

Windows NT wants to personalize your Windows NT installation and asks you the following information:

Name:
Organization:

The next window requests your ten-digit key which is on the back of the CD-ROM case.

The next topic you have to deal with is licensing. Windows NT is licensed on either a per server or per seat basis. You would select the licensing scheme that best meets the needs of your environment. I chose to support several concurrent connections to my server which requires a client access license for each concurrent connection.

You are next asked for the name of the Windows NT server which can be a maximum of 15 characters.

The next question relates to the server type. Your options are the following:

- Primary Domain Controller
- Backup Domain Controller
- Standalone Server

This is an area where some background is required. If your Windows NT systems worked in an autonomous manner, then you would not be able to share data, including data related to users. If you wanted to add a user to such an autonomous network, you would be required to add that user on each and every system in the network. If you have ten systems in your network and 20 users, you would have to keep track of 200 users! Fortunately Windows NT has a means by which accounts can be centrally managed called the Primary Domain Controller (PDC). The PDC holds the database of users that is shared among systems in the domain. There is actually a Security Accounts Manager (SAM) database in which the user information is kept.

Now, you can imagine a disaster in which your Primary Domain Controller is unaccessible and you have lost access to your database of users. You can back up your Primary Domain Controller with one, or multiple, Backup Domain Controllers (BDC). These systems can take over in the event you encounter a problem with your Primary Domain Controller. You also have the option to have a standalone server which will manage only itself. I recommend you use this option only if you have one Windows NT system and never plan to expand.

I chose to make the system a Primary Domain Controller during this installation.

The next step is to set up the Administrator account. I discuss the Administrator account, security, and system administration privileges in Chapter 7. The Administrator account is the top-level account on your system which has access to virtually all of your system resources. At the time of installation this account is automatically created and you will be asked for a password and asked to confirm the password. Use this account with care and don't give the password for it to people you don't think will need to perform advanced system administration work. You can create users with a variety of privileges, as discussed in Chapter 7 which covers Windows NT system administration, so use this account carefully and be sure to give it a password.

Next you are asked to select system components. There are six components you can select and when you highlight one of the components you are given a good description of the component. There is a box next to each component for you to check if you wish to install it. You can double click on a component and select subcomponents if you wish. These take up very little space so I usually select them. The following is a list of the six components and a brief description of each.

Accessibility Options   Options related to keyboard, sound, display, mouse, and others.

Accessories   Windows NT accessories and enhancements.

Communications   For connecting to other computers and on line services.

Games   No need to describe these. Just load them.

Multimedia   For sound, animation, video, and so forth.

Windows Messaging   For electronic mail and messaging.

For the relatively small amount of space consumed by these components, the biggest is 7.1 MBytes, I selected all of them. As time goes on
you may find additional components which are bigger in size and want to
select them more carefully.

Install Windows NT Networking (F7)

You next move on to step 2 of the Windows NT setup procedure which is
networking. If you have a network administration group in your organization you will want to work with them on this portion of the configuration.

Your first selection is the way in which your system is connected to
the network. Your choices are: Wired to the network; Remote access to the
network; or both. Windows NT supports remote access to the network
through a modem. Although I won't cover Remote Access Server (RAS) in
this book, the Windows NT network can be accessed through a modem
with RAS that would be selected at this point in the installation process. If
you think you may access your Windows NT network remotely through a
modem at some point, you want to select the option for remote access to
the network. Select the way(s) in which your Windows NT system will be
networked in this window.

Next you are asked whether or not you would like to install Microsoft Internet Information Server. This application is integrated into Windows NT. Select whether or not you wish to install this.

The next window allows you to have a search of your networking cards automatically performed by Windows NT with the *Start Search* button. The networking card on my system was not found so I used the *Select from list...* button to bring up a list of networking cards. The list from which I selected was complete and I was able to find my HP DeskDirect (J2585A) 10/100 LAN Adapter in the list. You can also use the *Have Disk...* button to use your own disk to load software to support the LAN interface.

Next you are asked which of the network protocols you wish to use: *TCP/IP Protocol; NWLink IPX/SPX Compatible Transport;* and *Net BEUI Protocol.* I selected TCP/IP and NetBEUI for my system. The computer networks on which I work use TCP/IP primarily and Net BEUI for existing personal computers. I will configure these onto my system and use them throughout this book.

Since I find many users of existing Microsoft operating systems haven't used TCP/IP, I'll provide some TCP/IP background information in the next section.

You now move up to the next networking level and select the network services you wish to load. The list I received was: *Microsoft Internet Information Server 2.0; RPC Configuration; NetBIOS Interface; Workstation;* and *Server.* The services you run depend on the functionality you wish to achieve. Because I find that networking requirements tend to grow and not to shrink, I usually load all services.

The networking installation will now take place based on the selections you have made. You have a selection during the installation process related to TCP/IP. You can use DHCP which will provide IP addresses dynamically, if indeed there is a DHCP server on the network or not. Since I will be assigning addresses manually to systems on the network, I chose not to use DHCP. Although I won't use DHCP throughout the book I'll just take a minute and provide a short overview of DHCP.

Dynamic Host Configuration Protocol (DHCP) is a means by which IP addresses, which I'll assign to the system shortly, are handed out by a system on a temporary basis. The environments in which I work always assign permanent IP addresses so DHCP does not play a role in these environments. The temporary addresses handed out by the DHCP server are sometimes referred to as "leased" addresses since they are not permanent. A Windows NT server can act as the DHCP server in a network, handing out and managing the temporary IP addresses. You may want to consider DHCP if you are just introducing IP addresses to your environment. Existing IP environments usually continue to distribute permanent IP addresses and don't use DHCP.

A window then appears in which you can enter your IP address, subnet mask, and default gateway.

Next you can select the order in which your computer finds network information and disable network bindings. Initially you probably want to go with the defaults and later determine if your networking scheme requires you to adjust these.

If you chose to have the system act a Primary Domain Controller, you will be asked the name of the domain your system will control.

TCP/IP Networking Background

There are seven layers of network functionality in the ISO/OSI model shown in Figure 1-10. I'll cover these layers at a cursory level so you have some background into this networking model. The top layers are the ones that you spend time working with because they are closest to the functionality you can relate to. The bottom layers are, however, also important to understand at some level so you can perform any configuration necessary to improve the network performance of your system which will have a major impact on the overall performance of your system.

Layer Number	Layer Name	Data Form	Comments
7	Application		User applications here.
6	Presentation		Applications prepared.
5	Session		Applications prepared.
4	Transport	Packet	Port to port transportation handled by TCP
3	Network	Datagram	Internet Protocol (IP) handles routing by either going directly to the destination or default router.
2	Link	Frame	Data encapsulated in Ethernet or IEEE 802.3 with source and destination addresses
1	Physical		Physical connection between systems. Usually thinnet or twisted pair

Figure 1-10 ISO/OSI Network Layer Functions

I'll start reviewing Figure 1-10 at the bottom with layer 1 and describe each of the four bottom layers. This is the International Standards Organization Open Systems Interconnection (ISO/OSI) model. It is helpful to visualize the way in which networking layers interact.

Physical Layer

The beginning is the physical interconnect between the systems on your network. Without the **physical layer** you can't communicate between systems and all of the great functionality you would like to implement will not be possible. The physical layer converts the data you would like to transmit to the analog signals that travel along the wire (I'll assume for now that whatever physical layer you have in place uses wires). The information traveling into a network interface is taken off the wire and prepared for use by the next layer.

Link Layer

In order to connect to other systems local to your system, you use the link layer which is able to establish a connection to all the other systems on your local segment. This is the layer where you have either IEEE 802.3 or Ethernet. These are "encapsulation" methods. This is called encapsulation because your data is put in one of these two forms (either IEEE 802.3 or Ethernet). Data is transferred at the link layer in frames (just another name for data) with the source and destination addresses and some other information attached. You might think that because there are two different encapsulation methods they must be much different. This, however, is not the case. IEEE 802.3 and Ethernet are nearly identical. So with the bottom two layers you have a physical connection between your systems and data that is encapsulated into one of two formats with a source and destination address attached. Figure 1-11 lists the components of an **Ethernet** encapsulation and includes comments about IEEE802.3 encapsulation where appropriate.

destination address	6 bytes	address data is sent to
source address	6 bytes	address data is sent from
type	2 bytes	this is the "length count" in 802.3
data	46-1500 bytes	38-1492 bytes for 802.3
crc	4 bytes	checksum to detect errors

Figure 1-11 Ethernet Encapsulation

One interesting item to note is the difference in the maximum data size between IEEE 802.3 and Ethernet of 1492 and 1500 bytes, respectively. This is the Maximum Transfer Unit (MTU). The data in Ethernet is called a *frame* (the re-encapsulation of data at the next layer up is called a *datagram* in IP, and encapsulation at two levels up is called a *packet* for TCP).

Keep in mind that Ethernet and IEEE 802.3 will run on the same physical connection, but there are indeed differences between the two encapsulation methods.

Network Layer

Next we work up to the third layer which is the network layer. This layer is synonymous with Internet Protocol (IP). Data at this layer is called a *datagram*. This is the layer which handles the routing of data around the network. Data that gets routed with IP sometimes encounters an error of some type which is reported back to the source system with an Internet Control Message Protocol (ICMP) message.

Unfortunately, the information IP uses does not conveniently fit inside an Ethernet frame so you end up with fragmented data. This is really re-encapsulation of the data so you end up with a lot of inefficiency as you work your way up the layers.

IP handles routing in a simple fashion. If data is sent to a destination connected directly to your system, then the data is sent directly to that system. If, on the other hand, the destination is not connected directly to your system, the data is sent to the default router. The default router, sometimes called a gateway, then has the responsibility to handle getting the data to its destination.

Transport Layer

This layer can be viewed as one level up from the network layer because it communicates with *ports*. TCP is the most common protocol found at this level and it forms packets which are sent from port to port. These ports are used by network programs such as **telnet, rlogin, ftp**, and so on. You can see that these programs, associated with ports, are the highest level we have covered while analyzing the layer diagram.

Internet Protocol (IP) Addressing

The Internet Protocol address (IP address) is either a class "A," "B," or "C" address (there are also class "D" and "E" addresses I will not cover). A class "A" network supports many more nodes per network than either a class "B" or "C" network. IP addresses consist of four fields. The purpose of breaking down the IP address into four fields is to define a node (or host) address and a network address. Figure 1-12 summarizes the relationships between the classes and addresses.

Address Class	Networks	Nodes per Network	Bits Defining Network	Bits Defining Nodes per Network
A	a few	the most	8 bits	24 bits
B	many	many	16 bits	16 bits
C	the most	a few	24 bits	8 bits
Reserved	-	-	-	-

Figure 1-12 Comparison of Internet Protocol (IP) Addresses

These bit patterns are significant in that the number of bits defines the ranges of networks and nodes in each class. For instance, a class A address uses 8 bits to define networks and a class C address uses 24 bits to define networks. A class A address therefore supports fewer networks than a class C address. A class A address, however, supports many more nodes per network than a class C address. Taking these relationships one step further, we can now view the specific parameters associated with these address classes in Figure 1-13.

Figure 1-13 Address Classes

Address Class	Networks Supported	Nodes per Network	Address Range		
A	127	16777215	0.0.0.1	-	127.255.255.254
B	16383	65535	128.0.0.1	-	191.255.255.254
C	2097157	255	192.0.0.1	-	223.255.254.254
Reserved	-	-	224.0.0.0	-	255.255.255.255
Looking at the 32-bit address in binary form, you can see how to determine the class of an address:					

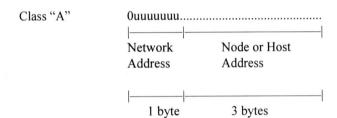

```
Class "A"           0uuuuuuu.............................................
                    |---------|----------------------------|
                    Network    Node or Host
                    Address    Address


                    |---------|----------------------------|
                      1 byte          3 bytes
```

net.host.host.host

A class "A" address has the first bit set to 0. You can see how so many nodes per network can be supported with all of the bits devoted to the node or host address. The first bit of a class A address is 0 and the remaining 7 bits of the network portion are used to define the network. There are then a total of 3 bytes devoted to defining the nodes with a network.

Figure 1-13 Address Classes (Continued)

Class "B"

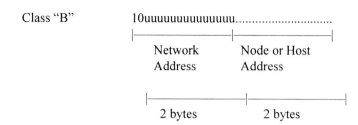

net.net.host.host

A class "B" address has the first bit set to a 1 and the second bit to a 0. There are more networks supported here than with a class A address, but fewer nodes per network. With a class B address there are 2 bytes devoted to the network portion of the address and 2 bytes devoted to the node portion of the address.

Class "C"

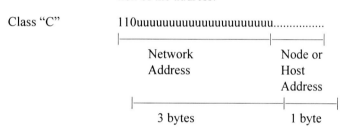

net.net.net.host

A class "C" address has the first bit and second bit set to 1 and the third bit is 0. The greatest number of networks and fewest number of nodes per network are associated with a class C address. With a class C address there are 3 bytes devoted to the network and 1 byte devoted to the nodes within a network.

Every interface on your network must have a unique IP address. Systems that have two network interfaces must have two unique IP addresses. I will cover some networking commands in Windows NT in an upcoming chapter.

Finish Setup (F8)

Step three now begins in which you finish Setup. You will receive information during this phase describing how the system is being configured. I was asked the location in which I would like Microsoft Internet Information Server and related products installed. All modules of this software consumed less than four MBytes of disk space at the time of my installation. I selected the default location of **D:\WINNT\System32\inetsrv** for installing this software.

I was also asked the ODBC drivers to install and selected SQL Server from the list.

A window appears in which you can select your time zone. This is just a matter of calling up the list of time zones and making the appropriate selection. When you select your time zone it automatically becomes the center of a world map that is shown which is as it should be - you are at the center of the world.

You then go through a process whereby your display properties are selected. If you hit the *OK* button to select the default settings the Setup program informs you that you have not hit *Test* to ensure that the graphics settings are correct. If you like what you see during *Test*, you can then hit *OK* and proceed with the installation.

The last activity in this step is to create the Emergency Repair Disk which will be discussed later in the book. You want to create this disk at this point.

When your system reboots, you can select the Windows NT operating you just installed for your operating system. You can log in by typing Ctrl+Alt+Del and provide your *Username* and *Password*. This would be the user *Administrator* for the first login. After your first login you will see a screen similar to that in figure 1-14.

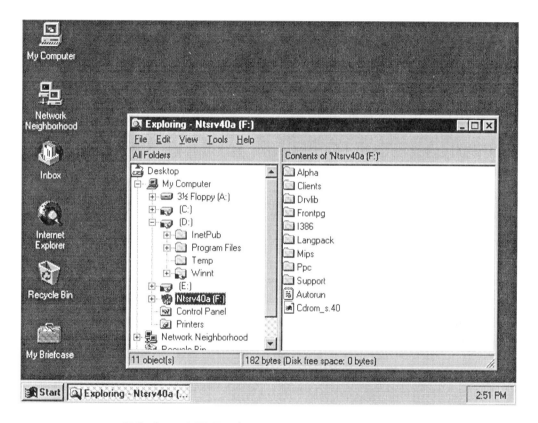

Figure 1-14   Windows NT Environment After First Login

With Windows NT now loaded you can view the Windows NT kernel that you have loaded in **D:\winnt\system32\ntoskrnl**. This file is only 843 KBytes on my system.

Let's now take a look at loading additional software.

Loading Other Software

The process I just covered will help you install the Windows NT operating system. There are probably several additional software packages you'll want to load on your system. What is it like to load nonoperating system software? The following example walks through some of the steps required to load a software package used in later chapters of the book. The product we will load in this section is the NFS Maestro product from Hummingbird Communications LTD.

To begin the load we'll use the Maestro CD-ROM. Figure 1-15 shows the CD-ROM mounted on **F:**.

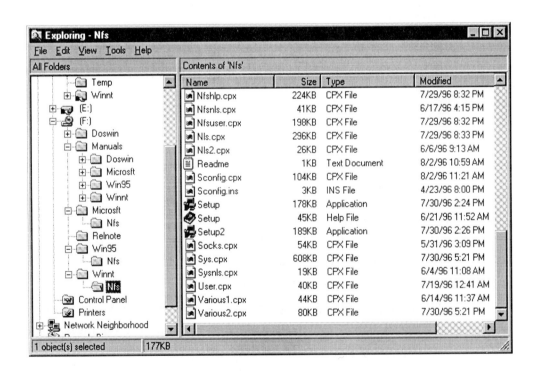

Figure 1-15 CD-ROM with Software Loaded on **F:**

Software you load on Windows NT systems usually has a **Setup** program used to run the installation program as shown in Figure 1-15. When we run the **Setup** program, a window appears asking me some setup related information. Then we are asked the location in which to load Maestro as shown in Figure 1-16.

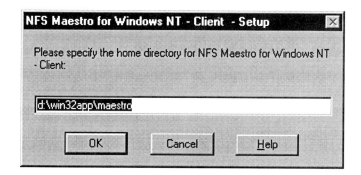

Figure 1-16 Location to Load Software

d:\win32app\maestro is the default location for loading the software. **win32app** is the directory where application software is typically loaded. You can set up any scheme you like for the location of software. In this example let's choose to go with the default location.

After having accepted the information shown in Figure 1-16, a useful window appears. This window shows the total disk space required for the Maestro application and the total disk space available. This leaves no uncertainty about whether or not the application will fit and whether or not there will be sufficient space left after the application is loaded. Figure 1-17 shows this window.

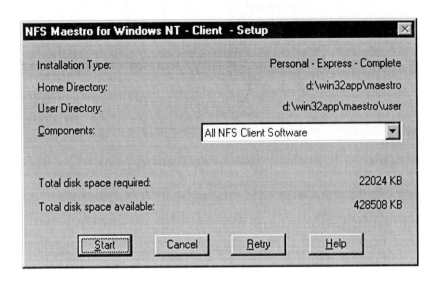

Figure 1-17 Window Showing Disk Space Information

Several more windows then appear asking specific information about the Maestro installation. When all of the necessary information has been provided, the software is installed in the default directory and a menu appears with all of the Maestro programs in it.

The installation of no two software products will be identical; however, I think you can see from this installation that loading software is a straight forward endeavor provided you know the basics of software instal-lation.

What I have covered in this chapter is the base, or essential Windows NT system setup. There are other tasks to be performed, many of which are covered in subsequent chapters. Topics such as the Windows NT file sys-tem and its management, Windows NT system management, and Windows NT performance are covered in upcoming chapters.

HP Netserver Navigator

The process of loading Windows NT covered in this chapter was per-formed on a small desktop system. The HP Netserver Navigator Kit con-tains several components to assist in the installation of HP Netservers including a CD-ROM that contains the following:

- Readme file that provides extensive background material on Net-servers.

- Configuration Assistant in which you: select a NOS; run EISA con-figuration; show configured cards; configure a disk array; install a utility partition; execute card utilities; create a drivers diskette, and install a NOS.

- Other configuration solutions and utilities.

The Navigator kit helps configure Netservers so your NOS installa-tion goes smoothly.

CHAPTER 2

Setting Up
Your HP-UX System

You are going to have a great time setting up your HP-UX system(s). I know you are because I have set up hundreds and hundreds of systems and my customers always enjoy it. Why? Because you think it's going to be one thing - pain and misery, and it turns out to be another - smooth, easy, and a great learning experience.

The systems I have helped set up have come in all shapes and sizes. They range from a network of hundreds of low-end desktop systems to massive data center systems with thousands of users. In the distributed environment networking is more of an issue; in the data center environment disk management is more of an issue. In either case, though, HP-UX is HP-UX and what you know about one system applies to the other. This is what I am hoping you get from the HP-UX parts of this book - **the common denominator of HP-UX system administration knowledge that applies to all systems**.

I am in a good position to help you with this knowledge. I have been setting up HP-UX systems since they were introduced. Before that I setup other UNIX systems. This means that although I haven't learned much else, I really know UNIX systems. In addition, I have a short memory so I write down most things that work. The result is this book and my other HP-UX books.

To help you understand the tasks you will have to perform, I have included a flowchart for setting up HP-UX systems. One of the most intimidating aspects to setting up a new system is that there are so many tasks to perform, it is easy to get lost in the detail. Figure 2-1 helps put in perspective the tasks to be performed and the sequence of performing them. I hope this helps make your setup more manageable.

The nature of learning HP-UX system administration is that in addition to the specific steps to be performed there is also some background information you need to know. What I have done is include the background in the appropriate setup step. This way you're not reading background information for the sake of reading background information. Instead, you're reading background information that applies to a specific setup step. An example of this is providing background information about the program used to load software and background on the HP-UX 10.x file system under the setup step called "Install HP-UX 10.x." You need to know about the software installation program in order to load software and you should also know the file system layout when you load software. It therefore makes sense to put this background information under this step of the setup flowchart.

Although I can't include every possible step you might need to perform, I have included the steps common to most installations. If a step is irrelevant to your site, you can skip it. Based on the many installations I have performed, I think I have discovered the common denominator of most installations. In any event, you can use this flowchart as an effective step-by-step approach to getting your system(s) up and running.

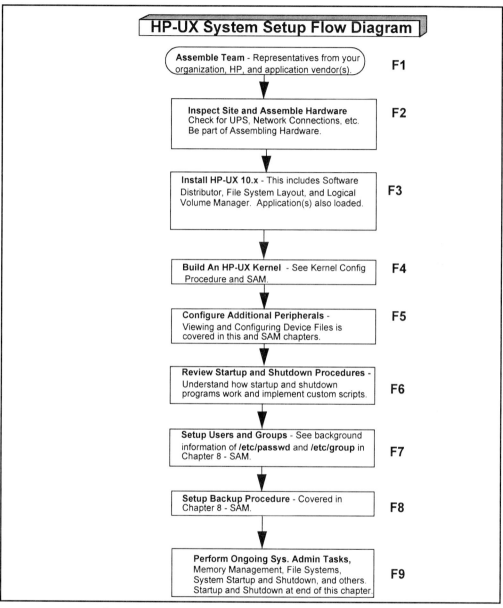

Figure 2-1 System Setup Flow Diagram

Using the Setup Flowchart

The goal is to get the system up and running as soon as possible, doing as little rework as possible after users are on the system. Although you might plan to have the system exclusively for setup-related work for a few weeks after it is delivered, you will probably find users are eager to get on the system. This usually means the setup gets compromised in the interest of getting users on the system. If possible, don't let this happen to you. Although the setup flowchart looks straightforward and gives you the impression you can get your system going step by step, there are invariably some steps you'll have to redo. This will, of course, affect any users who jump on the system before you have had a chance to complete the setup and do adequate testing.

This simplified setup flow diagram in Figure 2-1 can be of great value to you for three reasons:

1. It gives you an overview of the tasks you'll need to perform.

2. It serves as a check list as you complete activities.

3. It serves as a basis for your own custom flowchart, which includes your application installation procedures.

Although system administration books and manuals abound with information about how to perform a particular setup step such as adding users or performing backups, I have never seen a setup flowchart like the one in this chapter that encompasses HP-UX systems. I encourage you to copy this flowchart and edit it to reflect the process at your site.

This flowchart is by no means complete. This flowchart acts as a good common denominator. You may need to perform additional tasks, but virtually every new HP-UX installation involves the tasks shown in the flowchart.

The following sections cover the steps shown in the flowchart.

Assemble Team (F1)

What a fascinating process I have found this to be. When you consider the number of team members who might be required for a large, distributed project, this might seem to be an impossible task. I have found the converse to be true. In general, I have found application vendors, consultants, hardware vendors, customer representatives, and others involved in a project happy to have the opportunity to carefully plan a project and devote resources to ensure its success.

I think those of us involved in technology know the importance of both planning and working together as a team. I am often pleasantly surprised at how well planning can proceed when the right group of people are brought together. Although you are in the best position to determine who should be part of the team, I will list a few of my suggestions here.

- Within your organization you have a variety of people interested in the project including application developers; system administrators; managers responsible for the installation; help desk representatives; users, and others whom you may want to consider making part of your team.

- Hewlett Packard may have a number of representatives involved in making your installation successful including a sales representative, consultants in the Professional Services Organization; support people in the System Support Organization; and others.

- You may have several application vendors who will play a part in your project. If these representatives can be made part of your team rather than just software suppliers, you may find that you'll encounter fewer unforeseen problems such as software incompatibility, and when you do encounter problems, you may get a better response.

- You may have other consultants who fill a void within your organization. If they are part of the team, they may have prior experience they can share with the group that may be valuable.

You may have others you wish to be part of the team. As long as you have a team made up of people important to the project, you will know who is responsible for what and may end up with a smoother running project.

Inspect Site and Assemble Hardware (F2)

The systems used in the examples throughout this book were delivered with owner's manuals that included illustrated steps for setting up the system. There isn't really much to assembling the hardware. Just unpack the boxes, connect the cables, and power up. The manual for the Series 800 K class used in some of the examples went into some detail about the environment for the system, but in general there isn't much to setting up one of the smaller systems.

A large T class, on the other hand may require a lot of work to assemble. For a modest fee, the HP System Support Organization (SSO) will perform the hardware setup for you. I normally recommend my customers do this for a number of reasons. First, if you don't have a lot of experience with HP, you will meet your Customer Engineer (CE). Although HP equipment is highly reliable, you may need to see your CE for possible future hardware problems, so it makes sense to become acquainted with him or her. Secondly, it may be comforting to have a CE set up the system, tell you "it's working great," and give you some tips. Finally, the CE will take down all the serial numbers of the equipment and verify that all your hardware support is in order. It's good to take care of this when the system is set up and to ensure there won't be a delay when you need service.

The really important part of this step is what you do *BEFORE* you set up the equipment. I always recommend that the CE perform a site inspection to verify that your physical environment can accommodate the system(s) you have ordered. In the case of the systems used in the examples in this book, which operate in a standard office environment, you wouldn't think there is a lot to inspect. A trained eye, however, can uncover hidden problems. The most common of these is lack of sufficient power. Even though these systems consume a modest amount of power, some offices aren't wired for more than an adding machine and calculator charger! There is no greater disappointment than setting up your system only to find you have insufficient power to run it. Your CE can point out all such potential problems.

Consider all of the material you think you'll need to get your systems up and running. Here is a checklist of items I recommend my customers review.

Hardware Configuration

Cabling   LAN cable (twisted pair, thin net, etc.) of the length you require. Don't measure distance "as the crow flies." Remember that if your office is not prewired, you'll have to run wires up the wall, across the ceiling, and back down the wall to go from office to office.

Media Attachment Unit   MAU to attach cable to the connector on the back of the computer. An example is attaching twisted pair cable to the AUI connector on the back of the computer. HP workstations come with both a thin net connector and AUI. Order the system with the interface you want so you don't have to mess with this when you connect your systems.

Power   Make sure you have sufficient power and power outlets. Many offices already have PCs in them so you want to make sure you have enough power and outlets in the office. If your Series 800 system is going in a computer room, you will be pleasantly surprised by how little space it consumes compared to the dinosaurs for which computer rooms were originally developed.

Software Configuration

System Names   Think about system names. The most common delay I encounter when installing systems is waiting for users to select the names of their systems. It doesn't matter what theme you choose for system names. Just be sure you, the administrator, are happy with the theme. Some good system names are colors, planets, and sports teams. Choose a theme that can accommodate additional systems later.

Addresses   Have IP addresses ready. If you don't now use IP addresses, HP can provide you with class C addresses. Ask your HP Technical Consultant (TC) how to obtain these addresses from HP. Please don't make up IP addresses. Since you will be connected to the Internet, you want to use registered IP addresses.

Network Diagram   Since I recommend having your HP TC assist you with the installation on a consulting basis, I also recommend you ask your TC to give a rundown on what he or she will do to get your systems running. I normally produce a flowchart. A formal document isn't necessary, but it will be helpful to you to understand your TC's plan. TCs do this kind of work every day and can install your system quickly, but you won't know what he or she is doing unless you're involved.

Order Documentation

As part of preparing for your system you also want to consider your documentation needs when you buy your system. There is very little documentation delivered with either a new Series 800 or Series 700 unit; however, there are many manuals you can order with your system. The documentation is well organized into sets of manuals covering related topics. There is an extensive HP-UX 10.x documentation set. Be sure to order the documentation sets you need such as system administration,   programming reference, CDE, and so forth. when ordering your system. You can also order the manual set on CD-ROM.

Install HP-UX 10.x(F3)

Installing HP-UX means building an initial "barebones" HP-UX 10.x system and later building your complete full function HP-UX system. The initial system is loaded from the HP-UX Install media for both the Series 700 and Series 800 or from another system on the network for the Series 700 (not covered here). The full function system is loaded from the Core OS media and Applications media or from another system on the network.

You can have your system delivered with instant ignition, which means HP-UX has been loaded on your system and you'll only have to add to it the software you need. I'll cover the complete installation process for both a Series 700 and Series 800 from CD-ROM so you can see the process start to finish. If you have instant ignition on your system, you may need to install additional software on your system in the future or use some of the techniques described in this section to load additional software on your system.

The K class server systems I have worked with that were delivered with instant ignition did not have the **/SD_CDROM** directory which is used in the examples in this chapter to load software. Although I don't cover instant ignition much in this chapter, you may have your systems delivered with instant ignition and choose to not reinstall the operating system. If you have instant ignition and wish to load software using the /**SD_CDROM** directory, you may have to create **/SD_CDROM**.

The Install media that you use to install HP-UX 10.x on the Series 700 and Series 800 is self-contained; that is, it has on it everything you need for the initial installation. I will use CD-ROM media for the installation process for both the Series 700 and Series 800.

Before you start installing anything, make sure your configuration is a supported HP-UX 10.x configuration. If your system is not supported for HP-UX 10.x, you are taking a risk by installing it. There are a number of generic requirements that must be met such as a minimum of 16 MBytes of RAM and 400 MBytes of disk space for a standalone workstation. In addition, you want to make sure your processor is one of the supported devices for HP-UX 10.x

Loading HP-UX 10.x Software on Series 700

In order to install HP-UX software, place the HP-UX 10.x Install media into the device from which you want to install. In the upcoming example I am using a CD-ROM. Be sure to insert the CD-ROM Install media before you begin the installation. When you boot an older Series 700 unit and hit the ESCAPE key before it autoboots, a screen appears that looks something like Figure 2-2.

```
    Selecting a system to boot.
    To stop selection process, press and hold the ESCAPE key.

    Selection process stopped.

    Searching for Potential Boot Devices.
    To terminate search, press and hold the ESCAPE key

    Device Selection   Device Path   Device Type
    ---------------------------------------------------------

    P0                 scsi.6.0      HP       C2235
    P1                 scsi.3.0      TOSHIBA  CD-ROM  XM-3301TA
    P2                 scsi.0.0      TEAC     FC-1       HF   07


    b)    Boot from specified device
    s)    Search for bootable devices
    a)    Enter Boot Administration mode
    x)    Exit and continue boot sequence

    Select from menu: BOOT P1
```

Figure 2-2 Booting a Series 700 - Example 1

What is shown in Figure 2-2 (example 1) are the bootable devices found. Some workstations may show the menu of boot commands instead of the potential boot devices as shown in Figure 2-3 (example 2).

```
------------------------------------------------------------------
Command                          Description
-------                          -----------
Auto [boot|search] [on|off]      Display or set auto flag

Boot [pri|alt|scsi.addr][isl]    Boot from primary,alt or SCSI

Boot lan[.lan_addr][install][isl] Boot from LAN

Chassis [on|off]                 Enable chassis codes

Diagnostic [on|off]              Enable/disable diag boot mode

Fastboot [on|off]                Display or set fast boot flag

Help                             Display the command menu

Information                      Display system information

LanAddress                       Display LAN station addresses

Monitor [type]                   Select monitor type

Path [pri|alt] [lan.id|SCSI.addr] Change boot path

Pim [hpmc|toc|lpmc]              Display PIM info

Search [ipl] [scsi|lan [install]] Display potential boot devices

Secure [on|off]                  Display or set security mode
------------------------------------------------------------------

BOOT_ADMIN>
```

Figure 2-3 Booting a Series 700 - Example 2

If this is the case with your system, the **SEARCH** command will show the bootable devices presented in Figure 2-4.

```
BOOT_ADMIN> SEARCH

Searching for potential boot device.
This may take several minutes

To discontinue, press ESCAPE.


    Device Path                Device Type
    - - - - - - - - - - -      - - - - - - - - - - -
    scsi.6.0                   HP       C2247
    scsi.3.0                   HP       HP35450A
    scsi.2.0                   Toshiba  CD-ROM
    scsi.1.0                   HP       C2247

BOOT_ADMIN> BOOT SCSI.2.0
```

Figure 2-4 Series 700 Boot **SEARCH** Example

Once the bootable devices have been displayed, you may select an entry from the list. In this case I have the HP-UX 10.x Install media on CD-ROM so I can boot from P1 with the command shown in example 1 (**BOOT P1**). In example 2 I specify the CD-ROM at SCSI address 2 to boot from (**BOOT SCSI.2.0**) after running **SEARCH** to see what bootable devices exist. You may then be asked what language you want, such as U.S. English. After selecting your language, if indeed you were asked this question, the options in Figure 2-5 exist.

```
            [    Install HP-UX    ]

            [ Run a Recover Shell ]

            [   Cancel and Reboot ]

            [   Advanced Options  ]


                 [ Help ]
```

Figure 2-5 Installation Options on Series 700 HP-UX 10.x Install Media

From this menu I select *Install HP-UX*. The disks on the system are then listed and you can select from among this group to install HP-UX 10.x. In addition, on a workstation you are given the following two choices for system configuration:

• *Standard LVM configuration*

• *Standard Whole-disk (non-LVM) configuration*

If you have not reviewed the Logical Volume Manager section of Chapter 6, you want to do so before you make this selection (LVM is Logical Volume Manager). I am a strong advocate of using Logical Volume Manager whenever possible. There are many advantages to using Logical Volume Manager and you should be aware of these. In HP-UX 9.x Logical Volume Manager was not available on Series 700 units, so I expect some system administrators may select Standard Whole-disk configuration because this is what they have grown accustomed to for the Series 700. I would recommend using Logical Volume Manager. Among the many advantages of Logical Volume Manager is that a logical volume can span multiple physical disks.

The next information to be entered is information such as primary swap, secondary swap, software language, and so on. You want to consider your primary swap space very carefully. There is a detailed discussion about swap space later in this chapter. For HP-UX 10.0 the following default parameters were set, all of which you can modify:

Primary Swap Size	48Mb
Secondary Swap Size	100Mb
Software Selection	Runtime Environment
Software Language	English
/home Configuration	Minimal
Include all disks in root VG	False
Make volatile dirs separate	True

Create /export volume	False
File system file name length	Long

The decision you have to make at this point is the Software Selection. You have two Series 700 selections you can make:

- Runtime Environment

- Desktop Environment

The runtime environment is intended for most installations. The desktop environment is for client systems. At the time of this writing the runtime environment is roughly 280 MBytes and the desktop environment is roughly 224 MBytes (These were derived from the *Show Description of Software* from the *Actions* menu of swinstall.)

If indeed you have selected Logical Volume Manager, you can adjust the size of /, swap, and **/home** (if you specified that you would like a /**home**). You will get different default mount directory sizes depending on the size of the disk you have selected to load HP-UX 10.x onto. The mount directory default sizes in Table 2-1 were configured on my system for a 1 GByte disk.

TABLE 2-1   MOUNT DIRECTORY DEFAULT SIZES FOR 1 GBYTE DISK

Mount Directory	Size (Mb)	Usage	Disk Group
/	48	HFS	vg00.
(swap)	48	swap	vg00
(swap)	100	swap	vg00
/home	20	HFS	vg00
/opt	100	HFS	vg00
/tmp	24	HFS	vg00
/usr	300	HFS	vg00
/var	36	HFS	vg00

Keep in mind these defaults will vary depending on the size of your disk. You can select Modify Disk/FS Parameters and make disk and file system changes. At this point you can change the parameters associated with a mount directory including its size.

After making the appropriate selections, you reach a point where you are asked if you want to interact with **swinstall**. There is an overview of the Software Distributor-UX product used for installing all HP-UX 10.x software in this chapter. You may want to take a look at this overview to get a feel for the type of functionality Software Distributor offers. The **swinstall** program is the Software Distributor program used to install software. If you decide you want to interact with **swinstall,** you will be asked for code word information and select from among software to load. If your software is protected, you will have to enter code word information. If you need a code word, it should be printed on the CD-ROM certificate you received with your software. This code word is tied to the ID number of a hardware device on your system.

If you don't want to interact with **swinstall,** the software option you earlier selected, such as the Runtime Environment, will be loaded for you.

After the contents of the Install media have been copied to your system, you will be prompted to insert the Core OS media with a message like the following:

```
            USER INTERACTION REQUIRED

To complete the installation you must now remove the HP-UX
installation CD and insert the HP-UX Core Operating System CD.

Once this is done, press the <Return> key to continue:
```

When you interact with **swinstall,** you select the desired software to load from the Core OS media. You can mark software to be loaded from the Core OS media and then proceed to load the software. Software "bundles" may be selected and loaded. Software bundles are new to HP-UX 10.x so those of you who have HP-UX 9.x experience may not have heard this term before. Software bundles are a collection of filesets. A software bundle is sort of analogous to a partition in HP-UX 9.x, except a software bundle is more flexible in that a bundle can contain filesets from a variety of different products. If you do not interact with **swinstall,** the installation of the Runtime Environment takes place automatically. The process of loading the software consists of an analysis phase and an installation phase. Analysis may determine that you don't have enough disk space to load the desired software. After successfully completing the analysis phase, you can proceed with the installation. When the installation is complete, you exit **swinstall** and your HP-UX kernel is built.

Series 700 Boot After Installation

When the system comes up after installation, a series of windows appear that allow you to configure your system name, time zone, root password, Internet Protocol (IP) address, subnet mask, and other networking setup. This same information can be entered after your system boots by running **/sbin/set_parms**. This program can be used to set an individual system parameter or all of the system parameters that would be set at boot time. **/sbin/set_parms** uses one of the arguments in Table 2-2 depending on what you would like to configure.

TABLE 2-2   /sbin/set_parms ARGUMENTS

set_parms Argument	Comments
hostname	Set hostname.
timezone	Set time zone.
date_time	Set date and time.
root_passwd	Set root password.
ip_address	Set Internet Protocol address.
addl_network	Configure subnet mask, Domain Name System, and Network Information Service.

set_parms Argument	Comments
font_c-s	Use this system as a font server or font client.
initial	Go through the entire question and answer session you would experience at boot time.

If you use the **initial** argument, you'll interact with a variety of dialog boxes asking you for information. The system host name dialog box is shown in the Figure 2-6.

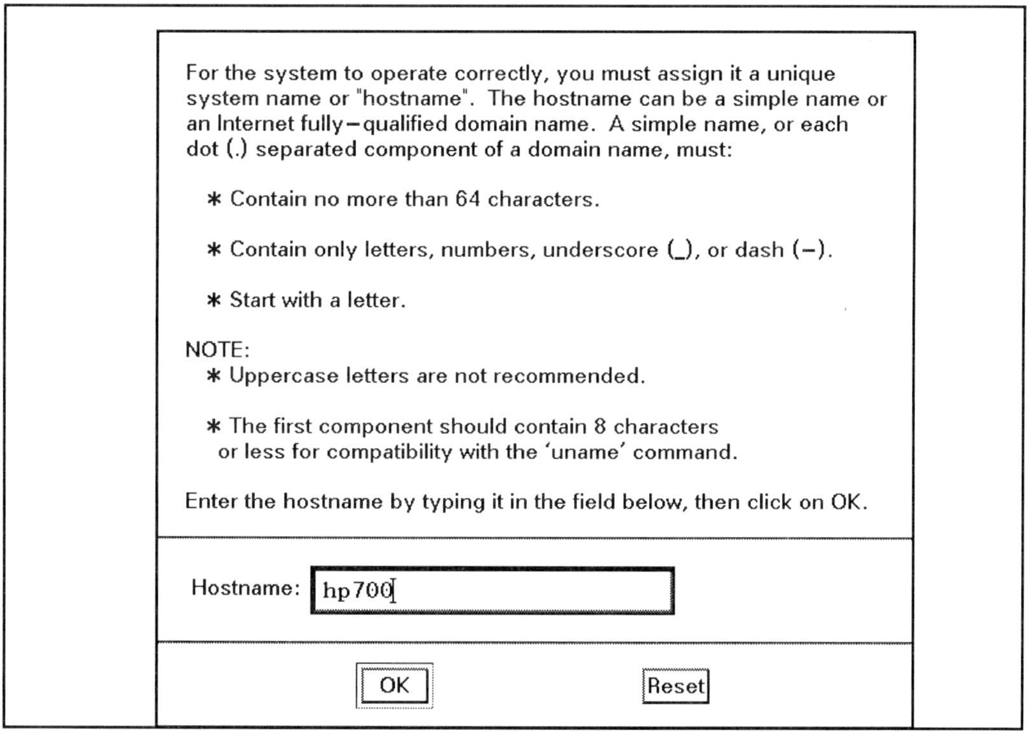

For the system to operate correctly, you must assign it a unique system name or "hostname". The hostname can be a simple name or an Internet fully–qualified domain name. A simple name, or each dot (.) separated component of a domain name, must:

* Contain no more than 64 characters.

* Contain only letters, numbers, underscore (_), or dash (–).

* Start with a letter.

NOTE:
* Uppercase letters are not recommended.

* The first component should contain 8 characters or less for compatibility with the 'uname' command.

Enter the hostname by typing it in the field below, then click on OK.

Hostname: hp700

OK   Reset

Figure 2-6 Entering Host Name on Series 700 with **set_parms**

You'll then be asked for your time zone and root password. Figure 2-7 shows the dialog box for entering your IP address.

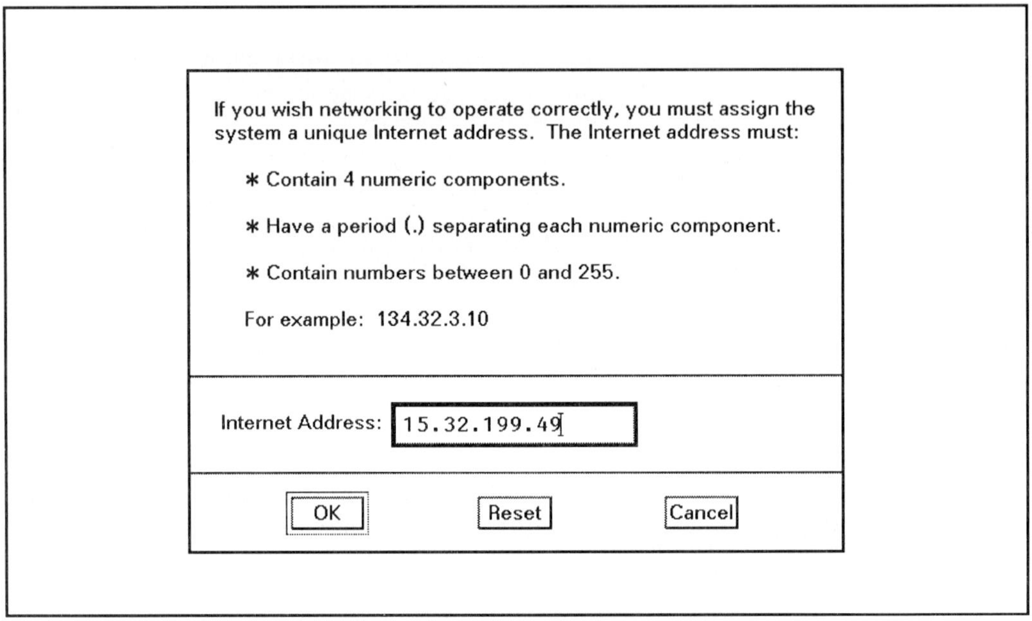

If you wish networking to operate correctly, you must assign the system a unique Internet address. The Internet address must:

* Contain 4 numeric components.

* Have a period (.) separating each numeric component.

* Contain numbers between 0 and 255.

For example: 134.32.3.10

Internet Address: 15.32.199.49

OK   Reset   Cancel

Figure 2-7 Entering IP Address on Series 700 with **set_parms**

You can then configure your subnet mask and other networking configuration.

Please be careful if you configure some of the additional networking parameters (**set_parms addl_netwrk**). Do not configure a system as an NIS client if it hasn't been set-up on the NIS server. I have encountered some interesting problems booting if you configure your system as an NIS client and select the option "Wait For NIS Server on Bootup: yes". This means your system will wait forever for the NIS server to respond before the system boot will complete. If you are having problems with your NIS server, you can forget about booting (this is a problem I encountered on a K class server acting as an NIS client). Your system won't boot and you'll have no way of running **set_parms** to change to "Wait For NIS Server on Bootup: no". I found there are two ways to make this change if your system won't complete the boot process. The first is to shut off the system and boot in single-user state from the ISL prompt with the following command:

```
ISL> hpux -is boot
```

When the system boots, it is in single-user mode with a login prompt. If you run **set_parms** and change to "Wait For NIS Server on Bootup: no", you think you have changed this variable to "no" but the file where this is changed (**/etc/rc.config.d/namesvrs**) has not been updated because you are in single-user mode and the commands required to make this change are on a logical volume which has not yet been mounted.

After finding out that the change had not been made by running **set_parms,** I decided to manually edit **/etc/rc.config.d/namesvrs** where I could make this change. The logical volume **/usr** is not mounted in single-user mode, however, so there isn't access to the **/usr/bin/vi** editor I wanted to use to make this change. To mount **/usr** I issued the following commands (the **fsck** is required because the system was improperly shutdown earlier):

```
$ fsck /dev/vg00/rlvol6
$ mount /dev/vg00/lvol6 /usr
```

I then edited **/etc/rc.config.d/namesvrs** and changed the variable in this file to WAIT_FOR_NIS_SERVER="FALSE" and proceeded with the boot process. This fixed the problem but not without a lot of monkeying around. This is an area where you must be careful when setting up your system(s).

Loading HP-UX 10.x Software on Series 800

Loading software on a Series 800 is different enough from a Series 700 that I decided to break these up into two different procedures. In this Series 800 example I will use a K class system.

In order to install HP-UX software, place the HP-UX 10.x Install media into the device from which you want to install. In the upcoming example I am using a CD-ROM. Be sure to insert the CD-ROM Install media before you begin the installation. As your Series 800 unit boots, you will see a variety of messages fly by including information about your processors, buses, boot paths, and so on. You are then given some time to hit any key before the system autoboots. If you do this, you'll see the menu shown in Figure 2-8.

```
--------------- Main Menu ----------------------------------

Command                          Descripton
-------                          ----------

BOot [PRI|ALT|<path>]            Boot from specified path

PAth [PRI|ALT| [<path>]          Display or modify a path

SEArch [DIsplay|IPL] [<path>]    Search for boot devices

COnfiguration menu               Displays or sets boot values

INformation menu                 Displays hardware information

SERvice menu                     Displays service commands

DIsplay                          Redisplay the current menu

HElp [<menu>|<command>]          Display help for menu or cmd

RESET                            Restart the system

--------

Main Menu: Enter command or menu >
```

Figure 2-8   Booting a Series 800

You can view the bootable devices with the **SEARCH** command as shown in Figure 2-9.

```
Main Menu: Enter command or menu > SEARCH

Searching for potential boot device(s)
This may take several minutes.

To discontinue search, press any key
(termination may not be immediate).

Path Number   Device Path (dec)   Device Type
-----------   -----------------   -----------
P0            10/0.6              Random access media
P1            10/0.5              Random access media
P2            10/0.4              Random access media
P3            10/0.3              Random access media
P4            10/12/5.2           Random access media
P5            10/12/5.0           Sequential access media
P6            10/12/6.0           LAN Module

Main Menu: Enter command or menu >
```

Figure 2-9 Series 800 Boot **SEARCH** Example

The information from this screen does not tell us what devices exist at each address. In fact, it is a guess at this point. I doubt people with little HP-UX experience know what such things as "Random access media" are; I know I don't. But since I know I ordered a system with four identical internal disk drives and I have what appear to be four indentical entries at P0, P1, P2, and P3, I assume that none of these is a CD-ROM. I'll guess that my CD-ROM is the next entry which is P4:

```
Main Menu: Enter command or menu > BOOT P4
Interact with IPL (Y or N)?> N
```

This was a lucky guess! This tells me that both hard disk drives and CD-ROMs are Random access media to the boot process. I'm sorry to say I actually cheated here and looked at the inside of the front door of the K class which listed the devices and their corresponding addresses. Going back to the Series 700 boot examples shown earlier, it was much clearer what devices were present. With the Series 800 it appears the categories of devices are much more broad.

After successfully selecting the CD-ROM, I get the screen in Figure 2-10.

```
┌──────────────────────────────────────────────────────────────────┐
│            Welcome to the HP-UX installation process              │
│                                                                    │
│                                                                    │
│                                                                    │
│                   [      Install HP-UX     ]                       │
│                                                                    │
│                   [ Run a Recover Shell ]                          │
│                                                                    │
│                   [   Cancel and Reboot ]                          │
│                                                                    │
│                   [   Advanced Options   ]                         │
│                                                                    │
│                                                                    │
│                          [ Help ]                                  │
│                                                                    │
└──────────────────────────────────────────────────────────────────┘
```

Figure 2-10 Installation Options on Series 800 HP-UX 10.x Install Media

From this menu I select *Install HP-UX*. You can install networking at this point or wait until the installation is further along. I normally wait. The disks on your system are then listed for you to select from. In this case the information in Figure 2-11 is shown for the K class.

```
The installation utility has discovered the following disks
attached to your system. You must select one disk to be your
root disk. When configured, this disk will contain (at least)
the boot area, a root file system and primary swap space.

Hardware                     Product                Size
Path                         ID                     (Megabytes [Mb] }
-----------------------------------------------------------------
10/0.6.0                     C2490WD                2033
10/0.5.0                     C2490WD                2033
10/0.4.0                     C2490WD                2033
10/0.3.0                     C2490WD                2033


[  OK  ]                     [ Cancel ]             [ Help ]
   -                            -                      -
```

Figure 2-11 Selecting a Series 800 Disk

After selecting the 2 GByte disk at 10/0.6.0, you're given the following two choices for system configuration:

• *Standard LVM configuration*

• *Standard Whole-disk (non-LVM) configuration*

If you have not reviewed the Logical Volume Manager section of Chapter 6, you will want to do so before you make this selection (LVM is Logical Volume Manager). I am a strong advocate of using Logical Volume Manager whenever possible with both the Series 800 and Series 700. There are many advantages to using Logical Volume Manager and you should be aware of these. Among the many advantages of Logical Volume Manager is its ability for a logical volume to span multiple physical disks.

The next information to be entered is information such as primary swap, secondary swap, software language, and so on. You want to consider your primary swap space very carefully. For HP-UX 10.0 the following default parameters were set for a 2 GByte disk, all of which you can modify:

Primary Swap Size	48Mb
Secondary Swap Size	500Mb.
Software Selection	Runtime Environment
Software Language	English
/home Configuration	Minimal
Include all disks in root VG	False
Make volatile dirs separate	True
Create /export volume	False
File system file name length	Long

Keep in mind that these defaults will vary depending on the size of your disk.

At this point you can load the runtime environment.

The mount directory default sizes shown in Table 2-3 existed for a 2 GByte disk.

TABLE 2-3   MOUNT DIRECTORY DEFAULT SIZES FOR 2 GBYTE DISK

Mount Directory	Size (Mb)	Usage	Disk Group
/	48	HFS	vg00.
(swap)	48	swap	vg00
(swap)	500	swap	vg00
/home	20	HFS	vg00
/opt	100	HFS	vg00
/tmp	24	HFS	vg00
/usr	300	HFS	vg00
/var	36	HFS	vg00

You can select Modify Disk/FS Parameters and make disk and file system changes. At this point you can change the parameters associated with a mount directory including its size. In this case with a K class with four processors and a lot of RAM, it would make sense to increase the size of primary swap.

After making the appropriate selections, you reach a point where you are asked if you want to interact with **swinstall**. There is an overview of the Software Distributor product used for installing all HP-UX 10.x software in this chapter. You may want to take a look at this overview to get a feel for the type of functionality Software Distributor offers. The **swinstall** program is the Software Distributor program used to install software. If you decide you want to interact with **swinstall,** you will be asked for code word information and select from among software to load. If your software is protected, you will have to enter code word information. If you need a code word, it should be printed on the CD-ROM certificate you received with your software. This code word is tied to the ID number of a hardware device on your system.

If you don't want to interact with **swinstall,** the software option you earlier selected, such as the Runtime Environment, will be loaded for you.

After the contents of the Install media have been copied to your system, you will be prompted to insert the Core OS media with a message like the following:

```
          USER INTERACTION REQUIRED

To complete the installation you must now remove the HP-UX
installation CD and insert the HP-UX Core Operating System CD.

Once this is done, press the <Return> key to continue:
```

When you interact with **swinstall,** you select the desired software to load from the Core OS media. You can mark software to be loaded from the Core OS media and then proceed to load the software. Software "bundles" may be selected and loaded. Software bundles are new to HP-UX 10.x so those of you who have HP-UX 9.x experience may not have heard this term before. Software bundles are a collection of filesets. A software bundle is sort of analogous to a partition in HP-UX 9.x except a software bundle is more flexible in that a bundle can contain filesets from a variety of different products. If you do not interact with **swinstall,** the installation of the Runtime Environment takes place automatically. The process of loading the software consists of an analysis phase and an installation phase. Analysis may determine that you don't have enough disk space to load the desired software. After successfully completing the analysis phase, you can proceed with the installation. When the installation is complete, you exit **swinstall** and your HP-UX kernel is built.

Series 800 Boot after Installation

When the system comes up after installation, the boot path will be displayed for you. For the K class system used in the example the following message appeared:

```
Boot:
: disc3(10/0.6.0;0)/stand/vmunix
```

Then a series of windows appear that allow you to configure your system name, time zone, root password, Internet Protocol (IP) address, subnet mask, and other networking setup. This same information can be entered after your system boots by running **/sbin/set_parms**. This program can be used to set an individual system parameter or all of the system parameters that would be set at boot time. You give **/sbin/set_parms** one of the arguments in Table 2-4 depending on what you would like to configure.

TABLE 2-4   **/sbin/set_parms** ARGUMENTS

set_parms Argument	Comments
hostname	Set host name.
timezone	Set time zone.
date_time	Set date and time.
root_passwd	Set root password.
ip_address	Set Internet Protocol address.

set_parms Argument	Comments
addl_network	Configure subnet mask, Domain Name System, and Network Information Service.
font_c-s	Use this system as a font server or font client.
initial	Go through the entire question and answer session you would experience at boot time.

If you use the **initial** argument, you'll interact with a variety of dialog boxes asking you for information. The dialog box asking your system host name is shown in Figure 2-12.

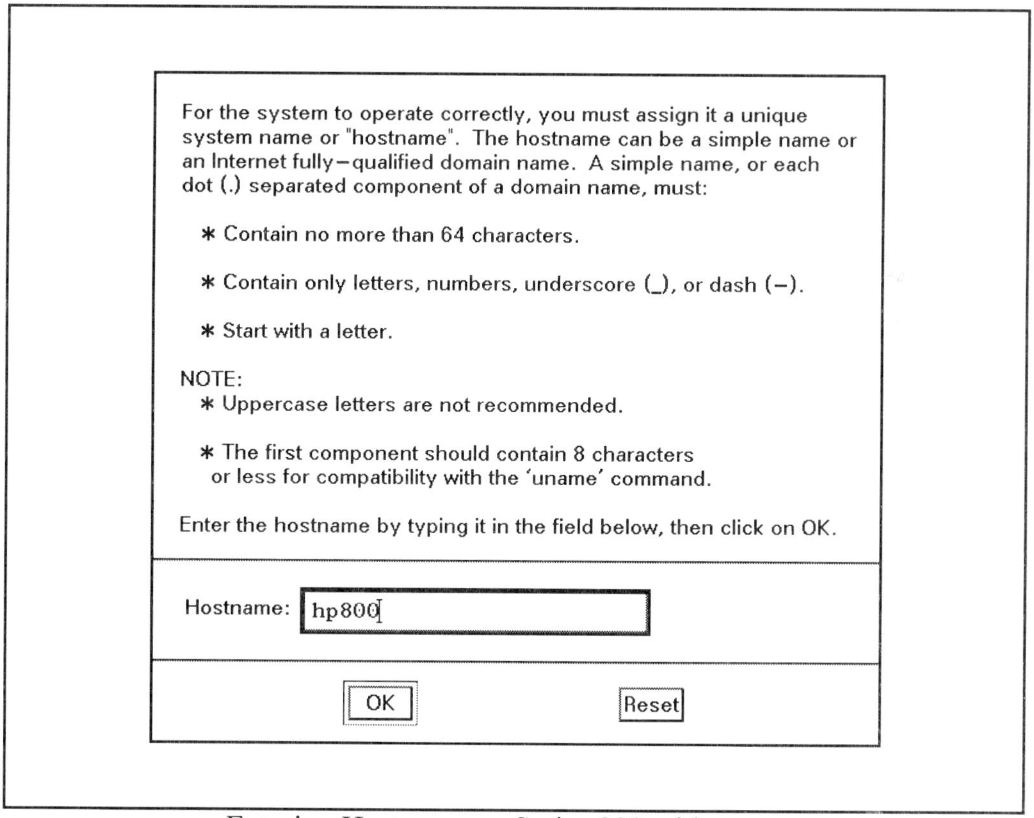

For the system to operate correctly, you must assign it a unique system name or "hostname". The hostname can be a simple name or an Internet fully-qualified domain name. A simple name, or each dot (.) separated component of a domain name, must:

   ✱ Contain no more than 64 characters.

   ✱ Contain only letters, numbers, underscore (_), or dash (−).

   ✱ Start with a letter.

NOTE:
   ✱ Uppercase letters are not recommended.

   ✱ The first component should contain 8 characters or less for compatibility with the 'uname' command.

Enter the hostname by typing it in the field below, then click on OK.

Hostname: | hp800 |

[OK]   [Reset]

Figure 2-12 Entering Hostname on Series 800 with **set_parms**

You'll then be asked for your time zone and root password. Figure 2-13 shows the dialog box for entering your IP address.

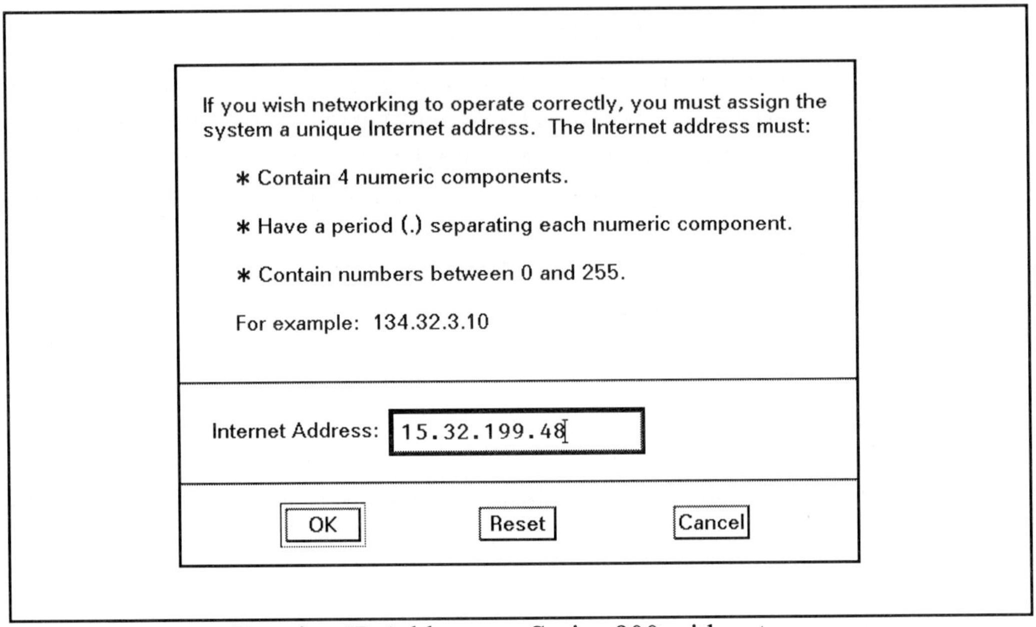

If you wish networking to operate correctly, you must assign the system a unique Internet address. The Internet address must:

      ✱ Contain 4 numeric components.

      ✱ Have a period (.) separating each numeric component.

      ✱ Contain numbers between 0 and 255.

      For example: 134.32.3.10

Internet Address: `15.32.199.48`

[OK]   [Reset]   [Cancel]

Figure 2-13 Entering IP Address on Series 800 with **set_parms**

You can then configure your subnet mask and other networking configuration.

Please be careful if you configure some of the additional networking parameters (**set_parms addl_netwrk**). Do not configure a system as an NIS client if it hasn't been set-up on the NIS server. I have encountered some interesting problems booting if you configure your system as an NIS client <u>and</u> select the option "Wait For NIS Server on Bootup: yes". This means your system will wait forever for the NIS server to respond before the system boot will complete. If you are having problems with your NIS server, you can forget about booting (this is a problem I encountered on a K series server acting as an NIS client). Your system won't boot and you'll have no way of running **set_parms** to change to "Wait For NIS Server on Bootup: no". I found there are two ways to make this change if your system won't complete the boot process. The first is to shut off the system and boot in single-user state from the ISL prompt with the following command:

```
ISL> hpux -is boot
```

When the system boots, it is in single-user mode with a login prompt. If you run **set_parms** and change to "Wait For NIS Server on Bootup: no", you think you have changed this variable to "no" but the file where this is changed (**/etc/rc.config.d/namesvrs**) has not been updated because you are in single-user mode and the commands required to make this change are on a logical volume which has not yet been mounted.

After finding out that the change had not been made by running **set_parms,** I decided to manually edit **/etc/rc.config.d/namesvrs** where I could make this change. The **/usr** logical volume is not mounted in single-user mode, however, so there isn't access to **/usr/bin/vi**, the editor I wanted to use to make this change. To mount **/usr** I issued the following commands (the **fsck** is required because the system was improperly shutdown earlier):

```
$ fsck /dev/vg00/rlvol6
$ mount /dev/vg00/lvol6 /usr
```

I then edited **/etc/rc.config.d/namesvrs** and changed the variable in this file to WAIT_FOR_NIS_SERVER="FALSE" and proceeded with the boot process. This fixed the problem but not without a lot of monkeying around. This is an area where you must be careful when setting up your system(s).

Installing Software with Software Distributor-HP-UX

Software Distributor-HP-UX (I'll call this Software Distributor throughout the book; HP documentation typically uses SD-UX) is the program used in HP-UX 10.x to perform all tasks related to software management. Software

Distributor will be used in an example to install software on a Series 700 and Series 800 shortly. Software Distributor is a standards-based way to perform software management. It conforms to the Portable Operating System Interface (POSIX) standard for packaging software and utilities related to software management. The Software Distributor product described in this section comes with your HP-UX system. There is additional functionality you can obtain by buying the OpenView Software Distributor (SD-OV) product. SD-OV provides support for additional platforms and allows you to "push" software out to target systems. In this section I won't cover SD-OV, but will make some comments about SD-OV functionality where appropriate.

Software Distributor can be invoked using the commands described in this section, by using SAM which is covered in Chapter 8, or by installing software for the first time as described earlier in this chapter. Although I don't cover upgrading from HP-UX 9.x to 10.x, or 10.x to 11.x, you can use Software Distributor to match what is on your HP-UX 9.x system to produce a 10.x system. This is described in detail in the HP-UX upgrade manual part number B2355-90050 for 9.x to 10.x.

The following are the four phases of software installation performed with Software Distributor:

- Selection - You can select the source and software you wish to load during this phase. In the upcoming example the graphical user interface of Software Distributor is used and you'll see how easy it is to select these. With SD-OV you could also select the target on which you wish to load software - remember the SD-OV "push" capability?

- Analysis- All kinds of checks are performed for you including free disk space; dependencies; compatibility; mounted volumes; and others. Among the very useful outputs of this phase is the amount of space the software you wish to load will consume on each logical volume. This will be shown in the example.

- Load - After you are satisfied with the analysis you may proceed with loading the software.

• Configuration - It is possible the software you load requires kernel rebuilding and a system reboot. Startup and shutdown scripts may also need to be modified.

There is some terminology associated with Software Distributor that I tend to use somewhat loosely. I have nothing but good things to say about Software Distributor, but I don't tend to conform to the official Software Distributor terminology as much as I should. I tend, for instance, to use the word system a lot which could mean many different things in the Software Distributor world. For instance, Software Distributor uses local host (a system on which Software Distributor is running or software is to be installed or managed by Software Distributor), distribution depot (a directory which is used as a place for software products), and development system (a place where software is prepared for distribution). I will use the word system to mean the system on which we are working in the examples because software is loaded onto the system from CD-ROM.

Here are some of the common software management-related tasks you can perform with Software Distributor.

Installing and Updating Software (Command Line or GUI)

The **swinstall** command is used to install and update software. The source of the software you are loading can come from a variety of places including a CD-ROM, magnetic tape, or a "depot" directory from which software can be distributed. Using the depot, you can load software into a directory and then install and update software on other nodes from this directory. Software loaded from the CD-ROM with Software Distributor must be loaded onto the local system; this technique is used in the upcoming example. You have a lot of flexibility with SD-OV only when selecting the target system onto which you want to load software and the source from which you will load the software. You can, for instance, load software from a depot which

is on another system on your network. This command can be run at the
command line or with the graphical user interface.

Copying Software to a Depot (Command Line or GUI)

The **swcopy** command is used to copy software from one depot to another.
The depot used in the upcoming examples is a CD-ROM. By setting up
depots, you can quickly install or update software to other nodes simultaneously with SD-OV only. This command can be run at the command line
or with the graphical user interface.

Removing Software from a System (Command Line or GUI)

The **swremove** command is used to remove software from a system that
has had software loaded with Software Distributor. This includes removing
installed and configured software from a system or removing software
from a depot. This command can be run at the command line or with the
graphical user interface.

List Information about Installation Software

The **swlist** command provides information about the depots that exist on a
system, the contents of a depot, or information about installed software.
Examples of using this command are provided shortly.

Configure Installed Software

The **swconfig** command configures or unconfigures installed software. Configuration of software normally takes place as part of **swinstall** but configuration can be deferred until a later time.

Verify Software

The **swverify** command confirms the integrity of installed software or software stored in a depot.

Package Software That Can Later Be Installed (Local System Only)

You may want to produce "packages" of software that you can later put on tape or in a depot with the **swpackage** command. This packaged software can then be used as a source for **swinstall** and be managed by other Software Distributor commands.

Control Access to Software Distributor Objects

You may want to apply restricted access to Software Distributor objects such as packaged software. Using the **swacl** command, you can view and change the Access Control List (ACL) for objects.

Modify Information about Loaded Software (Local System Only)

The Installed Products Database (IPD) and associated files are used to maintain information about software products you have loaded. **swmodify** can be run at the command line to modify these files.

Register Or Unregister a Depot

A software depot can be registered or unregistered with **swreg**. This means you don't have to remove a depot; if you temporarily don't want it used, you can unregister it.

Manage Jobs (Command Line or GUI, SD-OV Only)

Software Distributor jobs can be viewed and removed with **swjob**. The graphical user interface version of this command can be invoked with **sd** or **swjob -i**.

Software Distributor Example

The example of Software Distributor in this section describes the process of loading software from the CD-ROM to the local system. What I'll show here only begins to scratch the surface of functionality you have with Software Distributor, but, since I want to get you up and running fast, this overview should be helpful. You can load software from a variety of media as well as across the network. The graphical user interface that appears throughout this section makes the process of dealing with software easy. You don't, however, have to use this graphical user interface. You can use the **swinstall** command from the command line specifying source, options, target, and so forth. I would recommend using the graphical user interface because this is so much easier. If, however, you like to do things the "traditional UNIX" way, you can issue the **swinstall** command with arguments. You can look at the manual page for **swinstall** to understand its arguments and options and use this command from the command line. The graphical user interface of Software Distributor works with the **sd** (this is an SD-OV command and may also be invoked with **swjob -i**), **swcopy**, **swremove**, and **swinstall** commands. There is also an interactive terminal user interface for these commands if you don't have a graphics display.

The first step when loading software from the CD-ROM is to insert the media and mount the CD-ROM. The directory **/SD_CDROM** should already exist on your HP-UX 10.x system. If not, you can create this directory or use any name you like. You can use SAM to mount the CD-ROM for you or do this manually. I issued the following commands to mount a CD-ROM at SCSI address two on a workstation and start Software Distributor:

```
$ mount /dev/dsk/c0t2d0 /SD_CDROM

$ swinstall
```

Software Distributor may look for a software depot on your local system as a default source location for software. If this is not found, you'll receive a dialog box in which you can change the source depot path. In this case I changed the source depot path to the default for a CD-ROM,   / **SD_CDROM**. This is the selection process described earlier whereby you select the source and target for software to be loaded. You can now select the specific software you wish to load.

When the Software Selection Window is opened for you, you can perform many different operations. To identify software bundles you wish to load on your system, you can highlight these and *Mark For Install* from the *Actions* menu as I have done in Figure 2-14 for *The C/ANSI C Developers Bundle*.

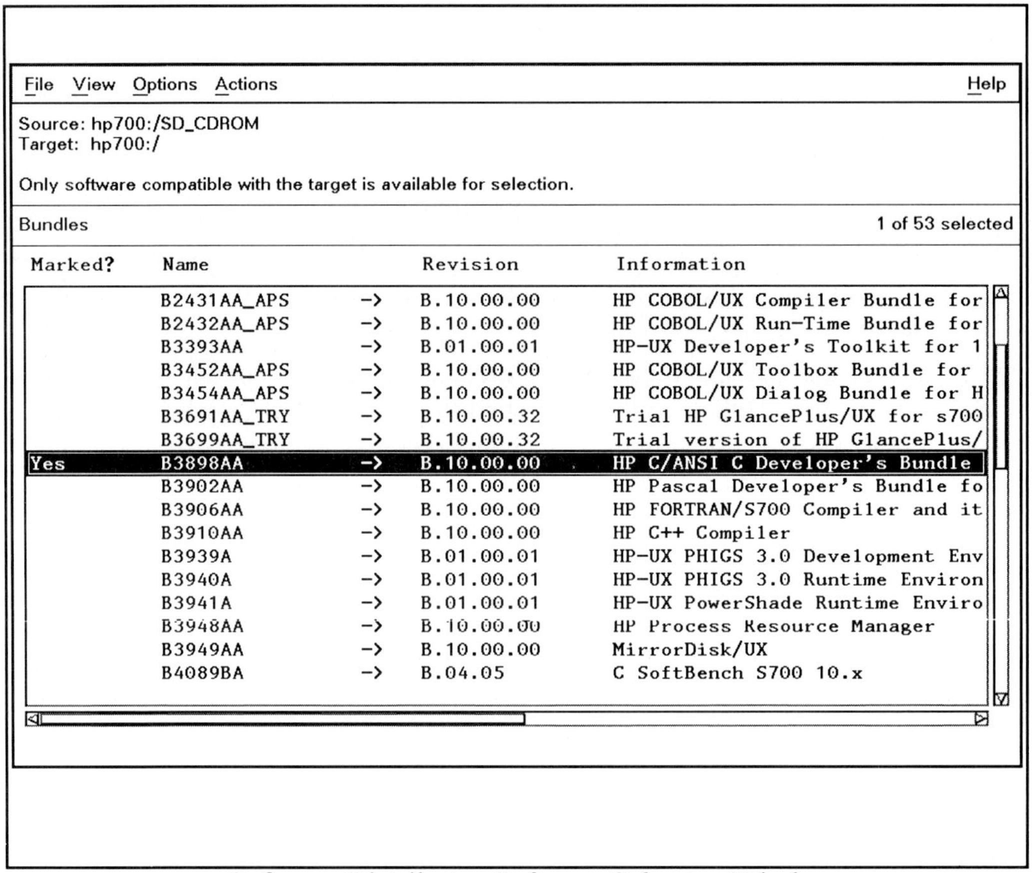

```
┌─────────────────────────────────────────────────────────────────────────┐
│                                                                           │
│  File  View  Options  Actions                                      Help   │
│  ───────────────────────────────────────────────────────────────────     │
│  Source: hp700:/SD_CDROM                                                  │
│  Target: hp700:/                                                          │
│                                                                           │
│  Only software compatible with the target is available for selection.     │
│  ───────────────────────────────────────────────────────────────────     │
│  Bundles                                              1 of 53 selected    │
│  ───────────────────────────────────────────────────────────────────     │
│   Marked?    Name              Revision        Information                │
│  ┌──────────────────────────────────────────────────────────────────┐▲   │
│  │            B2431AA_APS   ->  B.10.00.00   HP COBOL/UX Compiler Bundle for│
│  │            B2432AA_APS   ->  B.10.00.00   HP COBOL/UX Run-Time Bundle for│
│  │            B3393AA       ->  B.01.00.01   HP-UX Developer's Toolkit for 1│
│  │            B3452AA_APS   ->  B.10.00.00   HP COBOL/UX Toolbox Bundle for │
│  │            B3454AA_APS   ->  B.10.00.00   HP COBOL/UX Dialog Bundle for H│
│  │            B3691AA_TRY   ->  B.10.00.32   Trial HP GlancePlus/UX for s700│
│  │            B3699AA_TRY   ->  B.10.00.32   Trial version of HP GlancePlus/│
│  │ Yes        B3898AA       ->  B.10.00.00   HP C/ANSI C Developer's Bundle │
│  │            B3902AA       ->  B.10.00.00   HP Pascal Developer's Bundle fo│
│  │            B3906AA       ->  B.10.00.00   HP FORTRAN/S700 Compiler and it│
│  │            B3910AA       ->  B.10.00.00   HP C++ Compiler               │
│  │            B3939A        ->  B.01.00.01   HP-UX PHIGS 3.0 Development Env│
│  │            B3940A        ->  B.01.00.01   HP-UX PHIGS 3.0 Runtime Environ│
│  │            B3941A        ->  B.01.00.01   HP-UX PowerShade Runtime Enviro│
│  │            B3948AA       ->  B.10.00.00   HP Process Resource Manager    │
│  │            B3949AA       ->  B.10.00.00   MirrorDisk/UX                 │
│  │            B4089BA       ->  B.04.05      C SoftBench S700 10.x         │▼  │
│  └──────────────────────────────────────────────────────────────────┘    │
│  ◁▣▣▣▣▣▣▣▣▣▣▣▣▣▣▣▣▣▣▣▣▣▣▣▣▣▣▣▣▣▣▣▣▣▣▣▣▣▣▣▣▣▣▣▣▣▣▣▣▣▣▣▣▣▣▣▣▣▣▣▣▣▣▣▣▣▣▣▣▣▷  │
│                                                                           │
└─────────────────────────────────────────────────────────────────────────┘
```

Figure 2-14   Software Distributor *Software Selection* Window

A bundle, such as the one selected, may be comprised of products, subproducts and filesets. You can select *Open Item* from the *Actions* menu if you want to drop down one level to see the subproducts or filesets. Figure 2-15 shows *Open Item* for *C/ANSI C Developers Bundle*.

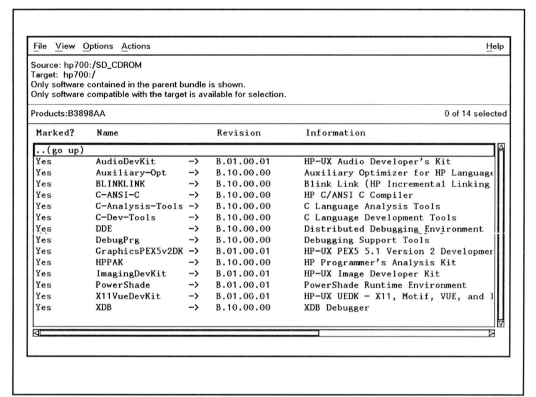

Figure 2-15 Software Distributor *Open Item*

After you have specified items to *Mark For Install,* you can select *Install (analysis)* from the *Actions* menu. Before starting analysis or before loading software, you should select *Show Description Of Software* from the *Actions* menu to see if a system reboot is required (you may have to scroll down the window to see the bottom of the description). You want to know this before you load software so you don't load software that requires a reboot at a time that it is inconvenient to reboot. Figure 2-16 is an example *Install Analysis* window for installing *Trail HP GlancePlus/UX for s700.*

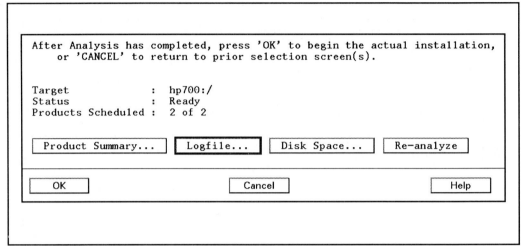

After Analysis has completed, press 'OK' to begin the actual installation,
    or 'CANCEL' to return to prior selection screen(s).

Target   :   hp700:/
Status   :   Ready
Products Scheduled :   2 of 2

    Product Summary...   Logfile...   Disk Space...   Re-analyze

    OK   Cancel   Help

Figure 2-16 Software Distributor *Install Analysis* Window

You can see that there are two products to be loaded in this bundle.
Among the many useful pieces of information analysis provides you is a
Logfile that contains a good review of the analysis and a *Disk Space* window that shows the amount of space that will be consumed by the software
you plan to load. Figure 2-17 shows the *Disk Space* window which
includes the amount of disk space available on the affected Logical Volumes both before and after the software load takes place.

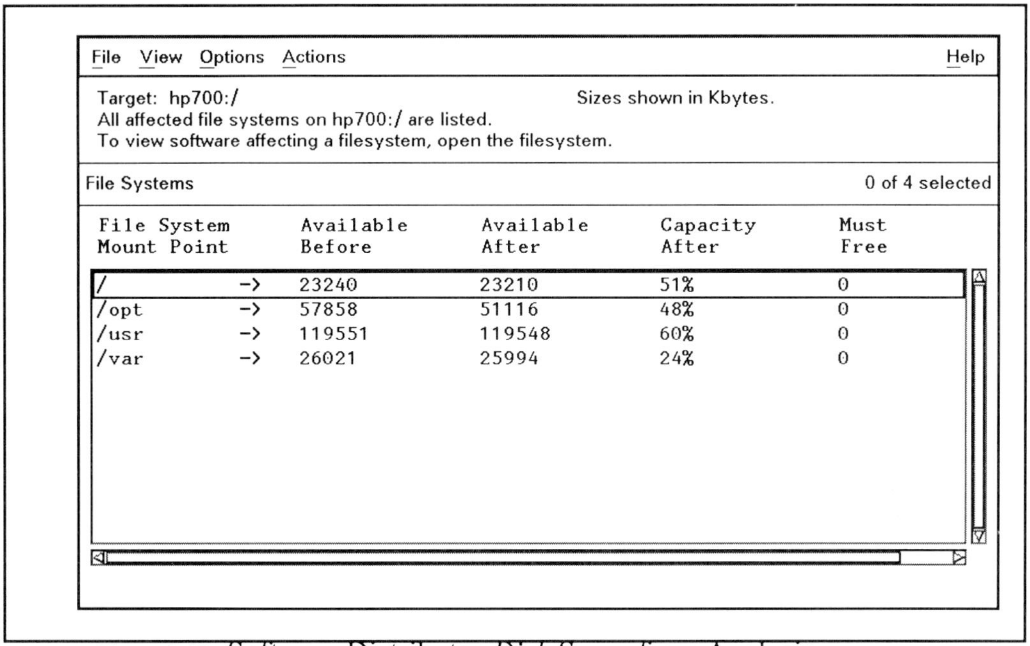

```
 File  View  Options  Actions                                    Help

 Target: hp700:/                          Sizes shown in Kbytes.
 All affected file systems on hp700:/ are listed.
 To view software affecting a filesystem, open the filesystem.

 File Systems                                            0 of 4 selected

    File System        Available      Available      Capacity      Must
    Mount Point        Before         After          After         Free

    /            ->    23240          23210          51%           0
    /opt         ->    57858          51116          48%           0
    /usr         ->    119551         119548         60%           0
    /var         ->    26021          25994          24%           0
```

Figure 2-17 Software Distributor *Disk Space* from Analysis

This window is a dream come true for system administrators who have traditionally not had a lot of good information about either the amount of space consumed by the software they are loading or the destination of the software they are loading. You also have menus here that allow you to further investigate the software you're about to load on your system.

After you are satisfied with the analysis information, you may proceed with loading the software.

Software Distributor Background

It is important to have some background on the way software is organized in Software Distributor. I earlier talked about software bundles in HP-UX 10.x being somewhat analogous to partitions in HP-UX 9.x except that software bundles are more flexible in that they can contain filesets from a variety of different products. Figure 2-18 shows the hierarchy of software bundles.

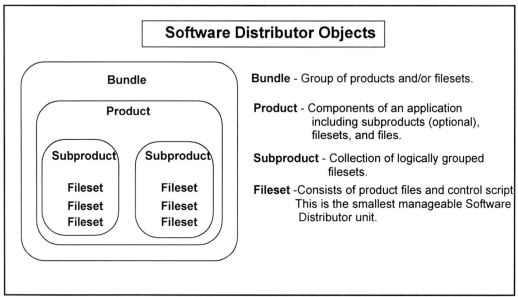

Figure 2-18   Software Distributor Objects

You can look at the bundle in Figure 2-18 as a group of software. This can be products, subproducts, and filesets as shown in the diagram. The concept here is to organize software in such a way that it is easy to manage. The diagram is somewhat over simplified in that a bundle can contain a whole or partial product. This allows a fileset to be in more than one product.

Listing Software

Although I like the graphical user interface of **swinstall,** you can also issue Software Distributor commands at the command line. One example is the **swlist** command. The **swlist** command is useful for viewing the software you have loaded on your system, the software you have loaded in a depot, or producing a list of depots. A graphical user interface to the **swlist** command is available in SAM. With the **swlist** command you perform many functions including the following:

- List the software you have at the specified level with the **-l** option. I will show several examples of this shortly. The levels you can specify are

  root
  depot
  bundle
  product
  subproduct
  fileset
  file

Levels are delineated by "." so you will see *bundle.[product].[subproduct].[fileset]*. You can get all kinds of useful information out of **swlist** and use this for other purposes. Some of the things you can do with **swlist** are:

- Display the table of contents from a software source.

- Specify which attributes you wish to see for a level of software such as name, size, revision, and so forth.

- Create a list of products that can be used as input to other Software Distributor commands such as **swinstall** and **swremove**.

When you run **swlist** with no options, you get a list of the software products installed on your system. Let's try a few **swlist** commands with the "-l" option to view software installed on a system (by default **swlist** will list installed products; you can use the "-s" option to specify a software depot or other source). The following example shows listing software at the bundle level.

```
$ swlist -l bundle

# various header information
#            .
#            .
#            .

B3691AA_TRY    B.10.00.32   Trail HP GlancePlus/UX for s700
B3782CA        B.10.00.00   HP-UX Media Kit (Ref Only)
B3910AA        B.10.00.00   HP C++ Compiler
HPUXEngRT700   B.10.00.00   English HP-UX Run-time Environment
```

This system has the HP-UX Runtime Environment, GlancePlus/UX trial software we loaded on it earlier, HP-UX Media Kit, and C++ compiler.

If we run **swlist** to the product level, the following is produced for GlancePlus/UX trial software; REV appears in place of the revision level.

```
$ swlist -l product B3691AA_TRY

# various header information
#            .
#            .
#            .

# B3691AA_TRY                   REV   Trail HP GlancePlus/UX
  B3691AA_TRY.Glance            REV   HP GlancePlus/UX
  B3691AA_TRY.MeasurementInt    REV   HP-UX Measurement Intfc

  (bundle)           (product)
```

GlancePlus/UX is comprised of the two products shown in this example. Are there any subproducts of which GlancePlus/UX is comprised? The following example will help us determine this.

```
$ swlist -l subproduct B3691AA_TRY

# various header information
#             .
#             .
#             .

# B3691AA_TRY                       REV   Trail HP GlancePlus/UX
  B3691AA_TRY.Glance                REV   HP GlancePlus/UX
  B3691AA_TRY.MeasurementInt REV   HP-UX Measurement Intfc


    (bundle)            (product)
```

The output of the product and subproduct levels are the same; there-fore, there are no subproducts in GlancePlus/UX. We can take this one step further and take this to the fileset level as shown in the following example.

```
$ swlist -l fileset B3691AA_TRY

# various header information
#             .
#             .
#             .

# B3691AA_TRY                       REV   Trail HP GlancePlus/UX
# B3691AA_TRY.Glance                REV   HP GlancePlus/UX
  B3691AA_TRY.Glance.GLANCE        REV   HP GlancePlus files
  B3691AA_TRY.Glance.GPM           REV   HP GlancePlus Motif
# B3691AA_TRY.MeasurementInt       REV   HP-UX Measurement Intfc
  B3691AA_TRY.MeasurementInt.MI REV   HP-UX Measurement Intfc


    (bundle)        (product)     (fileset)
```

With the **swlist** command and the **-l** option, we have worked our way down the hierarchy of HP GlancePlus/UX. Going down to the file level with the **-l file** option produces a long list of files associated with this prod-uct.

The other Software Distributor commands listed earlier can also be issued at the command line. You may want to look at the manual pages for these commands as you prepare to do more advanced Software Distributor work than loading software from a CD-ROM or tape.

To system administrators familiar with HP-UX 9.x, this is a different organization of software, but the graphical user interface of **swinstall** combined with the better organization of Software Distributor makes this an advantage of HP-UX 10.x.

Build an HP-UX Kernel (F4)

There are a variety of reasons to build a new HP-UX kernel on your system as well as a variety of ways to build the kernel. I would recommend you use the System Administration Manager (SAM) covered in Chapter 8 to build your kernel. There is, however, no substitute for understanding the process by which you would manually build an HP-UX kernel and therefore be more informed when you have SAM do this for you in the future. In this chapter I will discuss various commands related to kernel generation and cover the process by which you would manually create a kernel. As with most other system administration functions in HP-UX 10.x, creating an HP-UX kernel is the same for both a workstation and server system.

You may need to create a new HP-UX kernel in order to add device drivers or subsystems, to tune the kernel to get improved performance, or to change the dump and swap devices.

To begin, let's take a look at an existing kernel running on a Series 700. The **sysdef** command is used to analyze and report tunable parameters of a currently running system. You can specify a specific file to analyze if you don't wish to use the currently running system. The following is a partial listing of having run **sysdef** on the Series 700, used in the earlier installation example, showing some of the "max" parameters:

(on Series 700)

```
$  /usr/sbin/sysdef

NAME                  VALUE   BOOT      MIN-MAX      UNITS    FLAGS

maxdsiz               16384    -       256-655360    Pages     -
maxfiles                 60    -        30-2048                -
maxfiles_lim           1024    -        30-2048                -
maxssiz                2048    -       256-655360    Pages     -
maxswapchuncks          256    -          1-16384              -
maxtsize              16384    -       256-655360    Pages     -
maxuprc                  50    -         3-                    -
maxvgs                   10    -          -                    -
```

In addition to the tunable parameters, you may want to see a report of all the hardware found on your system. The **ioscan** command does this for you. Using **sysdef** and **ioscan**, you can see what your tunable parameters are set to and what hardware exists on your system. You will then know the way your system is set up and can then make changes to your kernel. The following is an **ioscan** output of the same Series 700 for which **sysdef** was run. (Using **-f** would have created a full listing; you should try with and without **-f**.)

(on Series 700)
```
$ /usr/sbin/ioscan

H/W Path     Class                Description
================================================================

             bc
1            graphics             Graphics
2            ba
2/0          unknown
2/0/1           ext_bus           Built-in SCSI
2/0/1.1            target
2/0/1.1.0           disk          HP        C2247
2/0/1.2            target
2/0/1.2.0           disk          TOSHIBA  CD-ROM XM-3301TA
2/0/1.6            target
```

```
2/0/1.6.0                   disk        HP          C2247
2/0/2           lan                     Built-in LAN
2/0/4           tty                     Built-in RS-232C
2/0/6           ext_bus                 Built-in Parallel Interface
2/0/8           audio                   Built-in Audio
2/0/10          pc                      Built-in Floppy Drive
2/0/10.1                 floppy         HP_PC_FDC_FLOPPY
2/0/11          ps2                     Built-in Keyboard
8               processor               Processor
9               memory                  Memory
```

The following is an **ioscan** output of a Series 800 (using **-f** would have created a full listing; you should try with and without **-f**). Note the four processors shown in this output.

                                                                    (on
Series 800)
$ **/usr/sbin/ioscan**

```
H/W Path      Class           Description
================================================================

              bc
8             bc              I/O Adapter
10            bc              I/O Adapter
10/0             ext_bus      GSC built-in Fast/Wide SCSI
10/0.3               target
10/0.3.0                disk  HP          C2490WD
10/0.4               target
10/0.4.0                disk  HP          C2490WD
10/0.5               target
10/0.5.0                disk  HP          C2490WD
10/0.6               target
10/0.6.0                disk  HP          C2490WD
10/4          bc              Bus Converter
10/4/0               tty      MUX
10/12         ba              Core I/O Adapter
10/12/0          ext_bus      Built-in Parallel Interface
10/12/5          ext_bus      Built-in SCSI
10/12/5.0            target
10/12/5.0.0             tape  HP          HP35480A
10/12/5.2            target
10/12/5.2.0             disk  TOSHIBA CD-ROM XM-4101TA
10/12/6          lan          Built-in LAN
10//12/7         ps2          Built-in Keyboard/Mouse
32            processor       Processor
34            processor       Processor
```

```
36              processor              Processor
38              processor              Processor
49              memory                 Memory
```

The file **/stand/vmunix** is the currently running kernel. Here is a long listing of the directory **/stand** on the Series 800 which shows the file **/stand/vmunix**:

```
$ ll   /stand

-rw-r--r--  1 root    sys          190 Jul 12 18:09 bootconf
drwxr-xr-x  2 root    root        1024 Jul 12 18:37 build
-rw-r--r--  1 root    root         684 Jul 12 18:05 ioconfig
-rw-r--r--  1 root    sys           82 Jul 12 18:31 kernel
-rw-r--r--  1 root    sys          609 Jul 12 18:15 system
-rwxr-xr-x  1 root    root     6938348 Jul 12 18:37 vmunix
```

In order to make a change to the kernel, we would change to the **/stand/build** directory (**cd /stand/build**) where all work in creating a new kernel is performed and issue the **system_prep** command as shown below:

```
$ /usr/lbin/sysadm/system_prep  -s   system
```

We can now proceed to edit the file **/stand/build/system** and make the desired changes to the kernel, including adding a driver or subsystem such as cdfs for CD-ROM file system.

With the desired changes having been made to the system file, we can create the new kernel which will be called **/stand/build/vmunix_test** with the command shown below:

```
$ mk_kernel  -s   system
```

At this point the new kernel exists in the **/stand/build** directory and can be moved to the **/stand** directory. I would first recommend moving the existing kernel (**/stand/vmunix**) to a backup file name and then moving the new kernel to the **/stand** directory as shown below:

```
$ mv   /stand/vmunix    /stand/vmunix.prev

$ mv   /stand/build/vmunix_test    /stand/vmunix
```

You can now shut down the system and automatically boot off of the new kernel.

In HP-UX 10.x you may want to rebuild the kernel for dynamic buffer cache. You can, for instance, specify a buffer cache boundary using dbc_min_pct as a lower boundary and dbc_max_pct as an upper boundary.

Figure 2-19 summarizes the process of building a new kernel in HP-UX 10.x.

Step	Comments
1) run **sysdef** and **ioscan -f**	Analyze and report tunable parameters of currently running kernel.
2) perform long listing of **/stand** directory	The file **vmunix** is the existing kernel and **system** is used to build new kernel.
3) **cd /stand/build**	This is the directory where the new kernel will be built.
4) **/usr/lbin/sysadm/system_prep -s system**	This extracts the **system** file from the currently running kernel.
5) edit **system** file and make desired changes	Takes place in the **/stand/build** directory.
6) **mk_kernel -s system**	Makes a new kernel in the **/stand/build** directory called **vmunix_test. conf.c, conf.o**, and **config.mk** are also produced.
7) **mv /stand/system /stand/system.prev** **mv /stand/build/system /stand/system**	Save the existing **system** file as **/stand/system.prev** and copy the new system file in **/stand/build/system** to **/stand/system.**
8) **mv /stand/vmunix /stand/vmunix.prev** **mv /stand/build/vmunix_test /stand/vmunix**	Save the existing **vmunix** file as **/stand/vmunix.prev** and copy the new kernel in **/stand/build** to **/stand/vmunix.**
9) **cd /** **shutdown -h 0**	Change directory to / and shut down the system so it comes up with the new kernel.

Figure 2-19 Creating a Kernel in HP-UX 10.x

Configure Additional Peripherals (F5)

As you progress through the installation flow, you reach a point where it makes sense to add the additional peripherals that are part of your system. A typical installation will have terminals, printers, a tape drive, a CD-ROM drive, and so forth. Some devices are "standard," meaning they are HP products or third-party products officially supported by HP. You have to be careful here, though, because what may seem as if it should work may not work after all and may not be supported. There is almost always a way to get things working eventually, but beware of devices you may be adding that aren't supported and may cause you trouble.

As you add additional peripherals to your system you will either have to add device files manually or use SAM to create them for you. Most all devices you add can be added through SAM. I find adding peripherals to be much like setting up networking; that is, I almost always use SAM but I find it important to know what is going on in the background. As an example, you could add a printer to your system using SAM and never know what has been done to support the new printer. In the event the printer does not work for some reason, you really can't begin troubleshooting the problem without an understanding of device files.

All About Device Files

What could be more confusing in the UNIX world than device files? Fortunately, in HP-UX device files for the Series 700 and Series 800 are nearly identical, so if you learn one it applies to the other. There were many more differences in device files in HP-UX 9.x. In this section I'll cover

- The structure of device files.

- Some commands associated with helping you work with device files.

• Some examples of creating device files.

A device file provides the HP-UX kernel with important information about a specific device. The HP-UX kernel needs to know a lot about a device before Input/Output operations can be performed. With HP-UX 10.x the device file naming convention is the same for workstations and server systems. Device files are in the **/dev** directory. There may also be a subdirectory under **/dev** used to further categorize the device files. An example of a subdirectory would be **/dev/dsk** where disk device files are usually located and **/dev/rmt** where tape drive device files are located. Figure 2-20 shows the HP-UX 10.x device file naming convention.

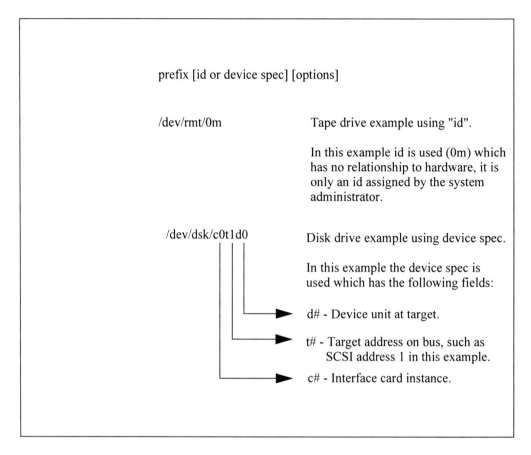

prefix [id or device spec] [options]

/dev/rmt/0m   Tape drive example using "id".

                                               In this example id is used (0m) which
                                               has no relationship to hardware, it is
                                               only an id assigned by the system
                                               administrator.

/dev/dsk/c0t1d0   Disk drive example using device spec.

                                               In this example the device spec is
                                               used which has the following fields:

                                               d# - Device unit at target.

                                               t# - Target address on bus, such as
                                                    SCSI address 1 in this example.

                                               c# - Interface card instance.

Figure 2-20 HP-UX 10.x Device File Naming Convention

There are a number of commands you use as you go about creating device files. The **ioscan** command is the first of these. This command was covered under "Build an HP-UX Kernel" in this chapter so you may want to flip back and review this material.

The next command that helps you when creating device files is **lsdev**. **lsdev** lists all of the drivers configured into your system. When adding a device file, you need to have the driver for the device you use configured into the system. If it is not configured into the system, you can use SAM to configure it or use the manual kernel configuration process covered earlier in this chapter. There is a column for the major number for a character device and block device, the driver name, and class of the driver. Here is an example of running **lsdev** on the same Series 700 **ioscan** was run on in an earlier section.

(on Series 700)
```
$ /usr/sbin/lsdev
```

```
Character      Block       Driver      Class
      0          -1        cn          pseudo
      1          -1        ansio0      tty
      3          -1        mm          pseudo
     16          -1        ptym        ptym
     17          -1        ptys        ptys
     46          -1        netdiag1    unknown
     52          -1        lan2        lan
     56          -1        ni          unknown
     60          -1        netman      unknown
     64          64        lv          lvm
     66          -1        audio       audio
     69          -1        dev_config  pseudo
     72          -1        clone       pseudo
     73          -1        strlog      pseudo
     74          -1        sad         pseudo
    112          24        pflop       floppy
    116          -1        echo        pseudo
    119          -1        dlpi        pseudo
    122          -1        inet_cots   unknown
    122          -1        inet_cots   unknown
    156          -1        ptm         strptym
    157          -1        ptm         strptys
    159          -1        ps2         ps2
    164          -1        pipedev     unknown
    168          -1        beep        graf_pseudo
    174          -1        framebuf    graf_pseudo
    188          31        sdisk       disk
    189          -1        klog        pseudo
    203          -1        sctl        pseudo
    205          -1        stape       tape
    207          -1        sy          pseudo
    216          -1        CentIF      ext_bus
    227          -1        kepd        pseudo
    229          -1        ite         graf_pseudo
```

Here is an example of running **lsdev** on the same Series 800 **ioscan** was run on in an earlier section.

(on Series 800)

```
$ /usr/sbin/lsdev
```

```
Character       Block      Driver        Class
     0           -1        cn            pseudo
     3           -1        mm            pseudo
    16           -1        ptym          ptym
    17           -1        ptys          ptys
    28           -1        diag0         diag
    46           -1        netdiag1      unknown
    52           -1        lan2          lan
    56           -1        ni            unknown
    60           -1        netman        unknown
    64           64        lv            lvm
    69           -1        dev_config    pseudo
    72           -1        clone         pseudo
    73           -1        strlog        pseudo
    74           -1        sad           pseudo
   116           -1        echo          pseudo
   119           -1        dlpi          pseudo
   122           -1        inet_cots     unknown
   122           -1        inet_cots     unknown
   136           -1        lpr0          unknown
   156           -1        ptm           strptym
   157           -1        ptm           strptys
   159           -1        ps2           ps2
   164           -1        pipedev       unknown
   168           -1        beep          graf_pseudo
   188           31        sdisk         disk
   189           -1        klog          pseudo
   193           -1        mux2          tty
   203           -1        sctl          pseudo
   205           -1        stape         tape
   207           -1        sy            pseudo
   216           -1        CentIF        ext_bus
   227           -1        kepd          pseudo
```

From these two **lsdev** outputs you can observe some minor differences in the devices. The Series 700, for instance, has such classes as audio and floppy and the Series 800 has a multiplexer.

You can use **ioscan** to show you the device files for a particular peripheral. Going back to the Series 800 that had four disks and a CD-

ROM attached to it, you could issue the following **ioscan** command to see the device files associated with disk:

(on Series 800)
```
$ /usr/sbin/ioscan -fn -C disk

Class  I  H/W Path    Driver  S/W State  H/W Type    Description
========================================================================
disk   0  10/0.3.0     sdisk   CLAIMED     DEVICE       HP C2490WD
                       /dev/dsk/c0t3d0  /dev/rdsk/c0t3d0

disk   1  10/0.4.0     sdisk   CLAIMED     DEVICE       HP C2490WD
                       /dev/dsk/c0t4d0  /dev/rdsk/c0t4d0

disk   2  10/0.5.0     sdisk   CLAIMED     DEVICE       HP C2490WD
                       /dev/dsk/c0t5d0  /dev/rdsk/c0t5d0

disk   3  10/0.6.0     sdisk   CLAIMED     DEVICE       HP C2490WD
                       /dev/dsk/c0t6d0  /dev/rdsk/c0t6d0

disk   3  10/12/5/2/0  sdisk   CLAIMED     DEVICE       CD-ROM
                       /dev/dsk/c1t2d0  /dev/rdsk/c1t2d0
```

You can see from this **ioscan** all of the devices files associated with disk including the CD-ROM.

You could find out more information about one of these devices with the **diskinfo** command and the character device you want to know more about as shown below (using the "-v" option for verbose provides more detailed information).

```
$ diskinfo /dev/rdsk/c0t5d0

SCSI describe of /dev/rdsk/c0t5d0
            vendor: HP
        product id: C2490WD
              type: direct access
              size: 2082636 bytes
   bytes per sector: 512
```

Before we construct a device file, let's view two existing device files on the Series 700 and see where some of this information appears. The first long listing is that of the tape drive and the second is the disk, both of which are on the Series 700 in the earlier listing.

(on Series 700)

```
$ ll /dev/rmt/0m


crw-rw-rw- 2 bin bin 205 0x003000 Feb 12 03:00 /dev/rmt/0m
```

(on Series 700)

```
$ ll /dev/dsk/c0t1d0


brw-r----- 1 root sys 31 0x001000 Feb 12 03:01 /dev/dsk/c0t1d0
```

The tape drive device file shows a major number of 205 corresponding to that shown for the <u>character</u> device driver stape from **lsdev**. The disk drive device file shows a major number of 31 corresponding to the <u>block</u> device driver sdisk from **lsdev**. Since the tape drive requires only a character device file and there is no major number for a block stape device, as indicated by the "-1" in the block column of **lsdev**, this is the only device file that exists for the tape drive. The disk, on the other hand, may be used as either block device or character device (also referred to as the raw device). Therefore, we should see a character device file with a major number of 188 as shown in **ioscan** for sdisk.

(on Series 700)

```
$ ll /dev/rdsk/c0t0d0


crw-r----- 1 root sys 188 0x001000 Feb 12 03:01 /dev/rdsk/c0t1d0
```

We can now create a device file for a second tape drive, this time at SCSI address 2, and a disk device file for a disk drive at SCSI address 5 using the **mksf** command. You can run **mksf** two different ways. The first form of mksf requires you to include less specific information such as the minor number. The second form requires you to include more of this specific information. Some of these arguments relate only to the specific form of **mksf** you use.

-d   Use the device driver specified. A list of device drivers is obtained with the **lsdev** command.

-C   The device specified belongs to this class. The class is also obtained with the **lsdev** command.

-H   Use the hardware path specified. Hardware paths are obtained with the **ioscan** command.

-m   The minor number of the device is supplied.

-r   Create a character, also known as a raw, device file

-v   Use verbose output which prints the name of each special file as it is created.

We could now create a block device file for a disk at SCSI address 5 using the following **mksf** command:

(on Series 700)

```
$ /sbin/mksf -v -C disk -m 0x005000 /dev/dsk/c0t5d0

    making /dev/dsk/c0t5d0 b 31 0x005000
```

Similarly, we could now create a <u>character</u> device file for a disk at SCSI address 5 using form two of **mksf**:

(on Series 700)

```
$ /sbin/mksf -v -r -C disk -m 0x005000 /dev/dsk/c0t5d0

    making /dev/rdsk/c0t5d0 c 188 0x005000
```

The "-v" option used in these examples prints out each device file as it is created. If you wanted to add a second tape drive at SCSI address 2 to your system in addition to the existing tape drive (/dev/rmt/0m), you might use the following **mksf** command:

(on Series 700)

```
$ /sbin/mksf  -v -C tape -m 0x002000 /dev/rmt/1m

    making /dev/rmt/1m c 205 0x002000
```

Character devices are automatically produced for these tape drives since no block device drivers are shown using the **lsdev** command as indicated by a -1 in the "Block" column.

System Startup and Shutdown (F6)

Startup and shutdown for HP-UX 10.x are based on a mechanism that sep-arates startup scripts from configuration information. In order to modify the way your system starts or stops, you don't have to modify scripts, which in general is considered somewhat risky; you can instead modify configuration variables. The startup and shutdown sequence is based on an industry standard that is similar to many other UNIX-based systems, so your knowledge on HP-UX applies to many other systems. If you have experience with HP-UX 9.x, you will find this new startup and shutdown structure much different (and improved).

Startup and shutdown are going to become increasingly more impor-tant to you as your system administration work becomes more sophisti-cated. As you load and customize more applications, you will need more startup and shutdown knowledge. What I'll do in this section is give you an overview of startup and shutdown and the commands you can use to shut-down your system.

There are the following three components in the startup and shutdown model:

Execution Scripts - Execution scripts read variables from configu-ration variable scripts and run through the startup or shutdown sequence. These scripts are located in **/sbin/init.d**.

Configuration Variable Scripts - These are the files you would modify to set variables that are used to enable or disable a subsystem or perform some other func-tion at the time of system startup or shutdown. These are located in **/etc/rc.config.d**.

Link Files -   These files are used to control the order in which
                    scripts execute. These are actually links to execu-
                    tion scripts to be executed when moving from one
                    run level to another. These files are located in the
                    directory for the appropriate run level such as /
                    sbin/rc0.d for run level zero, **/sbin/rc1.d** for run
                    level 1, and so on.

Sequencer Script - This script invokes execution scripts based on
                    run-level transition. This script is **/sbin/rc**.

Figure 2-21 shows the directory structure for startup and shutdown
scripts.

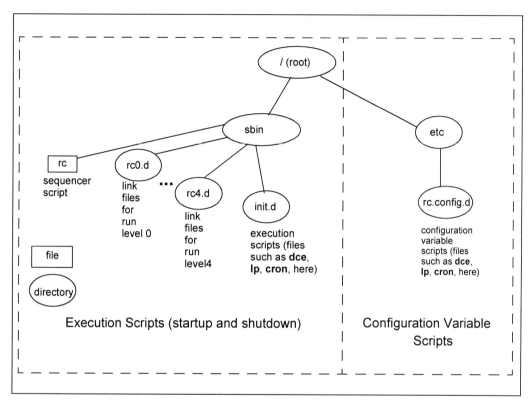

Figure 2-21 Organization of Startup and Shutdown Files

Execution scripts perform startup and shutdown tasks. **/sbin/rc** invokes the execution script, with the appropriate start or stop arguments, and you can view the appropriate start or stop messages on the console. The messages you see will have one of the three following values:

OK	This indicates that the execution script started or shut down properly.
FAIL	A problem occurred at startup or shutdown.
N/A	The script was not configured to start.

In order to start up a subsystem, you would simply edit the appropriate configuration file in **/etc/rc.config.d**. An example showing **/etc/rc.config.d/audio** is shown with the **AUDIO_SERVER** variable set to **1**.

```
#   ********** File:  /etc/rc.config.d/audio **************
# Audio server configuration.  See audio(5)
#
# AUDIO_SER:        Set to 1 to start audio server daemon
#

AUDIO_SERVER=1
```

This results in the following message being shown at the time the system boots:

```
Start audio server daemon .......................[ OK ]
```

And this message at the time the system is shut down:

```
Stopping audio server daemon ......................OK
```

Run levels have been mentioned several times in this discussion. Both the startup and shutdown scripts described here as well as the **/etc/inittab** file depend on run levels. In HP-UX 10.x the following run levels exist:

0	Halted run level.
s	Run level s, also known as single-user mode, is used to ensure no one else is on the system so you can proceed with system administration tasks.
1	Run level 1 starts various basic processes.

2	Run level 2 allows users to access the system. This is also known as multi-user mode.
3	Run level 3 is for exporting NFS file systems.
4	Run level 4 starts the HP Visual User Environment (HP VUE).
5 and 6	Not currently used.

/etc/inittab is also used to define a variety of processes that will be run and is used by **/sbin/init**. The **/sbin/init** process ID is 1. It is the first process started on your system and it has no parent. The **init** process looks at **/etc/inittab** to determine the run level of the system.

Entries in the **/etc/inittab** file have the following format:

id:run state:action:process

id:	The name of the entry. The id is up to four characters long and must be unique in the file. If the line in **/etc/inittab** is preceded by a "#", the entry is treated as a comment.
run state:	Specifies the run level at which the command is executed. More than one run level can be specified. The command is executed for every run level specified.
action:	Defines which of 11 actions will be taken with this process. The 11 choices for action are initdefault; sysinit; boot; bootwait; wait; respawn; once; powerfail; powerwait; ondemand; off.
process	The shell command to be run if the run level and/ or action field so indicates.

Here is an example of an **/etc/inittab** entry:

```
vue :4:respawn:/usr/vue/bin/vuerc
```

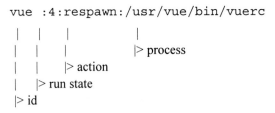

This is in the **/etc/inittab** file as opposed to being defined as a startup script because HP VUE may be killed and have to be restarted whenever it dies even if there is not a change in run level. **respawn** starts a process if it does not exist and restarts the process when it dies.

Another example is the first line from **/etc/inittab**:

```
init:4:initdefault:
```

The default run level of the system is defined as 4. You can change the run level interactively by executing **init** and specifying a run level as shown below:

```
$ init s
```

This command switches the system to single-user mode.

The basics of system startup and shutdown described here are important to understand. You will be starting up and shutting down your system and possibly even modifying some of the files described here. Please take a close look at the startup and shutdown files before you begin to modify these.

Now lets take a look at the commands you can issue to shutdown your system.

System Shutdown

What does it mean to shut down the system? Well, in its simplest form, a shutdown of the system simply means issuing the **/sbin/shutdown** command. The **shutdown** command is used to terminate all processing. It has many options including the following:

-r	Automatically reboots the system, that is, brings it down and brings it up.
-h	Halts the system completely.
-y	Completes the shutdown without asking you any of the questions it would normally ask.
grace	Specifies the number of seconds you wish to wait before the system is shut down in order to give your users time to save files, quit applications, and log out.

Here are some of the things your system does when you issue the **shutdown** command:

- Checks to see if the user who executed shutdown does indeed have permission to execute the command.
- Changes the working directory to root (/).
- Sets *PATH* to **/usr/bin/:/usr/sbin:/sbin**.
- Updates all superblocks.
- Informs the users that a **shutdown** has been issued and asks them to log out.
- **/sbin/rc** which does such things as unmount file systems and other tasks is run.
- **/sbin/reboot** is run if the **-h** or **-r** options were used.

So, to halt the system you would type

```
$ shutdown -h
```

You may then be asked if you want to type a message to users informing them of the impending system shutdown. After you type the message, it
is immediately sent to all users. After the specified time elapses, the system
begins the shutdown process. Once you receive a message that the system
is halted, you can power off all your system components.

To shut down the system in two minutes without being asked any
questions, type

```
$ shutdown -h -y 120
```

If the system is already in single-user mode or you like to live danger-
ously, you can execute **/usr/sbin/reboot**. I strongly suggest you issue **shutdown** which will call **reboot**. The **reboot** command terminates all
processes and then halts or reboots the system. **reboot** has many options
including the following:

-h	Shut down the system and halt the CPU.
-r	Shut down the system and automatically reboot.
-n	Do not sync the disks before reboot or halt.
-s	Sync the disks before reboot or halt (this is default).
-q	This is a quick reboot. No messages are sent and all processes are terminated.
-t time	Specify the time to bring down the system. Type either now or +number where number is the seconds in which to reboot or hour:min where hour:min is the time at which to reboot.
-m mesg	Sends the message specified to all terminals.

Again, I recommend using the **shutdown** command, not **reboot**. You
may, however, want to go into single-user mode with **shutdown**, perform

some task such as a backup, and then reboot the system to return it to its original state.

CHAPTER 3

Windows NT File System Layout

Windows NT File System Layout

There are a variety of considerations you have related to your Windows NT file system. The first, and most important, is the file system type to implement. The two primary trade-offs you have related to file system type are covered in the next section. You then have a whole set of issues related to using the Windows NT file system such as *Windows NT Explorer*; properties; attributes; security; permissions; and auditing. All of these topics will be covered in this chapter.

The two file system types to consider using with Windows NT are New Technology File System (NTFS) and File Allocation Table (FAT). There are some trade-offs to consider when deciding whether to use FAT or NTFS. The following is a brief comparison of NTFS versus FAT that also appears in the file system chapter.

NTFS and FAT

New Technology File System (NTFS)

New Technology File System (NTFS) is the best file system to select for running Windows NT on your system. If possible, I recommend using NTFS. The following bullet list describes some of the more important characteristics and features of NTFS:

- **NTFS File Names** can be up to 256 characters. This length includes any extensions you might use in a file name. You can use both upper and lower case in a name, however, file names are not case sensitive. The only reserved characters in NTFS file names that you can't use are the following:

  ? " / \ < > * ! :

- **NTFS is a recoverable file system**. There is a transaction log associated with NTFS that keeps track of directory and file updates. This means you can redo or undo an operation should your Windows NT system fail.

- **Windows NT security** can be used with NTFS. You can configure various auditing and permissions on files and directories in Windows NT if you use NTFS.

- **NTFS has no undelete utility** as a standard part of the operating system. To those of us with a lot of UNIX experience this is nothing new. If you have had the luxury of an undelete utility in the operating system(s) you have used in the past, then look at not having an undelete utility as adding much needed excitement to your life.

- **NTFS has substantially more file system overhead** than FAT. Along with all of the advantages of NTFS come the requirements for more of pretty much everything. As you work your way up the functional ladder of operating systems, it is a general rule that you will require more resources in general. A low-end, single-user personal computer needs minimal resources and one person to load and use it. A gigantic corporate mainframe may need a fleet of people just to handle security! It is therefore expected that NTFS would require more file system overhead than FAT.

- **NTFS requires large partition sizes**. Don't even play around with small partition sizes when using NTFS. Although 50 MBytes is the minimum file system size normally associated with Windows NT, you should have more than 100 MBytes of file system for NTFS if you are going to use the system for application or file or print purposes. This should not be a problem when you consider the typical configurations of today's systems. Even the "toy" system I used in the installation example had a 1 GByte hard disk drive.

- **NTFS has a large partition capacity**. Since I just spent some time talking about the minimum end of an NTFS partition size, I may as well cover the maximum size. An NTFS partition can be as large as 2^{64} bytes in Windows NT. This, of course, is outrageously large. Although today's systems are not going to have a partition of this size, it is possible that future systems may require a large partition size and it is admirable that Windows NT possesses such great head room for the future.

- **NTFS has a large file size**. The maximum file size for NTFS in Windows NT is also 2^{64} bytes.

- **No NTFS formatted floppies**. It is not now possible to have an NTFS formatted floppy disk. Along with all of the advantages of NTFS at the high end come some minor drawbacks at the low end. There is just too much overhead in NTFS to allow you to have an NTFS formatted floppy disk. This, however, is a small price to pay for all of the advantages of NTFS at the high end.

- **NTFS attempts to store files in contiguous space**. All things being equal, it would typically take longer to access a file if it is located in an uncontiguous area rather than a contiguous area of the disk. If NTFS is able to store files in a contiguous area, you will see a performance advantage as a result of this feature.

• **NTFS is only accessed through Windows NT**. You can use NTFS with Windows NT, but it is not now accessible through other operating systems.

File Allocation Table (FAT) File System

Although I recommend using NTFS if possible on your Windows NT system, millions of people have successfully used FAT for many years with most MS-DOS computers. FAT can also be used for Windows NT and OS/2. If you would like to boot your computer with both MS-DOS and Windows NT, then you will need a FAT partition. NTFS is more robust than FAT, but you may not need any of the additional features of NTFS. The following bullet list describes some of the more important characteristics and features of FAT:

• **FAT File Names** can take on two different forms in Windows NT. The standard MS-DOS FAT name can be used which is eight characters, a dot which acts as a delimiter, and then a three-character extension. **autoexec.bat** is a file name with eight characters, the dot delimiter, and a three-character extension. In this case the name must start with a letter or number. There are no spaces permitted in the name. Names are not case sensitive and case is not preserved in the file name. The following names are reserved:

NUL, PRN, LPT1 - LPT3, COM - COM4, AUX, CON

In addition, the following characters are reserved:

? " / \ ^ , = * ! : ; [ ]

- **Alternatively, you can use Long File Names (LFN)** with FAT under Windows NT. In this case you can have a name with 255 characters, which includes the full path but excludes the extension. This is a big advantage over the eight character name. In addition you have the flexibility of using spaces and multiple extensions with period delimiters in the name. Names are not case sensitive but do preserve case.

- **Windows NT security** cannot be used with FAT.

- **FAT has no undelete utility** when running under Windows NT. It may, however, be possible to use and MS-DOS FAT partition to undelete a file on a Windows NT FAT partition. I would not count on this and instead do everything possible to prevent files from being mistakenly deleted.

- **FAT uses very little file system overhead.**

- **FAT does not require partition sizes as large as NTFS.** If you will be using your Windows NT system to run a demanding application or for file and print services, you will still want to have a healthy size partition.

- **FAT also has a large partition capacity**. A FAT partition under Windows NT can be as large as 2^{32} bytes. This is also a large partition size.

- **FAT has a large file size**. The maximum file size in Windows NT using FAT is also 2^{32} bytes.

- **FAT formatted floppies are supported**.

- **FAT can be accessed through Windows NT, MS-DOS, and OS/2.**

Table 3-1 shows some of the features of FAT and NTFS.

TABLE 3-1   Some important FAT and NTFS characteristics

Characteristic	NTFS	FAT
File name and directory length:	255 characters	8 characters plus 3 character extension (w/o LFN)
		255 characters (with LFN)
Preserve case in file name?	yes	no
File name case sensitive?	no	no
Reserved file and directory name characters:	? " / \ < > * ! :	? " / \ ^ , = * ! : ; [ ]
Is it possible to format a floppy in this file system?	No NTFS formatted floppies.	No problem with FAT formatted floppies.
Associated operating system(s):	Windows NT	Windows NT, MS-DOS, OS/2
Security Features?	yes	no
Partition Size	2^{64}	2^{32}
File Size	2^{64}	2^{32}

Using the Windows NT File Systems

All of the background information just presented is important to know when you configure your system. You need to understand the different types of file systems and their characteristics. After having selected your file system type and configuring it, you now want to use it. Windows NT Explorer is the application through which you access your file system(s).

Windows NT Explorer is used to both view your file systems and control them. It is an advanced file system tool that provides almost all of the control over files and directories you need. The following sections describe some of the highlights of Windows NT Explorer. The following sections are not, however, a tutorial covering every aspect of *Windows NT Explorer*. Such rudimentary file related functions as moving, copying, and erasing files and directories are not covered. Some of the more advanced and system-related functions of file system-related work are covered. Some of the tasks you can perform with *Windows NT Explorer* include:

- Display directories and files and traverse the file systems graphically.

- Create and remove directories.

- Create, remove, and copy files.

- Determine file properties.

- Determine file attributes.

- Access CD-ROM drives.

- Access floppy disks.

- Manage shared devices on the network.

- Work with file and directory security.

Starting Windows NT Explorer

Figure 3-1 shows invoking *Windows NT Explorer* from the *Start* menu on my Windows NT Server system and Figure 3-2 shows what the Windows NT Explorer looks like after having been invoked.

Windows NT Explorer is a prominent program in Windows NT and therefore exists at the second level of menu hierarchy.

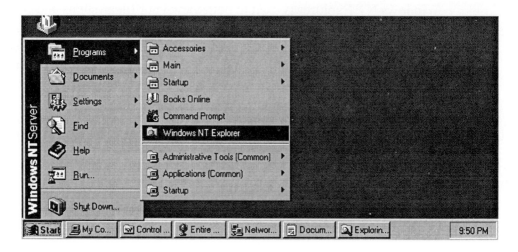

Figure 3-1   Starting *Windows NT Explorer*

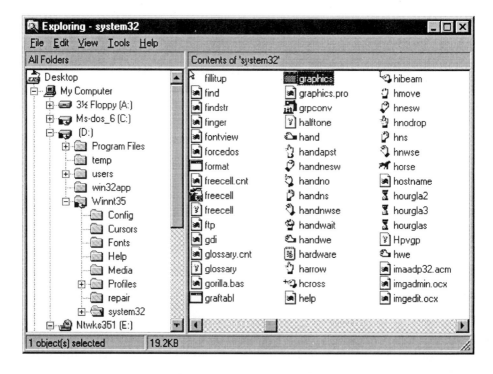

Figure 3-2   *Windows NT Explorer* with   **D:\Winnt35\system32\graphics**
Selected

The left side of the Explorer window shows "All Folders." This system has the following drives:

- 3 1/2 Floppy (A:) - Floppy disk drive.
- Ms-dos_6 (C:) - The disk partition on which MS-DOS is loaded.
- (D:) - The Windows NT partition on which we are running.
- (E:) - CD-ROM.

You can select any of these drives and traverse the hierarchy.

Of more interest are selecting a file and obtaining more detailed information about it and modifying its characteristics. The next sections investigate the file **graphics** and some of its characteristics.

Viewing Properties with Windows NT Explorer

An important aspect of the files on your system are their property assignments. Figure 3-3 shows the *Windows NT Explorer* with the file **graphics** selected.

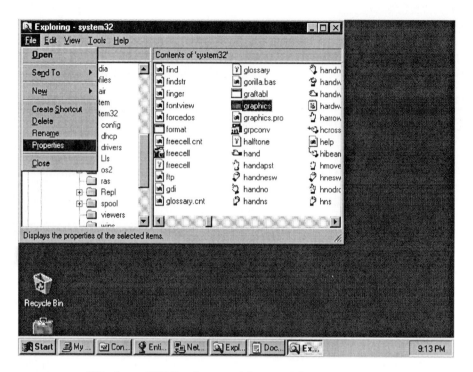

Figure 3-3 *Windows NT Explorer* with **graphics**

The *File-Properties* pulldown menu in Figure 3-3 is used to display the properties of graphics as shown in Figure 3-4. The pulldown menu is obscuring the full path in *Windows NT Explorer,* but the full path of the file **graphics** is **D:\Winnt35\system32\graphics.com**. After having selected the *File-Properties* pulldown menu pick, the window in Figure 3-4 appears.

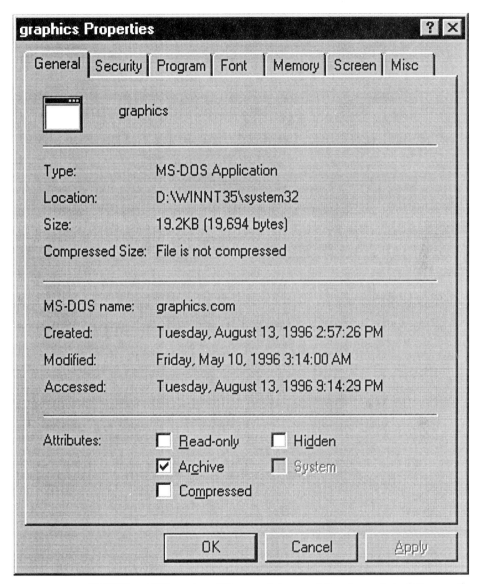

Figure 3-4 **D:\Winnt35\system32\graphics** and Its Associated Properties

There are several categories of file-related information you can view in *Properties*. By default, the General category is shown when you first open the *Property* window for a file. The following categories of properties you can view through this window:

- General

- Security

- Program

- Font

- Memory

- Screen

- Miscellaneous

In this section I am going to concentrate on only *General* and the *Permissions* and *Auditing* categories below *Security*.

Attributes (under General Area of Properties)

Figure 3-4 provides a lot of useful information about the file **graphics**. Most of the information is self explanatory, such as the *Type, Location, Size, Compressed Size, MS-DOS Name, Created, Modified, Accessed*, and so on. The *Attributes* are of particular interest because this is where you define the type of access users will have to a file. Table 3-2 is a summary of the Attributes categories shown in Figure 3-4:

TABLE 3-2   Summary of File Attributes

File Attribute	Description
Read Only	File can't be written to, it can only be read. This means that the user can't change the file; they can only view it.

File Attribute	Description
Archive	This file has been modified since the last time it was saved during a backup.
Compressed	The file is compressed. This means it consumes less disk space than it would if it were uncompressed.
Hidden	This file can't be seen in directory listings.
System	This is a system file.

These are important file-related attributes. You can use these as the system administrator to control access to any files. In general, the defaults set up by Windows NT are sufficient. As your users create many files and directories on the system, you may want to set these attributes in such a way that important files are protected.

These attributes are controlled through the General area. Let's now switch to the Security area and take a look at additional control mechanisms you have.

Security (under Properties)

Figure 3-5 shows the *Security* area under *Properties*. The attributes that you have access to are *Permissions, Auditing*, and *Ownership*. Let's take a closer look at *Permissions* and *Auditing*. I won't cover *Ownership* since the functionality of this area is limited to taking ownership of a file. *Permissions* and *Auditing* are important characteristics of any operating system and you may find the need to control these on your systems on a regular basis.

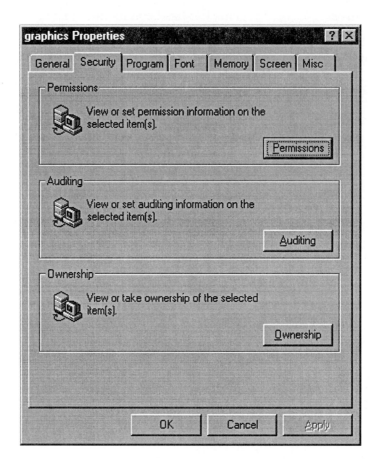

Figure 3-5 Security

These three control areas can be used in conjunction with the permissions over which you have control under *General*.

Permissions (under Security Area of Properties)

Figure 3-6 shows the permissions on the file **graphics** from the *Permissions* area under *Security*.

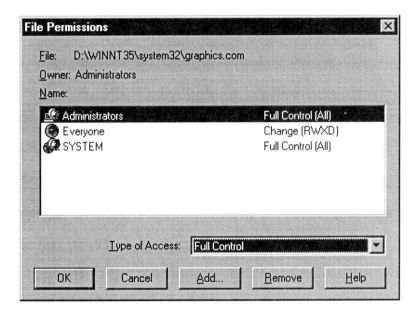

Figure 3-6 *Permissions* Area under *Security*

The *Permissions* area allows you to specify the access that a group or user has on a file. By default, a file will have the permissions specified by the directory in which it is located. In this case "Administrators" has *Full Control* over the file **graphics** and can therefore manipulate the file in any way including deleting it.

"Everyone" has somewhat more restricted control over the file called *Change*. Change means that "Everyone" can read, write, execute, and delete the file.

Here is a summary of the four types of standard permissions that can be set on a file:

Full Control

• Take ownership of file.

• Change permissions of file.

• Delete the file.

• Change the contents of the file.

• Execute the file if it is a program.

• View the contents of the file.

Change

• Delete the file.

• Change the contents of the file.

• Execute the file if it is a program.

• View the contents of the file.

Read

• Execute the file if it is a program.

• View the file.

No Access

• Prevents any access of any kind for this file.

You can also view and change permissions of files from the command line with **cacls**. Figure 3-7 shows the help screen for the **cacls** command.

Figure 3-7 **cacls** Help Screen

cacls is used to display and modify the access control lists of files. You can see in Figure 3-7 that you have four different types of access rights for files that were described in detail earlier. The following list shows the abbreviations for access rights that are associated with the **cacls** command.

N	None
R	Read
C	Change
F	Full Control

Figure 3-8 shows using both **cacls** and the *File Permissions* window to view the existing permissions for **D:\WINNT\REGEDIT.EXE**. This is one of the most important files on the system that is used in a later chapter to view and modify registry information on the system. This is a file that you want to carefully manage access rights to in order to avoid any operating system mishaps.

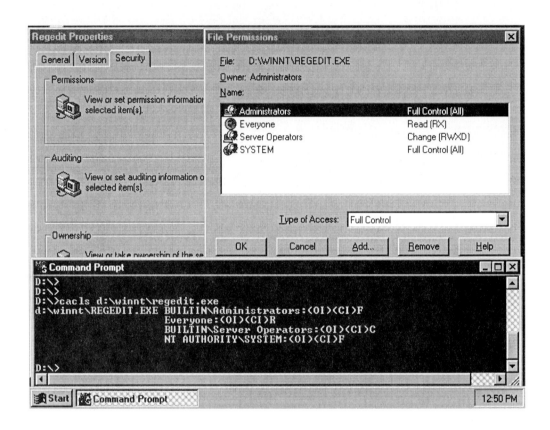

Figure 3-8   **D:\WINNT\REGEDIT.EXE** Permissions

Notice that *Server Operators* do indeed have *Change* rights to this file. You can, of course, modify the permissions on this, or any file, on the system. The *File Permissions* window and the output of the **cacls** command are in different formats; however, they contain the same information.

Auditing (under Security Area of Properties)

Auditing files and directories is a way of tracking their usage. To define audit policies, log in is a member of the Administrator's group, select the file you wish to audit from *Windows NT Explorer*, and select the *Auditing* area under *Security* as shown in Figure 3-7. This figure shows a copy of the graphics file that I have placed in **D:\temp**. The full path of the files is **D:\temp\graphics.com**.

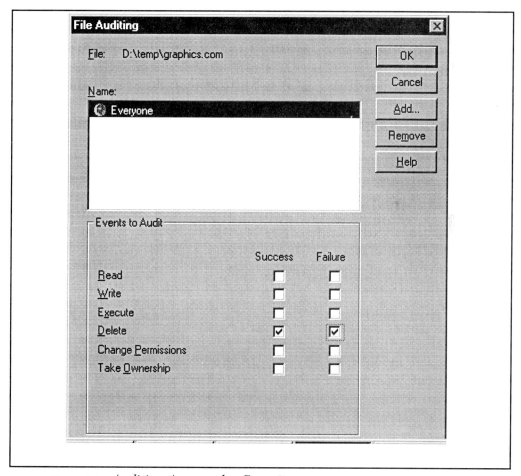

Figure 3-9 *Auditing* Area under *Security*

Select the *Name* box to choose the users you wish to audit. "Every-one" is selected in Figure 3-9 which means that all users will be audited. The only remaining information to include is what events will be audited. Both successful (*Success*) and unsuccessful (*Failure*) events can be monitored. In this case I have selected only successful and unsuccessful attempts to *Delete* as the *Events to Audit*. The following is a list and brief description of the events you can monitor in the same order in which they are shown in Figure 3-9:

- *Read* - Reading information about the file such as owner, permissions, attributes, and contents is audited.

- *Write* - Changes to the file such as owner, permissions, attributes, and contents are audited.

- *Execute* - Running the program is audited.

- *Delete* - Removing the file is audited.

- *Change Permissions* - Altering the permissions of the file is audited.

- *Take Ownership* - Changing the ownership of the file is audited.

If you hit OK in Figure 3-9 without having setup auditing on your system you will receive the dialogue box shown in Figure 3-10.

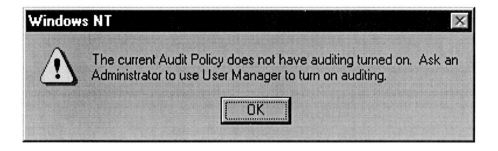

Figure 3-10 Audit Policy Failure.

Auditing must be turned on as part of the *User Manager* menu under *Policies - Audit.* You would select *Audit These Events* and *File and Object Access* as shown in Figure 3-11. Although I have made extensive use of the on-line help in Windows NT, there was no reference to this error or how to correct it in the version of Windows NT I used to initially set up auditing of the **D:\temp\graphics.com** file.

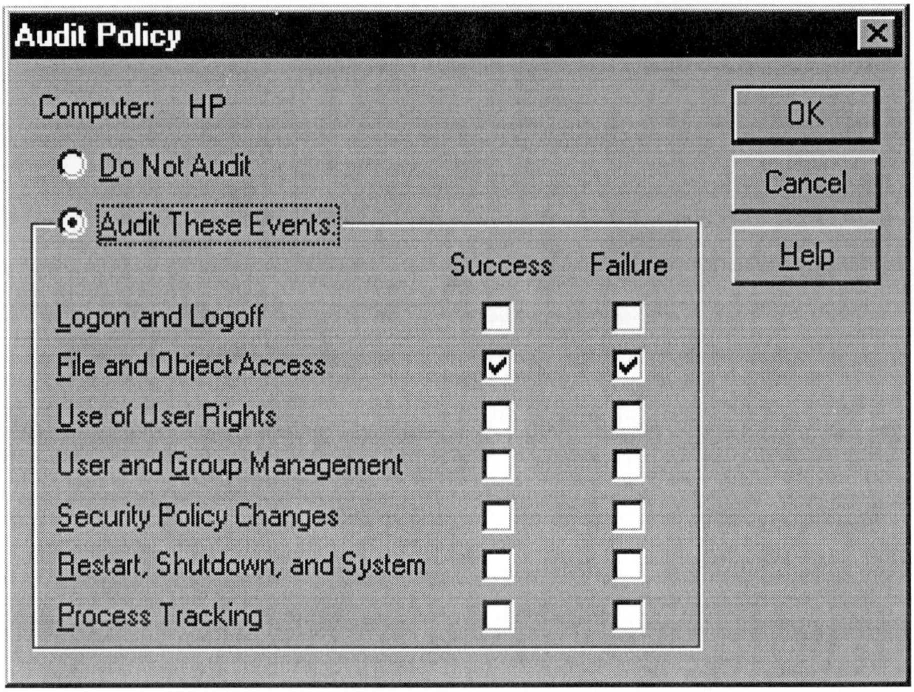

Figure 3-11 *Policies - Audit* setup under *User Manager*.

After having set up this *Audit Policy* I deleted **D:\temp\graphics.com** and went into the *Event Viewer*, under *Administrative Tools (Common)*, to review what audited activity had taken place. The menu pick *Log - Security* listed all of the security-related events and I selected *View - Detail* to obtain the window shown in Figure 3-12. The name of file is not shown in this figure but does appear in the *Description*.

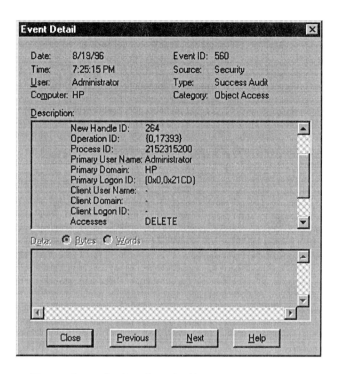

Figure 3-12 *Event Detail* of Deleted File

Auditing as described in this section can be useful in heading off potential security problems. Users who are continually trying to access files they should not be accessing may cause a potential security risk. Implementing auditing and reviewing the event log can prevent potential security problems.

Chapter 4

The HP-UX File System Layout

HP-UX File Types

A file is a means by which information is stored on an HP-UX system. The commands you issue, the applications you use, the data you store, and the devices you access such as printers and keyboard are all contained in files. This is one of the aspects of HP-UX that makes it both simple and complex; simple because you know everything out there is a file, complex because the contents of a file could be anything ranging from simple data you can read, to a device file that is created by your system administrator with a unique set of commands.

Every file on the system has a file name. The operating system takes care of all file system-related tasks; you just need to know the name of the file and how to use it. The file types we will look at are

- Text Files

- Data Files

- Source Code Files

- Executable Files

- Shell Programs

- Links

- Device Files

Text Files

What could be simpler than a file that contains characters, just like the ones you're now reading in this chapter? These ASCII characters are letters and numerals that represent the work you perform. If, for instance, you use an HP-UX editor to create an electronic mail message or a letter, you are creating a text file in most cases. Here is an example of part of a text file:

```
*                                                              *
  *                                                          *
    *                    HP LaserROM/UX                    *
      *                    README File                    *
        *********************************************************
```

```
This version of HP LaserROM/UX can only be installed and run
on HP-UX Operating System Release 10.x or better.

The graphical user interface of HP LaserROM/UX requires the X
Window System version 11, Release 5 or later.
```

This text file is easy to read, has no data or other information in it, and can easily be modified.

Data Files

A file that contains data used by one of your applications is a data file. If you use a sophisticated desktop publishing tool such as FrameMaker to write a book, you create data files that FrameMaker® uses. These data files contain data, which you can usually read, and formatting information, which you can sometimes read but is usually hidden from you. If your HP-UX installation uses a database program, then you may have data files which you can partially read.

Source Code File

A source code file is a text file that contains information related to a programming language such as C, C++, Pascal, Fortran, and so on. When a programmer develops a source code file, they create a file that conforms to the naming convention of the program language being used, such as adding a ".c" to the end of the file if creating a C program.

The following is an example of a C source code file:

```
/* this is K & R sort program */

# include <stdio.h>
# include <stdlib.h>

        int N;
        int v[1000000];          /* v is array to be sorted */
        int left = 0;            /* left pointer */
        int right;
        int swapcount, comparecount = 0;
                                 /* count swaps and compares*/
        int i, j, t;
        char print;
        char pr_incr_sorts;


main()

{
   printf("Enter number of numbers to sort : ");
   scanf("%10d", &N);                   /* 10d used for a BIG input */
   printf ("\n");                        /* select type of input to sort */
```

```
printf("Enter rand(1), in-order(2), or reverse order (3)    sort : ");
scanf("%2d", &type);
printf ("\n");                        /* select type of input to sort */

if (type == 3)
            for (i=0; i<N; ++i)       /* random       */
                 v[i] = (N - i);

else if (type == 2)
            for (i=0; i<N; ++i)
                 v[i]= (i + 1);         /* in order      */

else if (type == 1)
            for (i=0; i<N; ++i)
                 v[i]=rand();           /* reverse order */
fflush(stdin);
printf("Do you want to see the numbers before sorting (y or n)? : ");
scanf("%c", &print);
printf ("\n");                        /* View unsorted numbers?  */
if (print == 'y')
    {
          printf ("\n");
        for (i=0; i<N; ++i)
          printf("a[%2d]= %2d\n", i, v[i]);
          printf ("\n");
    }


    fflush(stdin);
    printf("Do you want to see the array at each step as it sorts? (y or n)? : ");
    scanf("%c", &pr_incr_sorts);
    printf ("\n");                    /* View incremental sorts?  */


     right = N-1;                     /* right pointer       */

                 qsort(v, left, right);




     {
       fflush(stdin);
       printf ("Here is the sorted list of %2d items\n", N);
          printf ("\n");
       for (i=0; i<N; ++i)
          printf ("%2d\n ", v[i]);
          printf ("\n");
          printf ("\n");              /* print sorted list      */
               }
               printf ("number of swaps = %2d\n ", swapcount);
               printf ("number of compares = %2d\n ", comparecount);
     }

/* qsort function */

          void qsort( v, left, right)
                     int v[], left, right;
     {
               int i, last;
               if (left > right)
                return;


               swap(v, left, (left + right)/2);
               last = left;
               for (i=left+1; i <= right; i++)
               {
                   comparecount = ++comparecount;
                     if (v[i] < v[left])
                   swap(v, ++last, i);
               }
               swap(v, left, last);
               qsort(v, left, last-1);
```

```
                          qsort(v, last+1, right);
                          }

                          /* swap function  */

                          swap(v, i, j)
                             int v[], i, j;

                             {int temp;
                                  swapcount = swapcount++;
                                  temp = v[i];
                                  v[i] = v[j];
                                  v[j] = temp;

          if (pr_incr_sorts == 'y')
             {
                          printf("Incremental sort of array = ");
             printf ("\n");
             for (i=0; i<N; ++i)
                printf("a[%2d]= %2d\n", i, v[i]);
                printf ("\n");
             }
          }
```

Executable Files

Executable files are compiled programs that can be run. You can't read executable files and you'll typically get a bunch of errors, unreadable characters, and beeps from your HP-UX system when you try to look at one of these. It is also possible you will lose your screen settings and cause other problems.

You don't have to go far in HP-UX to find executable files; they are everywhere. Many of the HP-UX commands you issue are executable files that you can't read. In addition, if you are developing programs on your system you are creating your own executables.

Here is an example of what you see if you attempt to send an executable to the screen:

```
unknown/etc/ttytyperunknown<@=>|<@=>|:unknown<@=>
callocLINESCOLUMNSunknownPackaged for
argbad aftger%3
parmnumber missing <@=>|<@=>|:
```

```
@ @ 3### @@@A:2TTO|>@#<|2X00R
EraseKillOOPS<@=>|<@=>|:
<@=>|<@=>|:
<@=>|<@=>|:<@=>|ATOO<@=>|:<@=>|<@=>|:<@=>|<@=>|:<@=>|<@=>|:
```

Shell Programs

A shell program is both a file you can run to perform a task and a file
that you can read. So yes, even though you can run this file because it is
executable, you can also read it. I'm going to describe shell programming in more detail in an upcoming chapter.

I consider shell programming to be an important skill for every user
to have. I'll spend some time going over the basics of shell programming. Some of the background I'm about to cover relating to file types
and permissions is important when it comes to shell programming, so
this is important information for you to understand.

Here is an example of part of a shell program from an old startup
file:

```
# Check if login script contains non-comment to "VUE"
# If it does, assume it's VUE safe, and set VUESOURCEPROFILE
# to true.

if [ "${SHELL:-}" -a -d "${HOME:-}; then
  case ${SHELL##*/} in
   sh | ksh ) shellprofile="$HOME/.profile" ;;
        csh ) shellprofile="$HOME/.login" ;;
          * ) shellprofile="" ;;

  esac
  if [[ -r "$shellprofile"]] ; then
    [ 'grep -c '^[^#:].*VUE' $shellprofile' !=0 ] &&
      VUERESOURCEPROFILE="true"
  fi
fi

# Place customization code beyond this point.
```

```
PATH="$PATH:/usr/local/bin:/usr/sbin:$HOME:."
export PATH

mesg y

umask 022
```

The shell program is text you can read and modify if indeed you have permissions to do so. In addition to programming information, shell programs contain comments indicated by lines beginning with a #.

Links

A link is a pointer to a file stored elsewhere on the system. Instead of having two or more copies of a file on your system, you can link to a file that already exists on your system.

One particularly useful way links have been used in HP-UX is related to new releases of the operating system. The locations of files sometimes change going from one release to another, and rather than learn all the new locations there are links produced from the old location to the new one. When you run a command using the old location, the link points to the new location.

Links are also useful for centralizing files. If a set of identical files has to be updated often, it is easier to link to a central file and update it rather than have to update several copies of the file in several different locations.

Device Files

Device files, sometimes called device special files, contain information about the hardware connected to your system. Devices on your system can often be accessed with different device files. A disk, for instance, can be accessed with either a block device file or a character device file. There is extensive coverage of device files in this book.

There are other types of files on your system as well, but for the purposes of getting started with HP-UX, the file types I will describe supply sufficient background to get you started.

The file Command

The **file** command is used to determine the file type. This command is useful because the name of a file does not always indicate its file type. The following examples perform a long listing of a file to provide some background information on the file, and then the **file** command is run to show the file type.

Text File

(Described by the **file** command as ascii text.)

```
# ll  .mosaic-global-history
-rw-r--r--   1 201      users        587 Dec 22  1994 .mosaic-global-history
# file  .mosaic-global-history
.mosaic-global-history: ascii text
#
```

Data File

(Described by the file command as data.)

```
# ll Static.dat
-rw-r--r--   1 201      users       235874 Aug 26  1993 Static.dat
# file Static.dat
Static.dat:     data
#
```

Source Code File

(Described by the file command as c program text.)

```
# ll krsort.c
-rwxrwxrwx  1 201      users         3234 Nov 16  1992 krsort.c
# file krsort.c
krsort.c:       c program text
#
```

Executable File

(Described by the file command as shared executable.)

```
# ll krsort
-rwxr-xr-x  1 201      users        34592 Nov 16  1992 krsort
# file krsort
krsort:         PA-RISC1.1 shared executable dynamically linked -not stripped
#
```

Shell Program

(Described by the file command as commands text.)

```
# ll llsum
-rwxrwxrwx   1 root     sys           1267 Feb 23  1993 llsum
# file llsum
llsum:          commands text
#
```

Link

(The link is not referenced by the file command; this is shown as a
shared executable dynamically linked. The reference to dynamically
linked does not mean this is a link.)

```
# ll /usr/bin/ar
lr-xr-xr-t   1 root     sys             15 Mar 23  1995 ar -> /usr/ccs/bin/ar
# file /usr/bin/ar
/usr/bin/ar:         s800 shared executable dynamically linked
#
```

Block Device File

(Described by the file command as block special.)

```
# ll /dev/dsk/c0t1d0
brw-r--r--   1 bin      sys          31 0x001000 Apr 17  1995 /dev/dsk/c0t1d0
# file /dev/dsk/c0t1d0
/dev/dsk/c0t1d0:     block special (31/4096)
#
```

Character Device File

(Described by the file command as character special.)

```
# ll /dev/rdsk/c0t1d0
crw-r-----   1 root      sys       188 0x001000 Mar 23  1995 /dev/rdsk/c0t1d0
# file /dev/rdsk/c0t1d0
/dev/rdsk/c0t1d0:      character special (188/4096)
#
```

File System Layout

Before I begin talking about the file system layout, it is important for you to know that there is not necessarily a single file system. You may have set up a variety of file system types on your system. I will briefly cover some of the different file system types. You care a lot about the different file system types because the commands you issue may have the option "-F" followed by the file system type. Some of the commands that support the -F option are **dcopy**, **fsck**, **mksf**, **mount**, **newfs**, and others. Here is a brief description of four file system types supported by HP-UX:

• High Performance File System (HFS) is HP's version of the UNIX File System. This is the most common file system and the one used in most of the examples.

• CD-ROM File System (CDFS) is used when you mount a CD-ROM. A CD-ROM is read-only so you can't write to it.

• Network File System (NFS) is a way of accessing files on other systems on the network from your local system. An NFS mounted file system looks as though it is local to your system even though it is located on another system.

• Loopback File System (LOFS) allows you to have the same file system in multiple places.

• VxFs is an extent-based Journal File System that supports fast file system recovery and on-line features such as backup.

I am going to cover only the HP-UX 10.x file system layout in this chapter. The 10.x file system layout is derived from the OSF/1 layout, which is based on the AT&T SVR4 layout.

You'll be very happy to read that all of the file system-related information in this section applies to both HP 9000 Series 800 and Series 700 systems (servers and workstations respectively.) This means that you can take the information in this section and apply it to all HP 9000 systems.

Figure 4-1 is a high-level depiction of the HP-UX 10.x file system.

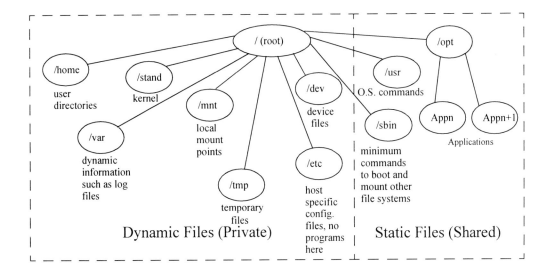

Figure 4-1 HP-UX 10.x File System Layout

Here are some of the more important features of the 10.x file system layout:

> • Files and directories are organized by category. The two most obvious categories that appear in Figure 4-1 are static vs. dynamic files. There are also other categories such as executable, configuration, data files, and so on. The static files are also labeled "shared" because other hosts on the network may share these. The directories **/usr**, **/sbin**, and **/opt** are shared directories.

> • The operating system and applications are kept separate from one another. Application vendors don't care where their applications are

loaded; that is up to you. But to a system administrator it is highly desirable to keep applications separate from the operating system, so you don't inadvertently have application files overwriting operating system files. In addition, if applications are loaded in a separate area, they are "modular," meaning a system administrator can add, remove, and modify them without affecting the operating system or other applications. Applications are kept in the **/opt** directory.

• Intrasystem files are kept in a separate area from intersystem, or network accessible, files. **/usr** and **/sbin** are shared operating system directories. There is no host specific information in these two directories. **/etc** is used to hold the host specific configuration files.

• Executable files are kept separate from system configuration files so that the executables may be shared among hosts. Having the configuration files separate from the programs that use them also means that updates to the operating system won't affect the configuration files.

I'll provide descriptions of some of the most important directories for HP-UX 10.x.

/   This is the root directory, which is the base of the file system's hierarchical tree structure. A directory is logically viewed as being part of root. Regardless of the disk on which a directory or logical volume is stored, it is logically viewed as a part of the root hierarchy.

/dev   Contains host-specific devices files.

/etc   Contains host-specific system and application
configuration files. The information in this
directory is important to the operation of the
system and is of a permanent nature. There are
also additional configuration directories below
/etc. There are two **/etc** subdirectories of particular interest:

/etc/rc.config.d contains configuration data
files for startup and shutdown programs.

/etc/opt contains host-specific application configuration data.

/export This is used for diskless file sharing only. Servers export root directories for networked cli-
ents.

/home Users' home directories are located here. Since
the data stored in users' home directories will
be modified often, you can expect this directory
to grow in size.

/lost+found This is the lost files directory. Here you
will find files that are in use but are not associated with a directory. These files typically
become "lost" as a result of a system crash that
caused the link between the physical information on the disk and the logical directory to be
severed. The program **fsck**, which is run at the

time of boot, finds these files and places them in the **lost+found** directory.

/mnt This directory is reserved as a mount point for local file systems. You can either mount directly to **/mnt** or have **/mnt** subdirectories as mount points such as **/mnt1**, **/mnt2**, **/mnt3**, and so on.

/net Name reserved as mount points for remote file systems.

/opt The directory under which applications are installed. As a rule, application vendors never specify a particular location for their applications to be installed. Now, with **/opt**, we have a standard directory under which applications should be installed. This is an organizational improvement for system administrators, because we can now expect applications to be loaded under **/opt** and the application name.

/sbin Contains commands and scripts used to boot, shut down, and fix file system mounting problems. **/sbin** is available when a system boots because it contains commands required to bring up a system.

/stand Contains kernel configuration and binary files that are required to bring up a system. Two significant files contained in this directory are the **system** and **vmunix** (kernel) files.

/tmp   This is a free-for-all directory where any user can temporarily store files. Because of the loose nature of this directory, it should not be used to store anything important, and users should know that whatever they have stored in /**tmp** can be deleted without notice. In 10.x, application working files should go in **/var/ tmp** or **/var/opt/appname**, not in **/tmp**.

/usr   Most of the HP-UX operating system is contained in **/usr**. Included in this directory are commands, libraries, and documentation. There are a limited number of subdirectories that can appear in **/usr**. Here is a list of **/usr** subdirectories:

/usr/bin - Common utilities and applications are stored here.

/usr/ccs - Tools and libraries used to generate C programs are stored here.

/usr/conf - Static directory containing the sharable kernel build environment.

/usr/contrib - Contributed software directory.

/usr/include - Contains header files.

/usr/lib - Contains libraries and machine dependent databases.

/usr/newconfig - Contains default operating system data files such as those found in **/etc/ newconfig** in HP-UX 10.x, although the directory structure of **/usr/newconfig** is different than that of **/etc/newconfig**.

/usr/old - Old files from an operating system update will be stored here.

/usr/sbin - System administration commands are in this directory, including many that had been in **/etc** in HP-UX 9.x.

/usr/share - Contains files that are architecture independent and can be shared.

/usr/share/man - Directory for manual pages.

/var   Holds files that are primarily temporary. Files such as log files, which are frequently deleted and modified, are stored here. Think of this as a directory of "variable" size. Files that an application or command create at runtime should be placed in this directory, including log and spool files. There may, however, be some applications which store state information in **/var**.

/var/adm - Directory for administrative files, log files, and databases such as kernel crash dumps will be stored here.

/var/adm/crash - Kernel crash dumps will be placed here.

/var/adm/sw - Software Distributor log files, and so forth.

/usr/var/cron - Log files for cron.

/var/mail - Incoming mail messages are kept here.

/var/opt - Application runtime files, such as log files, for applications mounted in **/opt** will be stored in **/var/opt** under the application name.

/var/spool - Spool files, such as those in **/usr/ spool** in HP-UX 10.x, are stored here.

Figure 4-2 is a window showing the top-level file system with the / **sbin** directory selected.

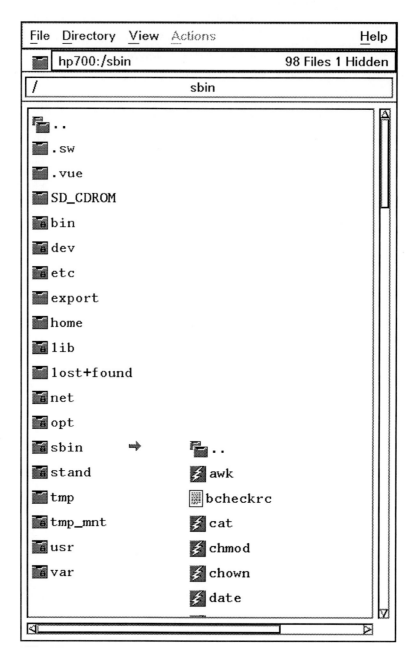

Figure 4-2   Window Showing HP-UX 10.x File System

You may find yourself spending a lot of time working in some of these directories and not so much time in others. In any event, you will surely spend a lot of time in file system management in general and should have a good overall understanding of the types of files on your system and the file system layout.

CHAPTER 5

Windows NT File System Management

Introduction

In Chapter 3 I covered Windows NT file systems. Information related to both background of the file system types (FAT and NTFS) as well as controlling files using attributes, properties, auditing, and other control mechanisms.

In this chapter I'll focus on information related to managing file systems. System administrators spend a lot of time managing file systems in advanced operating systems. As Windows NT is used for more and more important applications, managing file systems becomes a more complex and critical system administration function. The following sections cover the basics of managing file systems in Windows NT.

Disk Administration Tasks and Windows NT Disk Administrator

What is disk administration in general in the Windows NT environment? Unlike HP-UX, where the vast majority of disk administration takes place with Logical Volume Manager (LVM), disk administration in Windows NT involves primarily disks and partitions. The *Disk Administrator* of Windows NT is the tool through which the administration process takes place.

Before we jump into *Disk Administrator* and review its functionality I'll cover a few key terms that relate to disk management in Windows NT.

Windows NT Disk Management Terms

The following terms are used when performing disk management in Windows NT. This is only some of the terminology associated with disk management. Since the objective of this book is to get you started quickly with the operating systems covered, I want to make sure I give you the background required to administer Windows NT but I don't want to get bogged down in too much background detail.

Physical Drive	A disk that has been initialized for use by the operating system. A physical drive can be a disk drive, CD-ROM, or other drive used by Windows NT. A physical drive is a unit you can hold in your hand and is just that - a physical unit. For the most part I will be using disk drives as the physical devices in this discussion.
Partitions	A partition is a part of a physical disk. A partition is a way of dividing a physical drive into parts and making it look like several different physical drives.
Primary Partition	A primary partition is a part of the physical disk drive that has been configured as bootable by Windows NT. A single physical drive can have multiple primary partitions. You

have several primary partitions if you have multiple operating systems installed on a disk.

Extended Partition

An extended partition consists of free space on the disk which is used to create logical drives.

Logical Drive

A logical drive is a partition on the disk that is self-contained.

Volume Set

A volume set consists of parts of several physical drives that are combined to make a volume. This is different than a logical drive in that it consists of parts of more than one physical drive. This is both a good and bad technique to employ. It is good in that small areas of free space on several physical drives can be combined into a size that is useful. It is bad in that space is uncontiguous and heavy access to the volume set may result in poor performance. Another drawback to volume sets is that a failure on any disk in the volume set will result in the entire volume set being inaccessible. In any case it is good to know that small amounts of free space do not have to go to waste.

Mirror Set

A mirror set is a means by which you can have an identical copy of information on two different disks. Disk mirroring is a way of protecting information to a very high degree by having more than one copy on-line.

Stripe Set   A stripe set is a means of writing parts of
                          your data to different disks rather than writ-
                          ing all of your data to one disk. In this case
                          you would most likely employ parity to pro-
                          vide additional data integrity.

There is one more topic on which I want to supply some background
before we jump into disk administration. There is a general way of sharing
resources in a Windows NT environment called "share names." Directories
are resources commonly shared in Windows NT. You can take a directory
on your system such as **D:\programs\projectA** and give it a share name
such as **projA** and this can be shared among many Windows NT users
simultaneously. You can also assign different names to the shared resource
there by giving one set of privileges to one share name and a different set to
other share names. Shares are not limited to disks so other resources, such
as printers, can be shared as well. Although I won't cover share names in
this book, this is a potentially useful concept that is easy to implement in
Windows NT.

Windows NT Disk Administrator

Figure 5-1 shows starting the Windows NT *Disk Administrator* from the
Start menu.

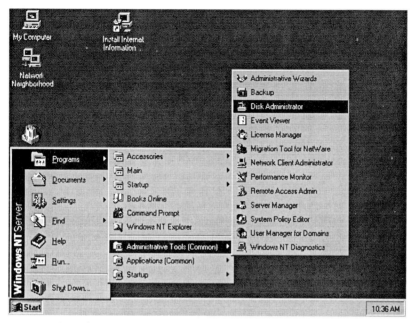

Figure 5-1 Starting Windows NT *Disk Administrator*

The *Disk Administrator* environment is shown in Figure 5-2.

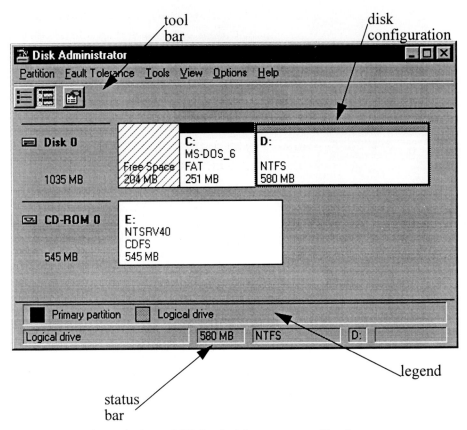

Figure 5-2   The Windows NT *Disk Administrator* Environment

Let's take a look at some of the elements in Figure 5-2. This is a simple system and therefore has only a few entries.

legend   The legend identifies the elements in the disk
                                    configuration area. In Figure 5-2 there are
                                    only two types of elements defined in the
                                    legend area: primary partition; and logical
                                    drive.

status bar	The status bar provides information about the disk configuration element that is currently selected. In Figure 5-2 **D:** is selected and the status of **D:** is provided in the status bar.
disk configuration	The disk configuration area shows the way in which disks are currently configured. Figure 5-2 shows disk 0 with 204 MBytes of free space, a FAT partition on **C:**, and an NTFS partition on **D:**. There is a also a CD-ROM on **E:** with Windows NT 4.x software on it.
tool bar	The tool bar contains icons which provide *Disk Administrator* tools. In this case there are three tools present: the first shows the volumes views; the second shows the disks view; and the third examines the properties of a volume or disk.

Volume Properties

You can view a lot of information about your volumes using the *Tools - Properties...* menu pick or using the properties icon (the third icon in Figure 5-2). Figure 5-3 shows the properties for **D:**.

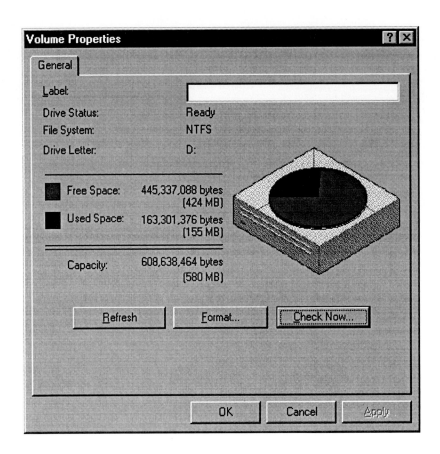

Figure 5-3 *Volume Properties*

As you can see there is a lot of useful information about this volume in Figure 5-3 such as the capacity, free space, used space, and so on. In addition you can use the *Check Now...* box that is currently selected in Figure 5-3 to bring up the *Check For Errors* window shown in Figure 5-4.

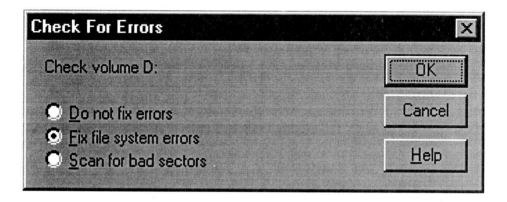

Figure 5-4 *Check For Errors* Window

If you proceed with the check process you may be told the volume is in use and therefore can't be checked. You can, however, schedule the volume to be checked the next time the system boots.

Create a Partition

Figure 5-2 shows 204 MBytes free on disk 0 that we can use for a variety of purposes. Among the activities you might want to perform is to create a partition using the *Partition - Create...* menu pick. When you select this menu pick you are asked to choose the size of the partition you wish to create as shown in Figure 5-5.

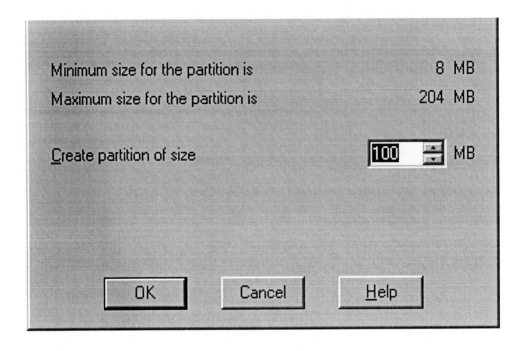

Minimum size for the partition is   8 MB

Maximum size for the partition is   204 MB

Create partition of size   100 ⬍ MB

            OK   Cancel   Help

Figure 5-5 Creating a Partition in *Disk Administrator*

204 MBytes came up as the default size and I changed this to 100 MBytes as shown in Figure 5-5.

After having created the partition, the disk manager shows an unformatted partition of 102 MBytes, close to the 100 MBytes I selected, that needs to be formatted.

To format the new 102 MByte partition you select the unformatted partition and the *Partition - Commit Changes Now...* menu pick. After committing the changes, there have been some name changes put into effect. Figure 5-6 shows the new names employed by *Disk Administrator*.

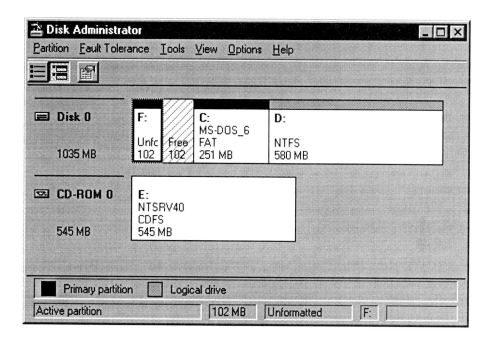

Figure 5-6 Creating a Partition in *Disk Administrator*

The CD-ROM has been renamed **E:** and our new 102 MByte partition is **F:**.

Selecting the *Tools - Format...* menu pick brings up the window shown in Figure 5-7 in which you can select a *Label* and *Format Type* for the new partition.

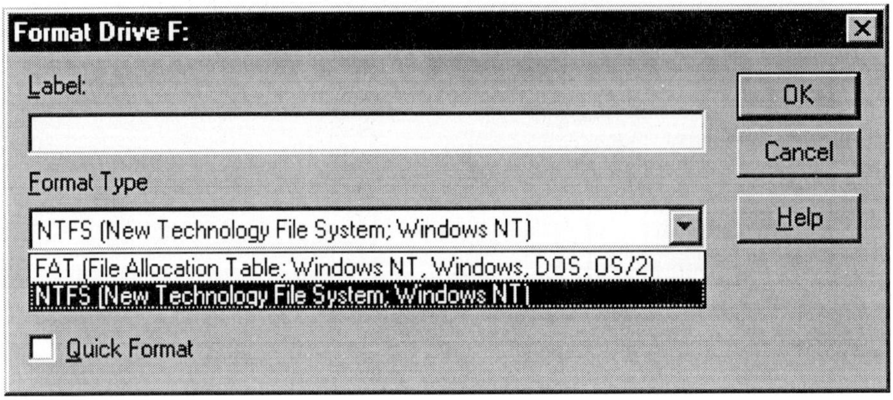

Figure 5-7 Format Drive **F:**

When you proceed with the formatting you receive the following warning message:

```
Warning: This operation will overwrite the data
contained on this volume. Are you sure you wish to
continue with this operation?
```

After the formatting the partition you see the good news shown in Figure 5-8 that you now have a 102 MByte NTFS formatted partition on which you can store data.

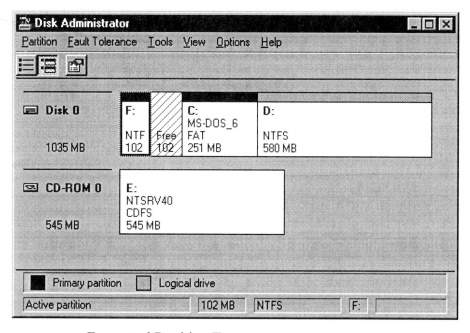

Figure 5-8 Formatted Partition **F:**

In addition you can view the properties of this new partition as well as shown in Figure 5-9.

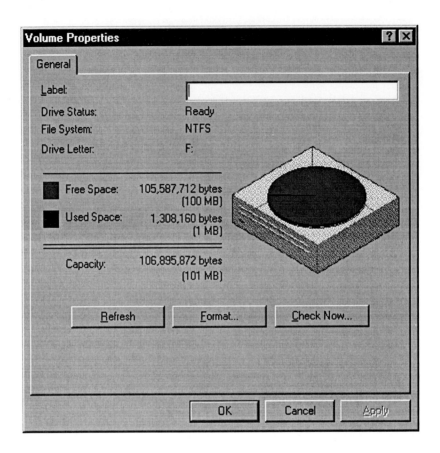

Figure 5-9 Properties of **F:**

Be Careful with *Mark Active*

One of the *Partition* menu picks is *Mark Active*. This is a menu pick to use carefully. When a partition is marked as active it is used for startup purposes when the system boots. In the case of the system used for the earlier examples in this chapter the **C:** drive is marked as active. Since your system may not boot if you mark the wrong partition as active, you want to be careful if you use this command. When you use the *Partition - Mark Active* menu pick you get the following message:

```
The requested partition has been marked active.
When you reboot your computer the operating system
on that partition will be started.
```

Be careful if, for any reason, you decide to mark a new partition as active.

Create a Repair Disk

After any changes are made to the disk configuration, it is a good idea to create a new repair disk. This disk contains information necessary to reconstruct a configuration if your system doesn't boot. The program **rdisk.exe** on your system is used to create a repair disk.

Figure 5-10 shows the window that appears when you invoke the *Repair Disk Utility*.

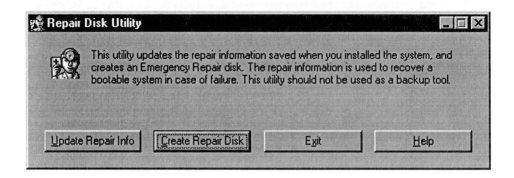

Figure 5-10 Properties of **F:**

There are several options as part of the *Repair Disk Utility*.

You would select *Update Repair Info* if you wanted to update repair information on your hard disk. You could also create an emergency repair disk with this option.

You would select *Create Repair Disk* if you wanted to use the information on your disk to create a repair disk.

This utility will automatically format the floppy you use for the emergency repair disk and create it. A number of configuration files will be placed on this disk. This disk is now ready to use in the event you have difficulty booting your system. I have found that the repair disk works sometimes and not other times depending on the type of system problem you are experiencing. In any event, make sure your emergency repair disk is up to date so you have it current if you do indeed need it.

CHAPTER 6

HP-UX File System Management

Logical Volume Manager Background

Logical Volume Manager is a disk management subsystem that allows you to manage physical disks as logical volumes. This means that a file system can span multiple physical disks. You can view Logical Volume Manager as a flexible way of defining boundaries of disk space that are independent of one another. Not only can you specify the size of a logical volume, but you can also change its size if the need arises. This is a great advancement over dedicating a disk to a file system or having fixed-size partitions on a disk. Logical volumes can hold file systems, raw data, or swap space. You can now specify a logical volume to be any size you wish, have logical volumes that span multiple physical disks, and then change the size of the logical volume if you need to!

So, what do you need to know in order to set up Logical Volume Manager and realize all these great benefits? First you need to know the terminology, and second you need to know Logical Volume Manager commands. As with many other system administration tasks you can use SAM to set up Logical Volume Manager for you. I recommend you use SAM to set up Logical Volume Manager on your system(s). But, as usual, I recommend you read this overview and at least understand the basics of Logical Volume Manager before you use SAM to set up Logical Volume Manager on your system. The SAM chapter has an example of using SAM to create logical volumes. After reading this section you may want to take a quick look at that example.

Logical Volume Manager Terms

The following terms are used when working with Logical Volume Manager. This is only some of the terminology associated with Logical Volume Manager, but it is enough for you to get started with Logical Volume Manager. You can work with Logical Volume Manager without knowing all of these terms if you use SAM. It is a good idea, however, to read the following brief overview of these terms if you plan to use Logical Volume Manager so you have some idea of what SAM is doing for you.

Volume	A volume is a device used for file system, swap, or raw data. Without Logical Volume Manager a volume would be either a disk partition or an entire disk drive.
Physical Volume	A disk that has been initalized for use by Logical Volume Manager. An entire disk must be initialized if it is to be used by Logical Volume Manger; that is, you can't initialize only part of a disk for Logical Volume Manager use and the rest for fixed partitioning.
Volume Group	A volume group is a collection of logical volumes that are managed by Logical Volume Manager.

You would typically define which disks on your system are going to be used by Logical Volume Manager and then define how you wish to group these into volume groups. Each individual disk may be a volume group, or more than one disk may form a volume group. At this point you have created a pool of disk space called a volume group. A disk can belong to only one volume group. A volume group may span multiple physical disks.

Logical Volume This is space that is defined within a volume group. A volume group is divided up into logical volumes. This is like a disk partition, which is of a fixed size, but you have the flexibility to change its size. A logical volume is contained within a volume group, but the volume group may span multiple physical disks. You can have a logical volume which is bigger than a single disk.

Physical Extent A set of contiguous disk blocks on a physical volume. If you define a disk to be a physical volume, then the contiguous blocks within that disk form a physical extent. Logical Volume Manager uses the physical extent as the unit for allocating disk space to logical volumes. If you use a small physical extent size such as 1 MByte, then you have a fine granularity for defining logical volumes. If you use a large physical extent size such as 256 MBytes, then you have a coarse granularity for defining logical volumes.

Logical Extents A logical volume is a set of logical extents. Logical extents and physical extents are the same size within a volume group. Although logical and physical extents are the same size, this doesn't mean that two logical extents will map to two contiguous physical extents. It may be that you have two logical extents that end up being mapped to physical extents on different disks!

Mirroring   Logical volumes can be mirrored one or more times creating an identical image of the logical volume. This means a logical extent can map to more than one physical extent if mirrored.

Figure 6-1 grapically depicts some of the logical volume terms I just covered. In this diagram it is clear that logical extents are not mapped to contiguous physical extents because some of the physical extents are used.

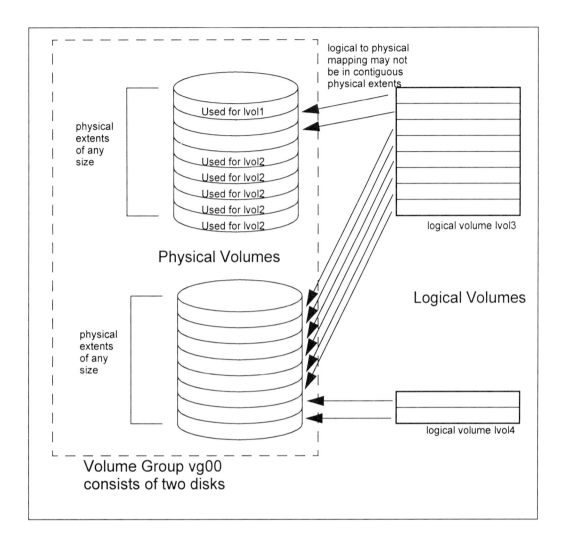

Figure 6-1 Logical Volume Manager Partial Logical to Physical Mapping

In addition to the setup of your logical volumes, you may have an environment where you wish to mirror some of these logical volumes. SAM can be used to set up disk mirroring for you. You must first, however, decide the characteristics of your mirroring. There is a mirroring policy called "strict." You define one of the following three strict policies when you create the logical volume using the following options:

n   This is not a strict allocation policy meaning that mirrored copies of a logical extent can share the same physical volume. This means that your original data and mirrored data may indeed be on the same physical disk. If you encounter a disk mechanism problem of some type you may lose both your original and mirrored data.

y   Yes, this is a strict allocation policy meaning that mirrored copies of a logical extent may not share the same physical volume. This is safer than allowing mirrored copies of data to share the same physical volume. If you have a problem with a disk in this scenario you are guaranteed that your original data is on a different physical disk from your mirrored data. Original data and mirrored data are always part of the same volume group even if you want them on different physical volumes.

g   Mirrored data will not be on the same Physical Volume Group (PVG) as the original data. This is called a PVG-strict allocation policy.

The strict allocation policy depends on your environment. Most installations that employ mirroring buy sufficient disk to mirror all data. In an environment such as this I would create two volume groups, one for the original data and one for the mirrored data, and use the "strict -g" option when creating logical volumes so that the original data is on one volume group and the mirrored data on the other.

Logical Volume Manager Commands

The following are definitions of some of the more common Logical Volume Commands. Many of these commands are found in the log file SAM creates when setting up logical volumes for you. I am giving a description of these commands here so that when you see them you'll have an idea of what each command is used for. Although these are not all of the Logical Volume Manager commands, these are the ones I use most often and are the commands you should have knowledge of when using Logical Volume Manager. The commands are broken down in logical volume (lv) commands, physical volume (pv) commands, and volume group (vg) commands. All of these commands are found in the manual pages. Some of the commands such as **lvdisplay**, **pvdisplay**, and **vgdisplay** were issued so you could see examples of these. The following output of **bdf** will be helpful to you when you view the output of Logical Volume Manager commands that are issued. The output of **bdf** shows several logical volumes mounted (lvol1, lvol3, lvol4, lvol5, lvol6, lvol7), all of which are in volume group vg00 (see **bdf** command overview in this chapter).

```
$ bdf
```

Filesystem	kbytes	used	avail	%used	Mounted on
/dev/vg00/lvol1	47829	18428	24618	43%	/
/dev/vg00/lvol7	34541	8673	22413	28%	/var
/dev/vg00/lvol6	299157	149449	119792	56%	/usr
/dev/vg00/lvol5	23013	48	20663	0%	/tmp
/dev/vg00/lvol4	99669	32514	57188	36%	/opt
/dev/vg00/lvol3	19861	9	17865	0%	/home
/dev/dsk/c0t6d0	802212	552120	169870	76%	/mnt/9.x

Logical Volume Commands

lvcreate   This command is used to create a new logical vol-
                           ume. A logical volume is created within a volume
                           group. A logical volume may span multiple disks
                           but must exist within a volume group. SAM will
                           execute this command for you when you create a
                           logical volume using SAM. There are many
                           options for this command and two that you would
                           often use are -L to define the size of the logical
                           volume and -n to define the name of the logical
                           volume.

lvchange   This command is used to change the logical volume
                           in some way. For example, you may wish to
                           change the permission on a logical volume to
                           read-write (w) or to read (r) with the **-p** option.
                           Or you may want to change the strict policy
                           (described under the **lvcreate** command) to strict
                           (y), not to strict (n), or to PVG strict (g).

lvdisplay   This command shows the status and characteris-
                           tics of every logical volume that you specify. If
                           you use the verbose (-v) option of this command,
                           you get a lot of useful data in many categories
                           including those in the paragraphs below

                           Information about the way in which the logical
                           volumes are set up such as the physical volume on
                           which the logical extents appear; the number of
                           logical extents on a physical volume; and the
                           number of physical extents on the physical vol-
                           ume.

                           Detailed information for logical extents including
                           the logical extent number and some information

about the physical volume and physical extent for the logical extent.

The following is an example of **lvdisplay** for the first of the logical volumes (lvol1) shown in the earlier **bdf** example:

```
$  lvdisplay -v /dev/vg00/lvol1

--- Logical volumes ---
LV Name                    /dev/vg00/lvol1
VG Name                    /dev/vg00
LV Permission              read/write
LV Status                  available/syncd
Mirror copies              0
Consistency Recovery       MWC
Schedule                   parallel
LV Size (Mbytes)           48
Current LE                 12
Allocated PE               12
Stripes                    0
Stripe Size (Kbytes)       0
Bad block                  off
Allocation                 strict/contiguous

   --- Distribution of logical volume ---
   PV Name                 LE on PV   PE on PV
   /dev/dsk/c0t1d0         12         12

   --- Logical extents ---
   LE    PV1                   PE1    Status 1
   0000  /dev/dsk/c0t1d0       0000   current
   0001  /dev/dsk/c0t1d0       0001   current
   0002  /dev/dsk/c0t1d0       0002   current
   0003  /dev/dsk/c0t1d0       0003   current
   0004  /dev/dsk/c0t1d0       0004   current
   0005  /dev/dsk/c0t1d0       0005   current
   0006  /dev/dsk/c0t1d0       0006   current
   0007  /dev/dsk/c0t1d0       0007   current
   0008  /dev/dsk/c0t1d0       0008   current
   0009  /dev/dsk/c0t1d0       0009   current
   0010  /dev/dsk/c0t1d0       0010   current
   0011  /dev/dsk/c0t1d0       0011   current
```

Although most of what is shown in this example is self-explanatory, there are some entries that require explanation. The size of the logical volume is 48 MBytes which consists of 12 Logical

Extents (LEs) and 12 Physical Extents (PEs). This means that each physical extent is 4 MBytes in size   (4 MBytes x 12 extents = 48 MBytes) which we can verify when we display the characteristics of the physical volume in an upcoming example. At the bottom of this listing you can see the mapping of logical extents onto physical extents. In this case there is a direct mapping between logical extents 0000 - 0011 and physical extents 0000 - 0011.

lvextend   This command is used to increase the number of physical extents allocated to a logical volume for a variety of reasons. We sometimes underestimate the size required for a logical volume and with this command you can easily correct this. You may want to extend a logical volume to increase the number of mirrored copies (using the -m option), to increase the size of the logical volume (using the -L option), or to increase the number of logical extents (using the -l option).

lvlnboot   Use this to set up a logical volume to be a root, primary swap, or dump volume (this can be undone with **lvrmboot**).

lvsplit & **lvmerge**   These commands are used to split and merge logical volumes respectively. If you have a mirrored logical volume, **lvsplit** will split this into two logical volumes. **lvmerge** merges two logical volumes of the same size, increasing the number of mirrored copies.

lvmmigrate   This command prepares a root file system in a partition for migration to a logical volume. You would use this if you had a partition to convert to a logical volume.

lvreduce   Use this to decrease the number of physical extents allocated to a logical volume. When creating logical volumes, we sometimes overestimate the size of the logical volume. This command can be used to set the number of mirrored copies (with the -m option), decrease the number of logical extents (with the -l option), or decrease the size of the logical volume (with the -L option).

lvremove   After closing logical volumes, you can use this command to remove logical volumes from a volume group.

lvrmboot   Use this if you don't want a logical volume to be root, primary swap, or a dump device (this is the converse of the **lvlnboot** command).

lvsync   There are times when mirrored data in a logical volume becomes "stale" or out of date. **lvsync** is used to synchronize the physical extents in a logical volume.

Physical Volume Commands

pvchange   This command is used to change the physical volume in some way. For example, you may wish to allow additional physical extents to be added to the physical volume if this is not permitted, or prohibit additional physical extents from being added to the physical volume if indeed this is allowed.

pvcreate   This command is used to create a physical volume that will be part of a volume group. Remember that a volume group may consist of several physical volumes. The physical volumes are the disks on your system.

pvdisplay   This command shows information about the physical volumes you specify. You can get a lot of information about the logical to physical mapping with this command if you use the verbose option (-v). With "-v", **pvdisplay** will show you the mapping of logical to physical extents for the physical volumes specified.

You will get a lot of other useful data from this command such as the name of the physical volume; name of the volume group to which the physical volume belongs; the status of the physical volume; the size of physical extents on the physical volume; the total number of physical extents; and the number of free physical extents.

The following is a partial example of running **pvdisplay**:

```
$  pvdisplay -v /dev/dsk/c0t6d0

--- Physical volumes ---
PV Name                     /dev/dsk/c0t1d0
VG Name                     /dev/vg00
PV Status                   available
Allocatable                 yes
VGDA                        2
Cur LV                      7
```

```
PE Size (Mbytes)        4
Total PE                157
Free PE                 8
Allocated PE            149
Stale PE                0

    --- Distribution of physical volume ---
    LV Name                 LE of LV      PE for LV
    /dev/vg00/lvol1         12            12
    /dev/vg00/lvol2         17            17
    /dev/vg00/lvol6         75            75
    /dev/vg00/lvol7         9             9
    /dev/vg00/lvol4         25            25
    /dev/vg00/lvol5         6             6
    /dev/vg00/lvol3         5             5

    --- Physical extents ---
    PE     Status   LV                       LE
    0000 current    /dev/vg00/lvol1          0000
    0001 current    /dev/vg00/lvol1          0001
    0002 current    /dev/vg00/lvol1          0002
    0003 current    /dev/vg00/lvol1          0003
    0004 current    /dev/vg00/lvol1          0004
    0005 current    /dev/vg00/lvol1          0005
    0006 current    /dev/vg00/lvol1          0006
    0007 current    /dev/vg00/lvol1          0007
    0008 current    /dev/vg00/lvol1          0008
    0009 current    /dev/vg00/lvol1          0009
    0010 current    /dev/vg00/lvol1          0010
    0011 current    /dev/vg00/lvol1          0011
    0012 current    /dev/vg00/lvol2          0000
    0013 current    /dev/vg00/lvol2          0001
    0014 current    /dev/vg00/lvol2          0002
    0015 current    /dev/vg00/lvol2          0003
    0016 current    /dev/vg00/lvol2          0004
    0017 current    /dev/vg00/lvol2          0005
    0018 current    /dev/vg00/lvol2          0006
    0019 current    /dev/vg00/lvol2          0007
    0020 current    /dev/vg00/lvol2          0008
    0021 current    /dev/vg00/lvol2          0009
    0022 current    /dev/vg00/lvol2          0010
    0023 current    /dev/vg00/lvol2          0011
    0024 current    /dev/vg00/lvol3          0000
    0025 current    /dev/vg00/lvol3          0001
    0026 current    /dev/vg00/lvol3          0002
    0027 current    /dev/vg00/lvol3          0003
    0028 current    /dev/vg00/lvol3          0004
    0029 current    /dev/vg00/lvol4          0000
    0030 current    /dev/vg00/lvol4          0001
    0031 current    /dev/vg00/lvol4          0002
    0032 current    /dev/vg00/lvol4          0003
    0033 current    /dev/vg00/lvol4          0004
```

```
0034 current   /dev/vg00/lvol4        0005
0035 current   /dev/vg00/lvol4        0006




                   .
                   .
                   .
0156 free                             0000
```

From this listing you can see that lvol1, which is roughly 48 MBytes, has many more physical extents assigned to it than lvol3, which is roughly 20 MBytes.

pvmove   You can move physical extents from one physical volume to other physical volumes with this command. By specifying the source physical volume and one or more destination physical volumes, you can spread data around to the physical volumes you wish with this command.

Volume Group Commands

vgcfgbackup   This command is used to save the configuration information for a volume group. Remember that a volume group is made up of one or more physical volumes.

vgcfgrestore   This command is used to restore the configuration information for a volume group.

vgchange | This command makes a volume group active or inactive. With the "-a" option, you can deactivate (-a n) a volume group or activate (-a y) a volume group.

vgcreate | You can create a volume group and specify all of its parameters with this command. You specify a volume group name and all of the associated parameters for the volume group when creating it.

vgdisplay | Displays all information related to the volume group if you use the verbose (-v) option including volume group name; the status of the volume group; the maximum, current, and open logical volumes in the volume group; the maximum, current, and active physical volumes in the volume group; and physical extent related information.

The following is an example of using **vgdisplay** for the volume group vg00:

```
$ vgdisplay /dev/vg00

--- Volume groups ---
VG Name             /dev/vg00
VG Write Access     read/write
VG Status           available
Max LV              255
Cur LV              7
Open LV             7
Max PV              16
Cur PV              1
Act PV              1
Max PE per PV       2000
VGDA                2
PE Size (Mbytes)    4
Total PE            157
Alloc PE            149
Free PE             8
Total PVG           0
```

vgexport   This command removes a logical volume group from the system but does not modify the logical volume information on the physical volumes. These physical volumes can then be imported to another system using **vgimport.**

vgextend   Physical volumes can be added to a volume group with this command by specifying the physical volume to be added to the volume group.

vgimport   This command can be used to import a physical volume to another system.

vgreduce   The size of a volume group can be reduced with this command by specifying which physical volume(s) to remove from a volume group.

vgremove   A volume group definition can be completely removed from the system with this command.

vgscan   In the event of a catastrophe of some type, you can use this command to scan your system in an effort to rebuild the **/etc/lvmtab** file.

vgsync   There are times when mirrored data in a volume group becomes "stale" or out of date. **vgsync** is used to synchronize the physical extents in each mirrored logical volume in the volume group.

Viewing File Systems with bdf

You can manually view the file systems you have mounted with the **bdf** command. **bdf** provides the following output:

File system	Block device file system name. In the following example there are several logical volumes shown.
KBytes	Number of KBytes of total disk space on the file system.
used	The number of used KBytes on the file system.
avail	The number of available KBytes on the file system.
%used	The percentage of total available disk space that is used on the file system.
Mounted on	The directory name the file system is mounted on.
iused	Number of inodes in use (only if you use the -i option with **bdf**).
ifree	Number of free inodes (only if you use the -i option with **bdf**).
%iuse	Percent of inodes in use (only if you use the -i option with **bdf**).

Here is an example of **bdf** that was also used earlier in this chapter:

```
$ /usr/bin/bdf
```

File system	kbytes	used	avail	%used	Mounted on
/dev/vg00/lvol1	47829	18428	24618	43%	/
/dev/vg00/lvol7	34541	8673	22413	28%	/var
/dev/vg00/lvol6	299157	149449	119792	56%	/usr
/dev/vg00/lvol5	23013	48	20663	0%	/tmp
/dev/vg00/lvol4	99669	32514	57188	36%	/opt
/dev/vg00/lvol3	19861	9	17865	0%	/home
/dev/dsk/c0t6d0	802212	552120	169870	76%	/mnt/9.x

File System Maintenance with fsck

fsck is a program used for file system maintenance on HP-UX systems. **fsck** checks file system consistency and can make many "life-saving" repairs to a corrupt file system. **fsck** can be run with several options including the following:

-F   This option allows you to specify the file system type (see explanation of file system types in Chapter 4). If you do not specify a file system type, then the **/etc/fstab** file will be used to determine the file system type. See **fstab** description in this section.

-m   This is a sanity check of the file system. If you run this, you'll be told if your file system is OK or not. I did the following to check lvol3 which is mounted as **/home**:

```
$ umount /home
$ fsck -m /dev/vg00/lvol3

fsck: sanity check,/dev/vg00/lvol3 okay
```

-y   **fsck** will ask questions if run in interactive mode and the **-y** option causes a "yes" response to all questions asked by **fsck**. Don't use this! If you have a serious problem with your file system, data will probably have to be removed and the **-y** indicates that the response to every question, including removing data, will be yes.

-n   The response to all questions asked by **fsck** will be "no." Don't use this either. If your file system is in bad shape, you may have to respond "yes" to some questions in order to repair the file system. All "no" responses will not do the job.

Since your system runs **fsck** on any file systems that were not marked as clean at the time you shut down the system, you can rest assured that when your system boots, any disks that were not properly shut down will be checked. It is a good idea to run **fsck** interactively on a periodic basis just so you can see firsthand that all of your file systems are in good working order.

Should **fsck** find a problem with a directory or file, it places these in the **lost+found** directory which is at the top level of each file system. If a file or directory appears in **lost+found,** you may be able to identify the file or directory by examining it and move it back to its original location. You can use the **file, what,** and **strings** commands on a file to obtain more information about a file to help identify its origin.

How are file system problems created? The most common cause for a file system problem is improper shutdown of the system. The information written to file systems is first written to a buffer cache in memory. It is later written to the disk with the **sync** command by unmounting the disk, or through the normal use of filling the buffer and writing it to the disk. If you walk up to a system and shut off the power, you will surely end up with a file system problem. Data in the buffer that was not synced to the disk will be lost. The file system will not be marked as properly shut down and **fsck** will be run when the system boots.

Proper shutdown of the system is described in this chapter. Although **fsck** is a useful utility that has been known to work miracles on occasion, you don't want to take any unnecessary risks with your file systems so be sure to properly shut down your system.

A sudden loss of power can also cause an unproper system shut down.

The **/etc/fstab** file mentioned earlier is used by **fsck** to determine the sequence of the file system check if it is required at the time of boot. The sequence of entries in **/etc/fstab** is important if there is not a "pass number" for any of the entries. Here is an example of the **/etc/fstab** file:

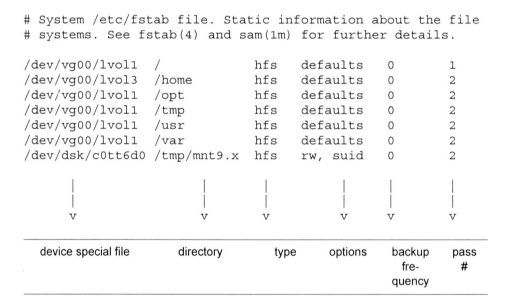

```
# System /etc/fstab file. Static information about the file
# systems. See fstab(4) and sam(1m) for further details.

/dev/vg00/lvol1    /            hfs    defaults    0        1
/dev/vg00/lvol3    /home        hfs    defaults    0        2
/dev/vg00/lvol1    /opt         hfs    defaults    0        2
/dev/vg00/lvol1    /tmp         hfs    defaults    0        2
/dev/vg00/lvol1    /usr         hfs    defaults    0        2
/dev/vg00/lvol1    /var         hfs    defaults    0        2
/dev/dsk/c0tt6d0   /tmp/mnt9.x  hfs    rw, suid    0        2
```

device special file	directory	type	options	backup frequency	pass #

device special file   This is the device block file, such as **/dev/vg00/ lvol1** in the example.

directory	Name of the directory under which the device special file is mounted.
type	Can be one of several types including: cdfs (local CD-ROM file system) hfs (high-performance local file system) nfs (network file system) vxfs swap swapfs
options	Several options are available including those shown in the example.
pass #	Used by **fsck** to determine order in which file system checks (**fsck**) will take place. If the same pass number is specified for two hfs file systems, then these will be checked in parallel with **fsck -p**.
comment	Anything you want, as long as it's preceded by a #.

For those of you who worked with HP-UX 9.x, you will notice the similarity between the **/etc/checklist** file (used in HP-UX 9.x) and the **/etc/**

fstab file (used in HP-UX 10.x). There is a transitional link between the **/etc/checklist** file and the **/etc/fstab** file as shown in the following example.

```
$ ll /etc/checklist

  lr-xr-xr-xT 1 root sys 10 Feb 7 13:39 /etc/checklist  -> /etc/fstab
```

Initialize with mediainit

Another command you should be aware of is **mediainit**. When you use SAM to set up disks for you, the **mediainit** command may be run.

Here are some of the options of **mediainit**:

-v	This is the verbose option. **mediainit** normally just prints error messages to the screen. You can get continuous feedback on what **mediainit** is doing with the -v option.
-i interleave	Allows you to specify the interleave factor, which is the relationship between sequential logical and physical records. **mediainit** will provide this if one is not specified.
-f format	The format option allows you to specify format options for devices such as floppy disks which support different format options. This is not required for hard disks.
pathname	The character device file to be used for **mediainit**.

newfs is used to create a new file system. **newfs** calls the **mksf** command earlier covered. **newfs** builds a file system of the type you specify (this is one of the commands that uses the "-F" option so you can specify the file system type).

CHAPTER 7

Windows NT System Administration Tools

Windows NT Administration

We have covered several system administration functions and there are more to come. The tools provided by Windows NT help you with virtually every aspect of system administration. You can manage everything from users to backups with a variety of tools. These tools, however, exist in a variety of places in the Windows NT environment. This does not make the tools any less effective; however, there is no central point of control for performing system administration tasks.

In this chapter I'll summarize the location of system administration tools in the Windows NT environment and cover some of these tools in this chapter. Some of the functions, such as disk administration and the performance tools, are covered in other chapters so I will just refer you to those chapters.

There are also two system administration products you may want to consider even though these do not come with Windows NT. The first is *Windows NT Resource Kit* and the second is *Technet*. Both of these provide advanced system administration material. I chose not to include these in the book because I tried to minimize the number of optional products covered.

There are exceptions to this rule in the book. For instance, the two interoperability chapters use X Windows and NFS products that are not part of the standard Windows NT oeprating system.

Windows NT Resource Kit is a Microsoft product that contains books and a CD-ROM with several useful utilities for Windows NT system administration. Many bookstores carry this product.

TechNet is a Microsoft service which includes CD-ROMs that are sent to you on a monthly basis which contain technical information, product resource kits, drivers, patches, and other useful material.

The Microsoft Web page (www.microsoft.com) contains detailed information about these and other Microsoft related products and topics.

True for Any Windows NT System Administration Tool

Most of the administration tools in Windows NT have the following two characteristics.

1. You are provided a summary of what your system currently looks like for the administration tool you are using. If you want to do something with the disks on your system, *Disk Administrator* shows the current configuration of disks on your system. When you invoke the *User Manager,* it first shows the *Username* and *Groups* for those on your system which you can view before making any modifications.

2. You can perform system administration tasks using administration tools. After you view your current configuration, all of the tools allow you to perform modifications to your system.

In general I would say that Windows NT allows you to perform almost all system administration functions through the many administration tools available to you.

Access to Common Administrative Tools

Windows NT provides a menu for the administrative tools you will most often use. As Administrator you have unlimited access to your system and these tools.

The menu pick you would use to get access to administration tools is *Start - Programs - Administrative Tools (Common)* as shown in Figure 7-1. The following is a list of programs available to you under this menu and those which are covered in this book:

- Administrative Wizards (covered)
- Backup (covered)
- Disk Administrator (covered)
- Event Viewer (covered)
- License Manager
- Migration Tool for Netware
- Network Client Administrator
- Performance Monitor (covered)
- Remote Access Admin
- Server Manager
- System Policy Editor
- User Manager for Domains (covered)
- Windows NT Diagnostics

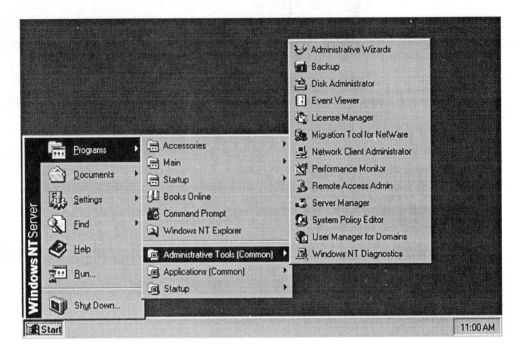

Figure 7-1 *Administrative Tools (Common)* Menu

There are many important administrative functional areas through which *Administrative Tools (Common)* gives you access. Are these all of the administrative areas to which you need access? The answer is no. There are other administrative tools, some of which you will use often and are very important, which are located in other areas of your Windows NT environment.

Another area in which several administrative tools are located is under the *Settings* menu. Figure 7-2 shows the *Settings* menu.

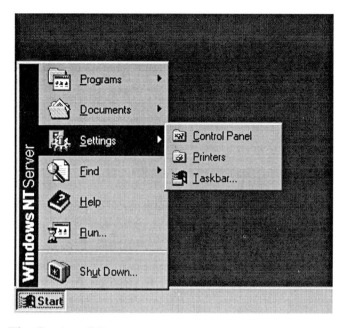

Figure 7-2 The *Settings* Menu

The *Control Panel* is used for many common administrative functions. The *Printers* pick shown in Figure 7-2 provides an interface through which printers can be configured which can also be reached through the *Control Panel*. As you can see, the administrative areas you will need to get access to are scattered throughout the Windows NT environment.

Let's now take a closer look at first the *Control Panel* and then *Administrative Tools (Common)*.

Control Panel

The *Settings - Control Panel* provides you access to many important administrative tools used to control your system in the following areas:

- Accessibility Options
- Add/Remove Programs
- Console
- Date/Time
- Devices
- Display
- Fonts
- Internet
- Keyboard
- Licensing
- Modems
- Mouse
- Multimedia
- Network
- PC Card (PCMCIA)
- Ports
- Printers
- Regional Settings
- SCSI Adapters
- Server
- Services
- Sounds

- System

- Tape Devices

- Telephony

- UPS

Figure 7-3 shows the Control Panel area.

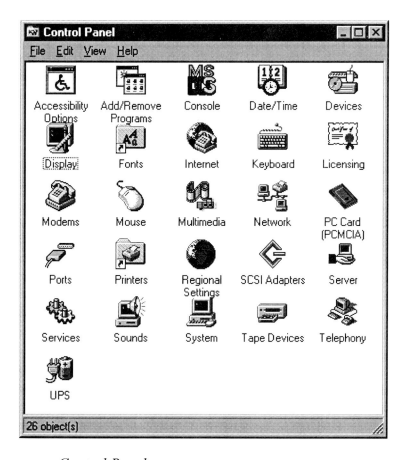

Figure 7-3 *Control Panel*

Let's take a quick look at the areas of the *Control Panel* often used by system administrators.

MS DOS Console

I can't live without typing commands. I like having a place to type. I like the Windows NT environment, but I still like to type commands. The *MS DOS Console* is available to you for typing commands when you select it from the *Start* menu. The look of it is controlled through *Control Panel*. Figure 7-4 shows the *MS DOS Console Windows Properties* that comes up when you select the *MS DOS Console* icon from the *Control Panel*.

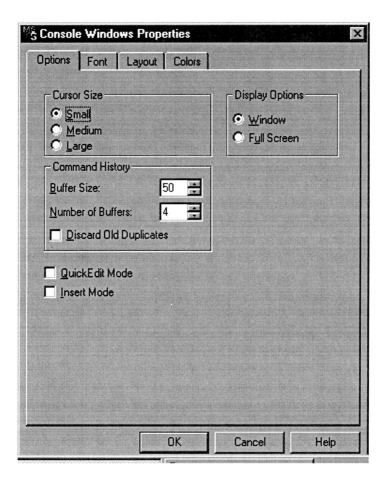

Figure 7-4 *MS DOS Console Windows Properties* from *Control Panel*

Figure 7-4 shows the *Options* window. There is also a window for *Font, Layout, and Colors*. The following is a list of the items you can control from these other windows.

Font

• Font

• Font size

Layout

• Screen Buffer Size

• Window Size

• Window Position

Colors

• Color of Screen Text

• Color of Screen Background

• Color of Popup Text

• Color of Popup Background

Devices

The *Devices* area of the *Control Panel* is used to start and stop devices. Figure 7-5 shows the *Devices* window.

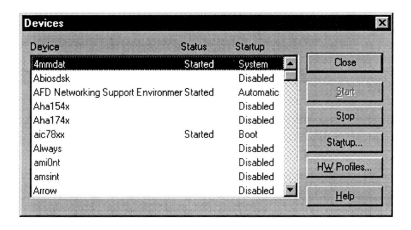

Figure 7-5 *Devices* from *Control Panel*

Devices can be started a variety of different ways. Devices that are started every time the system boots will have a *Boot, System*, or *Automatic* entry such as the 4mmdat shown in Figure 7-5. Others are *Disabled* such as several of those shown in Figure 7-5 which means they can't be started by a user. Still others have a *Manual* entry which means the device may be started by a user or another device. An example of a *Manual* device is a modem.

Network

You will, in all likelihood, connect your Windows NT system to a network and have to perform some configuration. This is discussed in other chapters

in some detail; however, it is worth noting that networking can be configured through the *Control Panel*. Here is a brief description of the five areas
of networking you can configure through the *Control Panel*.

Identification	This is the area in which information exists that is used to identify your computer on the network. You can specify such information as the *Computer Name* and *Workgroup* here.
Services	Services are networking functionalities that support the network operations you wish to perform. You can perform such functions as adding, removing, and updating services here.
Protocols	A protocol is a means by which computers communicate. They must run the same protocol in order to communicate. Two widely used protocols in the Windows NT world are NetBEUI and TCP/IP. You can perform such functions as adding, removing, and updating protocols here.
Adapters	Your network adapter is used to physically connect your computer to the network. You can perform such functions as adding, removing, and updating adapters here.
Bindings	Network Bindings are the way in which all the pieces of networking come together. When you play with bindings you are altering the connections between various networking components that can have a big effect on networking perfor-

mance. You can perform such functions as enabling, disabling, and changing the positions of bindings here.

Figure 7-6 shows the *Services* area under *Network*. The service that is highlighted, "NFS Maestro for Windows NT - Client," is a service that was installed on the system and used later in Chapter 14. The other services shown were installed on the system with Windows NT.

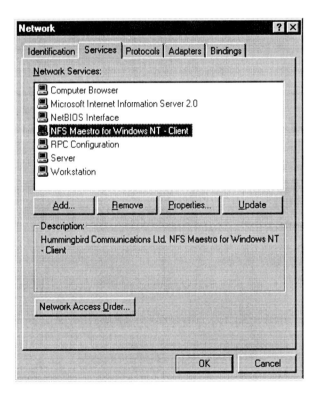

Figure 7-6 *Servcies* Under *Network*

There are a whole variety of TCP/IP networking related commands that you can issue from the command line. Although most of what you can accomplish in Windows NT can be done from the windows interface, there also many useful command line functions you can perform. The following section covers some of the TCP/IP commands available to you in Windows NT.

Networking Commands

You have access to many useful networking commands on the command line in Windows NT. Some of the commands not covered here that you may want to look into include the following:

- **lpr**
- **route**
- **finger**
- **rexec**
- **ftp**
- **telnet (opens a telnet window in the Windows NT environment)**
- **hostname**
- **lpq**
- **tracert**
- **rcp**
- **rsh**
- **tftp**

You can find out more about these commands by typing the command name /? at the command prompt such as **telnet /?**. There are some additional commands that I often use that are covered in the upcoming sections.

arp

arp is used to display and edit the Address Resolution Protocol (arp) cache. This cache maps IP addresses to physical hardware addresses. The cache has in it one or more addresses of recently accessed systems. The following example shows issuing the **arp** command on a Windows NT system at address 113 and the address of the system most recently accessed at 111 with its physical hardware address shown.

```
d: arp -a

Interface: 159.260.112.113 on Interface 2
   Internet Address      Physical Address        Type
   159.260.112.111       08-00-09-f0-bc-40       dynamic
```

There are several options to the **arp** command that you can view by issuing the **arp /?** command.

ipconfig

ipconfig is used to display the current networking interface parameters. The following example shows issuing the **ipconfig** command on a Windows NT system at address 113 with the **/all** option set which shows all information related to the networking interface.

```
d: ipconfig /all

Windows NT IP Configuration

        Host Name . . . . . . . . . : hpsystem1
        DNS Servers . . . . . . . . :
```

```
                  Node Type . . . . . . . . . : Broadcast
                  NetBIOS Scope ID. . . . . . :
                  IP Routing Enabled. . . . . : No
                  WINS Proxy Enabled. . . . . : No
                  NetBIOS Resolution Uses DNS : No

Ethernet adapter Hpddnd31:

                  Description . . . . . . . . : HP DeskDirect
                                            10/100 LAN Adapter
                  Physical Address. . . . . . : 08-00-09-D9-9A-8A
                  DHCP Enabled. . . . . . . . : No
                  IP Address. . . . . . . . . : 159.260.112.113
                  Subnet Mask . . . . . . . . : 255.255.255.0
                  Default Gateway . . . . . . : 159.260.112.250
```

There are several options to the **ipconfig** command that you can view by issuing the **ipconfig /?** command.

netstat

netstat provides network protocol statistics. The following **netstat** example uses the **-e** and **-s** options which show Ethernet statistics and statistics for various protocols, respectively. The ethernet statistics associated with the **-e** option are under "Interface Statistics" and end with "IP Statistics".

```
d: netstat -e -s

Interface Statistics

                              Received              Sent

Bytes                       3182007276            2446436
Unicast packets                  11046               9604
Non-unicast packets           21827982               7932
Discards                             0                  0
Errors                               0                  1
Unknown protocols              4946670

IP Statistics

   Packets Received                    = 20489869
   Received Header Errors              = 133441
```

```
         Received Address Errors          = 28222
         Datagrams Forwarded              = 0
         Unknown Protocols Received       = 0
         Received Packets Discarded       = 0
         Received Packets Delivered       = 20328206
         Output Requests                  = 12004
         Routing Discards                 = 0
         Discarded Output Packets         = 0
         Output Packet No Route           = 0
         Reassembly Required              = 0
         Reassembly Successful            = 0
         Reassembly Failures              = 0
         Datagrams Successfully Fragmented = 0
         Datagrams Failing Fragmentation  = 0
         Fragments Created                = 0

     ICMP Statistics

                                    Received    Sent
         Messages                   3702        23
         Errors                     0           0
         Destination Unreachable    4           5
         Time Exceeded              0           0
         Parameter Problems         0           0
         Source Quenchs             0           0
         Redirects                  3680        0
         Echos                      5           13
         Echo Replies               13          5
         Timestamps                 0           0
         Timestamp Replies          0           0
         Address Masks              0           0
         Address Mask Replies       0           0

     TCP Statistics

         Active Opens                     = 27
         Passive Opens                    = 8
         Failed Connection Attempts       = 1
         Reset Connections                = 15
         Current Connections              = 2
         Segments Received                = 1888
         Segments Sent                    = 1854
         Segments Retransmitted           = 3

     UDP Statistics

         Datagrams Received    = 607489
         No Ports              = 19718827
         Receive Errors        = 0
         Datagrams Sent        = 10124
```

There are several options to the **netstat** command that you can view by issuing the **netstat /?** command. If you wish to see the changes in the value of statistics, you can specify an interval after which the statistics will again be displayed.

ping

ping is used to determine whether or not a host is reachable on the network. **ping** causes an echo request that sends packets which are returned by the destination host you specify. There are several options to the ping command you can specify. The following example uses the **-n** option to specify the number of times you want to send the packets and **-l** specifies the length of packets for which the maximum of 8192 is used.

```
d: ping -n 9 -l 8192 system2

Pinging system2 [159.260.112.111] with 8192 bytes of data:

Reply from 159.260.112.111: bytes=8192 time=20ms TTL=255
Reply from 159.260.112.111: bytes=8192 time=20ms TTL=255
Reply from 159.260.112.111: bytes=8192 time=21ms TTL=255
Reply from 159.260.112.111: bytes=8192 time=20ms TTL=255
Reply from 159.260.112.111: bytes=8192 time=10ms TTL=255
Reply from 159.260.112.111: bytes=8192 time=30ms TTL=255
Reply from 159.260.112.111: bytes=8192 time=30ms TTL=255
Reply from 159.260.112.111: bytes=8192 time=20ms TTL=255
Reply from 159.260.112.111: bytes=8192 time=20ms TTL=255
```

There are several additional options to the **ping** command that you can view by issuing the **ping /?** command.

Services

You have access to a whole variety of services in the Control Panel. Figure 7-7 shows the *Services* window of the *Control Panel.*

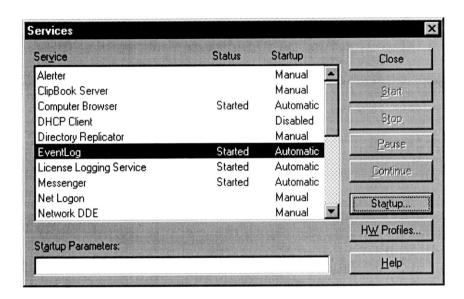

Figure 7-7 *Services* from *Control Panel*

You have a lot of control over the services on your Windows NT system in this dialog box. You can start, stop, pause, or continue services.

You also have control over the way in which a service is started just as you did under *Devices*. Services that are started every time the system boots will have an *Automatic* entry such as the *EventLog* in Figure 7-7. Others are *Disabled* which means they can't be started by a user or any other service. Still others have a *Manual* entry which means the service may be started by a user or another service.

The *Startup...* window for EventLog is shown in Figure 7-8.

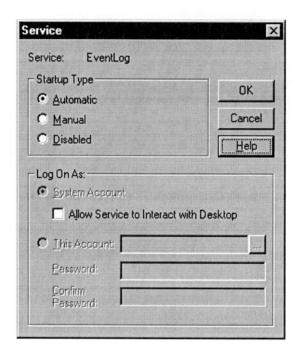

Figure 7-8 *Startup...* for EventLog

The EventLog is a particularly useful service. All kinds of events related to your Windows NT system are recorded by the EventLog service and can be viewed with the *Event Viewer*.

You'll see an example of an event that was captured by the EventLog and displayed with the *Event Viewer* under the *Event Viewer* section.

Printers

Adding printers through the *Control Panel* is trivial. The following are the steps you would perform to add a printer.

Select *Printers* Icon-

> Double-click *Printers* icon in *Control Panel*.

Select *Add Printers* Icon-

> Double-click *Add Printer* icon.

Printer Location - Select whether printer is attached to *My Computer* or *Network*. Use *My Computer* in this procedure.

Select Port   - Select from the available ports such as LPT1.

Select Printer   - Both manufacturer and printer must be selected such as HP and HP LaserJet 5MP.

Select Name   - Give the printer a name.

Shared or not   - Specify whether this is a shared or unshared printer.

This procedure is a simple walk through with all of the relevant windows popping up as you need them.

Tape Devices - An Example of Using Control Panel

With all of the good administrative tools shown under *Administrative Tools (Common)*, why would you need the *Control Panel*? Let's say you just hooked up a new HP SureStore tape drive for backup purposes. You go to *Programs - Administrative Tools (Common) - Backup* and you get the message shown in Figure 7-9.

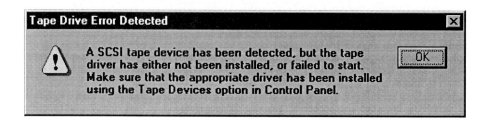

Figure 7-9 Tape Drive Error in *Programs - Administrative Tools (Common) Backup*

After this message appears, the backup window does not show the tape drive since it is not installed. At this point you cannot proceed with a backup to the tape drive. We can configure the tape drive by selecting *Settings - Control Panel* and then *Tape Devices*. Immediately upon selecting Tape Devices the window shown in Figure 7-10 appears.

Figure 7-10 *Control Panel* Detects New Tape Drive and Is Ready to Install

When OK is selected from Figure 7-10 the Windows NT CD-ROM is requested. After you install the Windows NT CD-ROM and specify the directory in which the driver is located (**F:\i386** in my case), you see the *Tape Devices* window from the *Control Panel* shown in Figure 7-11.

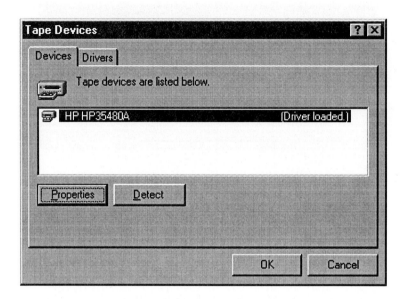

Figure 7-11 *Control Panel* Showing New Tape Drive Installed

If you select the *Properties* button in Figure 7-11 you get additional information about the tape drive. Figure 7-12 shows the General information.

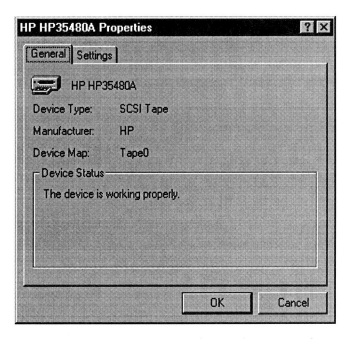

Figure 7-12 *Properties* of New Tape Drive under *General*

This screen shows general information about the tape drive. The bottom of the screen shows the status of the hardware. In this case the device is working properly. If there were a problem of some type, the nature of the problem would be displayed and a possible solution to the problem. There may also be a problem code and number which may be helpful in trouble shooting the problem.

I find this screen to be only moderately useful. When I shut off the tape drive, I still received the message that "The device is working properly."

Figure 7-13 shows the *Settings* information under *Properties.*

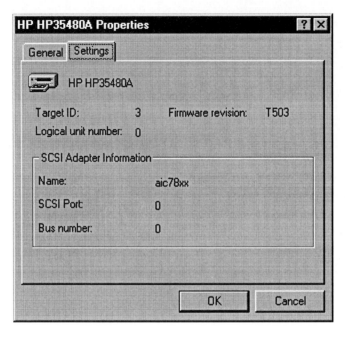

Figure 7-13 *Properties* of New Tape Drive Showing *Settings*

The information in this area relates to the SCSI adapter for the tape drive. In this case there is an aic78xx adapter.

Administrative Tools (Common)

I love areas like *Administrative Tools (Common)*. The operating system designers made a good attempt in Windows NT to give you, the system administrator, an area where your most often used tools are located. Although it is not complete, as we know from just having covered the *Control Panel* which is not part of *Administrative Tools (Common)*, it does contain many of the most often used system administration tools. Some of the tools in this area that fall under the umbrella of Windows NT system administration are covered in other chapters. These include *Disk Administrator* in Chapter 5; *Performance Monitor* in Chapter 9; and *Task Manager* in Chapter 11. There are, however, a few additional tools in this area that are useful to most every Windows NT system administrator. These include *Administrative Wizards, Backup, Event Viewer,* and *User Manager for Domains*. The other tools in this area may also be useful to some system administrators; however, I won't cover them in this book.

Administrative Wizards

Administrative Wizards is an interesting tool. It is a collection of eight system administration functions which can be launched from this area. It is a super introductory way of working with the eight areas covered. Figure 7-14 shows the window that pops up when you select Administrative Wizards.

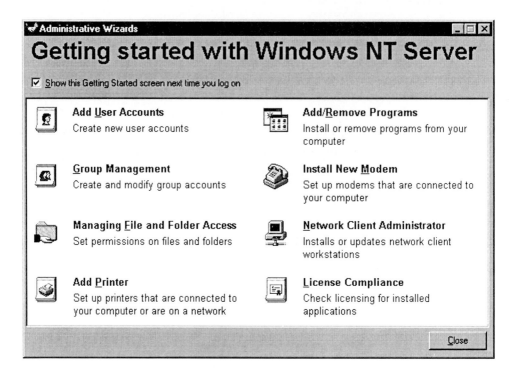

Figure 7-14 *Administrative Wizards* Screen

One of the reasons I find this area interesting is that if you select *Add Printer,* a screen comes up which is the same as that which you would see in the *Control Panel.* Although I think its great for *Administrative Wizards* to have some of the same functionality as *Control Panel,* I think it would be even better if there were "Printers" menu pick under *Administrative Tools (Common).* If you select *Install New Modem,* you will also see the same window that comes up under the *Control Panel.* If you select *Network Client Administrator,* you will see the same window that comes up when you pick this from *Administrative Tools (Common).* I imagine we may reach a point where *Administrative Wizards,* is the launch point for all system administration. In the meantime, it does contain some useful selections.

Backup

System and network backup seems to get more and more complex. This is for two reasons. Number one, system administrators are backing up more and more data. Disk is cheap, users create tons of files, and the system administrator gets stuck figuring out backup. Number two, you have to select from a wide variety of backup devices depending on your needs and your existing environment. I don't know how many times I have seen customers attempt centralized backup to a mainframe only to find out it's difficult to implement and even harder to restore files from in a timely fashion. Anyway, I digress. Let's get back to what Windows NT *Backup* can do for you.

Here are some of the common backup functions you can perform under *Backup*.

- Back up a variety of ways including full and incremental.

- Back up local and remote files.

- Back up NTFS and FAT files.

- Verify the backup.

- Span multiple tapes with a backup.

- Schedule backups.

- Produce a catalog of backup information.

Let's walk through a simple backup together to get a feel for the backup process. I'll cover the following common steps that are related to backup:

- Select a tape drive for the backup.

•Erase a foreign tape so it is suitable for a Windows NT backup.

•Fill in the dialog box used to specify backup parameters.

•Perform a backup.

•Review the backup log file.

•Fill in the dialog box used for restore.

•Perform a restore.

•Schedule future backups.

The *Backup* Screen

Selecting Backup produces a screen like that shown in Figure 7-15.

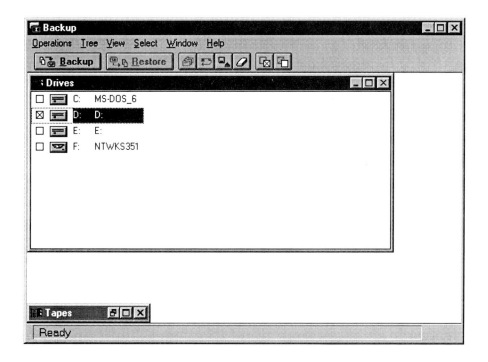

Figure 7-15 Top Level *Backup* Screen

The tapes icon appears in the lower left which you can select to view more information about the tape. At this time only **D:** is selected for backup as indicated by the "x" in the box on its left. You would click the box to the left of **C:** and **E:** if you wanted to include them in the backup. The *Operations* menu is used to control most aspects of the backup process. The menu picks under Operations are in the following list:

- Backup...

- Restore...

- Catalog

- Erase Tape...

- Format Tape...

- Hardware Setup...

- Exit

The *Hardware Setup* menu pick will show you the currently selected backup device as shown in Figure 7-16

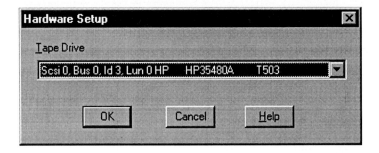

Figure 7-16 *Operations - Hardware Setup* Menu Pick

If you use a tape that has not been set up for Windows NT, you will see a window like that in Figure 7-17 pop up which tells you it is a foreign tape.

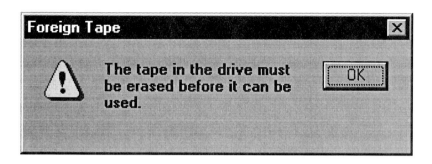

Figure 7-17 *Foreign Tape* Window

Operating systems do not like tapes used by other operating systems. It is like drinking a beverage from a glass used by someone else. Windows NT will want to erase the tape before it uses it. Selecting *Erase Tape...* from the *Operations* menu results in the dialog box in Figure 7-18.

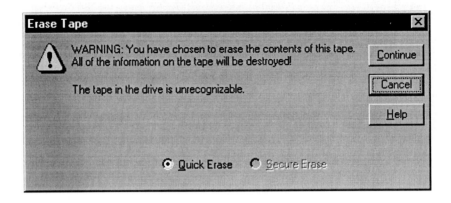

Figure 7-18 *Erase Tape* Dialog Box

When I select Continue in this dialog box, yet another appears asking me if I am sure I want to proceed with the erasing process. When I confirm I wish to proceed, the tape is erased and is now suitable for a Windows NT backup.

Now we can finally proceed to the backup. Figure 7-19 shows the Backup Information dialog box which we'll fill in to suit the needs of our backup.

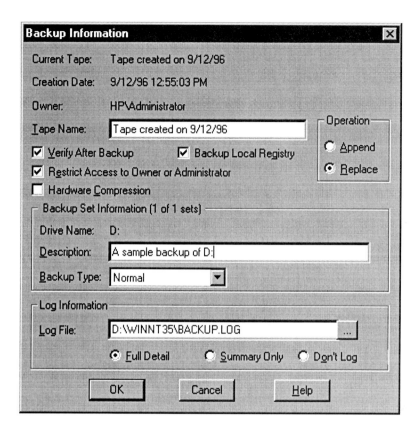

Figure 7-19 *Backup Information* Dialog Box

Let's take a closer look at some of the more important fields of this dialog box.

Current Tape   This provides information about the tape in the tape drive. The tape we are using in this example is blank. If we had used a tape from a previous backup, the date of the backup would have appeared in this field.

Creation Date   This field indicates when the tape was created.

Owner   The name and domain of the user who produced
                    the backup are shown here.

Tape Name   You can put any name of up to 50 characters in
                    this field. The example shows the default which is
                    "Tape created on [date]".

Verify After Backup

                    Verification of the backup ensures that the infor-
                    mation on the tape is identical to the information
                    on the disk. The verification process can add a
                    substantial amount of time to the backup. I like to
                    verify the backup because I have encountered
                    some cheap tapes that I found to be defective
                    when I tried to restore files.

Backup Local Registry

                    The *Local Registry* has in it a lot of important
                    information including information related to your
                    disk configuration. I normally check this box so
                    the backup contains information that may be valu-
                    able when recovering from a disaster. You may
                    need to restore the registry information in a crisis
                    situation.

Operation   To add the backup to the end of the tape, you
                    would select *Append*. It may be that you do not
                    have enough space on the tape for both backups.
                    You're much better off having more tapes on

hand than you could ever use and not have to worry about using *Append*. *Replace* will write the new data over the existing data on the tape.

Restrict Access to Owner or Administrator

If you select this only the owner of the files or the administrator will be able to access the files.

Hardware Compression

Your tape drive may be able to fit more data on less tape if it can compress that data. If you are certain you will be using the same tape drive to restore data, then you may want to use *Hardware Compression*. If you think you may be using a different tape drive to restore data, then you run the risk that compressed data may not be able to be restored on a different tape drive. Even tape drives that are the same model sometimes have a nuance which may prevent compressed data from being restored. One such nuance is a difference in the firmware on the tape drives. I once received two tape drives from the same manufacturer on the same day with very close serial numbers that had different firmware and could not therefore read a file that had been compressed on the other tape drive. I don't normally select *Hardware Compression*.

Drive Name   This is the name of the drive selected for backup. This was selected in the Backup window so you'll have to go to that screen to change the *Drive Name*.

Description   Put the description of the backup here. This field is for your information.

Backup Type   You have several selections for the Backup Type. Only Normal is shown here but you could select the arrow to the right of the arrow to select other backup types. The following bullet list describes the types of backup you can select:

- *Normal* - You will back up everything on your system. I'm not sure why this isn't called a "full" backup. The archive bit is set with Normal so you know that this file has been part of the backup. Many system administrators perform a normal backup periodically and perform incremental backups on a daily basis. On small systems I like to perform a normal backup regularly which saves a lot of time if you need to restore data because you know you can go back to a normal backup and the information will be there.

- *Copy* - This is also a full backup; however, the archive bit is not set so it is not clear whether or not the file has been part of the backup.

- *Differential* - This performs a backup of all the files with the archive bit set and does not reset it after the backup is complete.

- *Incremental* - This performs a backup of all the files with the archive bit set and resets it after the backup is complete.

- *Daily* - Performs a backup of all files that have been modified that day. The archive bit is not reset after a *Daily* backup.

Log File	This is the name of the file that will contain information about the backup. The default name of the *Log File* is shown in figure 7-19.
Full Detail	All information related to the backup will be logged including file and directory names. I would recommend using this selection so you can see everything that has taken place related to the backup. You may later decide this is too much information and revert to *Summary Only*.
Summary Only	Only major information is logged such as failure to open a file for backup. I would recommend selecting this option at a minimum so you can view the log file for backup related problems.
Don't Log	Information related to the backup is not logged.

Using the options in the *Backup Information* dialog box, I proceed with the backup. A Backup Status window appears which provides information about the backup. Figure 7-20 shows the *Backup Status* window just as the backup completed.

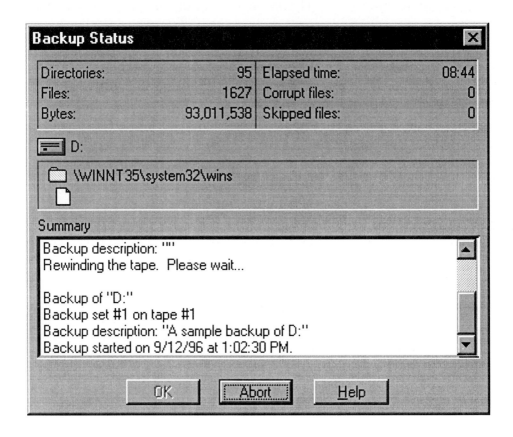

Figure 7-20 *Backup Status* Window

This window provides useful information about the status of the backup. This information is self explanatory so I won't cover this window in detail. The backup saved about 90 MBytes of data in about nine minutes.

One interesting note is that a *Verify Status* window appears during the verification stage. Its layout is the same as the *Backup Status* window. The Verify Status window may show differences encountered when the verification process is performed. This is because some files are being updated in real time as you use Windows NT. This means the files have changed between the time of the backup and the verification. Figure 7-21 shows a *Verify Status* Window.

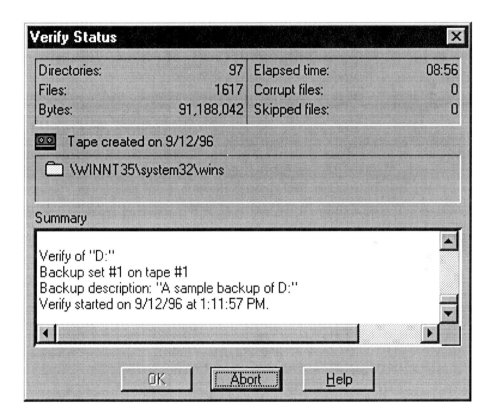

Figure 7-21 *Verify Status* Window

The verification process verified about 90 MBytes of data in about nine minutes.

The backup tape has on it a catalog which is used by the backup program to determine the tapes that are part of the backup set.

You can also issue the **ntbackup** command on the command line. To find out more about the **ntbackup** command type **ntbackup /?** at the command line.

Log File

The detailed log file produced as a result of this backup has a lot of useful information in it. The following are the first few lines of the log file from the backup we just performed.

```
Tape Erase started on 9/11/96 at 10:07:37 AM.
Erasing.
Tape Erase completed on 9/11/96 at 10:07:59 AM.

Backup Status

Tape Name: "Tape created on 9/11/97"
Backup of "D:"
Backup set #1 on tape #1
Backup description: "A sample backup of D:"
Backup Method: Normal

Backup started on 9/12/96 at 12:32:05 PM.
Directory D:\WINNT35\system32\config
default              <A>           163840    9/11/96    10:02 AM
SAM                  <A>            16384    9/11/96    10:03 AM
SECURITY             <A>            16384    9/11/96    10:02 AM
software             <A>           544768    9/12/96    12:30 PM
system               <A>           679936    9/11/96    10:03 AM
UserDef              <A>           114688    8/22/96    12:34 PM
userdiff             <A>            86016    8/22/96     1:13 PM
Directory D:\
Directory D:\Program Files
Directory D:\Program Files\Accessories
Directory D:\Program Files\Accessories\ImageVue
```

You can search through the log file to see if a specific file in which are interested was included in the backup. You can see that such useful information as the size of the file is included in the detailed log file.

Restore

You begin a restore by opening the *Backup* window and selecting the *Tapes* icon in the bottom left. For our restore we see the tape created as part of the earlier backup as shown in Figure 7-22.

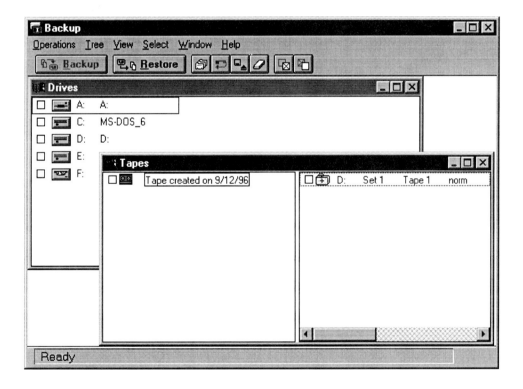

Figure 7-22 Beginning a Restore

You can select the files you wish to restore from tape by selecting the **D:** in the *Tapes* window. The **D:** in the *Tapes* window shows all of the files that are on the backup tape. The **D:** in the *Drives* window shows the files on the **D:** drive. Figure 7-23 shows a comparison of the **D:\temp\Screen Shots** directory on disk and tape. The disk contents are shown in the upper window and the tape contents are shown in the lower window. **backup1.bmp** (a bitmap file) appears on tape in the lower window but not on disk on the upper window

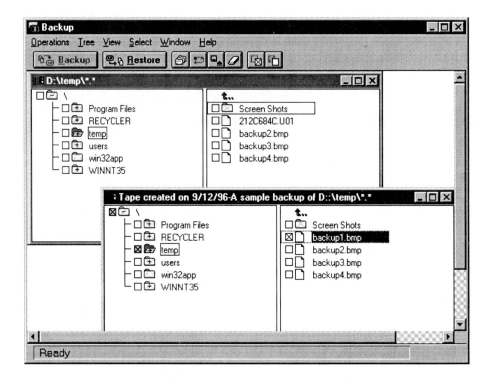

Figure 7-23   Selecting the File **backup1.bmp** for Restore

I have selected the file **backup1.bmp** as indicated by the "x" in the box next to the file in the bottom window. After *Restore* is selected from the *Backup* window the *Restore Information* window in Figure 7-24 appears.

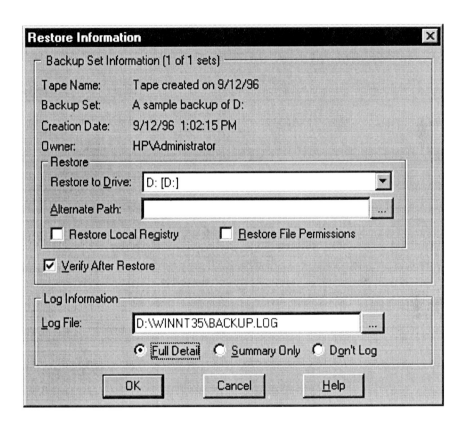

Figure 7-24 The *Restore Information* Window

There are many familiar fields from the *Backup Information* window that appeared earlier including the *Log File*. Since the *Log File* is the same file as that used to log backup information, the log information that is part of the restore will be appended to the log information that was part of the backup.

When you select *OK*, a Restore Status window appears which provides information about the restore. When the restore is complete, a *Verify Status* window appears because the *Verify After Restore* box was checked as part of the restore. The *Verify Status* window is shown in Figure 7-25.

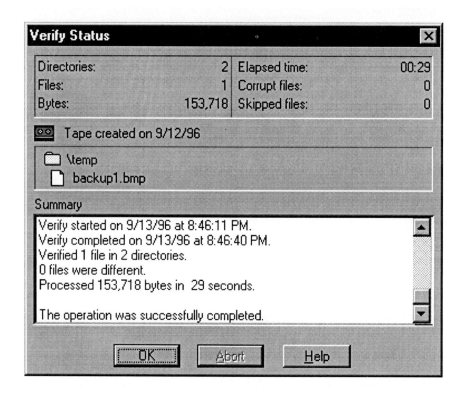

Figure 7-25 The *Verify Status* Window

The information appended to the end of the log file related to this restore and verification follows.

```
Restore Status


Tape #1: "Tape created on 9/12/96"

Backup performed on 9/12/96 at 1:02 PM

Backup set #1: "A sample backup of D:"

Restore started on 9/13/96 at 8:45:26 PM.

Directory D:\

Directory D:\temp

backup1.bmp                              153718      9/11/96      9:44 AM

Restore completed on 9/13/96 at 8:45:55 PM.

Restored 1 file in 2 directories.

Processed 153,718 bytes in  29 seconds.


Verify Status


Verify of "D:"

Backup set #1 on tape #1

Backup description: "A sample backup of D:"

Verify started on 9/13/96 at 8:46:11 PM.

Directory D:\

Directory D:\temp

backup1.bmp                              153718      9/11/96      9:44 AM

Verify completed on 9/13/96 at 8:46:40 PM.

Verified 1 file in 2 directories.

0 files were different.

Processed 153,718 bytes in  29 seconds.
```

This information appears at the very end of the log file. The file **backup1.bmp** was restored and verified successfully.

You may want to restore a file from tape and overwrite an existing file. The process is the same as that just covered for a restore; however, you will be asked to confirm that you wish to overwrite the existing file with the file from tape as shown in Figure 7-26.

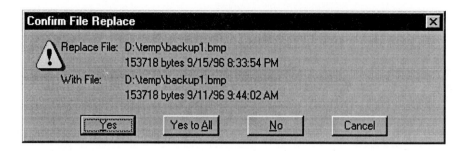

Figure 7-26 The *Confirm File Replace* Window

This window prevents you from inadvertently overwriting a file.

This chapter gives you a feel for the backup process in Windows NT. There are a variety of third-party backup tools you can use which go beyond the built-in backup capability of the *Backup* tool of Windows NT. You may want to back up to many devices at a time or have a variety of other backup needs for which the *Backup* program is not well suited. For many installations, especially newer installations, the Backup program works well and provides the functionality required.

Disk Administrator

Disk Administrator was covered in detail in Chapter 5. Chapter 5 is <u>Windows NT File System Management</u> and includes many important file system-related topics. The *Disk Administrator* is an important part of file system management so I strongly recommend you review Chapter 5.

Event Viewer

Every system administrator must keep track of what is taking place on his or her system. The better you document your system, using such simple methods as carefully documenting all system-related information in an system administration log book and closely monitoring the important activities taking place on your system, the closer you are to its operation. Should you encounter a catastrophic problem, your log book will help you in the rebuilding of your system. If you carefully monitor system events you are in a better position to proactively prevent system problems. The *Event Viewer* helps you with this all-important monitoring.

What is an event? An event is any significant occurrence that takes place on your system. Windows NT determines whether or not an event is indeed significant. If an event is significant and you chose to log it with the *Event Viewer* then all such events will be recorded. The *Event Viewer* has a *Log* menu through which you can specify the types of events to log including the following:

- *System* - System-related events are the most common types of events you want to log. We will review a system-related event that occurred shortly. This example shows a system component which was not present at the time the system booted. This is a typical system-related event which you would surely want to know about.

- *Security* - If you set up security auditing, then you can view security-related events using this menu pick. If, for instance, you set up some type of security under the *User Manager for Domains,* you can view events related to this setup here.

- *Applications* - You may have some important applications running on your system that you wish to log as well. Application-related events can be as important as system-related events when it comes to the successful operation of your system. You can view application-related events under this menu pick.

Figure 7-27 shows the *Event Viewer* with system events shown.

Date	Time	Source	Category	Event	User	Computer
i 9/19/96	8:18:37 AM	EventLog	None	6005	N/A	HP
9/15/96	8:24:01 PM	EventLog	None	6005	N/A	HP
9/15/96	8:22:31 PM	BROWSER	None	8033	N/A	HP
9/15/96	8:22:31 PM	BROWSER	None	8033	N/A	HP
9/15/96	8:22:06 PM	Service Control Mar	None	7026	N/A	HP
9/15/96	8:21:30 PM	EventLog	None	6005	N/A	HP
9/11/96	10:02:26 AM	EventLog	None	6005	N/A	HP
9/11/96	9:31:59 AM	EventLog	None	6005	N/A	HP
9/11/96	9:30:07 AM	BROWSER	None	8033	N/A	HP
9/11/96	9:30:07 AM	BROWSER	None	8033	N/A	HP
9/11/96	9:28:50 AM	Service Control Mar	None	7026	N/A	HP
9/11/96	9:28:16 AM	EventLog	None	6005	N/A	HP
9/11/96	9:26:44 AM	BROWSER	None	8033	N/A	HP
9/11/96	9:26:44 AM	BROWSER	None	8033	N/A	HP
9/11/96	9:24:18 AM	Service Control Mar	None	7026	N/A	HP
9/11/96	9:23:46 AM	EventLog	None	6005	N/A	HP
9/8/96	8:42:12 PM	EventLog	None	6005	N/A	HP
9/8/96	8:40:18 PM	BROWSER	None	8033	N/A	HP
9/8/96	8:40:04 PM	Service Control Mar	None	7026	N/A	HP
9/8/96	8:39:29 PM	EventLog	None	6005	N/A	HP
9/7/96	9:32:13 AM	Service Control Mar	None	7026	N/A	HP
9/7/96	9:31:43 AM	EventLog	None	6005	N/A	HP
9/7/96	9:29:39 AM	BROWSER	None	8033	N/A	HP
9/7/96	9:29:38 AM	BROWSER	None	8033	N/A	HP

Figure 7-27 *Event Viewer* Showing System Log

This figure has in it two different icons. The "i" in a circle is an informational icon indicating to you that a service is successfully operating. The "stop" in the icon indicates that there is an error of some type (there are five "stop" icons in this figure but the "stop" is hard to read.) There is also a "!" icon which is a warning; a "key" icon which indicates that a security event was successful; and a "lock" icon which indicates that a security event failed.

You have a lot of control over the events you will view. Figure 7-28 shows some of the filtering you can employ.

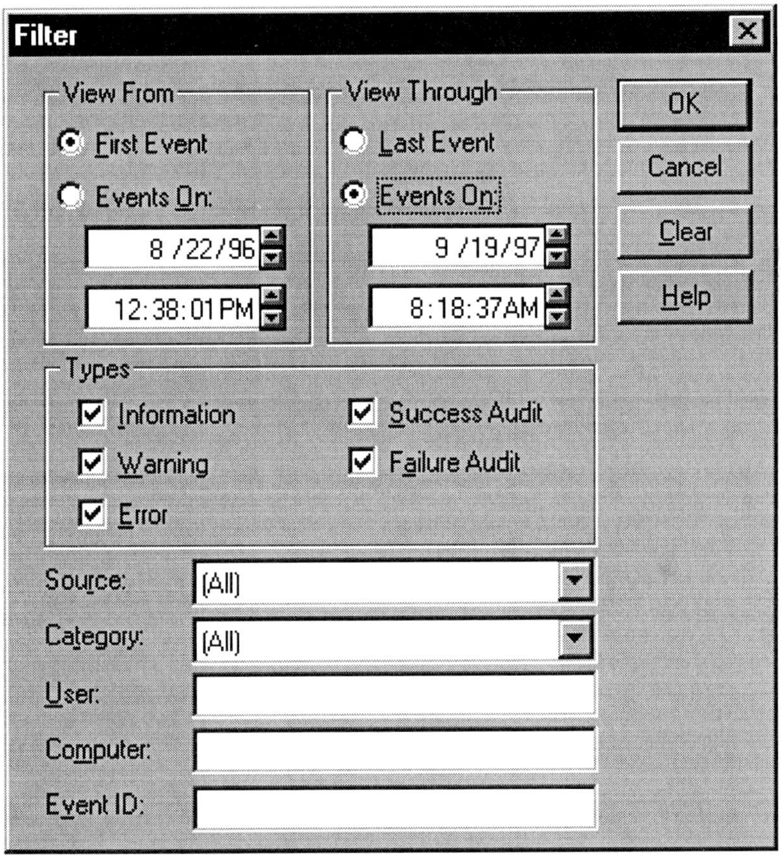

Figure 7-28 *Filter* Window from *Event Viewer*

This figure shows that we are viewing all events. You can limit the viewing to particular dates, which is useful when troubleshooting a problem that occurred at a particular time. You can also select the *Types* of events to display. Again we are displaying all events but you can view only some types of events such as *Error*. There are several other areas of control for viewing events such as *Category* which is the class of events you wish to view.

Using the Event Viewer

The tape drive we earlier configured under *Control Panel* is checked each time the system boots.

After we have loaded the device driver and performed various setup steps for a tape drive, the following message appeared when the system booted:

```
At least one service or driver failed during
system startup. Use Event Viewer to examine the
event log for details.
```

In order to view this event in more detail, you would select *Event Viewer* and select the event you wish. The event that was a problem during this boot is displayed in Figure 7-29.

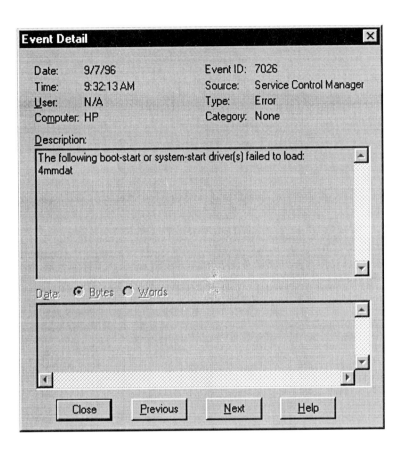

Figure 7-29 *Event Detail* Window from *Event Viewer*

This problem turned out to be nothing more than the tape drive powered down when I turned on the system. The *EventLog* service produces many such messages that you can view from the *Event Viewer*.

Performance Monitor

The *Performance Monitor* is covered in detail in Chapter 9.

User Manager for Domains

The *User Manager for Domains* is used to manage user accounts and groups in domains. *User Manager for Domains* runs on Windows NT server systems. On Windows NT workstation systems you run *User Manager* by default which has a subset of the functionality of *User Manager for Domains*.

In this section I will concentrate on user-related activity on a single machine. You can, however, manage users on a broader scale, or a domain, using *User Manager for Domains*. This means that all of the systems in a domain can have the users and groups on those systems managed through one system. This one system is the Primary Domain Controller (PDC). This is a powerful concept that greatly increases the ease with which users can be managed. You can also go beyond a domain and create relationships among domains which further enhance enterprise management functionality. During the installation process you can install the following three different types of Windows NT systems.

    - Primary Domain Controller
    - Backup Domain Controller
    - Standalone Server

This is an area where some background is required. If your Windows NT systems worked in an autonomous manner, then you would not be able to share data, including data related to users. If you wanted to add a user to such an autonomous network, you would be required to add that user on each and every system in the network. If you have ten systems in your network and 20 users, you would have to keep track of 200 users! Fortunately Windows NT has a means by which accounts can be centrally managed called the Primary Domain Controller (PDC). The PDC holds the database of users that is shared among systems in the domain. There is actually a Security Accounts Manager (SAM) database in which the user information is kept.

Now, you can imagine a disaster in which your Primary Domain Controller is unaccessible and you have lost access to your database of users. You can back up your Primary Domain Controller with one, or multiple, Backup Domain Controllers (BDC). These systems can take over in the event you encounter a problem with your Primary Domain Controller. You also have the option to have a stand alone server which will manage only itself. I recommend you use this option only if you have one Windows NT system and never plan to expand.

We can take this discussion one step further to "trust relationships." Although you don't establish trust relationships during the installation procedure, trust relationships are related to domain controllers so I'll give some background now. I'm not going to cover establishing trust relationships in the book but I will supply some background here.

Domains act as independent networks with their own user account databases. You can, however, have user accounts in one domain access resources in other domains through a trust relationship. Trust relationships can be either one way or two way. In a one way relationship you have one domain "trust" another domain. Only one domain trusts the other domain and not vice versa. In a two way trust relationship both domains trust each other. In a two way trust relationship users can log on from either domain to the other domain in the trust relationship.

All trust relationships are set up in *User Manager for Domains.*

The upcoming user-related section covers users on a specific system only, however, all of the topics covered can be expanded to apply to a domain and to trust relationships.

There are all kinds of activities we need to perform when working with users so let's jump right into it.

User Properties

To invoke the program, go to *Programs - Administrative Tools (Common) - User Manger for Domains*. The main *User Manager* window will appear and you can then select *Properties...* from the *User* menu to see the window shown in Figure 7-30.

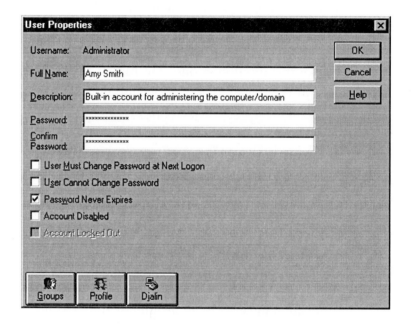

Figure 7-30 *User Properties...* Window from *User Manager for Domains*

You can view and manage most of the characteristics related to users in this window so let's take a look at the information in this window.

Username	This is the name of the user and is used to identify the account. This can be modified with *User - Rename*.
Full Name	The full name of the user appears here. I like to use the name as it appears in the company phone directory so if someone using the *User Manager for Domains* views the name and wishes to contact the user, their number can be easily found.
Description	Any information you want to include about the user. You could include the physical location of their desk or any relevant information here.
Password	The password is not viewable and only "*" appears in this field. The user must type his or her password in order to log in. Users should not share their password with anyone.

Confirm Password

The password is retyped in this field so as to ensure what was typed into the *Password* is correct.

User Must Change Password at Next Logon

The user will be instructed to change their password at the time of next logon.

User Cannot Change Password

> If an account is shared by several users, then there will be only one password for the account. You would check this box so one user using the account does not change the password, thereby locking out the other users from the account. My strong recommendation is to not have multiple users sharing an account. It is easy to track what a specific user has done, but if you have several users using the same account you lose control over that account.

Password Never Expires

> If there is a good reason for an account password to never change, then check this box. An example would be an account that is required to load software but is not used for other purposes. In general, you should have users change passwords on a regular basis.

Account Disabled

> You can disable an account using this box.

Account Locked Out

> An account that is locked for such reasons as too many failed attempts to logon will have this box available for unlocking. This is not used to lock an account; rather, it is used only to unlock a locked account.

There are two accounts that are installed on the system for you. These are "Administrator" and "Guest." You will see all the accounts that exist on the system when you invoke *User Manager for Domains* and you will see these two accounts if you just installed Windows NT. You may want to use *User - Properties...* to view the information related to these two users. "Administrator" is the user who has complete control over the system and the domain. The password for "Administrator" was assigned at the time you installed the Windows NT server but you could go ahead and change the password. You could change the name also but I consider password control a better means of security than user name control. Some people consider figuring out the name of the user to be half of what it takes to log in so they also keep user names a secret. If you subscribe to this way of thinking, then you will want to change the name of "Administrator" since this is a default name given at the time of installation.

Another matter to consider related to passwords is the system resources required to change passwords. When user passwords are changed, their accounts are updated on the Primary Domain Controller. These changes then have to be passed to the Backup Domain Controllers. This means you may have considerable network traffic because approximately 1 KByte of data is transferred for each user. For 10 users this is not a concern; for 10,000 it may be a concern. Security is the most important consideration here, however, so do what you think will best meet your security needs.

There is also a "Guest" account. The "Guest" account is disabled by default. I don't know of a good reason to enable this account. If you have guests on the system that need an account, it is easy enough with the *User Manager for Domains* to create the domain accounts you need.

Let's now go ahead and use *User Manager for Domains* to create a new user.

Creating New Users

To create a new user go to *User - New User* and the *New User* window appears. Figure 7-31 shows the *New User* window.

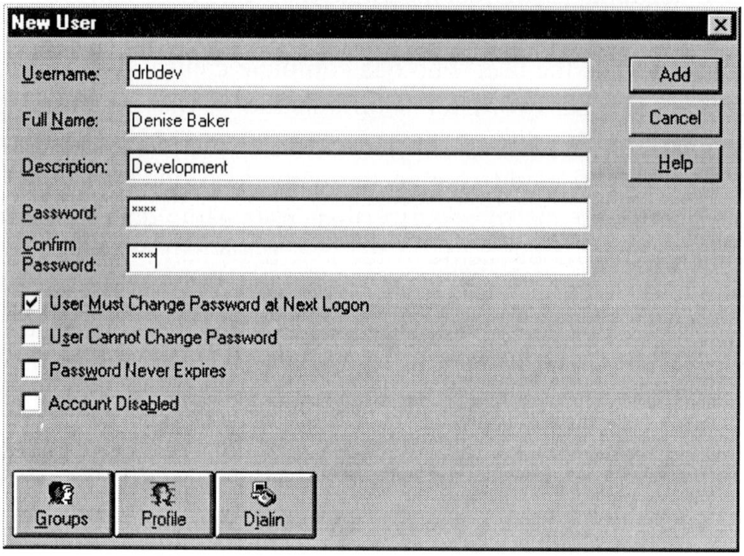

Figure 7-31 *New User* Window

We just covered these fields under the *User - Properties...* section. All of the same information applies to these fields. One aspect of adding users that tends to both simplify user management and provide some consistency to your environment is to maintain user names from other systems. Most users, especially in large organizations, have user accounts on other systems. In most cases you can use the user name from another system, or one close to it, on your Windows NT system. This makes it easier for users to move from system to system and it can also make such tasks as copying from the user area on one system to another easier.

If you assign new user names, try not to oversimplify by using a first name and last initial. Windows NT domains tend to grow and you may have many coworkers with the first name Denise and the last initial B. Also avoid using spaces in names and you can't use the following characters:

$$< \quad > \quad ? \quad * \quad + \quad , \quad = \quad | \quad : \quad ; \quad \{ \quad \} \quad \backslash \quad / \quad "$$

If you attempt to use one of these reserved characters and add the user you will see the message shown in Figure 7-32.

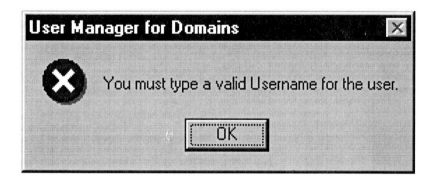

Figure 7-32   Window Indicating Invalid User Name

After you fill in the required information, you would then use the three buttons in the bottom to specify additional information about the user. You can also copy all of the information associated with this user to other users. You select the user in the *User Manager* window and *User - Copy...* from the menu. You can then type in a new user name and password and all of the other information will be copied. Let's take a look at *Groups*.

Groups

Groups can be global which means they are accessible to the entire network. They can also be local which means they are accessible only to the local domain. The icon in the *Group Memberships* window that has two people and a globe is global while the icon with two people and a computer is local (only local icons are shown figure 7-33.) Figure 7-33 shows the *Group Memberships* window for the user "drbdev" we are creating.

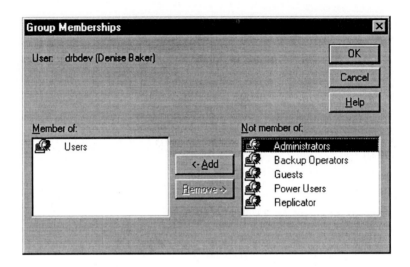

Figure 7-33   *Group Memberships* Window

When you create a user, it must be a member of at least one group. There are several predefined groups on a Windows NT system. You don't have to use only the default groups. You can use the *User - New Global Group...* and *User - New Local Group...* to create new groups.

There are several groups that exist on your Windows NT system. These are listed in the bottom of the User Manager window. To find out more about these groups, including the members of the group, highlight one of the groups and select the *User - Properties...* menu pick.

Policies - Account...

The *Policies* menu in the User Manager area allows you to control many aspects of user management. The first menu pick is *Policies - Account...* which is shown in Figure 7-34.

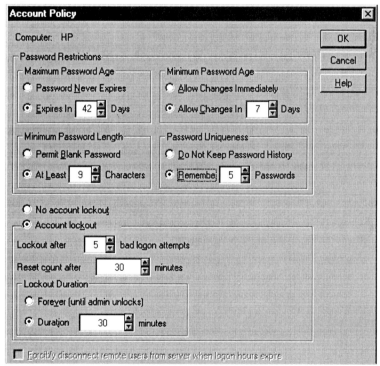

Figure 7-34 *Account Policy* Window

Although most of the fields in this window are self-explanatory, I would like to point out a few of the more important aspects of it.

Most of the fields shown in the figure are not filled in initially. By default most of the fields are blank and do not have the entries shown in this figure. At a minimum I recommend you specify a password length.

Blank passwords were permitted on my system. In addition, you should keep a password history. Many users will alternate between two passwords which can be dangerous if you don't keep a history. You should also lockout users after several bad login attempts and consider keeping a permanent lock out until you unlock the account. Security is becoming a bigger and bigger issue in all types of installations so you should spend some time in this window considering your policies.

Policies - User Rights...

The menu pick *Policies - User Rights...* allows you to select the functions that groups of users will be permitted to perform. Here is a list of some of the rights you can give to a group of users:

- Access this computer from network
- Add workstations to domain
- Back up files and directories
- Change the system time
- Force shutdown from a remote system
- Load and unload device drivers
- Log on locally
- Manage auditing and security log
- Restore files and directories
- Shut down the system
- Take ownership of files or other object

You carefully want to consider which rights you want to give groups of users. I found on my system that all users could shut down the system. Review the current rights on your system and adjust them as you see fit.

Policies - Audit...

There are a variety of events you can log. This is called security auditing because having a record of these events having occurred provides information that can be used to identify possible security-related problems. I have found that maintaining user accounts carefully to keep out intruders and other such functions are much more important to system security than auditing events. This does not mean, however, that keeping track of these events is not useful.

Figure 7-35 shows the Audit Policy window which you get access to the *Policies - Audit...*menu pick.

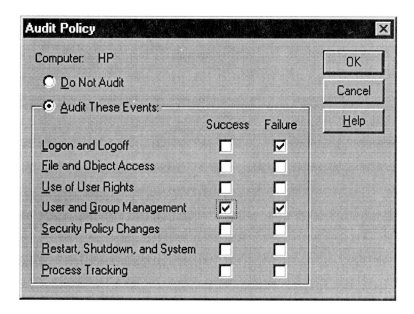

Figure 7-35 *Account Policy* Window

When you select the *Audit These Events* button, the events shown are highlighted. Here is a brief description of the events you can audit.

Logon and Logoff   Both successful and unsuccessful logon and logoff attempts are recorded as well as connections to other servers. The number of unsuccessful logon attempts is commonly recorded.

File and Object Access

Directories and files that have been selected for auditing will be tracked.

Use of User Rights   Tracks use of user rights.

User and Group Management

Records changes to user accounts and groups such as password changes.

Security Policy Changes

Keeps track of changes made to trust relationships, auditing, and user rights.

Restart, Shutdown, and System

Keeps track of all system shutdowns and reboots.

Process Tracking   Keeps track of information related to invoking programs.

What I have covered here is only the beginning of what you need to know to manage users. Creating users and groups and developing policies are iterative processes. You may start out with one set of requirements and find that they change over time. With Windows NT you have a substantial amount of flexibility you can exercise to adjust your users and groups.

The Registry

The *Registry* is a database that contains all of the configuration information for your Windows NT system. The information we have been working with in this chapter, such as the tape drive you have connected to your system and user information, are all in the *Registry*. In this section I'll provide a brief overview of the *Registry* so you get the feel for what information is in it and how to access information.

The Registry is a database that you view and manipulate through the **Registry Editor**. When you start a Windows 3.x system, run networking programs and applications, the system uses several configuration files scattered around in order to setup the operating environment. Windows NT, on the other hand, uses only the Registry for configuration information.

You can invoke the *Registry Editor* from the *Windows NT Explorer* with **winnt35\system32\regedt32.exe**. When you invoke the **Registry Editor** a whole series of windows will open as shown in Figure 7-36.

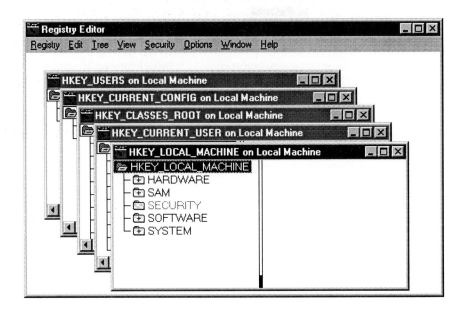

Figure 7-36   The *Registry Editor* Window

Before we go any further, here are some words of caution. Because there is so much important information in the *Registry,* I suggest you use the *Options - Read Only Mode* immediately after invoking the **Registry Editor** so you don't inadvertently change any information. In addition, the information in the Registry was put there with other tools such as the *Control Panel.* You do not, therefore, want to make any changes to the Registry entries until you are knowledgeable about the tool and feel comfortable doing so.

You can see in Figure 7-36 that information is grouped by users, current configuration, classes of root, current user information, and information about the local machine. Here is brief description of these categories.

HKEY_LOCAL_MACHINE

Lists information about your currently running hardware and applications.

HKEY_CLASSES_ROOT

Information about what application to invoke when a file is opened is kept here.

HKEY_USER   Contains user profile information.

HKEY_CURRENT_USER

Contains information about the user currently logged onto the system.

HKEY_CURRENT_CONFIG

The hardware profile of the system.

The information in the *Registry* is organized by keys and subkeys because the *Registry* is really a hierarchical database. Think of it as a database with a clear hierarchy that is comprised of keys and subkeys.

To get a feel for both the hierarchy of the *Registry* and the format of information in it, let's look at an entry. We can traverse the hierarchy in the *Registry* just as we do with *Windows NT Explorer*. We can look at the information in the *Registry* related to the local area network software with the *Registry Editor* path *HKEY_LOCAL_MACHINE - SOFTWARE - Hewlett-Packard - Hpfend - CurrentVersion* as shown in Figure 7-37.

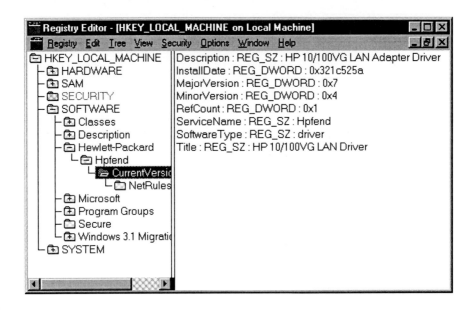

The right side of this window shows several *names*, *data types*, and *values*. The second entry from the bottom has a name of "Software Type", a data type of "REG_SZ", and a value of "driver". There are a variety of data types in the *Registry*. The value is of a type defined by the data type. The following list shows the data types.

REG_BINARY	This a binary data type. The value following the data type will be binary.
REG_SZ	This is a simple string. In our example the value "driver" is a string.
REG_DWORD	This is binary data type of four bytes.
REG_MULTI_SZ	This is a string with a number of parameters.

REG_EXPAND_SZ   This is a string of variable size such as a message
                   which may change depending on the circum-
                   stances.

You can find a key you are interested in with the *View - Find Key...*
command. This command, however, searches only for keys and not for values.

A database is a set of interrelated files. If indeed the *Registry* is a database, then it should be comprised mostly of a set of files.The *Registry* files
are called "hives." At the time you boot there are a set of binary files modified which comprise much of the *Registry*. If you use the *Windows NT
Explorer* and go to **winnt\system32\config,** you will see the hive files.
There is redundancy built into the hive files. You'll notice there are files
such as **security** and **security.sav**. These files work in conjunction to
ensure that changes to the hive files are saved in such a way that should a
system crash occur during the update to a hive file there is a mechanism to
ensure the system will have the necessary hive information to boot. This
redundancy is taken one step further with the system files. The system file
is especially well protected by having a complete copy of **system** in **sys-
tem.alt**.

If you view the details of the hive files in *Windows NT Explorer,* you
will see that many have the date and time of the last boot on them indicating that they were indeed modified at the time of the last system boot.

A piece of information that is particularly useful in the *Registry* is a
value that identifies the type of Windows NT you are running. The *Registry*
entry   \HKEY_LOCAL_MACHINE\SYSTEM\CURRENT\CON-
TROLSET\CONTROL\PRODUCTOPTIONS\PRODUCTTYPE   determines the type of Windows NT you are running. Figure 7-38 shows the
value of this *Registry* entry on my system.

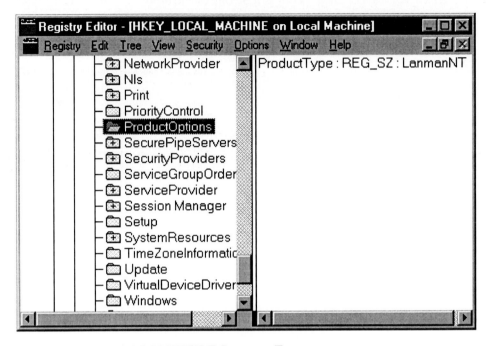

Figure 7-38 *PRODUCTTYPE Registry* Entry

The three possible values of this *Registry* entry are:

LANMANNT	Advanced Server
SERVERNT	Server
WINNT	Workstation

My system has a value of LANMANNT so I am running Advanced Server on my system.

CHAPTER 8

HP-UX System Administration Manager (SAM)

SAM Overview

SAM is a program you can use that automates performing various system administration tasks. I would like to go on record right now and suggest you use System Administration Manager (SAM) for performing routine system administration tasks. You'll talk to UNIX experts who say that any tool that automates system administration tasks is doing things behind your back and is therefore "evil." Don't believe them. SAM is a tool developed by HP-UX gurus who know as much about UNIX as anyone. I have met and worked with some of these people and they have labored long and hard to give you and me a tool that helps us do our job and doesn't hinder us from doing it. Does this mean that you blindly use SAM? Of course not. If you have no idea how TCP/IP works, then you shouldn't have SAM perform networking configuration for you. Similarly, you wouldn't want SAM to add users to your system without knowing what files will be updated. On the other hand, there is no reason to do this manually if SAM can do this for you. Let SAM help you perform your job better and don't feel guilty about it.

Four features of SAM make it particularly useful:

1. It provides a central point from which system administration tasks can be performed. This includes both the built-in tasks that come with SAM as well as those you can add into the SAM menu hierarchy. You can run SAM on a remote system and display it locally so you do truly have a central point of control.

2. It provides an easy way to perform tasks which are difficult in that you would have to perform many steps. SAM performs these steps for you.

3. It provides a summary of what your system currently looks like for any of the categories of administration tasks you wish to perform. If you want to do something with the disks on your system, SAM first lists the disks you currently have connected. If you want to play with a printer, SAM firsts lists all your printers and plotters for you. This cuts down on mistakes by putting your current configuration right in front of you.

4. You can assign non-root users to perform some of the system administration functions in SAM. If, for instance, you feel comfortable assigning one of your associates to manage users, you can give them permission to perform user-related tasks and give another user permission to perform backups, and so on.

There are some tasks SAM can't perform for you. SAM does most routine tasks for you, but troubleshooting a problem is not considered routine. Troubleshooting a problem gives you a chance to show off and to hone your system administration skills.

When SAM is performing routine tasks for you, it isn't doing anything you couldn't do yourself by issuing a series of HP-UX commands. SAM provides a simple user interface that allows you to perform tasks by selecting menu items and entering pertinent information essential to performing the task.

Running and Using SAM as Superuser

To run SAM, log in as root and type:

```
$ sam
```

This will invoke SAM. If you have a graphics display, SAM will run with the Motif interface. If you have a character-based display, SAM will run in character mode. You have nearly all the same functionality in both modes, but the Motif environment is much more pleasant to use.

If you have a graphics display and SAM does not come up in a Motif window, you probably don't have your DISPLAY variable set for root.

Type the following to set the DISPLAY variable for default POSIX, Korn, and Bourne shells:

```
$ DISPLAY=system_name:0.0
$ export DISPLAY
```

Just substitute the name of your computer for *system_name*. This can be set in your local **.profile** file. If you're running HP VUE, you may want to put these lines in your **.vueprofile** file.

Type the following to set the DISPLAY variable for C shell:

```
# setenv DISPLAY system_name:0.0
```

Again you would substitute the name of your computer for system_name. This would typically be done in your **.login** file but if you're running HP VUE, you may want to put this in your **.vueprofile** file.

Figure 8-1 shows the System Administration Manager running in graphics mode. This is the top-level window of the hierarchical SAM environment called the Functional Area Launcher (FAL). The 13 categories or areas of management shown are the default functional areas managed by SAM. You can select one of these functional areas and be placed in a sub-area. Because SAM is hierarchical, you may find yourself working your way down through several levels of the hierarchy before you reach the desired level. I'll cover each of these categories or areas in this chapter.

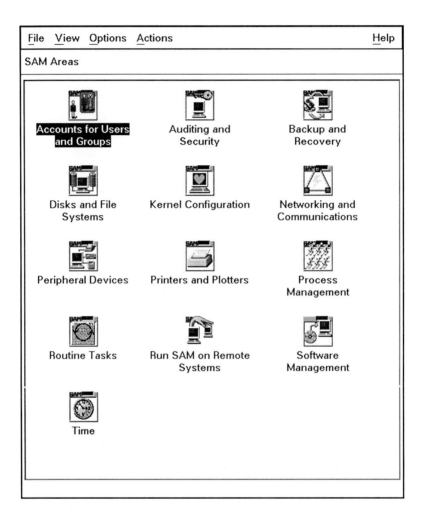

Figure 8-1   SAM Startup Window in Graphics Mode

In addition to selecting a functional area you can select from the pull down menu bar across the top of the SAM window. I will indicate selections made in SAM and keyboard keys in this chapter with italics. The five selections are *File, View, Options, Actions,* and *Help.* The title line shown in the figure reads *SAM Areas.* If you're running Restricted SAM Builder, you will also see a status line with the message "Privileges for user: <user-

name>". As you progress down the hierarchy the title line will change to reflect your level in the SAM hierarchy. You can move into one of the areas shown, such as *Backup and Recovery*, by double clicking the left mouse button on this functional area. You move back up the hierarchy by selecting the *Actions-Close Level* menu pick.

You don't need a graphics display to run SAM. You have access to nearly all the same functionality on a text terminal as you do on a graphics terminal. Figure 8-2 is SAM running in character mode with the same 13 functional areas you have in graphics mode.

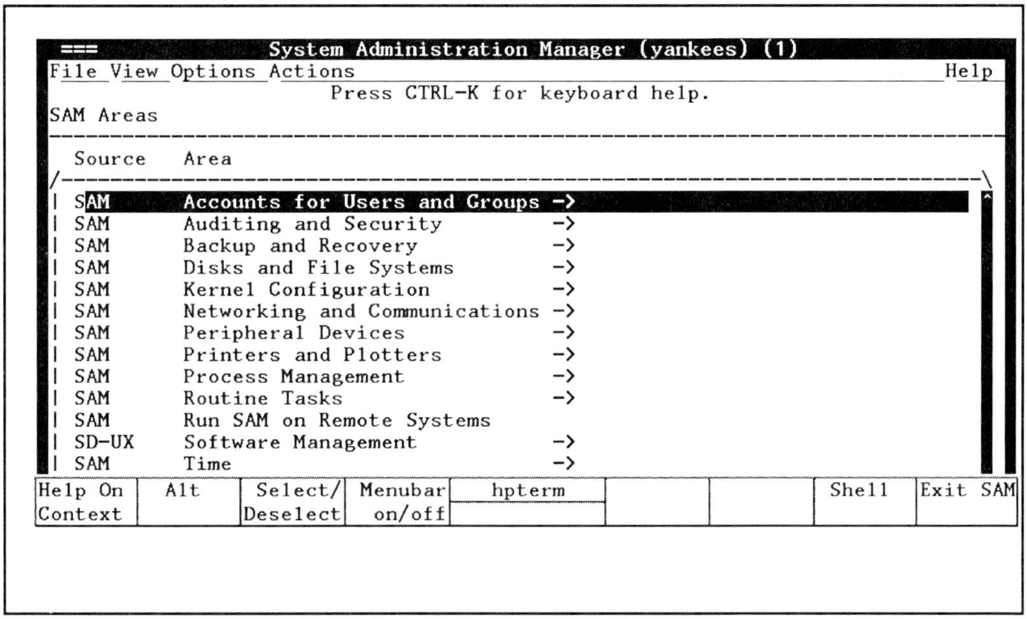

```
=== 	       System Administration Manager (yankees) (1)
File View Options Actions                                              Help
                        Press CTRL-K for keyboard help.
SAM Areas
------------------------------------------------------------------------
   Source    Area
/------------------------------------------------------------------------\
 |  SAM       Accounts for Users and Groups ->                          ^
 |  SAM       Auditing and Security          ->
 |  SAM       Backup and Recovery            ->
 |  SAM       Disks and File Systems         ->
 |  SAM       Kernel Configuration           ->
 |  SAM       Networking and Communications  ->
 |  SAM       Peripheral Devices             ->
 |  SAM       Printers and Plotters          ->
 |  SAM       Process Management             ->
 |  SAM       Routine Tasks                  ->
 |  SAM       Run SAM on Remote Systems
 |  SD-UX     Software Management            ->
 |  SAM       Time                           ->
 ------------------------------------------------------------------------
|Help On  | Alt    | Select/ | Menubar |   hpterm   |        | Shell | Exit SAM|
|Context  |        | Deselect| on/off  |            |        |       |         |
```

Figure 8-2 SAM Startup Window in Character Mode

The View menu can be used in character mode to tailor the information desired, filter out some entries, or search for particular entries.

Because you don't have a mouse on a text terminal, you use the keyboard to make selections. The point and click method of using SAM when in graphics mode is highly preferable to using the keyboard; however, the same structure to the functional areas exists in both environments. When you see an item in reverse video on the text terminal (such as *Accounts For*

Users and Groups in Figure 8-2), you know you have that item selected. After having selected *Accounts For Users and Groups* as shown in the Figure 8-2, you would then use the *tab* key (or *F4*) to get to the menu bar, use the <- -> keys to select the desired menu, and use the *space bar* to display the menu. This is where having a mouse to make your selections is highly desirable. Figure 8-3 shows a menu bar selection for both a text and graphic display. In both cases the *Actions* menu of *Disks and File Systems* has been selected.

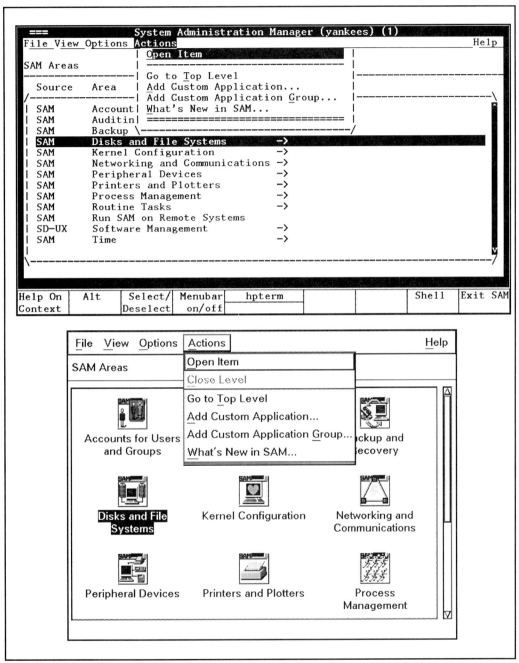

Figure 8-3 SAM Menu Selection for Text and Graphics Displays

Of particular interest on the pulldown menu are *Add Custom Application* and *Add Custom Application Group.* When you use *Add Custom Application Group,* you are prompted for the *Label* and optional *Help File* for the group. After you enter this information, a new icon appears, if you have a graphics display, with the name of your application group. You can then go into this application group and *Add Custom Applications*. This means that you can customize SAM to meet your specific administration needs by adding functionality to SAM. After you familiarize yourself with the aspects of system administration SAM can help you with, you'll want to test adding your own application to SAM. Adding a simple application like opening a log file or issuing the **/bin/find** command will take you only seconds to create.

You can also create users who have restricted access to SAM. You can specify areas within SAM that specific users can have access to. You may have users to whom you would like to give access to backup and restore, or managing users, or handling the print spooler. Invoking SAM with the "-r" option will allow you to select a user to whom you want to give access to a SAM area and then select the specific area(s) you want to enable that user to have access to. You can also give a user partial access to some areas such as providing access to backup and recovery but not providing access to handling automated backups. As you progress through the detailed descriptions of SAM areas in this chapter, you'll want to think about which of these areas may be appropriate for some of your users to have access to.

Running Restricted SAM Builder

SAM can be configured to provide a subset of its overall functionality to specified users such as operators. You may, for instance, wish to give a user the ability to start a backup but not the ability to manage disks and file systems. With the Restricted SAM Builder you have control of the functional areas specified users have access to.

When specifying the functionality you wish to give a user, you invoke SAM with the "-r" option initiating a Restricted SAM Builder session. After you have setup a user with specific functionality, you can then invoke SAM with both the "-r" and "-f" options with the login name of a user you wish to test. The functionality of the user can be tested using these two options along with the login name.

Initially Setting User Privileges

When you invoke SAM with the "-r" option, you are first asked to select the user to whom you want to assign privileges. You will then be shown a list of default privileges for a new restricted SAM user. Figure 8-4 shows the default privileges SAM recommends for a new restricted user. Note that custom SAM functional areas are disabled by default:

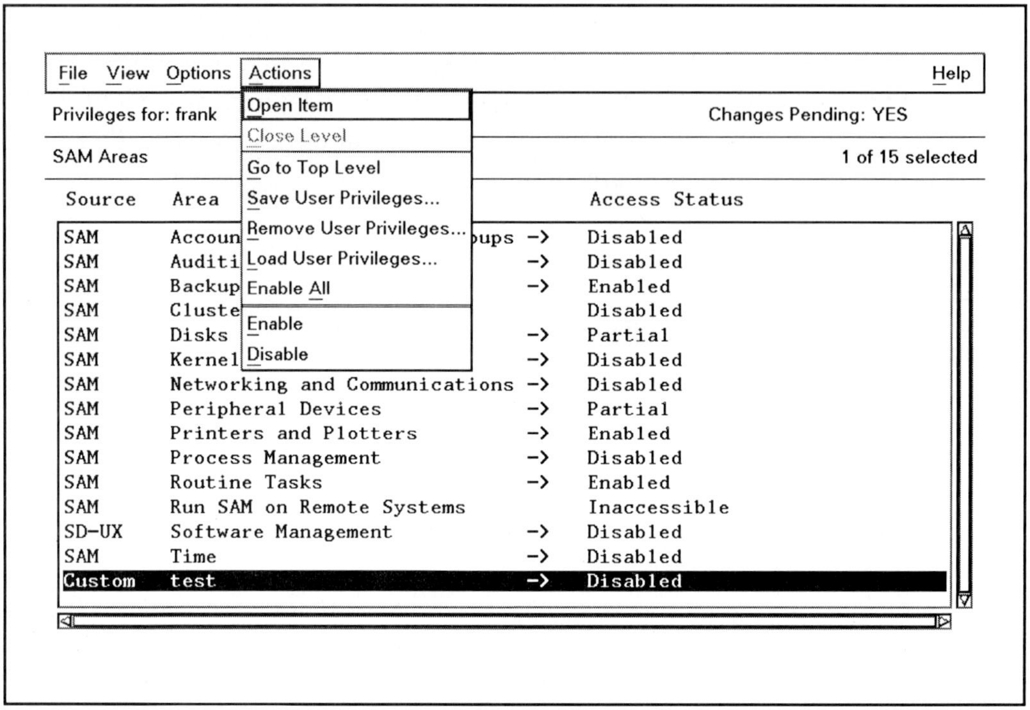

```
┌──────────────────────────────────────────────────────────────────────────────────┐
│  File  View  Options │ Actions │                                             Help  │
│                      ┌──────────────────────┐                                      │
│  Privileges for: frank│ Open Item            │          Changes Pending: YES       │
│                      ├──────────────────────┤                                      │
│  SAM Areas           │ Close Level           │              1 of 15 selected       │
│                      ├──────────────────────┤                                      │
│   Source   Area      │ Go to Top Level       │            Access Status            │
│  ┌──────────────────│ Save User Privileges… │─────────────────────────────────┐▲ │
│  │ SAM      Accoun   │ Remove User Privileges…│ups ->   Disabled               │  │
│  │ SAM      Auditi   │ Load User Privileges…  │   ->   Disabled               │  │
│  │ SAM      Backup   │ Enable All             │   ->   Enabled                │  │
│  │ SAM      Cluste   ├──────────────────────┤        Disabled               │  │
│  │ SAM      Disks    │ Enable                │   ->   Partial                │  │
│  │ SAM      Kernel   │ Disable               │   ->   Disabled               │  │
│  │ SAM      Networking and Communications ->   Disabled                      │  │
│  │ SAM      Peripheral Devices             ->   Partial                      │  │
│  │ SAM      Printers and Plotters          ->   Enabled                      │  │
│  │ SAM      Process Management             ->   Disabled                     │  │
│  │ SAM      Routine Tasks                  ->   Enabled                      │  │
│  │ SAM      Run SAM on Remote Systems           Inaccessible                 │  │
│  │ SD-UX    Software Management            ->   Disabled                     │  │
│  │ SAM      Time                           ->   Disabled                     │  │
│  │ Custom   test                           ->   Disabled                     │▽ │
│  └──────────────────────────────────────────────────────────────────────────┘  │
│  ◁▐════════════════════════════════════════════════════════════════════════▷   │
└──────────────────────────────────────────────────────────────────────────────────┘
```

Figure 8-4 Restricted SAM Builder Screen

You can select from the *Actions* shown in the figure to control access to functional areas. Of particular interest is the ability to save the privileges which you may later use as a template for other users with *Load User Privileges* from the *Actions* menu.

Verify Restricted Access

After having selected the appropriate privileges for a user by invoking SAM with the "- r" option, you can then use the "-f" option and login name to test the privileges for a user. The command shown below can be used to test user frank's privileges:

$ sam -r -f frank

When the user invokes SAM, they see only the functional areas to which they have been given access. They can then proceed to perform tasks under one of these functional areas.

Accounts for Users and Groups

In this chapter I'll take a two-step approach to working with users and groups. The first is to provide background on users and groups. The second is to show how the System Administration Manager (SAM) is used to work with users and groups.

You need to make a few basic decisions about users. Where should user's data be located? Who needs to access data from whom, thereby defining "groups" of users? What kind of particular startup is required by users and applications? Is there a shell that your users will prefer? Then you can proceed with your user setup.

You will want to put some thought into these important user-related questions. I spend a lot of time working with my customers rearranging user data for several reasons. It doesn't fit on a whole disk (this is one reason I strongly recommend using Logical Volume Manager), users can't freely access one another's data, or even worse, users *can* access one another's data too freely.

We will consider these questions, but first, let's look at the basic steps to adding a user, whether you do this manually or rely on SAM. Here is a list of activities:

- Select a user name to add
- Select a user ID number
- Select a group for the user
- Create an **/etc/passwd** entry (you can specify such options as minimum and maximum times between password changes)

- Assign a user password
- Select and create a home directory for user
- Select shell the user will run (I strongly recommend the default POSIX shell)
- Place startup files in user's home directory
- Test the user account

This may seem like a lot of work, but there is nothing to it if you run SAM and answer the questions. Most of what you do is entered in the file /**etc/passwd** where information about all users is stored. You can make all of these entries to the **/etc/passwd** file with the **/usr/sbin/vipw** command. The following is a sample **/etc/passwd** entry:

marty:*:155:20:Marty P:/home/marty:/usr/bin/sh

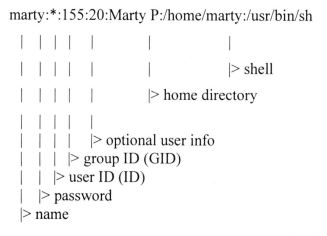

Here is a description of each of these fields:

name.   The user name you assign. This name should be easy for the user and other users on the system to remember. When sending electronic mail or copying files from one user to another, the easier it is to remember the user name, the better. If a user has a user name on another system and it is an easy name for others to remember, you may want to assign the same user name on your HP-UX system. Some systems don't permit nice, easy user names, so you may want to break the tie with the old system and start using sensible, easy-to-remember user names on your HP-UX system. Remember, there is no security tied to the user name; security is handled through the user's password and the file permissions.

password. This is the user's password in encrypted form. If an asterisk appears in this field the account can't be used. If it is empty, the user has no password assigned and can log in by typing only his or her user name. I strongly recommend each user have a password which he or she changes periodically. Every system has different security needs, but at a minimum every user on every system should have a password. Some features of a good password are:

- A minimum of six characters that should include special characters such as slash, dot, asterisk, etc.

- No words should be used for a password.

- Don't make the password personal such as name, address, favorite sports team, etc.

- Don't use something easy to type such as 123456, or qwerty.

- Some people say misspelled words are acceptable, but I don't recommend using them. Spell check programs that match misspelled words to correctly spelled words can be used to guess at words that might be misspelled for a password.

- A password generator that produces unitelligible passwords works the best.

user ID (UID). The identification number of the user. Every user on your system should have a unique UID. There are no conventions for UIDs. SAM will assign a UID for you when you add users, but you can always change this. I would recommend you reserve UIDs less than 100 for system-level users.

group ID (GID).   The identification number of the group. The members of the group, and their GID, are in the **/etc/group** file. You can change the GID assigned if you don't like it, but you may also have to change the GID of many files. As a user creates a file, their UID is assigned to the file as well as the GID. This means if you change the GID well after users of the same group have created many files and directories, you may have to change the GID of all these. I usually save GIDs less than 10 for system groups.

optional user info.   In this space you can make entries, such as the user's phone number or full name. SAM asks you for this information when you create a user. You can leave this blank, but if you manage a system or network with many users you may want to add the user's full name and extension so if you need to get in touch with him or her, you'll have the information at your fingertips.

home directory.   The home directory defines the default location for all the users' files and directories. This is the present working directory at the time of login.

shell.   This is the startup program the user will run at the time of login. The shell is really a command interpreter for all of the commands the user issues from the command line. I recommend using the default POSIX shell (**/usr/bin/sh**), but there are also three traditional popular shells in the HP-UX environment: C shell (**/usr/bin/csh**); Bourne shell   (**/usr/old/bin/sh**); and Korn shell (**/usr/bin/ksh**).

Assigning Users to Groups

After defining all user-related information, you need to consider groups. Groups are often overlooked in the HP-UX environment until the system administrator finds that all his or her users are in the very same group, even though from an organizational standpoint they are in different groups. Before I cover the groups in general, let's look a file belonging to a user and the way access is defined for a file:

```
$ ll
-rwxr-x--x   1 marty      users      120 Jul 26 10:20 sort
```

For every file on the system HP-UX supports three classes of access:

- User access (u). Access granted to the owner of the file

- Group access (g). Access granted to members of the same group as the owner of the file

- Other access (o). Access granted to everyone else

These access rights are defined by the position of r (read), write (w), and execute (x) when the long listing command is issued. For the long listing (**ll**) above, you see the following permissions in Table 8-1.

TABLE 8-1   LONG LISTING PERMISSIONS

Access	User Access	Group Access	Othe r
Read	r	r	-
Write	w	-	-
Exe-cute	x	x	x

You can see that access rights are arranged in groups of three. There are three groups of permissions with three access levels each. The owner, in this case marty, is allowed read, write, and execute permissions on the file. Anyone in the group users is permitted read and execute access to the file. Others are permitted only execute access of the file.

These permissions are important to consider as you arrange your users into groups. If several users require access to the same files, then you will want to put those users in the same group. The trade-off here is that you can give all users within a group rwx access to files, but then you run the risk of several users editing a file without other users knowing it, thereby causing confusion. On the other hand, you can make several copies of a file so each user has his or her personal copy, but then you have multiple versions of a file. If possible, assign users to groups based on their work.

When you run SAM and specify the groups to which each user belongs, the file **/etc/group** is updated. The **/etc/group** file contains the group name, encrypted password, group ID, and list of users in the group. Here is an example of an **/etc/group** file:

```
root::0:root
other::1:root, hpdb
bin::2:root,bin
sys::3:root,uucp
adm::4:root,adm
daemon::5:root,daemon
mail::6:root
lp::7:root,lp
tty::10:
nuucp::11:nuucp
military::25:jhunt,tdolan,vdallesandro
commercial::30:ccascone,jperwinc,devers
nogroup:*:-2:
```

This **/etc/group** file shows two different groups of users. Although all users run the same application, a desktop publishing tool, some work on documents of "commercial" products while others work on only "military" documents. It made sense for the system administrator to create two groups, one for commercial document preparation and the other for military document preparation. All members of a group know what documents are current and respect one another's work and its importance. You will have few problems among group members who know what each other is doing and will find these members don't delete files that shouldn't be deleted. If you put all users into one group, however, you may find that you spend more time restoring files because users in this broader group don't find files that are owned by other members of their group to be important. Users can change group with the **newgrp** command.

Another important entry in the **/etc/passwd** file is the location of his or her home directory. You have to select a location for the user's "home" directory in the file system where the user's files will be stored. With some of the advanced networking technology that exists, such as NFS, the user's home directory does not even have to be on a disk that is physically connected to the computer he or she is using! The traditional place to locate a user's home directory on an HP-UX system is the **/home** directory.

The **/home** directory is typically the most dynamic in terms of growth. Users create and delete files in their home directory on a regular basis. This means you have to do more planning related to your user area than in more static areas, such as the root file system and application areas. You would typically load HP-UX and your applications and then perform relatively few accesses to these in terms of adding and deleting files and directories. The user area is continuously updated, making it more difficult to maintain.

Managing users and groups in SAM is easy. The *Accounts for Users and Groups* top-level SAM category or area has beneath it only two picks: *Groups* and *Users*. The menu hierarchy for "Users and Groups" is shown in the Figure 8-5.

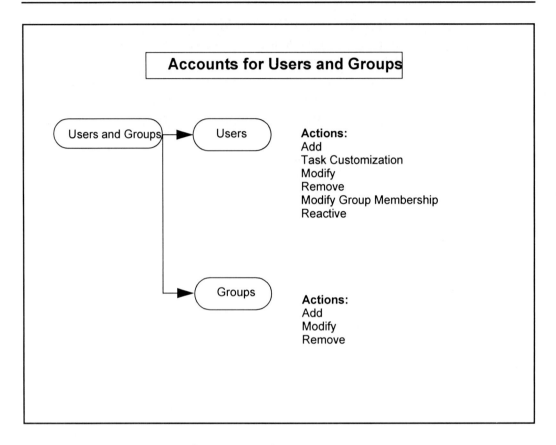

Figure 8-5 Accounts for Users and Groups

When you select *Accounts for Users and Groups* and then *Users* from the SAM menu, you are provided a list of all the users on your system. Table 8-2 is a partial list of users provided by SAM on my system.

Login Name	User ID (UID)	Real Name	Primary Group	Office Phone	Office Location
root	0		sys		
daemon	1		daemon		
bin	2		bin		
adm	4		adm		
uucp	5		sys		

Login Name	User ID (UID)	Real Name	Primary Group	Office Phone	Office Location
lp	9		lp		
vinny	204	Vinny D.	users	Internal 5611	Stmfd
marty	219	Marty P.	users	Internal 5613	Stmfd
tftp	510	Trivial FTP user	other		
sas	205		users		

TABLE 8-2   LIST OF USERS

Adding a User

SAM is ideal for performing administration tasks related to users and groups. These are routine tasks that are not complex but require you to edit the **/etc/passwd** and **/etc/group** files, make directories, and copy default files, all of which SAM performs for you. Finally, take a minute to check what SAM has done for you, especially if you modify an existing user or group.

To add an additional user, you would select *Add* from the *Actions* menu under *Users* and then fill in the information as shown in Figure 8-6:

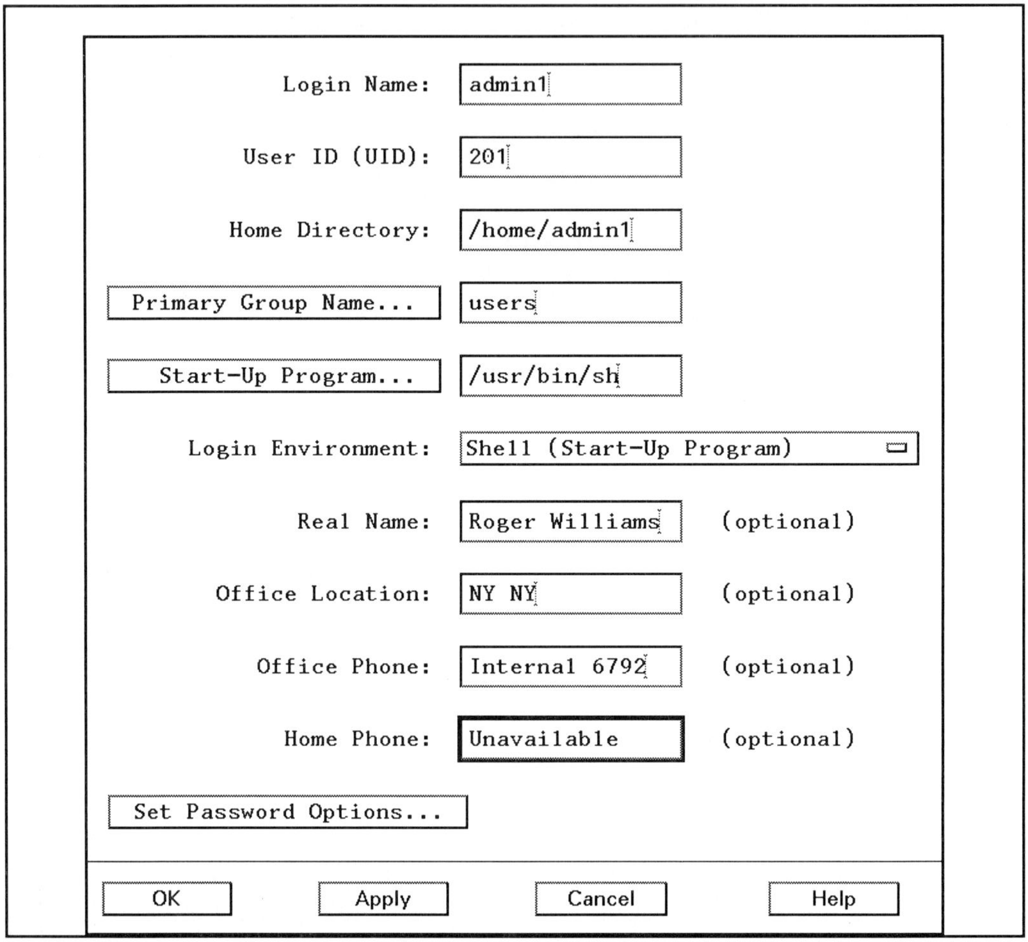

```
                Login Name:  │ admin1│

             User ID (UID):  │ 201│

           Home Directory:   │ /home/admin1│

    │ Primary Group Name... │ │ users│

    │   Start-Up Program... │ │ /usr/bin/sh│

        Login Environment:   │ Shell (Start-Up Program)        ▭ │

                Real Name:   │ Roger Williams│   (optional)

           Office Location:  │ NY NY│           (optional)

              Office Phone:  │ Internal 6792│   (optional)

               Home Phone:   │ Unavailable │    (optional)

    │ Set Password Options... │

    │   OK   │    │   Apply   │    │   Cancel   │    │   Help   │
```

Figure 8-6 Example of Adding a New User

There are some restrictions when entering this information. For instance, a comma and colon are not permitted in the Office Location field. When I tried to enter a comma, SAM informed me this was not permitted.

As a result of adding user admin1, the following **/etc/passwd** entry was made. (Notice there is no entry for password; please make sure you always enter a password on your system.)

admin1::201:20:Roger Williams,NY NY,Internal 6792,Unavailable:/ home/admin1:/usr/bin/sh

Adding this user gives us an opportunity to look at one of the best features of SAM - the ability to review what took place when this user was added with the "SAM Log Viewer" as shown in Figure 8-7.

Figure 8-7 SAM Log Viewer for Adding a User

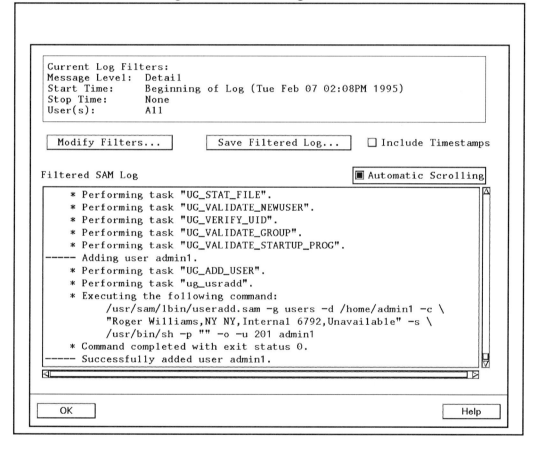

The log file is viewed by selecting *View SAM Log* from the *Actions* menu bar.

The scroll bar on the right-hand side of the SAM Log Viewer allows you to scroll to any point in the log file. We are viewing only the part of the log file that pertains to adding the user Roger Williams. You can select the level of detail you wish to view with the log file. The four levels are *Summary, Detail, Verbose,* and *Commands Only*. The level shown in Figure 8-7 is *Detail*. I like this level because you can see what has taken place without getting mired down in too much detail.

Adding a Group

Adding an additional group is similar to adding a new user. To add an additional group, you would select *Add* from the *Actions* menu under *Groups*. Figure 8-8 shows the Add a New Group window.

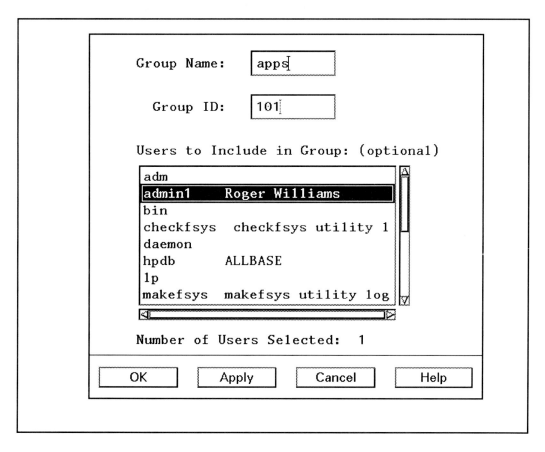

Figure 8-8 Example of Adding a New Group

In this example I added a new group called "apps" with a group ID of 101 and into that group I added the user admin1.

Auditing and Security

Under *Auditing and Security* you manage the security of your system. This is becoming an increasingly important aspect of system management.

Some installations care very little about security because of well-known, limited groups of users who will access a system. Other installations, such as those connected to the Internet, may go to great pains to make their systems into fortresses with fire walls, checking each and every user who attempts to access a system. I suggest you take a close look at all of the ramifications of security, and specifically a trusted system, before you enable security. You'll want to review the "Managing System Security" chapter of the *HP-UX System Administration Tasks Manual*. Although SAM makes creating and maintaining a trusted system easy, there are a lot of files created for security management that take place under the umbrella of auditing and security. Among the modifications that will be made to your system, should you choose to convert to a trusted system, is the **/etc/rc.config.d/auditing** file that will be updated by SAM. In addition, passwords in the **/etc/passwd** file will be replaced with "*" and the encrypted passwords will be moved to a password database. All users are also given audit ID numbers. Figure 8-9 shows the hierarchy of Auditing and Security.

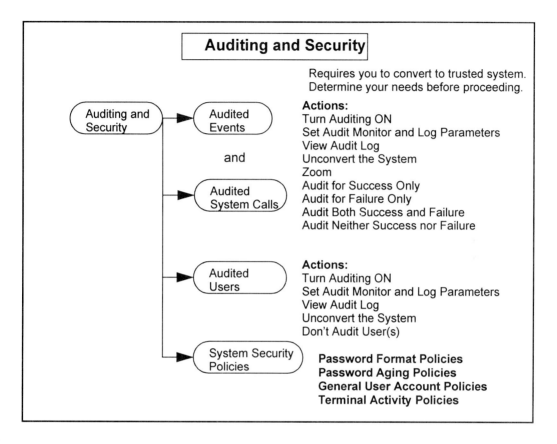

Figure 8-9 Auditing and Security

One choice to observe in this figure is an *Actions* menu choice to *Unconvert the System*. This means to reverse the trusted system environment. I have tried this on various systems and it seems to work fine, but you should have a good idea of what a trusted system can do for and to you before you make the conversion.

I hope I have given you a reasonably good overview of auditing and security because in order to investigate it yourself, you must first convert to a trusted system. Before you do this, please read this section to get an idea of the functionality this will provide and then convert to a trusted system if you think there is adequate benefit.

Audited Events and Audited System Calls

Under *Audited Events* you can select the particular events you wish to analyze and detect which may cause security breaches. Under *Audited System Calls* you can monitor system calls. This is a function of the trusted system which you must convert to in order to perform auditing. You may have in mind particular events and system calls that are most vital to your system's security that you wish to audit and not bother with the balance. There are a number of events and system calls that you may wish to keep track of for security reasons.Figure 8-10 shows the *Audited Events* window with the *Actions* menu shown as well.

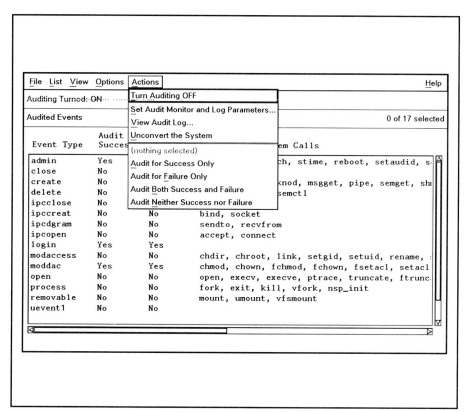

Figure 8-10 *Audited Events* Window

Auditing these events gives you a detailed report of the event. The same is true of system calls. Notice from the *Actions* menu that you have many options for the conditions you do and don't want to monitor. SAM uses the auditing commands of HP-UX such as **audsys**, **audusr**, **audevent**, **audomon**, and **audisp** to perform auditing.

Audited Users

Under *Audited Users* you can use the *Actions* menu to turn auditing on and off for specific users. Since the audit log files, which you can also control and view through the *Actions* menu, get big very fast, you may want to select specific users to monitor to better understand the type of user audit information that is created.

System Security Policies

The most important part of HP-UX security are the policies you put in place. If, for instance, you choose to audit each and every system call but don't impose any restrictions on user passwords, then you are potentially opening up your system to any user. You would be much better off restricting users and not worrying so much about what they're doing. Being proactive is more important in security than being reactive.

You have several options for passwords under *Password Format Policies* shown in Figure 8-11.

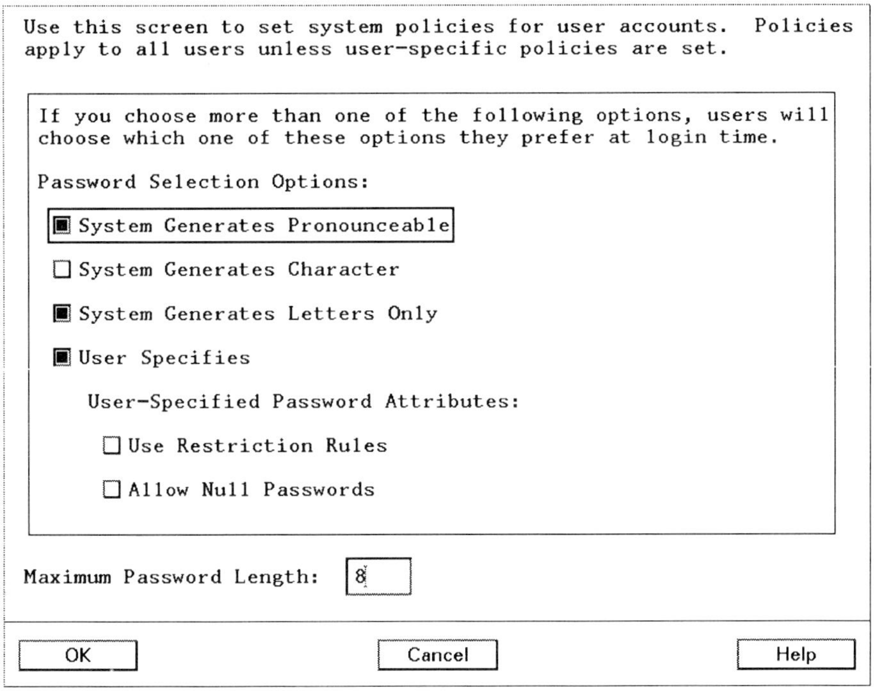

```
Use this screen to set system policies for user accounts.  Policies
apply to all users unless user-specific policies are set.

  If you choose more than one of the following options, users will
  choose which one of these options they prefer at login time.

  Password Selection Options:

  ■ System Generates Pronounceable

  □ System Generates Character

  ■ System Generates Letters Only

  ■ User Specifies

      User-Specified Password Attributes:

      □ Use Restriction Rules

      □ Allow Null Passwords


Maximum Password Length:   8

  ┌──────────┐        ┌──────────┐              ┌──────────┐
  │    OK    │        │  Cancel  │              │   Help   │
  └──────────┘        └──────────┘              └──────────┘
```

Figure 8-11 *Password Format Policies* Window

Password Aging Policies, when enabled, allows you to select:

- Time between Password Changes

- Password Expiration Time

- Password Expiration Warning Time

- Password Life Time

- Expire All User Passwords Immediately

General User Account Policies, when enabled, allows you to specify the time in which an account will become inactive and lock it. In addition, you can specify the number of unsuccessful login tries that are permitted.

Terminal Security Policies allows you to set

• Unsuccessful Login Tries Allowed

• Delay between Login Tries

• Login Timeout Value in seconds

Backup and Recovery

The most important activities you'll perform as a system administrator are system backup and recovery. The SAM team put a lot of thought into giving you all the options you need to ensure the integrity of your system through backup and recovery. Figure 8-12 shows the hierarchy of the "Backup and Recovery" SAM menu.

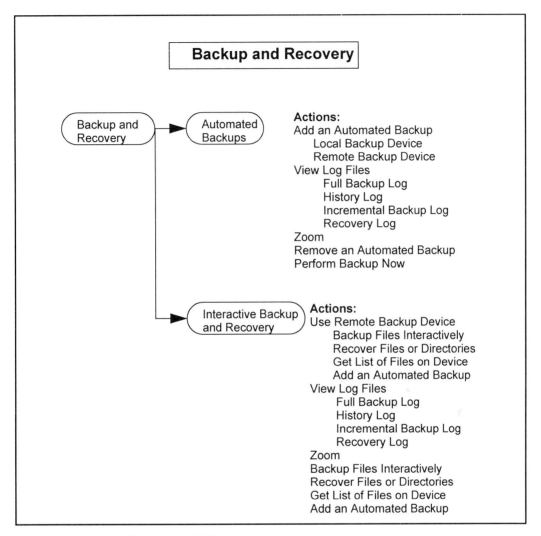

Figure 8-12 Backup and Recovery

Scheduling a Backup

The first step is to enter the *Automated Backups* subarea. You won't see any automated backups appear in the list until you have specified one. Using the *Actions* menu and selecting *Add an Automated Backup,* you can specify all the information about your automated backup. When you select

Add an Automated Backup, you have to specify whether your backup will be to a local or remote backup device. You will have to enter information pertaining to the backup scope, backup device, backup time, and additional parameters.

Select Backup Scope

You can view the backup scope as the files that will be included and excluded from the backup. This can include Network File System (NFS) mounted file systems as well. Figure 8-13 shows the window used to specify files to be included and excluded from the backup.

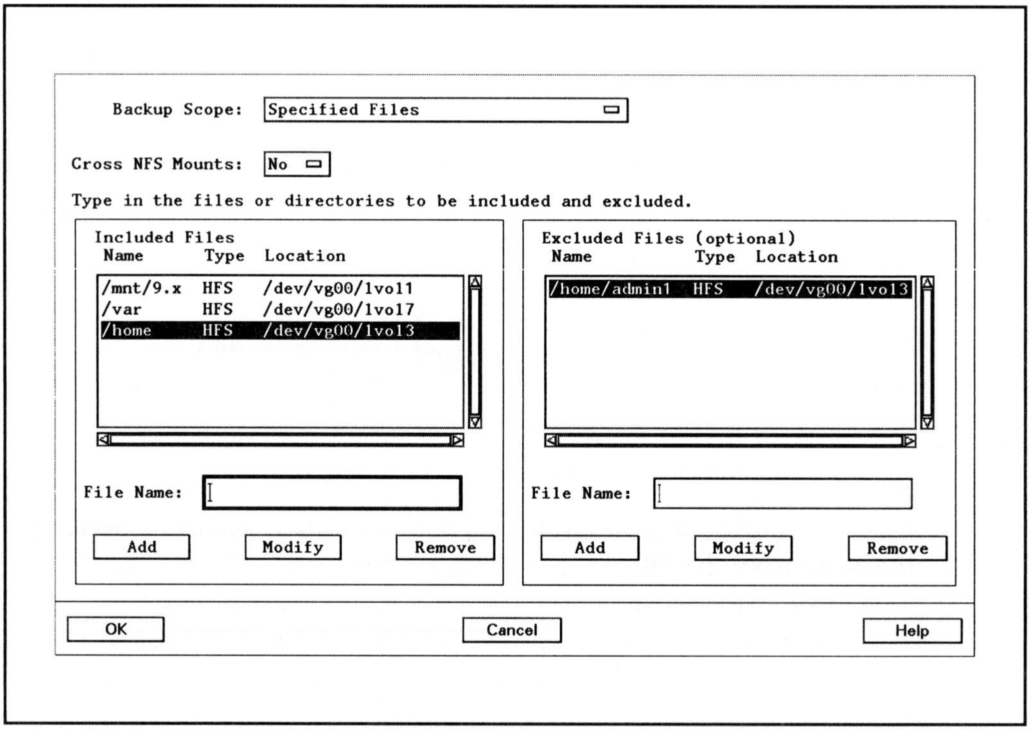

Figure 8-13   Selecting the Backup Scope

In the selections shown in Figure 8-13 there are three directories specified under included files. You can specify entire directories or individual files to be included or excluded from the backup. Although I want **/home** to be included in the backup, I don't want the home directory of **admin1**, the user we earlier created, to be included in the backup.

Instead of *Specified Files* as shown above, I could have selected *Local File Systems Only,* in which case all local file systems would have appeared in the *Included Files* list. If I had specified *All File Systems,* then all local file systems and NFS file systems (this will include **/net** by default) would have appeared in the list.

Select Backup Device

If you plan to back up to a local backup device, then those attached to your system will be listed and you select the desired device from the list.

If you plan to use a remote backup device, then you will be asked to specify the remote system name and device file.

Select Backup Time

As with the backup scope, you are provided with a window in which you can enter all of the information about backup time for both full and incremental backups as shown in Figure 8-14. If *Incremental Backup* is *Enabled,* then you must provide all pertinent information about both the full and incremental backup as shown in the figure.

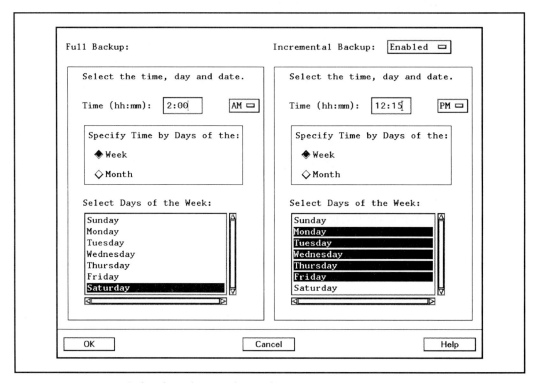

Figure 8-14 Selecting the Backup Time

A key point to keep in mind here is that the incremental backup that SAM creates for you includes files that have been changed <u>since the last full backup</u>. This means that you need only the full backup and last incremental backup to recover your system; that is, you do not need to restore the full backup and each incremental backup.

Set Additional Parameters

You can also specify additional parameters such as whether or not to create an index log, which I strongly suggest you do, and to whom to mail the results of the backup. We can now view the **crontab** entry SAM has made for root for these backups. The **crontab** file is used to schedule jobs that are automatically executed by **cron**. **crontab** files are in the **/var/spool/ cron/crontabs** directory. **cron** is a program that runs other programs at the specified time. **cron** reads files that specify the operation to be performed and the date and time it is to be performed. Since we want to perform backups on a regular basis, SAM will activate **cron**.

The format of entries in the **crontab** file are as follows:

minute   hour   monthday   month   weekday   user name   command

minute - the minute of the hour, from 0-59
hour - the hour of the day, from 0-23
monthday - the day of the month, from 1-31
month - the month of the year, from 1-12
weekday - the day of the week, from 0 (Sunday) - 6 (Saturday)
user name - the user who will run the command if necessary (not used in example)
command - specifies the command line or script file to run

You have many options in the **crontab** for specifying the *minute, hour, monthday, month,* and *weekday* to perform a task. You could list one entry in a field and then a space, several entries in any field separated by a comma, two entries separated by a dash indicating a range, or an asterisk, which corresponds to all possible entries for the field.

To list the contents of the **crontab** file you would issue the following command. The output of this command is the **crontab** file created for the user root in the SAM backup example.

```
$ crontab -l
```

```
00 2 * * 6 /usr/sam/lbin/br_backup DAT FULL Y /dev/rmt/0m /etc/sam/br/
graphDCAa02410 root Y 1 N > /tmp/SAM_br_msgs 2>&1 #sambackup

15 12 * * 1-5 /usr/sam/lbin/br_backup DAT PART Y /dev/rmt/0m /etc/sam/
br/graphDCAa02410 root Y 1 N > /tmp/SAM_br_msgs 2>&1 #sambackup
```

Although these seem to be excruciatingly long lines, they do indeed conform to the format of the **crontab** file. The first entry is the full backup; the second entry is the incremental backup. In the first entry the *minute* is 00; in the second entry the *minute* is 15. In the first entry the *hour* is 2; in the second entry the *hour* is 12. In both entries the *monthday* and *month* are all legal values (*), meaning every *monthday* and *month*. In the first entry the *weekday* is 6 for Saturday (0 is Sunday); in the second entry the *weekdays* are 1-5 or Monday through Friday. The optional *user name* is not specified in either example. And finally, the SAM backup command (**/usr/sam/lbin/br_backup**) and its long list of associated information is provided.

minute	*hour*	*monthday*	*month*	*weekday*	*user name*	*command*
00	*12*	*all*	*all*	*6*	*n/a*	*br_backup*
15	*12*	*all*	*all*	*1-5*	*n/a*	*br_backup*

The *graph* file that is used by **/usr/sam/lbin/br_backup** is a list of files to be included and excluded from the backup. The following is the contents of the graph file **/etc/sam/br/graphDCAa02410** that was created for the full and incremental backups:

> i /mnt/9.x
>
> i /var
>
> i /home
>
> e /home/admin1

Lines that start with an "i" are files and directories to be included in the backup and those starting with an "e" will be excluded from the backup.

You will see various crontab **commands** when you use the *SAM Log Viewer* to see what SAM has done for you to create the **crontab** files. For instance, if you change your backup plan SAM will remove the old crontab file with the command:

```
$ crontab -r
```

This will remove the **crontab** file for the user from the **/var/spool/cron/crontabs** directory.

To place a file in the **crontab** directory you would simply issue the **crontab** command and the name of the **crontab** file:

```
$ crontab crontabfile
```

You can schedule cron jobs using SAM. The section in this chapter covering *Process Management* has a subsection called *Scheduling Cron Jobs*.

Interactive Backup and Recovery

The *Interactive Backup and Recovery* subarea is used to perform a backup interactively or restore information that was part of an earlier backup. When you enter this area, you are asked to select a backup device from a list that is produced in the same way you are asked to select a backup device when you first enter the **Automated Backups** subarea.

After selecting a device from the list, you may select an item from the *Actions* menu shown earlier. If you decide to use *Backup Files Interactively,* you are again provided a window in which you can specify files to be included and excluded from the backup. You are asked to *Select Backup Scope, Specify Tape Device Options*, and *Set Additional Parameters*. You are not, however, asked to *Select Backup Time* since the backup is taking place interactively.

The steps in this area will vary depending on the tape devices you have selected.

The log file **/var/sam/log/br_log** reports on the backup. The index files can be reviewed from the *Actions* menu. These are stored in the /**var/sam/log** directory. The following shows the very top and bottom of an index file that is 800 KBytes in size:

```
#  1 /
#  1 /.profile
#  1 /.rhosts
#  1 /.sh_history
#  1 /.sw
#  1 /.sw/sessions
#  1 /.sw/sessions/swinstall.last
#  1 /.sw/sessions/swlist.last
#  1 /.sw/sessions/swmodify.last
#  1 /.sw/sessions/swreg.last
#  1 /.vue
#  1 /.vue/.trashinfo
#  1 /.vue/Desktop
#  1 /.vue/Desktop/Five                    TOP
#  1 /.vue/Desktop/Four
#  1 /.vue/Desktop/One
#  1 /.vue/Desktop/Six
#  1 /.vue/Desktop/Three


                    .
                    .
                    .


#  1 /var/uucp/.Log/uucico
#  1 /var/uucp/.Log/uucp
#  1 /var/uucp/.Log/uux
#  1 /var/uucp/.Log/uuxqt
#  1 /var/uucp/.Old
#  1 /var/uucp/.Status
#  1 /var/vue                              BOTTOM
#  1 /var/vue/Xerrors
#  1 /var/vue/Xpid
#  1 /var/vue/recserv.langconfig
#  1 /var/yp
#  1 /var/yp/Makefile
#  1 /var/yp/binding
#  1 /var/yp/securenets
```

```
#   1  /var/yp/secureservers
#   1  /var/yp/updaters
#   1  /var/yp/ypmake
#   1  /var/yp/ypxfr_1perday
#   1  /var/yp/ypxfr_1perhour
#   1  /var/yp/ypxfr_2perday
```

Performing a Restore

A full or incremental backup, however, is only as good as the files it restores. To retrieve a file from the backup tape, you supply information in three areas: *Select Recovery Scope; Specify Tape Device Options*; and *Set Additional Parameters*. The device options you specify will depend on the tape device you are using.

Select Recovery Scope allows you to either enter a file name that contains the files to be recovered or manually list the files to be included in the recovery. You can optionally list files to be excluded from the recovery as well.

A list of tape device files is provided in *Specify Tape Device Options* from which you can select the tape device. In this step you may select the tape device file; in other cases you might make selections such as a magneto-optical surface or have nothing to select at all.

Under *Set Additional Parameters* you can select any of the following options:

Overwrite Newer Files

Preserve Original File Ownership

Recover Files Using Full Path Name

Place Files in Non-Root Directory

After you make all of the desired selections, the recovery operation begins. If a file has been inadvertently deleted and you wish to restore it from the recovery tape, you would select the *Preserve Original File Ownership* and *Recover Files Using Full Path Name* options. You will receive status of the recovery as it takes place and may also *View Recovery Log,* from the *Actions* menu after the recovery has completed. If you *View Recovery Log,* you will receive a window which provides the name of the index log and the name of the files recovered:

```
Recovery Log (/var/sam/log/br_index.rec)

-rw-r--r--  admin1  users  /home/admin1/fortran/makefile
```

Disks and File Systems

Disks and File Systems helps you manage disk devices, file systems, logical volumes, swap, and volume groups (you may also manage HP disk arrays through SAM if you have these installed on your system). There is no reason to manually work with these since SAM does such a good job of managing these for you. Figure 8-15 shows the hierarchy of *Disks and File Systems.*

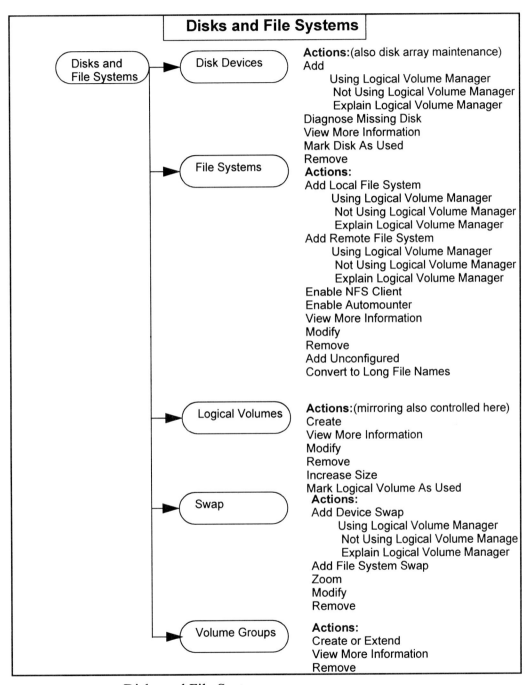

Figure 8-15 Disks and File Systems

Disk Devices

When you enter this subarea, SAM shows you the disk devices connected to your system. Figure 8-16 shows a listing of the disks for a Series 800 unit (this is the same system used in several examples in Chapter 1).

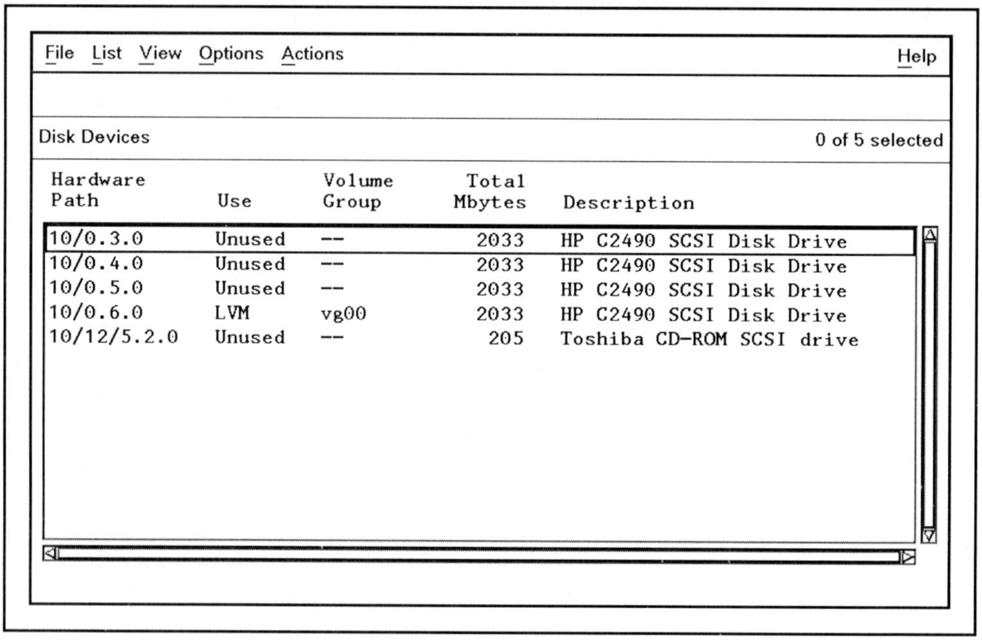

```
 ┌──────────────────────────────────────────────────────────────────────┐
 │  File  List  View  Options  Actions                             Help   │
 │                                                                        │
 │  Disk Devices                                           0 of 5 selected │
 │                                                                        │
 │  Hardware              Volume      Total                               │
 │  Path         Use      Group       Mbytes    Description               │
 │  10/0.3.0     Unused   --            2033     HP C2490 SCSI Disk Drive  │
 │  10/0.4.0     Unused   --            2033     HP C2490 SCSI Disk Drive  │
 │  10/0.5.0     Unused   --            2033     HP C2490 SCSI Disk Drive  │
 │  10/0.6.0     LVM      vg00          2033     HP C2490 SCSI Disk Drive  │
 │  10/12/5.2.0  Unused   --             205     Toshiba CD-ROM SCSI drive │
 │                                                                        │
 └──────────────────────────────────────────────────────────────────────┘
```

Figure 8-16 *Disk Devices* Window

The first four entries are the Fast/Wide 2 GByte SCSI disks in the system. Only the disk at SCSI address 6 is in use at this time. The last entry is the CD-ROM. The following **ioscan** command shows these disk devices:

(on Series 800)

```
$ /usr/sbin/ioscan -fn -C disk

Class  I  H/W Path      Driver  S/W State  H/W Type    Description
==================================================================
disk   0 10/0.3.0       sdisk   CLAIMED    DEVICE      HP C2490WD
                        /dev/dsk/c0t3d0  /dev/rdsk/c0t3d0

disk   1 10/0.4.0       sdisk   CLAIMED    DEVICE      HP C2490WD
                        /dev/dsk/c0t4d0  /dev/rdsk/c0t4d0

disk   2 10/0.5.0       sdisk   CLAIMED    DEVICE      HP C2490WD
                        /dev/dsk/c0t5d0  /dev/rdsk/c0t5d0

disk   3 10/0.6.0       sdisk   CLAIMED    DEVICE      HP C2490WD
                        /dev/dsk/c0t6d0  /dev/rdsk/c0t6d0

disk   3 10/12/5/2/0 sdisk   CLAIMED    DEVICE      CD-ROM
                        /dev/dsk/c1t2d0  /dev/rdsk/c1t2d0
```

You can see from this **ioscan** all of the device files associated with disks including the CD-ROM. Using SAM to view and manipulate these devices is easier and clearer than typing such commands as **ioscan**. This doesn't mean you don't have to know the **ioscan** command or that it is not useful, but SAM certainly makes viewing your system a lot easier. We can now add one of the unused disks in SAM by selecting *Add* from the *Actions* menu. Using Logical Volume Manager we can create a new volume group or select the volume group we wish to add the new disk to. We would then select the new logical volumes we wanted on the volume group or extend the size of existing logical volumes. Other information such as the mount directory and size of the logical volume would be entered.

Another common disk device that you may configure through SAM is Redundant Arrays of Inexpensive Disks (RAID). RAID from HP can be configured directly through SAM under Disk Devices. These devices have a Storage Control Processor (SP) and disk which can be configured in a variety of ways. Using SAM you can specify the RAID level, and which disks will bind to which SPs.

After the RAID has been configured, you can access it as you would any other disks by specifying logical volumes and so on.

File Systems

File Systems shows the *Mount Directory, Type* of file system, and *Source Device or Remote Directory*. Figure 8-17 shows the information you see when you enter *File Systems* for the Series 800 used in earlier examples.

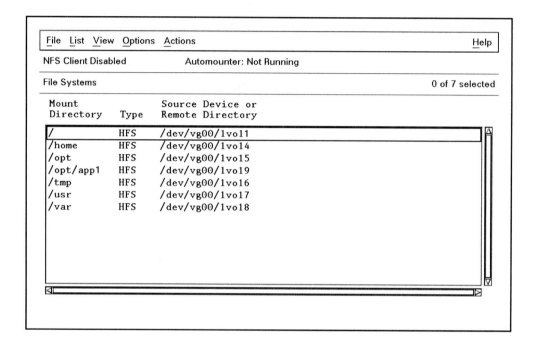

Figure 8-17 *File Systems* Window

At this level you could perform such tasks as *Add Local File System, Add Remote File System*, and others from the *Actions* menu.

There are several types of file systems that may be listed under the Type column. The most common are

Auto-Indirect   Directory containing auto-mountable remote NFS file systems. You may see the **/net** directory here if you have auto-mounter running.

Auto-Mount   Auto-mountable remote NFS file system.

CDFS   CD-ROM file system if it is currently mounted. If, for instance, you have a CD-ROM mounted as /SD_CDROM, you will see this as type CDFS in the list.

HFS   Local HFS file system. These are local HFS file systems that are part of your system.

NFS   Remote NFS file system that is currently mounted.

LOFS   Loopback file system that allows you to have the same file system in multiple places.

VxFS   Extent-based Journal File System that supports fast file system recovery and on-line features such as backup.

Logical Volumes

You can perform several functions related to logical volume manipulation in SAM. Such tasks as *Create, Modify, Remove,* and *Increase Size* can be performed in SAM. Figure 8-18 shows increasing the size of lvol4   (/ **home**) from 20 MBytes to 500 MBytes.

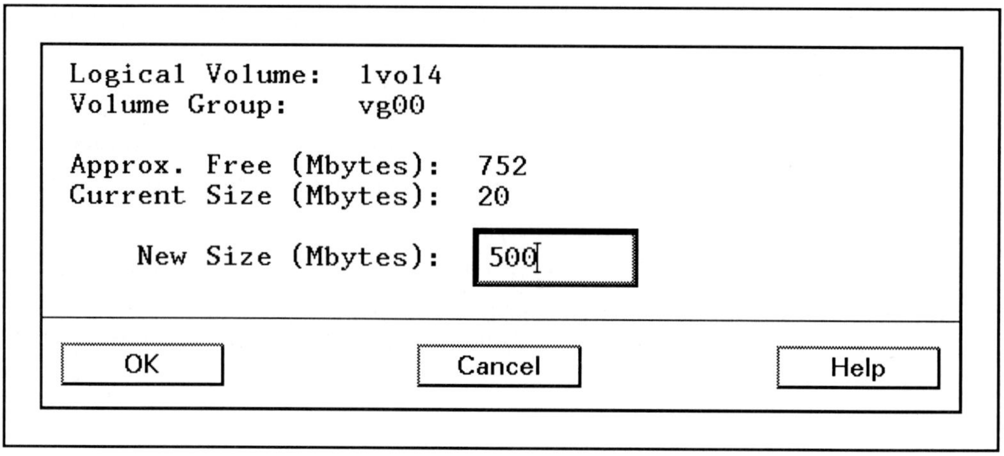

```
Logical Volume:    lvol4
Volume Group:      vg00

Approx. Free (Mbytes):    752
Current Size (Mbytes):    20

    New Size (Mbytes):    [500]


    OK                    Cancel                    Help
```

Figure 8-18 *Increase Size* Window

SAM will only increase the size of the logical volume if it can be unmounted. Viewing the log file after this task has been completed shows SAM ran such commands as **/sbin/lvextend** and **/sbin/extendfs** to extend the size of the logical volume and file system, and **/usr/sbin/umount** and **/usr**.

Increasing The Size Of A Logical Volume In SAM

SAM may create a unique set of problems when you attempt to increase the size of a logical volume. Problems may be encountered increasing the size of a logical volume if it can't be unmounted. If, for instance, you wanted to increase the size of the **/opt** logical volume, it would first have to be unmounted by SAM. If SAM can't umount **/opt,** you will receive a message from SAM indicating the device is busy. You can go into single user state but you will have to have some logical volumes mounted in order to get SAM to run such as **/usr** and **/var.** You would then bring the system up to the appropriate run level when you have completed your work. This works for directories such as **/opt** which SAM does not need in order to run.

Alternatively, you could exit SAM and kill any processes accessing the logical volume you wish to extend the size of and then manually unmount that logical volume. You could then use SAM to increase the size of the logical volume. This also works for **/opt**.

Swap

Both device swap and file system swap are listed when you enter *Swap*. Listed for you are the *Device File/Mount Directory, Type, Mbytes Available*, and *Enabled*. You can get more information about an item by highlighting it and selecting *Zoom* from the *Actions* menu.

Volume Groups

Listed for you when you enter volume groups are *Name, Mbytes Available, Physical Volumes*, and *Logical Volumes*. If you have an unused disk on your system, you can extend an existing volume group or create a new volume group.

Kernel Configuration

Your HP-UX kernel is a vitally important part of your HP-UX system that is often overlooked by HP-UX administrators. Perhaps this is because administrators are reluctant to tinker with such a critical and sensitive part of their system. Your HP-UX kernel, however, can have a big impact on system performance, so you want to be sure you know how it is configured. This doesn't mean you have to make a lot of experimental changes, but you should know how your kernel is currently configured so you can assess the possible impact that changes to the kernel may have on your system.

SAM allows you to view and modify the four basic elements of your HP-UX kernel. There is a great deal of confusion among new HP-UX system administrators regarding these four elements. Before I get into the details of each of these four areas, I'll first give you a brief description of each.

- *Configurable Parameters* - These are parameters that have a value associated with them. When you change the value, there is a strong possibility you will affect the performance of your system. An example of a *Configurable Parameter* is **nfile** which is the maximum number of open files on the system.

- *Drivers* - Drivers are used to control the hardware on your system. You have a driver called **CentIF** for the parallel interface on your system, one called **sdisk** for your SCSI disks, and so on.

- *Dump Devices* - A dump device is used to store the contents of main memory in the event that a serious kernel problem is encountered. If no dump device is configured, then the contents of main memory are saved on the primary swap device. A dump device is different than a swap device.

- *Subsystems* - A subsystem is different from a driver. A subsystem is an area of functionality or support on your system such as **CD-ROM/9000** which is CD-ROM file system support, **LVM** which is Logical Volume Manager support, and so on.

When you go into one of the four subareas described above, the configuration of your system for the respective subarea is listed for you. The first thing you should do when entering *Kernel Configuration* is to go into each of the subareas and review the list of information about your system in each.

In *Kernel Configuration* there is a *current* kernel and *pending* kernel. The *current* kernel is the one you are now running and the *pending* kernel is the one for which you are making changes.

Figure 8-19 shows the SAM menu hierarchy for *Kernel Configuration.*

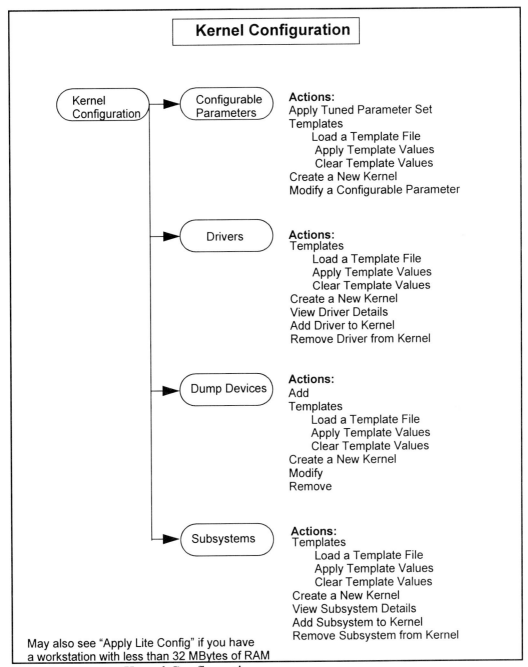

Kernel Configuration

Kernel Configuration → Configurable Parameters

Actions:
Apply Tuned Parameter Set
Templates
    Load a Template File
    Apply Template Values
    Clear Template Values
Create a New Kernel
Modify a Configurable Parameter

Drivers

Actions:
Templates
    Load a Template File
    Apply Template Values
    Clear Template Values
Create a New Kernel
View Driver Details
Add Driver to Kernel
Remove Driver from Kernel

Dump Devices

Actions:
Add
Templates
    Load a Template File
    Apply Template Values
    Clear Template Values
Create a New Kernel
Modify
Remove

Subsystems

Actions:
Templates
    Load a Template File
    Apply Template Values
    Clear Template Values
Create a New Kernel
View Subsystem Details
Add Subsystem to Kernel
Remove Subsystem from Kernel

May also see "Apply Lite Config" if you have
a workstation with less than 32 MBytes of RAM

Figure 8-19 Kernel Configuration

Configurable Parameters

Selecting *Configurable Parameters* lists all of your configurable kernel parameters. For each configurable parameter the following information is listed:

- Name - Name of the parameter.

- Current Value - Value of parameter in **/stand/vmunix**.

- Pending Value - Value of parameter in kernel to be built.

- Description - A few words describing parameter.

You can then take a number of *Actions* including the following:

Apply Tuned Parameter Set

There are several sets of configurable parameters that have been tuned for various environments. When you select this from the *Actions* menu, the tuned parameter sets on your system, such as a database server system, are listed for you and you can select from among these.

Templates   You can select a kernel template to load which is basically a different kernel configuration than you are currently running.

Create a New Kernel After making whatever changes you like to the *Pending Value* of a configurable parameter, you can have SAM create a new kernel for you.

Modify Configurable Parameter

> You can change the value of parameter in the *pending* kernel. You simply highlight a parameter and select this from the *Actions* menu.

Modifying a configurable parameter is made much easier by SAM. But although the logistics of changing the parameter are easier, determining the value of the parameter is still the most important part of this process.

Many applications recommend modifying one or more of these parameters for optimal performance of the application. Keep in mind, though, that many of these parameters are related; modifying one may adversely affect another parameter. Many applications will request that you change the *maxuprc* to support more processes. Keep in mind that if you have more processes running, you may end up with more open files and also have to change the *maxfiles* per process. If you have a system primarily used for a single application, you can feel more comfortable in modifying these. But if you run many applications, make sure you don't improve the performance of one application at the expense of another.

When you do decide to modify the value of a configurable parameter, be careful. The range on some of these values is broad. The *maxuprc* (maximum number of user processes) can be reduced as low as three processes. I can't imagine what a system could be used for with this low a value, but SAM ensures the parameter is set to within supported HP-UX ranges for the parameter. "Let the administrator beware" when changing these values. You may find that you'll want to undo some of your changes. Here are some tips. Keep careful notes of the values you change in case you have to undo a change. In addition, change as few values at a time as possible. That way if you're not happy with the results, you know which configurable parameter caused the problem.

Drivers

When you select *Drivers*, the drivers for your current kernel, the template file on which your current kernel is based, and the pending kernel are listed. You'll know that the drivers displayed are for more than your current kernel because you'll see that some of the drivers listed are *Out* of both your current and pending kernels. The following information is listed for you when you enter the *Drivers* subarea:

- Name - Name of the driver.

- Current State - Lists whether the driver is *In* or *Out* of **/stand/vmunix**.

- Pending State - Lists whether the driver is *In* or *Out* of the pending kernel to be built.

- Description - A few words describing driver.

The Current State indicates whether or not the driver selected is in **/stand/vmunix.**

The Pending State indicates whether or not you have selected this driver to be added to or removed from the kernel. *In* means the driver is part of the kernel or is pending to be part of the kernel. *Out* means the driver is not part of the kernel or is pending to be removed from the kernel.

Using the *Actions* menu, you can select one of the drivers and add or remove it. You can also pick *View Driver Details* from the *Actions* menu after you select one of the drivers. You can select *Create a New Kernel* from the *Actions* menu. If you have indeed modified this screen by adding or removing drivers, you want to re-create the kernel. SAM asks if you're sure you want to rebuild the kernel before it does this for you. The only recommendation I can make here is to be sure you have made your selections carefully before you rebuild the kernel.

Dump Devices

When you enter this subarea, both the *Current Dump Devices* and *Pending Dump Devices* are listed for you. A dump device is used when there is a serious kernel problem with your system and all of main memory is written to disk. This information is a core dump which can later be read from disk and used to help diagnose the kernel problem.

The sizes of the dump areas should be at least as large as main memory in your system. You can specify a disk or logical volume as a dump device (you can also specify a disk section, but I don't recommend you use disk sections at all). The entire disk or logical volume is then reserved as a dump device.

If no dump device is specified, then the core dump is written to primary swap. This has sometimes been a point of confusion; that is, primary swap may indeed be used as a dump device but a dump device is used specifically for core dump purposes whereas primary swap fills this role in the event there is no dump device specified.

Since you probably won't be allocating an entire disk as a dump device, you may be using a logical volume. You must select a logical volume in the root volume group that is unused or is used for non-file-system swap. This is done by selecting *Add* from the *Actions* menu to add a disk or logical volume to the list of dump devices.

Subsystems

Selecting *Subsystems* lists all of your subsystems. For each subsystem the following information is listed:

- Name - Name of the subsystem.
- Current Value - Lists whether the subsystem is *In* or *Out* of   /
  stand/vmunix.
- Pending Value -   Lists whether the subsystem is *In* or *Out* of the
  pending kernel.
- Description - A few words describing parameter.

You can then take a number of *Actions* including the following:

    Templates   You can select a kernel template to load which is basically a different kernel configuration than you are currently running.

Create a New Kernel After making whatever changes you like to the *Pending State* of a subsystem, you can have SAM create a new kernel for you.

View Subsystem Details

You get a little more information about the subsystem when you select this.

Add Subsystem to Kernel

When you highlight one of the subsystems and select this from the menu, the *Pending State* is changed to *In* and the subsystem will be added to the kernel when you rebuild the kernel.

Remove Subsystem from Kernel

When you highlight one of the subsystems and select this from the menu, the *Pending State* is changed to *Out* and the subsystem will be removed from the kernel when you rebuild the kernel.

After making selections, you can rebuild the kernel to include your pending changes or back out of this without making the changes.

Networking and Communications

The menu hierarchy for *Networking and Communications* is shown in Figure 8-20.

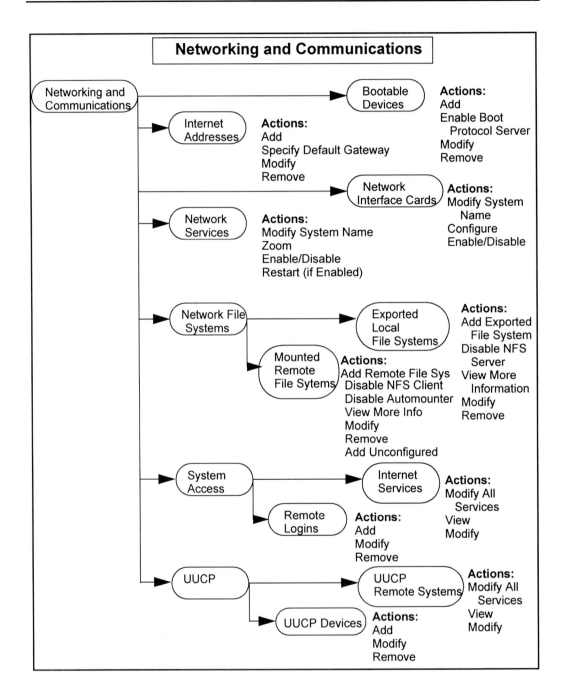

Figure 8-20 Networking and Communications

Bootable Devices

In the *Bootable Devices* subarea you can specify systems which will boot from your system using Bootstrap Protocol (Bootp). Bootp is a means by which a system can discover network information and boot automatically. The Bootp software must be loaded on your system in order for other devices to use it as a boot source. Among the many devices that use Bootp are HP X Stations. In this subarea you can add, modify, or remove a Bootp device. In addition you can enable or disable the Boot Protocol Server.

When you enter the *Bootable Devices* subarea you immediately receive a list of devices which can boot off your system. You can choose *Add* from the *Actions* menu and you'll be asked to enter the following information about the device you are adding:

- Bootp Client Device Name

- Internet Address

- Subnet Mask (this is optional)

- Station Address in hex (this is optional)

- Boot File Name

- Whether you'll be using Ethernet or IEEE 802.3 for booting

You can select *Enable Boot Protocol Server* or *Disable Boot Protocol Server* from the *Actions* menu, depending on whether your system is currently disabled or enabled to support this functionality. When you *Enable Boot Protocol Server,* you also enable Trivial File Transfer Protocol (TFTP) which boot devices use to get boot files. When you enable or disable this, the **/etc/inetd.conf** is edited. This file contains configuration information about the networking services running on your system. If a line in **/etc/inetd.conf** is preceded by a "#", then it is viewed as a comment. The daemon that reads the entries in this file is **/usr/sbin/inetd**. Before enabling or disabling Bootp, you may want to view the **/etc/inetd.conf** file and see what services are enabled. After you make your change through SAM, you can again view **/etc/inetd.conf** to see what has been modified. See *System*

Access for security related to **/etc/inetd.conf.** The following is the beginning of the **/etc/inetd.conf** file from a system showing Bootp and TFTP enabled. There is also a brief explanation of the fields in this file at the beginning of the file:

```
## Configured using SAM by root on Sat Aug 25 10:12:51 1995
##
#
# Inetd  reads its configuration information from this file upon ex-
# ecution and at some later time if it is reconfigured.
#
# A line in the configuration file has the following fields separated
# by tabs and/or spaces:
#
#    service name            as in /etc/services
#    socket type             either "stream" or "dgram"
#    protocol                as in /etc/protocols
#    wait/nowait              only applies to datagram sockets, stream
#                            sockets should specify nowait
#    user                     name of user as whom the server should run
#    server program          absolute pathname for the server inetd
#                            will execute
#  server program args.      arguments server program uses as they
#                             normally are starting with argv[0] which
#                            is the name of the server.
#
# See the inetd.conf(4) manual page for more information.
##


##
#
#               ARPA/Berkeley services
#
##
ftp           stream tcp nowait root /usr/lbin/ftpd       ftpd -l
telnet        stream tcp nowait root /usr/lbin/telnetd    telnetd

# Before uncommenting the "tftp" entry below, please make sure
# that you have a "tftp" user in /etc/passwd. If you don't
# have one, please consult the tftpd(1M) manual entry for
# information about setting up this service.

tftp          dgram  udp wait    root  /usr/lbin/tftpd       tftpd
bootps        dgram  udp wait    root  /usr/lbin/bootpd      bootpd
#finger       stream tcp nowait bin   /usr/lbing/fingerd   fingerd
login         stream tcp nowait bin   /usr/lbin/rlogind    rlogind
shell         stream tcp nowait bin   /usr/lbin/remshd     remshd
exec          stream tcp nowait root  /usr/lbin/rexecd     rexecd
#uucp         stream tcp nowait bin   /usr/sbin/uucpd      uucpd
```

•
•
•

If you select one of the Bootp client device names, you can then select *Modify* or *Remove* from the *Actions* menu and either change one of the parameters related to the client, such as its address or subnet mask, or completely remove the client.

Internet Addresses

This subarea is for maintaining the default gateway and remote hosts on your system. When you enter this subarea, you receive a list of hosts specified on your system as shown in Figure 8-21.

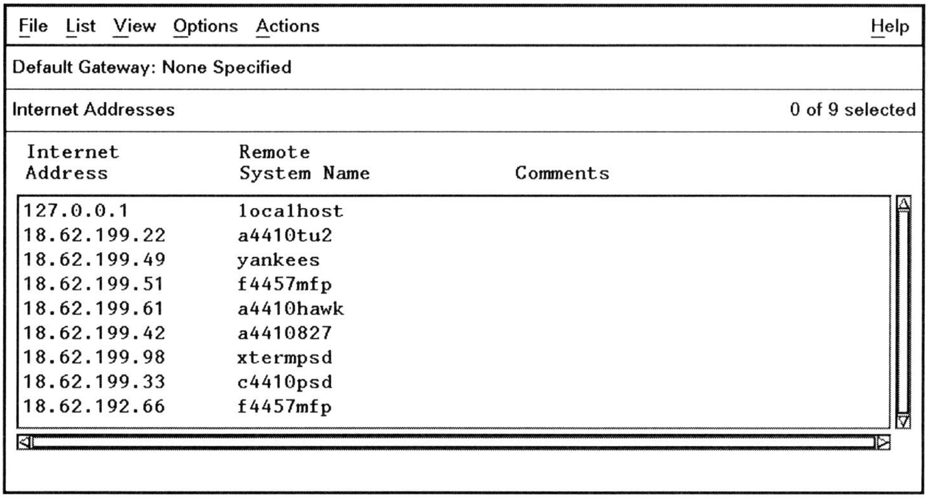

```
 File  List  View  Options  Actions                                  Help

 Default Gateway: None Specified

 Internet Addresses                                      0 of 9 selected

   Internet         Remote
   Address          System Name           Comments

  127.0.0.1         localhost
  18.62.199.22      a4410tu2
  18.62.199.49      yankees
  18.62.199.51      f4457mfp
  18.62.199.61      a4410hawk
  18.62.199.42      a4410827
  18.62.199.98      xtermpsd
  18.62.199.33      c4410psd
  18.62.192.66      f4457mfp
```

Figure 8-21 Internet Addresses

You can then *Add* a new host, *Specify Default Gateway*, *Modify* one of the hosts, or *Remove* one of the hosts, all from the *Actions* menu. When adding a host, you'll be asked for information pertaining to the host including Internet address; system name; aliases for the system; and comments.

Network Interface Cards

This subarea is used for configuring any networking cards in your system. You can *Enable, Disable*, and *Configure* networking cards as well as *Modify System Name,* all from the *Actions* menu.

The Network Interface Cards screen lists the network cards installed on your system including the following information. You may have to expand the window or scroll over to see all of this information.

- Card Type such as Ethernet, IEEE 802.3, Token Ring, FDDI, etc.

- Card Name

- Hardware Path

- Status, such as whether or not the card is enabled

- Internet Address

- Subnet Mask

- Station Address in hex

Included under *Configure* for Ethernet cards is *Advanced Options,* which will modify the Maximum Transfer Unit for this card. Other cards included in your system can also be configured here such as ISDN, X.25, ATM, and so on.

Network Services

This subarea is used to enable or disable some of the network services on your system. This screen has three columns which are the name, status, and description of the network services. Figure 8-22 from the *Network Services* subarea shows the network services that can be managed.

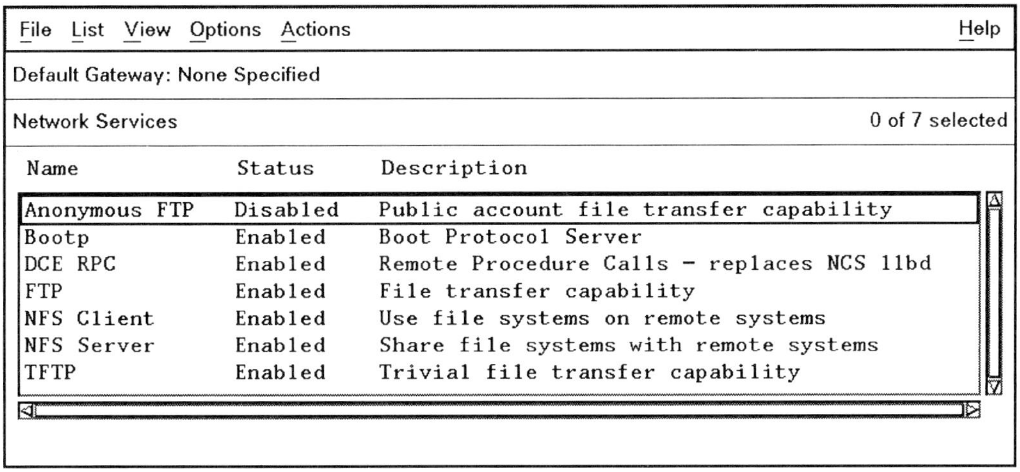

File List View Options Actions		Help
Default Gateway: None Specified		
Network Services		0 of 7 selected

Name	Status	Description
Anonymous FTP	Disabled	Public account file transfer capability
Bootp	Enabled	Boot Protocol Server
DCE RPC	Enabled	Remote Procedure Calls — replaces NCS 11bd
FTP	Enabled	File transfer capability
NFS Client	Enabled	Use file systems on remote systems
NFS Server	Enabled	Share file systems with remote systems
TFTP	Enabled	Trivial file transfer capability

Figure 8-22 Network Services

After selecting one of the network services shown, you can *Enable* or *Disable* the service depending on its current status, *Restart* the service if it is currently enabled, get more information about the service with *Zoom*, or *Modify System Name*, all from the *Actions* menu.

Network File Systems

This subarea is broken down into *Exported Local File Systems* and *Mounted Remote File Systems*. NFS is broken down into these two areas because you can export a local file system without mounting a remote file system and vice versa. This means you can manage these independently of one another. You may have an NFS server in your environment that won't mount remote file systems, and you may have an NFS client that will mount only remote file systems and never export its local file system.

Under *Exported Local File Systems* you can select the file systems you want exported. The first time you enter this screen you have no exported file systems listed. When you select *Add Exported File System* from the *Actions* menu you enter such information as.

- local directory name

- user ID

- whether or not to allow asynchronous writes

- permissions

When this exported file system has been added, you can select it and choose from a number of *Actions* including *Modify* and *Remove*.

Under *Mounted Remote File Systems,* you have listed for you all of the directories and files that are mounted using NFS. These can be either mounted or mounted on demand with auto-mounter. After selecting one of the mounted file systems, you can perform various *Actions*. For every remote file system mounted you have the following columns:

- Mount Directory which displays the name of the local directory name used to mount the remote directory.

- Type which is either *NFS* for standard NFS or *Auto* for automounter (see the paragraph below).

- Remote Server which displays the name of the remote system where the file or directory is mounted.

- Remote Directory which is the name of the directory under which the directory is remotely mounted.

You should think about whether or not you want to use the NFS automounter. With automounter you mount a remote file or directory on demand, that is, when you need it. Using a master map you can specify which files and directories will be mounted when needed. The files and directories are not continuously mounted with automounter, resulting in more efficiency as far as how system resources are being used. There is, however, some overhead time associated with mounting a file or directory on demand as opposed to having it continuously mounted. From a user standpoint this may be slightly more undesirable, but from an administration standpoint, using the automounter offers advantages. Since the automounter is managed through SAM, there is very little additional work you need to perform to enable it.

System Access

This subarea is broken down into *Internet Services* and *Remote Logins*.

When you select *Internet Services,* the screen lists the networking services that are started by the Internet daemon **/usr/sbin/inetd**. I earlier covered the **/etc/inetd.conf** which is a configuration file that lists all of the network services supported by a system that is read by **inetd**. There is also a security file **/var/adm/inetd.sec** that serves as a security check for **inetd**. Although there are many other components involved, you can view **inetd**, **/etc/inetd.conf**, and **/var/adm/inetd.sec** as working together to determine what network services are supported and the security level of each.

Listed for you in the *System Access* subarea are *Service Name, Description, Type*, and *System Permission*. In Figure 8-23 the *System Permission* for **shell** is "Denied"; for **ftp** is *Selected-Denied*; for **login** is *Selected-Allowed*; and for all others is *Allowed*.

```
 File  List  View  Options  Actions                                    Help

 Internet Services                                          0 of 15 selected

  Service                                        System
  Name        Description                 Type   Permission

 printer     Remote spooling line printer   rlp    Allowed
 recserv     HP SharedX receiver service    SharedX Allowed
 spc         User Defined                   N/A     Allowed
 bootps      Bootstrap Protocol requests    ARPA    Allowed
 chargen     Inetd internal server          ARPA    Allowed
 daytime     Inetd internal server          ARPA    Allowed
 discard     Inetd internal server          ARPA    Allowed
 echo        Inetd internal server          ARPA    Allowed
 exec        Remote command execution       ARPA    Allowed
 ftp         Remote file transfer           ARPA    Selected-Denied
 login       Remote user login              ARPA    Selected-Allowed
 shell       Remote command execution, copy ARPA    Denied
 telnet      Remote login                   ARPA    Allowed
 tftp        Trivial remote file transfer   ARPA    Allowed
```

Figure 8-23 System Access - Internet Services

I changed the permission for **shell** by selecting it and using the *Modify* pick from the *Actions* menu and selecting "Denied." The following are three entries from **/var/adm/inetd.sec**. Note that no entry exists for all of the network services that are *Allowed.*

```
ftp         deny        system1
login       allow       system2
shell       deny
```

The four permissions are

• Denied - All systems are denied access to this service.

• Allowed - All systems are allowed access to the service.

• Selected Denied - Only the selected systems are denied access to this service (**system1** under **ftp**).

• Selected Allowed - Only the selected systems are allowed access to this service (**system2** under **login**).

Remote Logins is used to manage security restrictions for remote users who will access the local system. There are two HP-UX files that are used to manage users. The file **/etc/hosts.equiv** handles users and **/.rhosts** handles superusers (root). When you enter this subarea you get a list of users and the restrictions on each. You can then *Add, Remove*, or *Modify* login security.

UUCP

The final subarea under *Networking and Communications* is UUCP. UUCP is a means of transferring files and executing commands on remote systems. UUCP is UNIX-to-UNIX Copy, which means you would use this software when going between UNIX systems. With a modem you can make a direct connection between UNIX systems and perform your system administration tasks.

SAM helps you with UUCP in two ways: by setting up management of remote systems under *UUCP Remote Systems*, and by managing devices to connect to remote systems under *UUCP Devices*.

The first time you enter *UUCP Devices* you won't have any device files listed. You can select *Add Modem Device* from the *Actions* menu and then select the *Modem Type* and *Modem Device* from the *Add Modem Device* window that appears. If no Modem Devices are present in the list, you can go under *Peripheral Devices* and *Terminals and Modems* and add a modem device.

Under *UUCP Remote Systems* you can *Add, Modify*, or *Remove* a system from the list that appears. The modifications you can make include the following categories of information:

• Set System Information

• Set Calling Out Times

• Set Calling In Configuration

• Set Calling In Directories

• Set Calling Out Configuration

• Set Calling Out Directories

Peripheral Devices

With *Peripheral Devices* you can view any I/O cards installed in your system and peripherals connected to your system. This includes both used and unused. You can also quickly configure any peripheral including printers, plotters, tape drives, terminals, modems, and disks. This is a particularly useful area in SAM because configuring peripherals in HP-UX is tricky. You perform one procedure to connect a printer, a different procedure to connect a disk, and so on when you use the command line. In SAM these procedures are menu driven and therefore much easier.

Two of the six subareas, *Disks and File Systems* and *Printers and Plotters,* have their own dedicated hierarchy within SAM and are covered in this chapter. I won't cover these again in this section. The other four subareas *Cards, Device List, Tape Drives*, and *Terminals and Modems* will be covered in this section.

It's impossible for me to cover every possible device that can be viewed and configured in SAM. What I'll do is give you examples of what you would see on a workstation and a server so you get a feel for what you can do under **Peripheral Devices** with SAM. From what I show here, you should be comfortable that SAM can help you configure peripherals.

Figure 8-24 shows the hierarchy of *Peripheral Devices.*

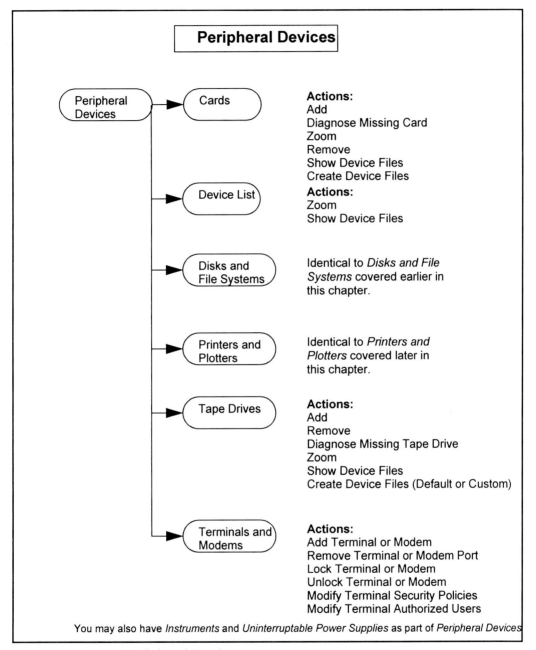

Figure 8-24 Peripheral Devices

Cards

When you select *Cards* you are provided with a list of I/O cards in your system. You can also perform such tasks as adding and removing cards. Having this list of I/O cards is useful. Figures 8-25 and 8-26 show a listing of I/O cards for a workstation and server, respectively.

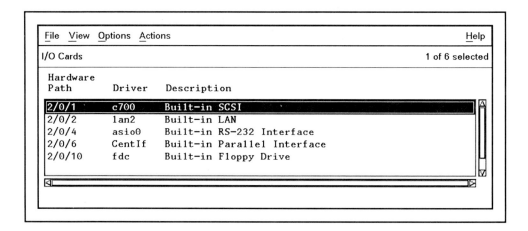

Figure 8-25   *I/O Cards* Window for Workstation

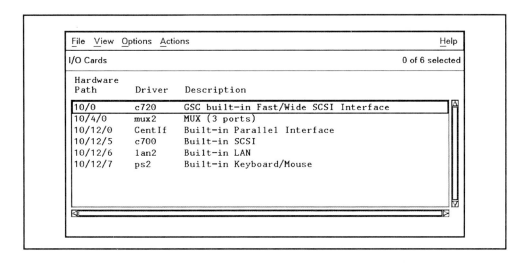

Figure 8-26 *I/O Cards* Window for Server

In *Cards* you can perform the following *Actions*:

Add   You can add a new I/O card in the window that is
                            opened for you.

Diagnose Missing Card

                            If a card you have installed is not included in the
                            list, you can select this to determine the reason.

Zoom   If you highlight a card and select *Zoom,* you will
                            be provided such information as the hardware
                            path, driver, and description of the card.

Remove   If you highlight a card and select *Remove,* a win-
                            dow will appear which walks you through remov-
                            ing the card from the system.

Show Device Files

>If you select this, a window will be opened in which the device files associated with the card will be listed.

Create Device Files

>Creates device files for the selected card. This takes place without any user interaction.

Device List

Device List shows all of the peripherals configured into the system. Figures 8-27 and 8-28 show a device list for a workstation and server, respectively.

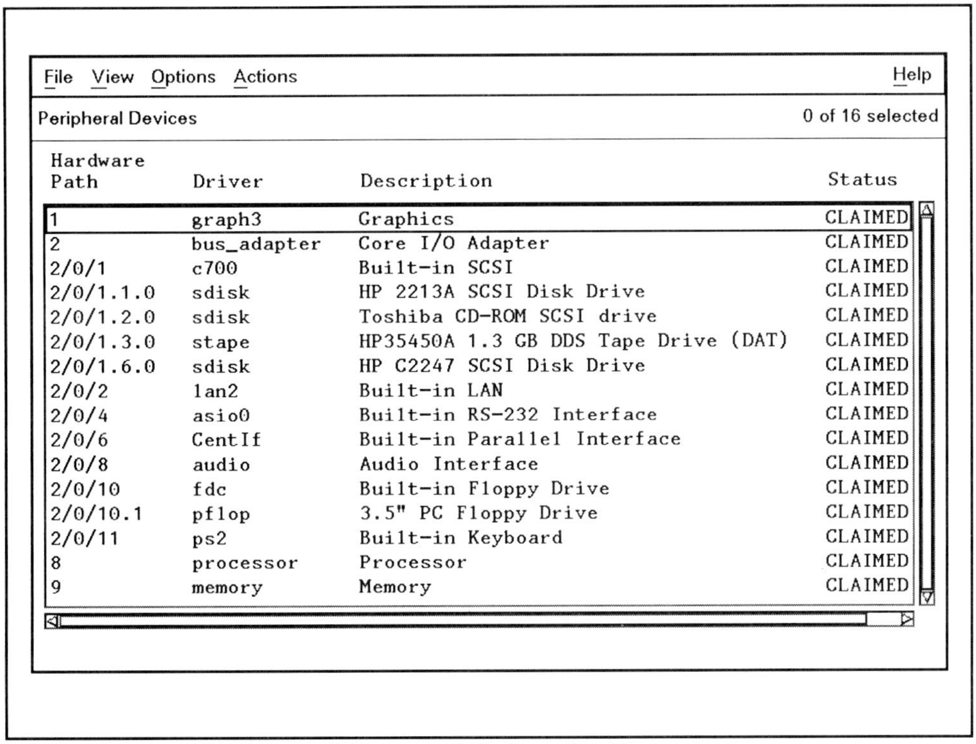

```
 File  View  Options  Actions                                          Help

 Peripheral Devices                                        0 of 16 selected

 Hardware
 Path          Driver        Description                      Status

 1             graph3        Graphics                         CLAIMED
 2             bus_adapter   Core I/O Adapter                 CLAIMED
 2/0/1         c700          Built-in SCSI                    CLAIMED
 2/0/1.1.0     sdisk         HP 2213A SCSI Disk Drive         CLAIMED
 2/0/1.2.0     sdisk         Toshiba CD-ROM SCSI drive        CLAIMED
 2/0/1.3.0     stape         HP35450A 1.3 GB DDS Tape Drive (DAT)  CLAIMED
 2/0/1.6.0     sdisk         HP C2247 SCSI Disk Drive         CLAIMED
 2/0/2         lan2          Built-in LAN                     CLAIMED
 2/0/4         asio0         Built-in RS-232 Interface        CLAIMED
 2/0/6         CentIf        Built-in Parallel Interface      CLAIMED
 2/0/8         audio         Audio Interface                  CLAIMED
 2/0/10        fdc           Built-in Floppy Drive            CLAIMED
 2/0/10.1      pflop         3.5" PC Floppy Drive             CLAIMED
 2/0/11        ps2           Built-in Keyboard                CLAIMED
 8             processor     Processor                        CLAIMED
 9             memory        Memory                           CLAIMED
```

Figure 8-27 *Peripheral Devices* Window for Workstation

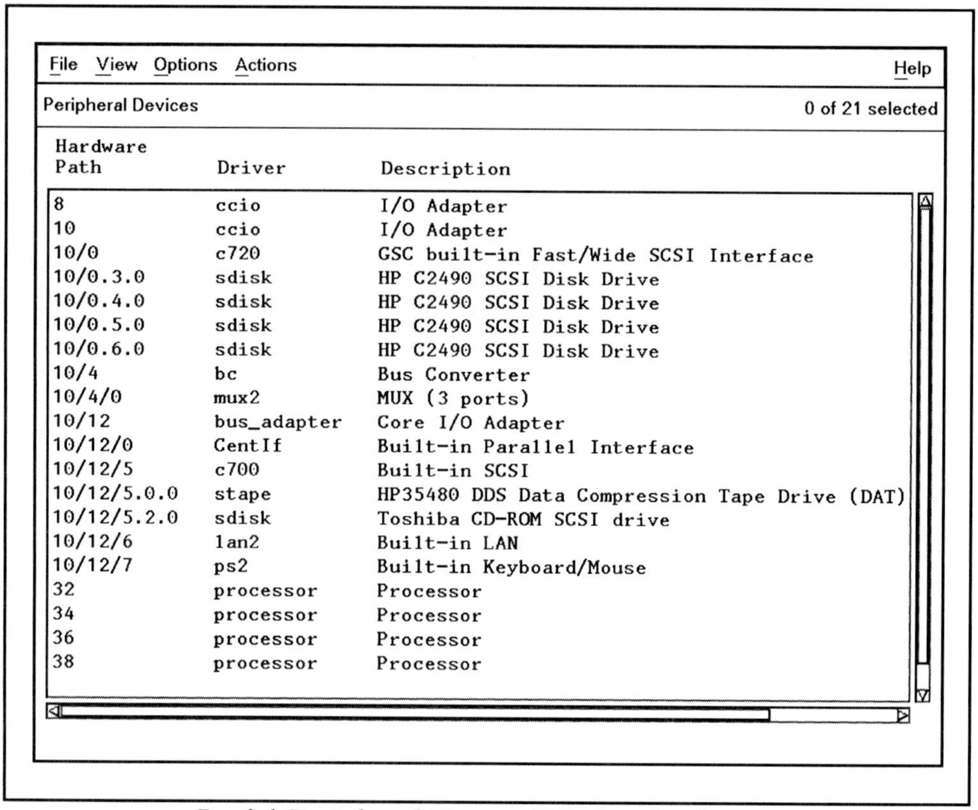

```
 File   View  Options  Actions                                        Help

 Peripheral Devices                                         0 of 21 selected

  Hardware
  Path            Driver         Description

  8               ccio           I/O Adapter
  10              ccio           I/O Adapter
  10/0            c720           GSC built-in Fast/Wide SCSI Interface
  10/0.3.0        sdisk          HP C2490 SCSI Disk Drive
  10/0.4.0        sdisk          HP C2490 SCSI Disk Drive
  10/0.5.0        sdisk          HP C2490 SCSI Disk Drive
  10/0.6.0        sdisk          HP C2490 SCSI Disk Drive
  10/4            bc             Bus Converter
  10/4/0          mux2           MUX (3 ports)
  10/12           bus_adapter    Core I/O Adapter
  10/12/0         CentIf         Built-in Parallel Interface
  10/12/5         c700           Built-in SCSI
  10/12/5.0.0     stape          HP35480 DDS Data Compression Tape Drive (DAT)
  10/12/5.2.0     sdisk          Toshiba CD-ROM SCSI drive
  10/12/6         lan2           Built-in LAN
  10/12/7         ps2            Built-in Keyboard/Mouse
  32              processor      Processor
  34              processor      Processor
  36              processor      Processor
  38              processor      Processor
```

Figure 8-28 Partial *Peripheral Devices* Window for Server

The two *Action* menu picks here are *Zoom* and *Show Device Files.* Selecting *Zoom* produces a window with such information as hardware path, driver, description, and status. The device files associated with the item you have highlighted will be shown if you select *Show Device Files.*

Disks and File Systems was covered earlier in this chapter.
Instruments may appear if your system supports HP-IB cards.
Printers and Plotters is covered later in this chapter.

Tape Drives

Tape Drives lists the tape drives connected to your system. You are shown the Hardware Path, Driver, and Description for each tape drive. You can add, remove, diagnose tape drives, list tape drive device files, and add new tape drive device files.

Terminals and Modems

Your system's terminals and modems are listed for you when you enter this subarea. You can perform a variety of tasks from the *Actions* menu including the following:

- Add Terminal
- Add Modem
- Remove Terminal or Modem Port
- Lock Terminal or Modem Port
- Unlock Terminal or Modem Port
- Modify Terminal Security Policies
- Modify Terminal Authorized Users
- Additional Information

Uninterruptable Power Supplies

Your system's uninterruptable power supplies are listed for you when you enter this area including the UPS type, device file of the UPS, hardware path, port number, and whether or not shutdown is enabled. The *Actions* you can select are; *Modify Global Configuration*; *Add; Zoom; Remove*; and *Modify*.

Figure 8-29 shows the *Modify Global Configuration* window.

```
┌─────────────────────────────────────────────────────────┐
│  ┌───────────────────────────────────────────────────┐  │
│  │   ┌─────────────────────────────┐                 │  │
│  │   │ UPS Daemon Status:          │                 │  │
│  │   │  ◇ Activate Daemon          │                 │  │
│  │   │  ◆ Deactivate Daemon        │                 │  │
│  │   └─────────────────────────────┘                 │  │
│  │                                                    │  │
│  │     Shutdown Delay (minutes):    │ 1 │            │  │
│  │                                                    │  │
│  │     Shutdown Timeout (minutes):  │ 5 │            │  │
│  │                                                    │  │
│  │        Configuration File Name: │/etc/ups_conf│   │  │
│  │                                                    │  │
│  ├───────────────────────────────────────────────────┤  │
│  │  ┌─────────┐   ┌─────────┐      ┌─────────┐       │  │
│  │  │   OK    │   │ Cancel  │      │  Help   │       │  │
│  │  └─────────┘   └─────────┘      └─────────┘       │  │
│  └───────────────────────────────────────────────────┘  │
└─────────────────────────────────────────────────────────┘
```

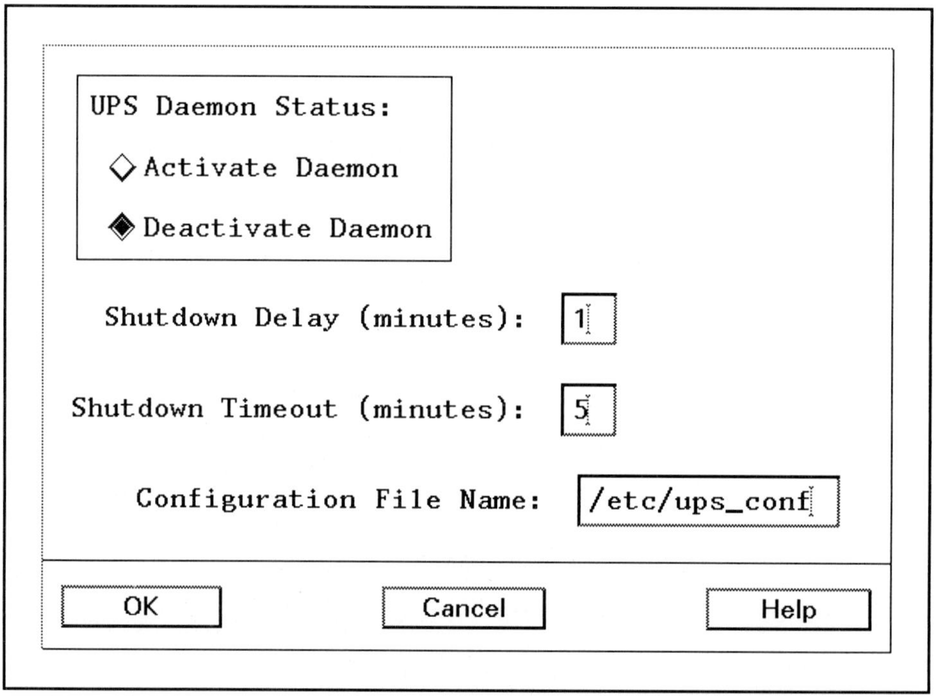

Figure 8-29 *Modify Global Configuration* Window For UPS

Printers and Plotters

Figure 8-30 shows the hierarchy of *Printers and Plotters*.

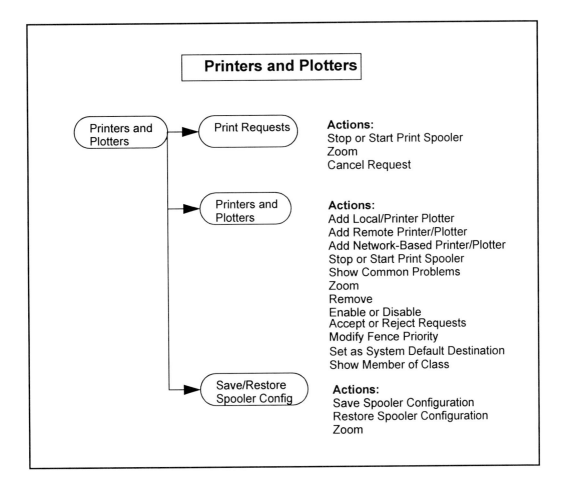

Figure 8-30 Printers and Plotters

Print Requests

Under *Print Requests* you can manage the print spooler and specific print jobs. You can start or stop the print spooler and cancel print jobs. The following information on print requests is listed for you:

Request ID   There is an ID associated with each print job. This is the Printer Name followed by a number.

Owner   Name of the user who requested the print job.

Priority   The priority of a print job is assigned when the job is submitted. The **-p** option of **lp** can be used to assign a priority to a job. Each print destination has a default priority that is assigned to jobs when **-p** is not used on the **lp** command.

File   Name of the file sent to the print queue.

Size   Size of the print job in bytes.

The *Actions* menu allows you to act on print jobs by canceling them. In addition, the print spooler can be stopped and started.

Printers and Plotters

You can configure both local and remote printers in *Printers and Plotters*. When you select *Add Local Printer/Plotter* from the *Actions* menu and then the appropriate type of printer, a window is opened for you in which you can supply the specifics about the printer. Before this window is opened, however, you must specify whether the *type* of printer to be added is: parallel serial; HP-IB; non-standard device file; or a printer connected to a TSM terminal as well as which I/O card to add the printer to. One huge advantage to adding the printer using SAM is that this process is entirely menu driven, so you only have to select from among the information that is supplied you.

The window that appears asks you for the following information:

Printer Name   You can pick any name for the printer. I usually like to use a name that is somewhat descriptive, such as ljet4 for a LaserJet 4. The name is limited to 14 alphanumeric characters and underscores.

Printer Model/Interface   SAM supplies a list of all interface models for you when this window is opened. These models are located in the **/usr/lib/lp/model** directory. Each printer has an interface program that is used by the spooler to send a print job to the printer. When an interface model is selected, the model is copied to **/etc/lp/interface/**\<printername> where it becomes the printer's interface program. Models can be used without modification or you can create customized interface programs.

Printer Class   You can define a group of printers to be in a class, which means print requests won't go to a specific printer but instead they will go to the first available printer within the class. This is optional.

Default Request Priority   This defines the default priority level of all requests sent to this printer.

Default Destination   Users who do not specify a printer when requesting a print job will have the print request sent to the default printer.

Figure 8-31 is an example *Add Local Printer/Plotter* window.

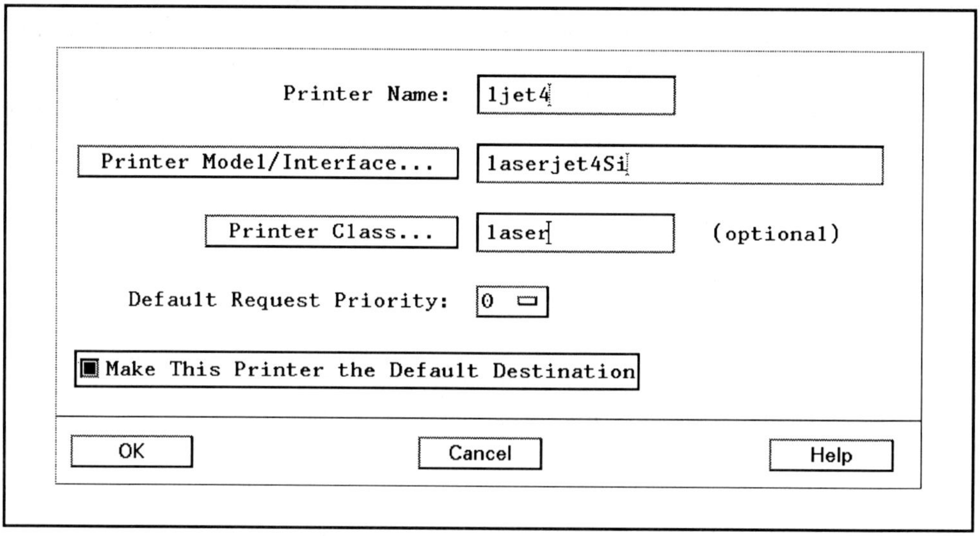

Figure 8-31 *Add Local Printer/Plotter* Window

After this printer has been added, I could use SAM to show me its status or use the **lpstat** command. Here is an example of the **lpstat** command showing ljet4 which was added in the last example.

```
$ /usr/bin/lpstat -t
scheduler is running
system default destination: ljet4
members of class laser:
        ljet4
device for ljet4: /dev/c1t0d0_lp
ljet4 accepting requests since Nov 21 22:45
```

```
printer ljet4 is idle. enabled since Nov 21 22:45
        fence priority : 0
no entries
```

As with all the other tasks SAM helps you with, you can manage printers and plotters manually. Doing this manually, however, is a real pain in the neck and I would strongly recommend you use SAM for managing printers and plotters. Not only does SAM make this easier for you, but I have also had nothing but good results having SAM do this for me. As you go through the SAM Log file you will see a variety of **lp** commands issued. Some of the more common commands, including the **lpstat** command issued earlier, are listed in Table 8-3.

TABLE 8-3 lp COMMANDS

COMMAND	DESCRIPTION
/usr/sbin/accept	Start accepting jobs to be queued
/usr/bin/cancel	Cancel a print job that is queued
/usr/bin/disable	Disable a device for printing
/usr/bin/enable	Enable a device for printing
/usr/sbin/lpfence	Set minimum priority for spooled file to be printed
/usr/bin/lp	Queue a job or jobs for printing
/usr/sbin/lpadmin	Configure the printing system with the options provided
/usr/sbin/lpmove	Move printing jobs from one device to another
/usr/sbin/lpsched	Start the **lp** scheduling daemon
/usr/sbin/lpshut	Stop the **lp** scheduling daemon
/usr/bin/lpstat	Show the status of printing based on the options provided
/usr/sbin/reject	Stop accepting jobs to be queued

Save/Restore Spooler Configuration

Occasionally the spooler can get into an inconsistent state (usually something else has to go wrong with your system that ends up somehow changing or renaming some of the spooler configuration files). SAM keeps a
saved version of the spooler's configuration each time SAM is used to
make a change (only the most recent one is saved). This saved configuration can be restored by SAM to recover from the spooler's having gotten
into an inconsistent state. Your latest configuration is automatically saved
by SAM, provided you used SAM to create the configuration as opposed to
issuing **lp** commands at the command line and can be restored with *Restore
Spooler Configuration* from *Save/Restore Spooler Config*. This screen
allows you to save your current spooler configuration or restore previously
saved spooler configuration information.

Process Management

Process Management is broken down into three areas which allow you to
monitor, control, and schedule processes. Under *Performance Monitors*
you can view the performance of your system in several different areas
such as disk and virtual memory. *Process Control* allows you to control an
individual process by performing such tasks as viewing it, changing its nice
priority, killing it, stopping it, or continuing it. You can also view and
schedule **cron** jobs under *Scheduled Cron Jobs*. Figure 8-32 shows the
menu hierarchy of *Process Management*.

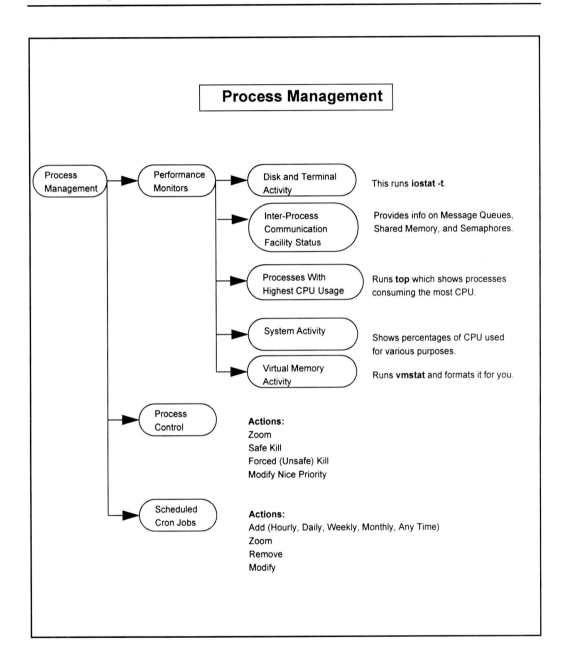

Figure 8-32 Process Management

Performance Monitors

Performance Monitors provides you with a window into several areas of your system. If you are serious about becoming familiar with the tools available on your system to help you understand how your system resources are being used, you should take a close look at the HP-UX Performance Overview chapter. That chapter is devoted to getting a handle on how your system resources are being used, including many built-in HP-UX commands. Some of the performance monitors you can select in this sub-area are HP-UX commands which you'll need some background in before you can use them. I'll cover these areas only briefly because this material will be covered in more detail in HP-UX Performance Overview.

Selecting *Disk and Terminal Activity* opens a window which shows the output of **iostat -t**. When the *Disks and Terminal Activity* window with the output of **iostat** is opened for you, it shows a single **iostat** output. When you hit *return,* the window is automatically closed for you.

The **iostat** command gives you an indication of the level of effort the CPU is putting into I/O and the amount of I/O taking place among your disks and terminals. The following example shows the **iostat -t** command, which will be executed every three seconds, and associated output from an HP-UX 10.x system. The "#" shown is the HP-UX prompt.

```
# iostat -t 3
              tty              cpu
          tintout        us   ni   sy   id
           78   42        2    0   28   70
/dev/dsk/c0t1d0  /dev/dsk/c0t4d0      /dev/dsk/c0t6d0
bpssps msps          bps sps msps       bps sps msps
  0   0    0          33 8.3 25.2         7   1 19.5
              tty              cpu
          tintout        us   ni   sy   id
           66   24        0    0   30   70
/dev/dsk/c0t1d0  /dev/dsk/c0t4d0      /dev/dsk/c0t6d0
```

```
bpssps msps              bps  sps msps            bps sps msps
 5 12 15.9               36  9.7   21             7 1.2 13.8
                tty                   cpu
              tintout          us   ni   sy  id
               90  29           1    0   25  73
/dev/dsk/c0t1d0  /dev/dsk/c0t4d0      /dev/dsk/c0t6d0
bpssps msps              bps  sps msps            bps sps msps
12 1.7 15.5              24    3 19.1            14 2.1 14.6
                tty                   cpu
              tintout          us   ni   sy  id
               48  16           1    0   16  83
/dev/dsk/c0t1d0  /dev/dsk/c0t4d0      /dev/dsk/c0t6d0
bpssps msps              bps  sps msps            bps sps msps
 0  0   0                62  9.3   18             12   2 17.2
                tty                   cpu
              tintout          us   ni   sy  id
               32  48           7    0   14  79
/dev/dsk/c0t1d0  /dev/dsk/c0t4d0      /dev/dsk/c0t6d0
bpsspsmsps               bps  sps msps            bpssps  msps
10.3 14.4                 5   .9 16.2             17129.418.2
                tty                   cpu
              tintout          us   ni   sy  id
                2  40          20    1   42  27
/dev/dsk/c0t1d0  /dev/dsk/c0t4d0      /dev/dsk/c0t6d0
bpssps msps              bps  sps  msps           bps sps msps
24830.920.8              20329.2 18.8            16530.622.1
```

Descriptions of the reports you receive with **iostat** for terminals, the CPU, and mounted file systems follow.

For every terminal you have connected (tty), you see a "tin" and "tout", which represent the number of characters read from your terminal and the number of characters written to your terminal, respectively. The **-t** option produces this terminal report.

For your CPU, you see the percentage of time spent in user mode ("us"), the percentage of time spent running user processes at a low priority called nice ("ni"), the percentage of time spent in system mode ("sy"), and the percentage of time the CPU is idle ("id").

For every locally mounted file system, you receive information on the kilobytes transferred per second ("bps"), number of seeks per second ("sps"), and number of milliseconds per average seek ("msps"). For disks that are NFS-mounted or disks on client nodes of your server, you will not receive a report: **iostat** reports only on locally mounted file systems.

Interprocess Communication Facility Status shows categories of information related to communication between processes. You receive status on Message Queues, Shared Memory, and Semaphores. This is a status window only, so again you would hit *return* and the window will close.

Processes with Highest CPU Usage is a useful window that lists the processes consuming the most CPU on your system. Such useful information as the Process ID, its Resident Set Size, and the Percentage of CPU it is consuming are listed.

System Activity provides a report of CPU utilization. You receive the following list:

%usr	Percent of CPU spent in user mode.
%sys	Percent of CPU spent in system mode.
%wio	Percent of CPU idle with some processes waiting for I/O such as virtual memory pages moving in or moving out.
%idle	Percent of CPU completely idle.

Virtual Memory Activity runs the **vmstat** command. Some of the columns of **vmstat** are moved around a little when the *Virtual Memory Activity* window is opened for you.

vmstat provides virtual memory statistics. It provides information on the status of processes, virtual memory, paging activity, faults, and the breakdown of the percentage of CPU time. In the following example, the output was produced ten times at five-second intervals. The first argument to the **vmstat** command is the interval; the second is the number of times you would like output produced.

```
# vmstat 5 10:
```

procs			memory		page						faults			cpu		
r	b	w	avm	free	r e	at	pi	po	f r	de	sr	in	sy	cs	us	sy	id
4	0	0	1161	2282	6	22	48	0	0	0	0	429	289	65	44	18	38
9	0	0	1161	1422	4	30	59	0	0	0	0	654	264	181	18	20	62
6	0	0	1409	1247	2	19	37	0	0	0	0	505	316	130	47	10	43
1	0	0	1409	1119	1	10	19	0	0	0	0	508	254	180	69	15	16
2	0	0	1878	786	0	1	6	0	0	0	0	729	294	217	75	17	8
2	0	0	1878	725	0	0	3	0	0	0	0	561	688	435	67	32	1
2	0	0	2166	98	0	0	20	0	0	0	66	728	952	145	8	14	78
1	0	0	2310	90	0	0	20	0	0	0	171	809	571	159	16	21	63
1	0	0	2310	190	0	0	8	1	3	0	335	704	499	176	66	14	20
1	0	0	2316	311	0	0	3	1	5	0	376	607	945	222	4	11	85

You will get more out of the **vmstat** command than you want. Here is a brief description of the categories of information produced by **vmstat**.

Processes are classified into one of three categories: runnable ("r"), blocked on I/O or short term resources ("b"), or swapped ("w").

Next you will see information about memory. "avm" is the number of virtual memory pages owned by processes that have run within the last 20 seconds. If this number is roughly the size of physical memory minus your kernel, then you are near paging. The "free" column indicates the number of pages on the system's free list. It doesn't mean the process has finished running and these pages won't be accessed again; it just means they have not been accessed recently. I suggest you ignore this column.

Next is paging activity. Only the first field (re) is useful. It shows the pages that were reclaimed. These pages made it to the free list but were later referenced and had to be salvaged. Check to see that "re" is a low number. If you are reclaiming pages which were thought to be free by the system, then you are wasting valuable time salvaging these. Reclaiming pages is also a symptom that you are short on memory.

Next you see the number of faults in three categories: interrupts per second, which usually come from hardware ("in"); system calls per second ("sy"); and context switches per second ("cs").

The final output is CPU usage percentage for user ("us"), system ("sy"), and idle ("id"). This is not as complete as the **iostat** output, which also shows **nice** entries.

Process Control

When you pick *Process Control,* SAM lists the processes on your system and allows you to perform various actions. Using *Process Control* is a much easier way of controlling the processes on your system than executing commands such as **ps**, **nice**, etc. Figure 8-33 shows a partial listing of processes.

```
 File  List  View  Options  Actions                                        Help

 Process Control                                                  1 of 68 selected

                          Nice
 User        Priority   Priority    Command
|root          154         20       /usr/sbin/biod 4                           |▲|
|root          154         20       /usr/sbin/biod 4                           | |
|root          154         20       /usr/sbin/rpc.statd                        | |
|root          154         20       /usr/sbin/rpc.lockd                        | |
|root          154         20       /usr/sbin/inetd                            |▓|
|daemon        154         20       sendmail -bd -q30m -accepting connections  |▓|
|root          154         20       /usr/sbin/snmpd                            |▓|
|root          154         20       /opt/dce/sbin/rpcd                         | |
|root          154         20       /opt/ifor/ls/bin/i41md                     | |
|root          154         20       /usr/sbin/vtdaemon                         | |
|root          154         20       /usr/sbin/cron                             | |
|root          154         20       /opt/audio/bin/Aserver                     | |
|root          154         20         /opt/audio/bin/Aserver                   | |
|root          154         20       /usr/sbin/rpc.mountd                       | |
|root          154         20       /usr/sbin/nfsd 4                           | |
|root          154         20         /usr/sbin/nfsd 4                         | |
|root          154         20         /usr/sbin/nfsd 4                         | |
|root          154         20         /usr/sbin/nfsd 4                         | |
|root          156         20       /usr/sbin/getty console console            | |
|root          154         20       /usr/vue/bin/vuelogin                      |▽|
|◁|▦▦▦▦▦▦▦▦▦▦▦▦▦▦▦▦▦▦▦▦▦▦▦▦▦▦▦▦▦▦▦▦▦▦▦▦▦▦▦▦▦▦         |▷|
```

Figure 8-33 Partial *Process Control* Listing.

There are the four following columns of information listed for you.

• *User* - The name of the user who owns the process.

• *Priority* - The priority of the process determines its scheduling by the CPU. The lower the number, the higher the priority. Unless you have modified these priorities, they will be default priorities. Changing the priority is done with the **nice** command which will be covered shortly.

• *Nice Priority* - If you have a process that you wish to run at a lower or higher priority, you could change this value. The lower the value, the higher the CPU scheduling priority.

• *Command* - Lists the names of all the commands on the system.

In addition to these four columns, there are several others you can specify to be included in the list by selecting *Columns* from the *View* menu. You could include such information as the *Process ID, Parent Process ID, Processor Utilization, Core Image Size*, and so on. Adding *Processor Utilization* as a column, for instance, shows me how much of the processor all processes are consuming including SAM.

You can now go select one of the processes and an *Actions* to perform.

When you select a process to kill and pick *Safe Kill* from the *Actions* menu, you get a message which indicates the process number killed and that it may take a few minutes to kill it in order to terminate cleanly. If you select a process to kill and pick *Forced Kill* from the *Actions* menu, you don't get any feedback; SAM just kills the process and you move on.

The **kill** command can be either **/usr/bin/kill** or **kill** that is part of the POSIX shell. The POSIX shell is the default shell for HP-UX. The other shells provide their own **kill** commands as well. We use the phrase "kill a process" in the UNIX world all the time, I think, because it has a powerful connotation associated with it. What we are really saying is we want to terminate a process. This termination is done with a signal. The most common signal to send is "SIGKILL" which terminates the process. There are other signals you can send to the process, but SIGKILL is the most common. As an alternative to sending the signal, you could send the corresponding signal number. A list of signal numbers and corresponding signals is shown below:

Signal Number	Signal
0	SIGNULL
1	SIGHUP
2	SIGINT
3	SIGQUIT
9	SIGKILL
15	SIGTERM
24	SIGSTOP

| 25 | SIGTSTP |
| 26 | SIGCONT |

I obtained this list of processes from the **kill** manual page.

To **kill** a process with a process ID of 234, you would issue the following command:

```
$ kill -9 234
    |   |  |
    |   |  |> process id (PID)
    |   |> signal number
    |> kill command to terminate the process
```

The final selection from the *Actions* menu is to *Modify Nice Priority* of the process you have selected. If you were to read the manual page on **nice,** you would be very happy to see you can modify this with SAM. Modifying the **nice** value in SAM simply requires you to select a process and specify its new **nice** value within the acceptable range.

Scheduling Cron Jobs

The *Scheduled Cron Jobs* menu selection lists all of the **cron** jobs you have scheduled and allows you to *Add, Zoom, Remove*, and *Modify* **cron** jobs through the *Actions* menu. **cron** was described earlier in this chapter under *Backup and Recovery*. I have included some of the **cron** background covered earlier to save you the trouble of flipping back.

The **crontab** file is used to schedule jobs that are automatically executed by **cron. crontab** files are in the **/var/spool/cron/crontabs** directory. **cron** is a program that runs other programs at the specified time. **cron** reads files that specify the operation to be performed and the date and time it is to be performed. Going back to the backup example earlier in this chapter, we want to perform backups on a regular basis. SAM was used to activate **cron** in the backup example using the format described below.

The format of entries in the **crontab** file are as follows:

minute   hour monthday   month   weekday   user name   command

minute - the minute of the hour, from 0-59

hour - the hour of the day, from 0-23

monthday - the day of the month, from 1-31

month - the month of the year, from 1-12

weekday - the day of the week, from 0 (Sunday) - 6 (Saturday)

user name - the user who will run the command if necessary (not used in example)

command - specifies the command line or script file to run

You have many options in the **crontab** file for specifying the *minute, hour, monthday, month,* and *weekday* to perform a task. You could list one entry in a field and then a space, several entries in any field separated by a comma, two entries separated by a dash indicating a range, or an asterisk, which corresponds to all possible entries for the field.

To list the contents of the **crontab** file, you would issue the following command. The output of this command is the **crontab** file created for the user root in the SAM backup example earlier in the chapter:

```
$ crontab -l

00 2 * * 6 /usr/sam/lbin/br_backup DAT FULL Y /dev/rmt/0m /etc/sam/br/
graphDCAa02410 root Y 1 N > /tmp/SAM_br_msgs 2>&1 #sambackup

15 12 * * 1-5 /usr/sam/lbin/br_backup DAT PART Y /dev/rmt/0m /etc/sam/
br/graphDCAa02410 root Y 1 N > /tmp/SAM_br_msgs 2>&1 #sambackup
```

Although these seem to be excruciatingly long lines, they do indeed conform to the format of the **crontab** file. The first entry is the full backup, the second entry is the incremental backup. In the first entry the *minute* is 00; in the second entry the *minute* is 15. In the first entry the *hour* is 2; in the second entry the *hour* is 12. In both entries the *monthday* and *month* are all legal values (*), meaning every *monthday* and *month*. In the first entry the *weekday* is 6 for Saturday (0 is Sunday); in the second entry the *weekdays* are 1-5 or Monday through Friday. The optional *username* is not specified in either example. And finally, the SAM backup command (**/usr/sam/lbin/br_backup**) and its long list of associated information is provided.

minute	hour	monthday	month	weekday	user name	command
00	12	all	all	6	n/a	br_backup
15	12	all	all	1-5	n/a	br_backup

This was done as part of the full and incremental backups that were covered earlier in the chapter. You can, however, schedule **cron** to run any kind of job for you. Using *Add* from the *Actions* menu you can add *Hourly, Daily, Weekly, Monthly*, or jobs to run *Any Time*. You can also *Remove, Modify*, or *Zoom* in on one of the existing **cron** entries from the *Actions* menu.

Routine Tasks

The following subareas exist under *Routine Tasks* in SAM:

- Backup and Recovery
- Find and Remove Unused Filesets
- Selective File Removal
- System Log Files
- System Shutdown

The hierarchy of *Routine Tasks* is shown in Figure 8-34. Please note that *Backup and Recovery* is identical to the SAM top-level *Backup and Recovery* area discussed earlier in this chapter.

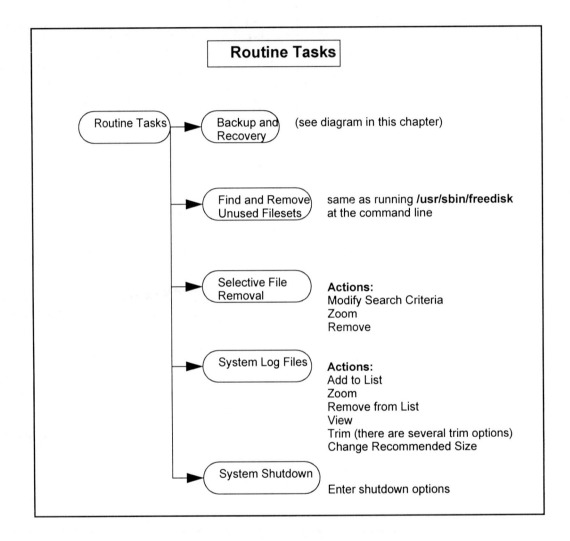

Figure 8-34 Routine Tasks

Backup and Recovery

This is identical to the *Backup and Recovery* area covered earlier in this chapter.

Find and Remove Unused Filesets

Find and Remove Unused Filesets runs the **/usr/sbin/freedisk** utility that is used to recover disk space by locating filesets which can be removed. **freedisk** is a command that identifies filesets that have not been used since they were installed and will remove them for you. The filesets in question would have been installed with **swinstall**.

When you run **freedisk,** it looks for filesets that have not been used since installed. If you use the **-a** option and specify a usage time, then **freedisk** will find the filesets that have not been used since that time. Filesets that have not been used but are depended on by filesets that have been used are treated as though they have been used. Here is an example of the **freedisk** command to identify files that have not been used in 60 days:

```
$ /usr/sbin/freedisk -a 60
```

freedisk then removes filesets by invoking **swremove,** at which time you can unselect filesets which are slated for removal.

Using SAM, **freedisk** is run for you and reports on what filesets have not been used. This process takes some time. Such activities as collecting filesets, counting filesets, screening files, and checking access times are performed. During the phase where access times are checked, SAM reports on the percent complete of this process. When SAM has completed this phase, it reports the number of filesets which appear to be unused and the total number of filesets. You will also receive a list of filesets which are unused but depended on by other filesets. In an example run I received the following list of filesets which were unused but were not passed to **swre-move** because other filesets which were in use depended on these.

AudioSubsystem.AUDIO-SHLIBS
UUCP.UUCP
OS-Core.C-MIN
GraphicsCommon.FAFM-RUN
GraphicsCommon.FAFM-SHLIBS
ProgSupport.PROG-MIN

SAM then allows you to remove any or all of the filesets identified as unused. Then **swremove** is run and you can proceed with removing any filesets you wish.

Selective File Removal

Selective File Removal allows you to search for files to remove. You can specify a variety of criteria for selecting files to remove including the following:

Type of file   There are three different file types you can search for: *Large Files, Unowned Files*, and *Core Files*. A pop-up menu allows you to select which of these to search for. Figure 8-35 shows *Large Files* selected. With *Large Files,* you are searching for files of a minimum size that haven't been modified in the specified time. *Unowned Files* are those files owned by someone other than a valid system user. *Core Files* contain a core image of a terminated process when the process was terminated under certain conditions. Core files are usually related to a problem with a process and contain such information as data, stack, etc.

Mount Points   Specify whether or not you want to search across non-NFS mount points. If you select *Yes*, this means the search will include mount points on your system but not extend to NFS mount points. I chose not to include other mount points in the example.

Beginning Path   Your search can begin at any point in the system hierarchy. You can specify the start point of the search in this field. If you want to search only the **/home** directory for files, then change this entry to **/home** and you will search only that directory as I did in the example.

Minimum Size   Specify the smallest size file in bytes that you want searched for. Files smaller than this size will not be reported as part of the search. The minimum size in the example is 500,000 bytes.

Last Modification

If you select *Large Files*, you can make an entry in this field. You enter the minimum number of days since the file was last modified and files that have been modified within that time period will be excluded from the search. This is 30 days in the example.

Figure 8-35 shows an example of specifying which files to search for.

```
┌─────────────────────────────────────────────────────────────────┐
│                                                                   │
│                        Search For:  │Large Files    ▭│            │
│                                                                   │
│     Search Across non-NFS Mount Points:  │No  ▭│                  │
│                                                                   │
│             Beginning of Search Path:  │/home│                    │
│                                                                   │
│             Minimum Size (Bytes):  │500000                    │   │
│                                                                   │
│   Time Since Last Modification (Days):  │30│                      │
│                                                                   │
├─────────────────────────────────────────────────────────────────┤
│   ┌──────────┐          ┌──────────┐              ┌──────────┐    │
│   │    OK    │          │  Cancel  │              │   Help   │    │
│   └──────────┘          └──────────┘              └──────────┘    │
└─────────────────────────────────────────────────────────────────┘
```

Figure 8-35   Searching for Files to Remove

The list of files reported for removal was too long with a minimum size of only 500 KBytes. I increased the minimum size to 5 MBytes and received the list of files in Table 8-4 after my search.

TABLE 8-4   Files Reported For Removal

File Name	Size (Bytes)	Last Modified
/home/denise/demo.mpg	5215336	Jun 19 1995
/home/denise/rock.mpg	17698880	Aug 12 1995
/users/tomd/tst.sasdata2	15666920	Sep 11 1995
/home/joe/testdatabase	23496520	Sep 13 1995

The way to approach removing files is to start with an exceptionally large file size and work your way down in size. It may be that you have a few "unexpected" large files on your system that you can remove and ignore the smaller files.

System Log Files

System Log Files is used to manage the size of your system log files. Log files are generated by HP-UX for a variety of reasons including backup, shutdown, cron, etc. Your applications may very well be generating log files as well. Some of these log files can grow in size indefinitely, creating a potential catastrophe on your system by growing and crashing your system. You can be proactive and manage these log files in this subarea.

SAM is aware of many of the log files generated by HP-UX. When you enter the *System Log Files* subarea, information related to log files is listed. You can add to the list of log files SAM knows about and have a complete list of log files presented to you each time you enter this subarea. SAM lists the following information related to log files each time you enter this subarea. (You may have to increase the size of the window to see all this information.)

File Name	Full path name of log file.
Percent Full	SAM has what it thinks should be the maximum size of a log file. You can change this size by selecting *Change Recommended Size* from the *Actions* menu. The percent full is the percentage of the recommended size the log file consumes.
Current Size	The size of the file in bytes is listed for you. You may want to take a look at this. The current size of a log file may be much bigger than you would like. You could then change the recommended size and quickly see which files are greater than 100 percent. The converse may also be true. You

may think the recommended size for a log file is far too small and change the recommended size to a larger value. In either case you would like to quickly see which files are much bigger than recommended.

Recommended Size

This is what you define as the recommended size of the file. Check these to make sure you agree with this value.

Present on System

Yes if this file is indeed present on your system; *No* if it is not present on your system. If a file is not present on your system and it simply does not apply to you, then you can select *Remove from List* from the *Actions* menu. For example, you may not be running UUCP and therefore want to remove all of the UUCP-related log files.

File Type

The only file types listed are *ASCII* and *Non-ASCII*. I found it interesting that **/var/sam/log/ samlog** was not one of the log files listed. This is not an ASCII file and must be viewed through *View SAM Log* from the *Actions* menu, but it is indeed a log file which I thought would appear in the list.

You can trim a log file using the *Trim* pick from the *Actions* menu. You then have several options for trimming the file.

System Shutdown

SAM offers you the following three ways to shut down your system:

- *Halt the System*
- *Reboot (Restart) the System*
- *Go to Single User State*

In addition, you can specify the number of minutes before shutdown occurs.

Run SAM on Remote Systems

I think SAM is great. If it works well on one system then you, as the system administrator, may as well use it on other systems from a central point of control. *Run SAM on Remote Systems* allows you to setup the system on which you will run SAM remotely from a central point of control.

You can specify any number of remote systems to be controlled by a central system. With the *Actions* menu you can:

Add System	A window opens up in which you can specify the name of the remote system you wish to administer locally.
Run SAM	You can select the remote system on which you want to run SAM.

Remove System(s)

> Remote systems can be removed from the list of systems on which you will run SAM remotely.

Software Management

Software Management under SAM uses Software Distributor-HP-UX (I'll call this Software Distributor) which was covered in detail in an earlier chapter. I will go over the basics of *Software Management* in SAM so you can see how some of these tasks are performed in SAM. If you read Chapter 2, you will recognize a lot of the information presented here. The following subareas exist under *Software Management* in SAM:

- Copy Software to Local Depot
- Install Software to Local Host
- List Software
- Remove Software

The hierarchy of *Software Management* is shown in Figure 8-36.

Figure 8-36 Software Management

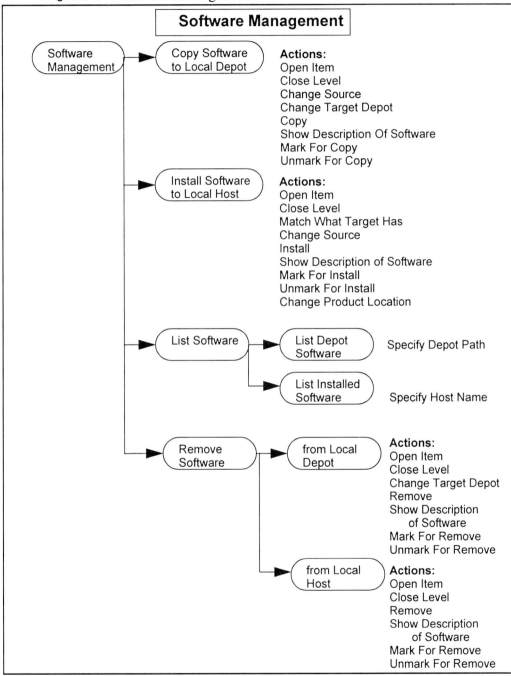

Copy Software to Local Depot

The first task to perform under *Copy Software to Local Depot* is to specify the target depot path. This is the location on your system where software will be stored or managed. Keep in mind that the CD-ROM from which you may be loading software can also be a depot. This is a directory from which your system and other systems can install software. SAM asks if you would like to use **/var/spool/sw** as the directory of the target depot path. I have selected **/var/spool/swdepot** as the target depot path in the upcoming example. You can use this directory or specify another directory name. SAM then asks for the source host name and source depot path. Using the CD-ROM on the system, we would perform the following steps.

The first step when loading software from CD-ROM is to insert the media and mount the CD-ROM. The directory **/SD_CDROM** should already exist on your system. You can use SAM to mount the CD-ROM for you or do this manually. I issued the following command to mount a CD-ROM at SCSI address 2 on a workstation:

```
$ mount /dev/dsk/c0t2d0 /SD_CDROM
```

The dialog box that appears in SAM where you specify the source is shown in Figure 8-37.

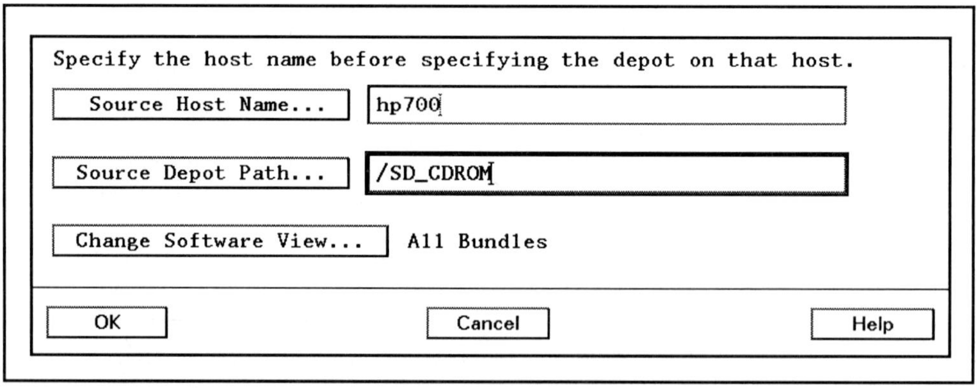

```
┌──────────────────────────────────────────────────────────────────────┐
│  ┌──────────────────────────────────────────────────────────────────┐ │
│  │ Specify the host name before specifying the depot on that host.  │ │
│  │   ┌─────────────────────────┐  ┌──────────────────────────────┐  │ │
│  │   │   Source Host Name...   │  │ hp700                        │  │ │
│  │   └─────────────────────────┘  └──────────────────────────────┘  │ │
│  │   ┌─────────────────────────┐  ┌──────────────────────────────┐  │ │
│  │   │   Source Depot Path...  │  │ /SD_CDROM                    │  │ │
│  │   └─────────────────────────┘  └──────────────────────────────┘  │ │
│  │   ┌─────────────────────────────┐                                │ │
│  │   │  Change Software View...    │   All Bundles                  │ │
│  │   └─────────────────────────────┘                                │ │
│  │  ┌──────────────┐      ┌──────────────┐      ┌──────────────┐     │ │
│  │  │     OK       │      │    Cancel    │      │    Help      │     │ │
│  │  └──────────────┘      └──────────────┘      └──────────────┘     │ │
│  └──────────────────────────────────────────────────────────────────┘ │
└──────────────────────────────────────────────────────────────────────┘
```

Figure 8-37 *Specify Source* Window

At this point you select the software you wish to copy to the software depot from the source. This is done by highlighting the names you wish to be loaded and selecting *Mark For Copy* from the *Actions* menu and then *Copy* from the *Actions* menu. This places the software in the local depot. Figure 8-38 shows the *Software Selection Window* with the HP C++ Compiler highlighted with a source of **/SD_CDROM** and target depot directory **/var/spool/swdepot**.

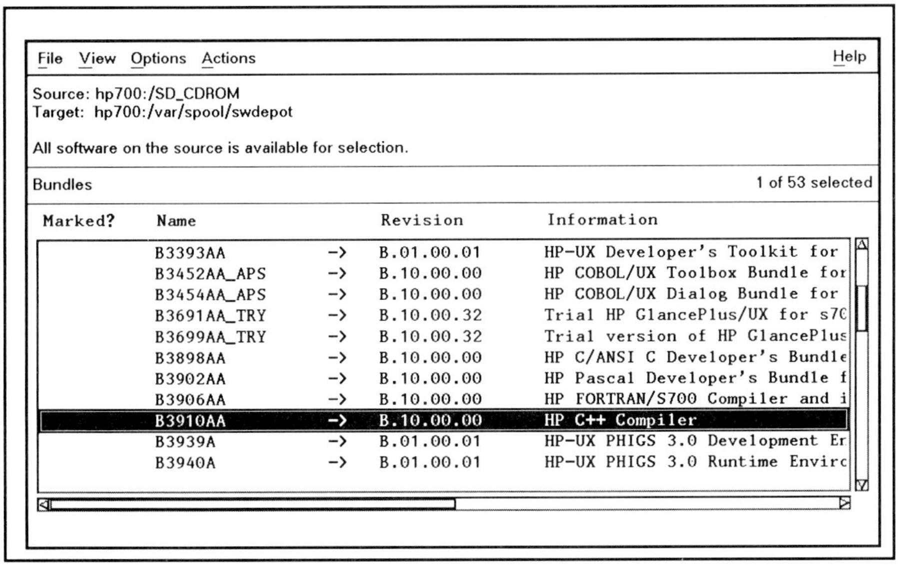

```
┌─────────────────────────────────────────────────────────────────────────┐
│                                                                           │
│  File  View  Options  Actions                                      Help   │
│  ───────────────────────────────────────────────────────────────────     │
│  Source: hp700:/SD_CDROM                                                  │
│  Target: hp700:/var/spool/swdepot                                         │
│                                                                           │
│  All software on the source is available for selection.                   │
│  ───────────────────────────────────────────────────────────────────     │
│  Bundles                                            1 of 53 selected      │
│  ───────────────────────────────────────────────────────────────────     │
│   Marked?    Name              Revision      Information                   │
│                                                                           │
│              B3393AA     ->    B.01.00.01    HP-UX Developer's Toolkit for▲│
│              B3452AA_APS ->    B.10.00.00    HP COBOL/UX Toolbox Bundle for│
│              B3454AA_APS ->    B.10.00.00    HP COBOL/UX Dialog Bundle for │
│              B3691AA_TRY ->    B.10.00.32    Trial HP GlancePlus/UX for s7C│
│              B3699AA_TRY ->    B.10.00.32    Trial version of HP GlancePlus│
│              B3898AA     ->    B.10.00.00    HP C/ANSI C Developer's Bundle│
│              B3902AA     ->    B.10.00.00    HP Pascal Developer's Bundle f│
│              B3906AA     ->    B.10.00.00    HP FORTRAN/S700 Compiler and i│
│  ████████████B3910AA█████->████B.10.00.00████HP C++ Compiler██████████████│
│              B3939A      ->    B.01.00.01    HP-UX PHIGS 3.0 Development En│
│              B3940A      ->    B.01.00.01    HP-UX PHIGS 3.0 Runtime Envirc▼│
│  ◁                                                                    ▷    │
│                                                                           │
└─────────────────────────────────────────────────────────────────────────┘
```

Figure 8-38 *Software Selection* Window

Copy first performs an analysis in which a lot of useful information is produced such as the amount of disk space in the depot directory both before and after the installation takes place, as shown in Figure 8-39.

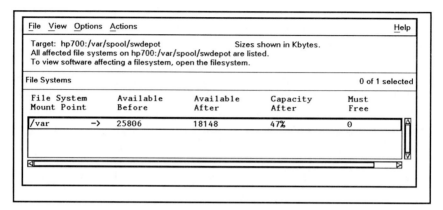

Figure 8-39 *Disk Space Analysis* Window

If you are satisfied with the analysis information, you can load the software. A window showing the status of the installation will appear. It is now in a depot on the hard disk, as opposed to the CD-ROM depot it was loaded from, that this and other systems can access for installing software.

You can select *Save Session As* from the *Actions* menu if you wish to save the list of depots and software.

Install Software to Local Host

Install Software To Local Host is similar to *Copy Software to Local Depot* in that you must specify the Source Host Name and Source Depot Path. The Source Depot Path could be the CD-ROM from which you are loading software, as shown in the previous example or it could be a directory depot. We just created a directory depot from which software can be copied in the previous example so we could use that directory rather than the CD-ROM. If that directory name is specified as the Source Depot Path, the software Figure 8-40 is shown in the depot.

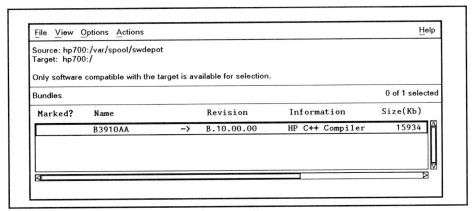

Figure 8-40 Copying From Directory Depot

The <u>HP C++ Compiler</u> is the software we loaded into this directory in the previous example. Before loading software you should select *Show Description Of Software* from the *Actions* menu to see if a system reboot is required (you may have to scroll down the window to see the bottom of the description). You want to know this before you load software so you don't load software that requires a reboot at a time that it is inconvenient to reboot. We can now install this software onto the local host by selecting *Mark For Install* and *Install* from the *Actions* menu.

When this installation is complete, after only about four minutes when installing from a local disk on the local host, a system reboot is not required.

List Software

You can select either *List Depot Software* or *List Installed Software*.

Under *List Depot Software,* you specify the host and depot path to receive a complete list of software. This can be listed at the bundle, product, subproduct, fileset, or file level. If you have even a small amount of software installed in a depot, the file level is probably going to be too much detail. Listing HP C++ Compiler we loaded earlier to the fileset level is both manageable to read and informative. The file level is just too much detail.

List Installed Software allows you to list the software installed on your system to the bundle, product, subproduct, fileset, or file level also. Selecting the bundle level and listing through SAM produces the same output as typing **swlist** at the command line. You can try this on your system to see how the two compare.

Remove Software

You can *Remove Software from Local Depot* or *Remove Software from Local Host*.

We can use the directory depot in **/var/spool/swdepot** we created earlier to delete software. The HP C++ Compiler we loaded in this directory can be highlighted, and *Mark For Remove* from the *Actions* menu. Selecting *Remove* from the *Actions* menu will remove the software from the directory depot. You can also *Remove Software From Local Host* using the same procedure.

Time

Not covered.

NFS Diskless Concepts

Rather than cover NFS diskless as an area to managed, I'm going to deviate from the format found throughout this chapter and instead provide a brief description of NFS diskless.

This is a topic new to HP-UX 10.x. Diskless nodes were implemented with Distributed HP-UX (DUX) in HP-UX 9.x and earlier releases. Distributed HP-UX was first introduced in HP-UX 6.0 in 1986 and was successfully used in many HP installations. The new implementation of diskless nodes in HP-UX 10.x is NFS Diskless. It has many desirable features including the following:

- NFS diskless is the current de facto standard.

- It is not a proprietary solution.

- High-end diskless servers and clients can be symmetric multiprocessing systems.

- Many file system types and features are available such as UNIX File System, Journaled File System, Logical Volume Manager, disk mirroring, etc.

- The System V Release 4 file system layout described throughout this book is implemented. This file system layout is conducive to extensive file sharing which is used in NFS Diskless.

- Read-only NFS mounts such as **/usr**, **/bin**, and **/opt/**<application> are supported.

- Distributed HP-UX functionality such as context-dependent files have been removed.

- Servers can be both Series 700 and Series 800 units.

- The physical link doesn't matter so servers can use many interfaces such as IEEE 802.3 and FDDI. A server can also assign some diskless systems to one network card, and other systems to other network cards.

- Diskless systems can boot across a gateway thereby allowing subnets to be used.

- Booting is implemented with standard Boot Protocol (BOOTP) and Trivial File Transfer Protocol (TFTP) protocols.

- Clients can swap to a local disk or swap using NFS to a remote disk.

There are many additional features of NFS diskless; however, since our focus is on management let's take a closer look at this. Using SAM, all tasks related to NFS diskless administration can be performed. This means you have a single point of administration for the cluster. You have cluster wide resources, such as printers and file systems, that can be managed from any node in the cluster. You can defer some operations until a later point in time if a node is unreachable. And, of course, you can add and delete clients in SAM.

Using SAM you get a single point of administration for several NFS Diskless systems. This means that performing an operation in SAM affects all systems in the cluster. The single point of administration areas in SAM include:

- Printers/Plotters

- File Systems

- Users/Groups

- Home Directories

- Electronic Mail

- Backups

Although there is a great deal that could be covered on NFS diskless and the many improvements in this area over Distributed HP-UX, the key point from an administrative perspective is that SAM provides a central point of administration for NFS Diskless administration. All tasks related to NFS Diskless administration can be performed through SAM.

ENWARE X-station Administration (optional)

When you install the ENWARE software on your system, you'll have *ENWARE X-station Administration* as one of your top-level menu picks.

This is not a standard area of SAM but makes X-station administration easier. This does not appear unless you install the ENWARE software. You can perform the following X-station-related functions from within SAM:

1) Add an X-station
2) Remove an X-station
3) Printers, plotters
4) Installation testing and version control
5) XDM Administration

Configuring and X-station in SAM is identical to running **/opt/ enware/lbin/xtadm**.

To add an X-station, you would add provide the following information in SAM:

Name
IP address
LAN hardware address
Subnet mask
Default Gateway IP address

CHAPTER 9

Windows NT Performance Overview

Performance Monitor - Charting

To be a system administrator means, among other things, to understand the uniqueness of your environment. Among the unique characteristics of a computing environment are the applications you run; the user hogs who consume the greatest amount of system resources; the times of the day, week, month, and year when your systems are taxed most heavily; the configuration of your disks which greatly affects overall system performance; the configuration of your network including which segments are most heavily used; and a million other characteristics that no author could cover in any book. How then is a performance overview covered? I will provide an overview of the Windows NT *Performance Monitor* and show a couple of examples from installations on which I work. The rest is really up to you. No one else has even a small fraction of the knowledge you have of your installation, therefore giving you a tool to go about handling performance is the best that anyone could do.

The Windows NT *Performance Monitor* is indeed a good tool for getting started analyzing your system performance. For one thing, it is not limited to a system in your domain. You can run it locally and display information from other systems. You can perform some measurements and make the appropriate adjustments.

You invoke the *Performance Monitor* with *Programs - Administrative Tools (Common) - Performance Monitor*. The first time you invoke *Performance Monitor* you have a blank chart. The designers of Windows NT made no assumptions about what you might like to monitor; therefore they left it up to you. Most of the other Windows NT tools have defaults that come up when you invoke them, but performance management is so unique to your environment you are left to your own devices. You can, however, chart many useful items.

When you select *Edit - Add To Chart...*, a dialog window pops up with an extensive list of items you can add to the chart. Figure 9-1 shows the *Add to Chart* window.

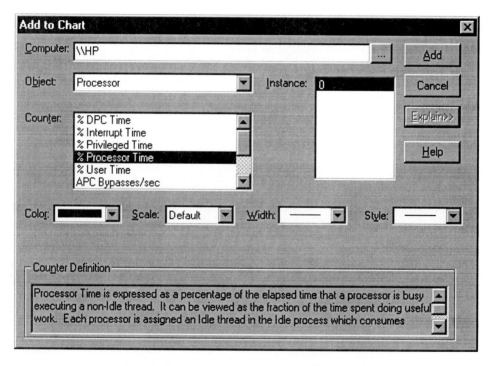

Figure 9-1 *Add to Chart* Window of Performance Monitor

The first entry in the window is the computer you wish to monitor. You can monitor systems on your network, not just the one on which you are sitting. This is one of the areas with which I am impressed with Windows NT. I was one of the early adopters of distributed computing and this is an area where Windows NT is particularly strong. Without getting into discussions over what does and does not constitute a standard, I am impressed with such functionality as the ability to monitor the performance of another Windows NT system across the network. Getting back to our computer entry, you can select the "..." next to *Computer* in which case a *Select Computer* window appears. This allows you to select other computers on which you can monitor the performance. Other domains and work groups to which you have access will appear. It may take some time to identify these remote networks. Let's stick with our local computer for monitoring an item or two.

The next entry in the window is *Object*. There are a variety of objects you can monitor. The *Object* is the way Windows NT identifies and uses system resources. In the hierarchy of system resources the *Object* is a higher-level item. Moving down the hierarchy from *Object* would be *Counter*, which we will get into shortly. Several *Counters* can be associated with an *Object* in the same way that several files can be associated with a directory.

An *Object* is not necessarily limited to being a single item. There can be several instances of an *Object* in the same way there can be several instances of a database running on a system. If you have multiple disks or processors on the system, then there will be multiple instances of these *Objects* on the system.

There are other types of hierarchy you should be aware of as well. A process is created by programs. One of your applications, such as X server software, starts a process. The process then consumes memory and has a minimum of one thread of execution associated with it. Some processes spawn multiple threads of execution. A thread executes a set instructions. Multiple threads can be executing multiple sets of instructions on different processors in a multiprocessor system.

Because of the many parameters associated with performance this tends to get to be a complex issue. My objective here is to get you started with the *Performance Monitor* and not get into excruciating detail in performance management.

Here is a bullet list of *Objects* that appeared on my system:

- Browser
- Cache
- LogicalDisk
- Memory
- NBT Connection
- NetBEUI
- NetBEUI Resource
- Objects
- Paging File
- PhysicalDisk
- Process
- Processor
- Redirector
- Server
- Server Work Queues
- System
- Thread

Some of these are obvious system resources you have seen before; others are not. I recommend you start with the painfully obvious ones such as Memory and Processor and then start to investigate some of the others as your installation matures.

Next you would select a *Counter*. The *Counter* is context sensitive. If you select the *Object* Processor to monitor, then you will receive one list of

Counters. If you select the *Object* Memory, then you will receive a different list of *Counters*.

The *Counter* you have selected may not be familiar to you. After you highlight a *Counter*, you can then hit *Explain* and a good description of that *Counter* will appear for you as shown in Figure 9-1.

When you select *Add* in the *Add To Chart* window, your selection is automatically added to the Performance Monitor.

Figure 9-2 shows the *Add to Chart* dialog box with the *Object* "Processor" and the *Counter* "% Processor Time" selected which are the defaults when you open this dialog box.

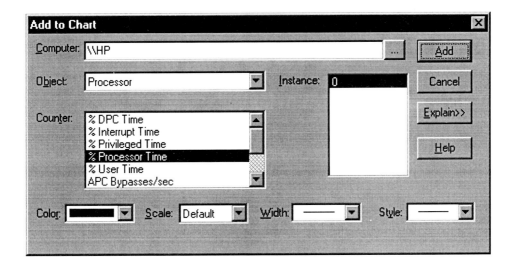

Figure 9-2 *Add to Chart* Window

When I added *% Processor Time* to the Performance Monitor it automatically began charting this for me. Figure 9-3 shows the result of charting this.

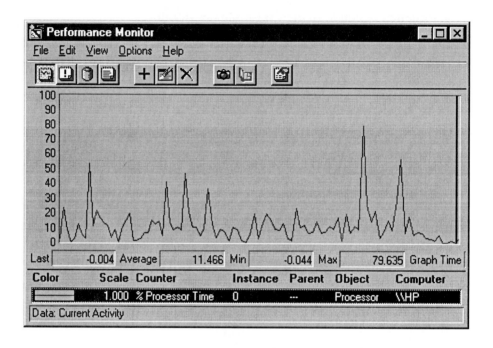

Figure 9-3 *Performance Monitor* Window

Note at the bottom of the screen shot in Figure 9-3 is a table that shows the Color, Scale, Counter, Instance, Parent, Object, and Computer related to our performance plot. Although you can't see the color, I selected red for *% Processor Time*. You are not limited to charting only one item. You can have several Counters on the screen simultaneously with different colors so they are easy to discern. The "Graph Time," which is the time it takes to create a complete chart across the window in Figure 9-3, was cut off in the figure. This time is 100 seconds.

You also have a lot of flexibility over the layout of the *Performance Manager* screen. Figure 9-3 shows graph mode. You can easily switch to histogram which has always been my preference because the performance tools I have used on other systems have used histograms. You can also change the time it takes to complete the chart across the window. Figure 9-4 shows the *Chart Options* window which allows you to change these and many other parameters. You can easily go from graph to histogram and change the update time from updating every one second to any number of seconds. There are also many other parameters you can change to customize you *Performance Monitor* window.

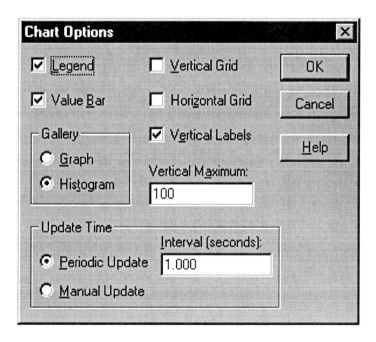

Figure 9-4 *Chart Options* Window

When I sit down on at an existing system for the first time, I want to know about four aspects of system resource utilization immediately. These are processor, disk, memory, and networking utilization. The *Performance Monitor* can give you a snapshot of these immediately to give you a feel for how the system is being used.

There are short bursts of time shown in Figure 9-3 in which the processor on my system was very active. There were also times when processor activity was low. Since the screen consists of only 100 seconds of data capture, these bursts are probably not important. You can, however, change the time during which data is captured to a much greater interval than 100 seconds and monitor system performance over long time periods.

Performance Monitor - Proactive with Alerts

What we discussed so far is using *Performance Monitor* in a reactive fashion by selecting the information we want to view and the time period over which we want to view it. We will then go about reacting to the results in the appropriate manner. We are not, however, limited to only viewing what has taken place in chart mode. We can also set up *Performance Monitor* to look for specific information and alert us when the specified conditions are met. This is alert mode.

To set up alert mode, use *View - Alert*. We can then enter the specific conditions we wish to proactively monitor with the *Edit - Add To Alert...* menu pick. Figure 9-5 shows setting up an alert for processor utilization greater than 10 percent.

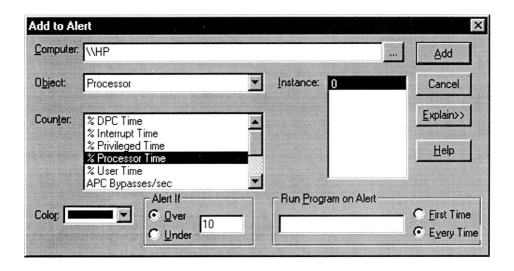

Figure 9-5 *Add to Alert* Window

You can specify the same objects and counters within objects that you could in chart mode. You therefore have a lot of control over the items you wish to monitor. Note also in Figure 9-5 that you can select a program to run if the specified alert takes place. This means you cannot only monitor for a specified set of conditions but you can also automatically take action if indeed that set of conditions is met.

Figure 9-6 shows the Performance Monitor window with alerts listed.

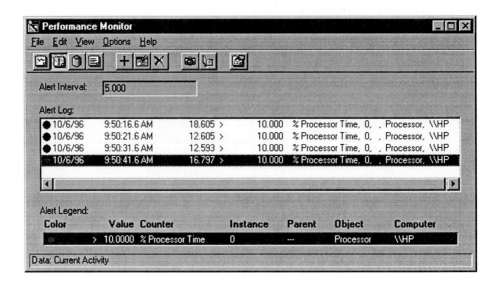

Figure 9-6 *Performance Monitor* Window with Alerts Shown

Performance Monitor - Logging

You can log information over long periods of time and later display it with *Performance Monitor*. You select *View - Log* in the *Performance Monitor* to specify the information about logging. The *Options - Log...* menu pick allows you to select a log file in which performance information will be placed. This window is shown in Figure 9-7.

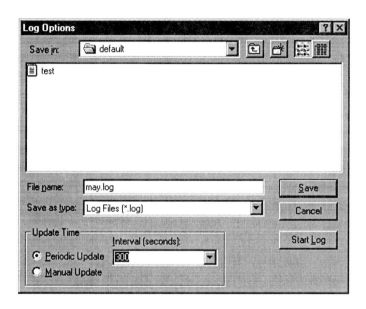

Figure 9-7 *Log Options* Window

In addition to the name I have picked (**may.log**), there is also an old **test.log** file. There is also a *Start Log* button in this window which begins logging. You can also specify an interval for saving log information. The default is 15 seconds which I have changed to 300 seconds in Figure 9-7.

After specifying this information you would then use the *Edit - Add to Log...* menu pick to specify the information you wish to log. This window is shown in Figure 9-8.

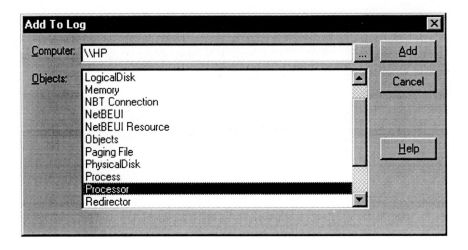

Figure 9-8 *Add To Log* Window

The information you have logged can then be viewed by selecting the *Options - Data From...* menu pick. A dialog box appears in which you can specify the log file from which to view data. The logged information will then be charted for you. If you wish to go back to seeing real-time data, you would select *Current Activity* from the *Data From...* dialog box.

There is a *Performance* tab in the *Task Manager* that has both memory and CPU usage graphs in it that is covered briefly in Chapter 11.

CHAPTER 10

HP-UX Performance Overview

Where Are Your HP-UX System Resources Going?

In this chapter we'll cover some techniques for determining how your HP-UX system resources are being used. Some of the material in this chapter was developed using HP-UX 9.x; however, the same principles and commands apply to later revisions of HP-UX.

Everyone likes setting up new systems and the excitement of seeing the system run for the first time. With system setup you get a great deal in return for your investment of time. With an instant ignition system, for instance, you spend a short amount of time in setup and you get a big return - your system is up and running. Similarly, when you perform routine system administration functions with SAM, you spend a short time running SAM and you end up completing a vital task, such as adding a user or performing a system backup.

In Chapter 2, I described a process whereby you spend about two hours unpacking boxes and connecting cables, and then you turn on the power and your HP-UX system boots. You've done a lot in a short time and it feels great. At this point it's not even lunch time and you can justify taking off the rest of the day!

If a new user were to walk up to your desk and ask you for an account, you say you would be happy to do so but this is a complex process which will take a while. Then you run SAM and in about 30 seconds the new user is added to the system! Again you're quite pleased with yourself for having done so much so quickly.

In this chapter we get into some of the "gray" areas of system administration. System resource utilization and performance monitoring are less straightforward endeavors than others covered, such as system setup and SAM. You play detective some of the time when determining how systems resources are being used and sometimes you guess at what is taking place. That's the reason I think this is where the fun begins.

When determining where system resources are going, I often find system administrators dealing with their computer systems as **SYSTEMS** for the first time. Computer systems are too often thought of as independent components. What may look like the source of a system bottleneck may just be a symptom of some other problem. Keep in mind that components of the system work together; a small problem in one area may manifest itself as a bigger problem in other areas. I'll provide some examples of what to look for throughout this chapter, but keep in mind your system is indeed unique. You have to consider your environment as you use the tools described here.

Understanding where your HP-UX system resources are going is indeed an art. There are great built-in HP-UX commands such as **iostat** and **vmstat**. There are also some fine performance monitoring tools such as HP GlancePlus/UX and HP PerfView to help you. Which tools you use and how you use them are not as clean and orderly as the topics earlier covered.

Why is it so difficult to determine where your system resources are going if there are so many great tools to assist you? To begin with, this is the information age. No one knows better than those of us who deal with information systems that the problem is there is too much information. This can be the problem when you try to determine where your system resources are going. You may end up gathering information about your system in off hours when it is not in use, thereby getting erroneous results. You may end up with long accounting reports with too much data to digest. You may end up with so many network statistics that a fleet of system administrators wouldn't have time to analyze them, let alone one overworked, albeit enthusiastic, administrator.

Since every system and network are different, I can't recommend just one approach to determining where your system resources are going. I can recommend, however, that you understand all of the tools I cover here and then determine which are best suited for your environment. You may decide that you can get all the information you need from the built-in HP-UX commands. You may, on the other hand, determine that you need the best performance tools available. Once you know what each of these techniques does and does not offer, you will be in a much better position to make this decision.

System Components

Now the big question: *What are the components of your system?* At one time we viewed the components of a system as

- **CPU**
- **Memory**
- **I/O**

Well, like all other things in this world, system components have become more complex. All of the components of your system work together, or in some cases against one another. You must, therefore, take an inventory of system components before you can begin to determine how your system resources are being used. Here is more current list of system components:

1. Applications

- **local** - These applications run locally and don't rely on other systems for either the applications or data.

- **remote** - These are applications that either run remotely or are copied from a remote system to a local system and then run locally. I consider both of these remote applications because an application that has to be copied to the local system before it is run consumes a lot of networking resources, sometimes more than an application which runs remotely would consume.

- **license servers** - Many applications require license servers to be running to ensure that you have a license available for a user who wants to run an application. In a distributed environment you may have an application with several license servers running so that if one or two license servers go down, you still have a third license server running. Because you can have many license servers running for many applications, these may be consuming substantial system resources

2. **Data** - Listing your data as a system resource may be a surprise to you. I think, however, that since most computers and applications are a means to create the data that keeps your company in business, you should indeed consider it as a system resource. In some cases, system and database administrators spend many hours planning how data will be stored in order to achieve the fastest response time. In a distributed engineering application, the location and number of data servers can have a major impact on overall system and network performance. In this respect data is indeed a system resource.

- **local data** - On local system, consumes primarily system resources.

- **remote data** - On remote system, consumes resources on local system, remote system, and network.

3. **Windowing environment and user interface**

- **X, Motif, CDE** - You will want to take a close look at the amount of system resources that can be consumed by X, Motif, and CDE. Later in this chapter when we look at programs that are consuming system resources, you will see the substantial impact these programs have.

4. **Networking** - Networking is the perceived or real bottleneck in more and more installations. Because of the increasing demand placed on networking resources by client/server applications and

other distributed environments, you need to have an understanding of the amount of networking resources your system is consuming and how busy your network is in general. Because I don't cover such advanced network management tools as HP OpenView in this book, we are going to take a look at the commands you can issue to see how busy the network interface is on a particular system and get an idea of the overall amount of traffic on the network.

5. **CPU -** Of course the CPU is a system resource. I just chose not to list it first because until you know how your system is set up in terms of applications, data, user interface, etc., it is pointless to start looking at the CPU.

6. **Memory -** Memory is the system resource I find most often needs to be increased. What sometimes looks to be a shortage of CPU capacity sometimes turns out to be a lack of memory.

7. **Input/Output (I/O) -** The real question with I/O as a system resource is how long does it take to get my applications or data to and from disk. We'll look at various ways to see what kind of I/O activity you have going on.

Commands and Tools for Determining How System Resources Are Being Used

There are a variety of approaches you can take to determine how system resources are being used. These choices range from quick snapshots that take but a few seconds to create, to long-range capacity planning programs that you may want to run for weeks or months before you even begin to analyze the data they produce. Figure 10-1 shows the level of data produced by some of the possible approaches to determining how your system resources are being consumed.

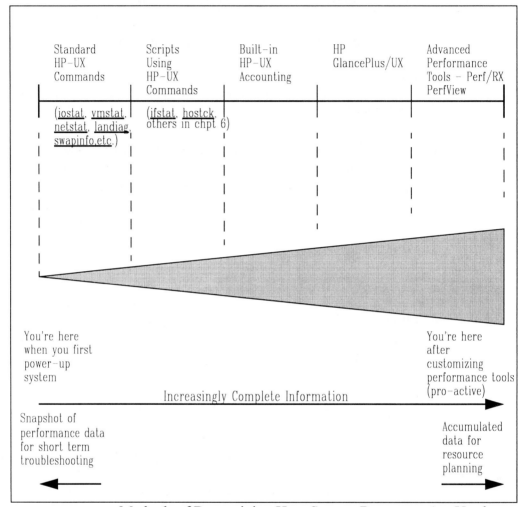

Figure 10-1   Methods of Determining How System Resources Are Used

This figure shows some commonly used techniques for determining how system resources are being used. We'll cover two of these techniques:

1. Introducing some standard HP-UX commands that give you information about system resources. These are also embedded in some scripts that are included in the last chapter.

2. Using the performance monitoring tool HP GlancePlus/UX.

These two approaches are covered in upcoming sections.

Taking Inventory

In an existing computing environment it is essential to first take an inventory of your computing resources before you begin to determine the level of system resources. The minimum you should include in this inventory are the system resources I listed earlier in this chapter (applications, data, user interface, etc.) so you will know how your network is setup before you begin to determine how your system resources are being used.

I will show examples of systems and portions of networks throughout this chapter. In order to show how system resources are being used, it is essential to know the system components you are dealing with, especially if they are scattered among systems in a distributed environment.

With existing networks this may be a long and painful process, but a process that is well worth the time. A network that has evolved over the course of 20 years will have vast inefficiencies in it that will become apparent immediately upon taking inventory. I have been asked to help improve the performance of such networks and after taking inventory I have developed a list of ways to improve the performance of systems without issuing a single HP-UX command! When you see a user's home directory on one system, her application on another, her data on a third, her application's license server on a fourth, and all of these systems on different subnets, you can quickly develop ways to improve system performance.

You may find some similarities between the examples I use in this chapter and your own computing environment. In any event, I suggest you take an inventory of what you have if you haven't already done so.

There are degrees to which you can take an inventory. You may choose a high-level inventory with little detail that is simply a drawing of your network including systems and major software. A highly detailed inventory, on the other hand, might be a detailed network diagram including all of the hardware components of which each system is comprised and a detailed list of software including what data is located on what disks and so on. The granularity of your inventory depends on what you would like to accomplish. If your goal is to visualize what systems are used for which purpose, then a high-level network diagram may be sufficient. If you need to troubleshoot a disk I/O problem, then you may need to produce a detailed inventory of a system including what files and directories are located on each disk.

Standard HP-UX Commands

To begin, let's look at some commands you can issue from the HP-UX prompt to give you some information about your system. The commands I'll cover are

- **iostat**
- **vmstat**
- **netstat**
- **landiag**
- **ps**
- **swapinfo**
- **showmount and mount**

We'll first look at each of these commands so you get an understanding of the output produced by each and how this output may be used. Later in the chapter we'll then use some of these commands in conjunction with HP GlancePlus/UX to help uncover an interesting performance problem.

I/O and CPU Statistics with iostat

The **iostat** command gives you an indication of the level of effort the CPU is putting into I/O and the amount of I/O taking place among your disks and terminals. The following example shows the **iostat -t** command, which will be executed every three seconds, and associated output from an HP-UX system. The "#" shown is the HP-UX prompt

```
# iostat -t 3
```

```
                    tty            cpu
                  tintout     us   ni   sy   id
                  78   42      2    0   28   70

device        bps sps    msps

c0t1d0          0    0       0
c0t4d0         33   .3    25.2
cot6d0          7    1    19.5

                    tty            cpu
                  tintout     us   ni   sy   id
                  66   24      0    0   30   70

device        bps sps    msps

c0t1d0         15   12    15.9
c0t4d0         36  9.7      21
cot6d0          7  1.2    13.8

                    tty            cpu
                  tintout     us   ni   sy   id
                  90   29      1    0   25   73

device        bps sps    msps

c0t1d0         12  1.7    15.5
c0t4d0         24    3    19.1
cot6d0         14  2.1    19.6

                    tty            cpu
                  tintout     us   ni   sy   id
                  48   16      1    0   16   83
```

```
device          bps sps      msps

c0t1d0            0    0         0
c0t4d0           62  9.3        18
cot6d0           12    2      17.2


                  tty                cpu
               tintout        us    ni   sy   id
                32   48        7     0   14   79

device          bps sps      msps

c0t1d0            1  0.3      14.4
c0t4d0            5  0.9      16.2
cot6d0          17129.4       18.2


                  tty                cpu
               tintout        us    ni   sy   id
                 2   40       20     1   42   27

device          bps sps      msps

c0t1d0          24830.9       20.8
c0t4d0          20329.2       18.8
cot6d0          16530.6       22.1
```

Here are descriptions of the reports you receive with **iostat** for terminals, the CPU, and mounted file systems.

For every terminal you have connected (tty), you see a "tin" and "tout", which represents the number of characters read from your terminal and the number of characters written to your terminal, respectively. The **-t** option produces this terminal report.

For your CPU, you see the percentage of time spent in user mode ("us"), the percentage of time spent running user processes at a low priority called nice ("ni"), the percentage of time spent in system mode ("sy"), and the percentage of time the CPU is idle ("id").

For every locally mounted file system, you receive information on the kilobytes transferred per second ("bps"), number of seeks per second ("sps"), and number of milliseconds per average seek ("msps"). For disks that are NFS-mounted or disks on client nodes of your server, you will not receive a report; **iostat** reports only on locally mounted file systems.

When viewing the output of **iostat,** there are some parameters to take note of.

First, note the time your CPU is spending in the four categories shown. I have worked on systems with poor performance that the administrator assumed to be a result of a slow CPU when the "id" number was very high indicating the CPU was actually idle most of the time. If the CPU is mostly idle, the chances are the bottleneck is not the CPU but I/O, memory, or networking. If the CPU is indeed busy most of the time ("id" is very low), see if any processes are running "nice" (check the "ni" number). It may be that there are some background processes consuming a lot of CPU time that can be changed to run "nice."

Second, compare the milliseconds per average seek ("msps") for all of the disks you have mounted. If you have three identical disks mounted, yet the "msps" for one of the disks is substantially higher than the others, then you may be overworking it while the others remain mostly idle. If so, distribute the work load evenly among your disks so that you get as close to the same number of accesses per disk as possible. Note that a slower disk will always have a higher "msps" than a faster disk, so put your most often accessed information on your faster disks. The "msps" for a disk is usually around 20 milliseconds, as in all three disks (1s0, 4s0, and 6s0) in the last example. A CD-ROM would have a much higher msps of approximately 200 milliseconds.

Virtual Memory Statistics with vmstat

vmstat provides virtual memory statistics. It provides information on the status of processes, virtual memory, paging activity, faults, and the breakdown of the percentage of CPU time. In the following example, the output was produced ten times at five-second intervals. The first argument to the

vmstat command is the interval; the second is the number of times you would like output produced:

```
# vmstat 5 10:
```

procs			memory		page					faults			cpu		
r	b	w	avm	free	re	at	pi	po	fr	de	sr	in	sy	cs	us	sy	id
4	0	0	1161	2282	6	22	48	0	0	0	0	429	289	65	44	18	38
9	0	0	1161	1422	4	30	59	0	0	0	0	654	264	181	18	20	62
6	0	0	1409	1247	2	19	37	0	0	0	0	505	316	130	47	10	43
1	0	0	1409	1119	1	10	19	0	0	0	0	508	254	180	69	15	16
2	0	0	1878	786	0	1	6	0	0	0	0	729	294	217	75	17	8
2	0	0	1878	725	0	0	3	0	0	0	0	561	688	435	67	32	1
2	0	0	2166	98	0	0	20	0	0	0	66	728	952	145	8	14	78
1	0	0	2310	90	0	0	20	0	0	0	171	809	571	159	16	21	63
1	0	0	2310	190	0	0	8	1	3	0	335	704	499	176	66	14	20
1	0	0	2316	311	0	0	3	1	5	0	376	607	945	222	4	11	85

You will get more out of the **vmstat** command than you want. Here is a brief description of the categories of information produced by **vmstat**.

Processes are classified into one of three categories: runnable ("r"), blocked on I/O or short-term resources ("b"), or swapped ("w").

Next you will see information about memory. "avm" is the number of virtual memory pages owned by processes that have run within the last 20 seconds. If this number is roughly the size of physical memory minus your kernel, then you are near paging. The "free" column indicates the number of pages on the system's free list. It doesn't mean the process is done running and these pages won't be accessed again; it just means they have not been accessed recently. I suggest you ignore this column.

Next is paging activity. Only the first field (re) is useful. It shows the pages that were reclaimed. These pages made it to the free list but were later referenced and had to be salvaged. Check to see that "re" is a low number. If you are reclaiming pages which were thought to be free by the system, then you are wasting valuable time salvaging these. Reclaiming pages is also a symptom that you are short on memory.

Next you see the number of faults in three categories: interrupts per second, which usually come from hardware ("in"), system calls per second ("sy"), and context switches per second ("cs").

The final output is CPU usage percentage for user ("us"), system ("sy"), and idle ("id"). This is not as complete as the **iostat** output, which also shows **nice** entries.

You want to verify that the runnable processes ("r") value is higher than the blocked ("b") value and runnable but swapped ("w") processes value. If too many processes are blocked and swapped, your users will get a slower response time. In the example we'll review later in this chapter you'll see many swapped ("w") process and no runnable ("r") or blocked ("b") processes, indicating a great deal of swapping is taking place.

Whenever you see entries in the blocked ("b") or runnable but swapped ("w") columns, you see evidence that processes are standing still. You want to identify the source of the blocked and runnable but swapped processes. The reason will usually be insufficient RAM in your system. Swapped processes are those that have been moved from RAM to disk in an effort to free up RAM for other processes. You may want to look at GlancePlus to do more detailed troubleshooting of memory under the "Memory Detail" screen.

Network Statistics with netstat

netstat provides information related to network statistics. Since network bandwidth has as much to do with performance as the CPU and memory in some networks, you want to get an idea of the level of network traffic you have.

There are two forms of **netstat** that I use to obtain network statistics. The first is **netstat -i** which shows the state of interfaces that are autoconfigured. Since I am most often interested in getting a summary of lan0, I issue this command. Although **netstat -i** gives a good rundown of lan0, such as the network it is on, its name and so on, it does not show useful statistical information.

The following diagram shows the output of **netstat -i**.

```
# netstat -i

Name    Mtu     Network     Address     Ipkts     Ierrs   Opkts     Oerrs   Col

lan0    1497    151.150     a4410.e.h.c  242194    120     107665    23      19884
```

netstat doesn't provide as much extraneous information as **iostat** and **vmstat**. Put another way, most of what you get from **netstat** is useful. Here is a description of the nine fields in the **netstat** example.

Name	The name of your network interface (Name), in this case "lan0".
Mtu	The "maximum transmission unit" which is the maximum packet size sent by the interface card.
Network	The network address of the LAN to which the interface card is connected (151.150).
Address	The host name of your system. This is the symbolic name of your system as it appears in the **/etc/hosts** file.

Start of statistical information:

Ipkts	The number of packets received by the interface card, in this case lan0.
Ierrs	The number of errors detected on incoming packets by the interface card.
Opkts	The number of packets transmitted by the interface card.
Oerrs	The number of errors detected during the transmission of packets by the interface card.
Collis	The number of collisions (Collis) that resulted from packet traffic.

netstat provides cumulative data since the node was last powered up; you might have a long elapsed time over which data was accumulated. If you are interested in seeing useful statistical information, you can use **netstat** with different options. You can also specify an interval to report statistics. I usually ignore the first entry since it shows all data since the system was last powered up. This means the data includes non-prime hours when the system was idle. I prefer to view data at the time the system is working its hardest. This second **netstat** example provides network interface information every five seconds.

```
# netstat -I lan0 5

(lan 0) -> input                      output

packets        errs      packets       errs       colls

14600725       14962     962080        0          9239

    217        0         202           0          2

    324        0         198           0          0

    275        0         272           0          3

    282        0         204           0          4

    297        0         199           0          2

    277        0         147           0          1

    202        0         304           0          2
```

With this example you get multiple outputs of what is taking place on the LAN interface. I am showing only half the output. There are another five columns that show the "Total" of all the same information. As I mentioned earlier, you may want to ignore the first output since it includes information over a long time period. This may include a time when your network was idle and therefore the data is not important to you.

You can specify the network interface on which you want statistics reported by using **-I interface**; in the case of the example it was **-I lan0**. An interval of five seconds was also used in this example.

Analyzing **netstat** statistical information is intuitive. You want to verify that the collisions (Coll) are much lower than the packets transmitted (Opkts). Collisions occur on output from your LAN interface. Every collision your LAN interface encounters slows down the network. You will get varying opinions on what is too many collisions. If your collisions are less than 5 percent of "Opkts," you're probably in good shape and better off spending your time analyzing some other system resource. If this number is high, you may want to consider segmenting your network in some way such as by installing networking equipment between portions of the network that don't share a lot of data.

As a rule of thumb, if you reduce the number of packets you are receiving and transmitting ("Ipkts" and "Opkts"), then you will have less overall network traffic and fewer collisions. Keep this in mind as you plan your network or upgrades to your systems. You may want to have two LAN cards in systems that are in constant communication. That way these systems have a "private" LAN over which to communicate and do not adversely affect the performance of other systems on the network. One LAN interface on each system is devoted to intrasystem communication. This provides a "tight" communication path among systems which usually act as servers. The second LAN interface is used to communicate with any systems which are usually clients on a larger network.

You can also obtain information related to routing with **netstat** (see the interoperability chapter covering networking.) The **-r** option to **netstat** shows the routing tables, which you usually want to know, and the **-n** option can be used to print network addresses as numbers rather than as names. In the following examples **netstat** is issued with the **-r** option (this will be used when describing the **netstat** output) and the **-rn** options so you can compare the two outputs.

```
$ netstat -r
```

Routing tables

Destination	Gateway	Flags	Refs	Use	Interface	Pmtu
hp700	localhost	UH	0	28	lo0	4608
default	router1	UG	0	0	lan0	4608
128.185.61	system1	U	347	28668	lan0	1500

```
$ netstat -rn
```

Routing tables

Destination	Gateway	Flags	Refs	Use	Interface	Pmtu
127.0.0.1	127.0.0.1	UH	0	28	lo0	4608

Routing tables

Destination	Gateway	Flags	Refs	Use	Interface	Pmtu
default	128.185.61.1	UG	0	0	lan0	4608
128.185.61	128.185.61.2	U	347	28668	lan0	1500

With **netstat** there is some information provided about the router which is the middle entry. The **-r** option shows information about routing but there are many other useful options to this command. Of particular interest in this output is "Flags," which defines the type of routing that takes place. Here are descriptions of the most common flags from the HP-UX manual pages.

1=U   Route to a *network* via a gateway that is the local host itself.

3=UG   Route to a *network* via a gateway that is the remote host.

5=UH   Route to a *host* via a gateway which is the local host itself.

7=UGH   Route to a *host* via a remote gateway which is a host.

The first line is for the local host or loopback interface called **lo0** at address 127.0.0.1 (you can see this address in the **netstat -rn** example). The UH flags indicate the destination address is the local host itself. This class A address allows a client and server on the same host to communicate with one another with TCP/IP. A datagram sent to the loopback interface won't go out onto the network; it will simply go through the loopback.

The second line is for the default route. This entry says send packets to router1 if a more specific route can't be found. In this case the router has a UG under Flags. Some routers are configured with a U; others, such as the one in this example, with a UG. I've found that I usually end up determining through trial and error whether a U or UG is required. If there is a U in Flags and I am unable to ping a system on the other side of a router, a UG usually fixes the problem.

The third line is for the system's network interface **lan0**. This means to use this network interface for packets to be sent to 128.185.61.

Network Statistics with landiag and lanadmin

/usr/sbin/landiag (lanadmin and landiag are the same program; I'll use landiag in this explanation) provides additional information related to network statistics. When you run landiag, a menu appears that gives you the option to perform various functions, one of which is display information related to the LAN interface. The following page shows the output of landiag when this option is selected.

```
                    LAN INTERFACE STATUS DISPLAY
                         Tues, 15:47:20
Network Management ID              = 4
Description                        = lan0 Hewlett-Packard LAN Intfc
Type (value)                       = active
MTU Size                           = 1500
Speed                              = 10000000
Station Address                    = 0x80009874511
Administration Status (value)      = up(1)
Operation Status (value)           = up(1)
Last Change                        = 3735
Inbound Octets                     = 912
Inbound Unicast Packets            = 0
Inbound Non-Unicast Packets        = 4518
Inbound Discards                   = 0
Inbound Errors                     = 0
Inbound Unknown Protocols          = 0
Outbound Octets                    = 569144
Outbound Unicast Packets           = 4
Outbound Non-Unicast Packets       = 4518
Outbound Discards                  = 0
Outbound Errors                    = 0
Outbound Queue Length              = 0
Specific                           = 655367

Ethernet-like Statistics Group

Index                              = 4
Alignment Errors                   = 0
FCS Errors                         = 0
Single Collision Frames            = 0
Multiple Collision Frames          = 0
Deferred Transmissions             = 0
Late Collisions                    = 0
Excessive Collisions               = 0
Internal MAC Transmit Errors       = 0
Carrier Sense Errors               = 0
Frames Too Long                    = 0
Internal MAC Errors                = 0
```

```
LAN Interface test mode. LAN Interface Net Mgmt ID = 4
clear                     = Clear statistics registers
display                   = Display LAN intfc status and registers
end                       = End LAN Interface Administration
menu                      = Display this menu
nmid                      = Network Management ID of the LAN intfc
quit                      = Terminate diagnostic, return to shell
reset                     = Reset LAN Interface to execute self-test
Enter Command:
```

landiag gives more detailed information about the LAN interface than **netstat**. The type of interface, Maximum Transfer Unit (MTU), speed, administration and operation status (a quick way to see if your interface is up), and the LAN interface address in hex. The hex address is often used when access codes are generated for application software or for generating client kernels.

landiag also gives much more detailed error information. Although any error slows down your network, having more detailed information on the type of errors and collisions may be helpful in troubleshooting a problem.

With **landiag** you can also "reset" the network interface which is sometimes helpful when the network interface doesn't seem to be working such as when the LAN interface does not **ping** itself.

Check Processes with ps

To find the answer to "What is my system doing?", use **ps -ef**. This command provides information about every running process on your system. If, for instance, you wanted to know if NFS is running, you would simply type **ps -ef** and look for NFS daemons. Although **ps** tells you every process that is running on your system, it doesn't provide a good summary of the level of system resources being consumed. The other commands we have covered to this point are superior resource assessment commands. On the other hand, I would guess **ps** is the most often issued system administration command. There are a number of options you can use with **ps**. I normally use **e** and **f** which provide information about every ("e") running process and lists this information in full ("f"). The following example is a partial **ps -ef** listing.

```
# ps -ef
```

UID	PID	PPID	C	STIME	TTY	TIME	COMMAND
root	0	0	0	Jan 2	?	0:00	swapper
root	1	0	0	Jan 2	?	0:01	/etc/init
root	2	0	0	Jan 2	?	0:01	vhand
root	3	0	0	Jan 2	?	0:02	statdaemon
root	8	0	0	Jan 2	?	0:01	unhashdaemon
root	6	0	0	Jan 2	?	0:02	sockregd
root	11	0	0	Jan 2	?	0:01	syncdaemon
root	45	0	0	Jan 2	?	0:02	syncer
lp	49	0	0	Jan 2	?	0:04	lpsched
root	129	1	0	08:07:33	?	0:00	/etc/cron
oracle	2079	2071	0	07:34:22	?	9:22	oracle
daemon	2088	98	0	08:23:11	ttyp0	8:23	/usr/bin/X11
becker	278	57	0	09:22:45	ttyp2	5:21	ANSYS
lori	234	67	0	08:23:43	ttyp3	6:33	ileaf

Here is a brief description of the headings:

UID	The user ID of the process owner.
PID	The process ID. (You can use this number to kill the process.)
PPID	The process ID of the parent process.
C	Process utilization for scheduling.
STIME	Start time of the process.
TTY	The controlling terminal for the process.
TIME	The cumulative execution time for the process.
COMMAND	The command name and arguments.

ps gives a quick profile of the processes running on your system. If you issue the **ps** command and find a process is hung, you can issue the **kill** command. **kill** is a utility that sends a signal to the process you identify. The most common signal to send is "SIGKILL" which terminates the process. There are other signals you can send to the process, but SIGKILL is the most common. As an alternative to sending the signal, you could send the corresponding signal number. The **kill** described here is either **/usr/bin/kill** or **kill** from the default POSIX shell in HP-UX. The other shells also have **kill** commands. A list of signal numbers and corresponding signals is shown next.

Signal number	Signal
0	SIGNULL
1	SIGHUP
2	SIGINT
3	SIGQUIT
9	SIGKILL
15	SIGTERM
24	SIGSTOP
25	SIGTSTP
26	SIGCONT

To kill the last process shown in this **ps** example, you would issue the following command:

```
$ kill -9 234
    |    |   |
    |    |   |> process id (PID)
    |    |> signal number
    |> kill command to terminate the process
```

Show Remote Mounts with showmount

showmount is used to show all remote systems (clients) that have
mounted a local file system. **showmount** is useful for determining the file
systems that are most often mounted by clients with NFS. The output of
showmount is particularly easy to read because it lists the host name and
the directory which was mounted by the client

NFS servers often end up serving many NFS clients that were not
originally intended to be served. This ends up consuming additional HP-
UX system resources on the NFS server as well as additional network
bandwidth. Keep in mind that any data transferred from an NFS server to
an NFS client consumes network bandwith and in some cases may be a
substantial amount of bandwith if large files or applications are being
transferred from the NFS server to the client. The following example is a
partial output of **showmount** taken from a system that is used as an example later in this chapter.

```
# showmount -a

hp100.ct.mp.com:/applic

hp101.ct.mp.com:/applic

hp102.cal.mp.com:/applic

hp103.cal.mp.com:/applic

hp104.cal.mp.com:/applic

hp105.cal.mp.com:/applic

hp106.cal.mp.com:/applic

hp107.cal.mp.com:/applic

hp108.cal.mp.com:/applic

hp109.cal.mp.com:/applic

hp100.cal.mp.com:/usr/users

hp101.cal.mp.com:/usr/users
```

```
# showmount -a
```

hp102.cal.mp.com:/usr/users

hp103.cal.mp.com:/usr/users

hp104.cal.mp.com:/usr/users

hp105.cal.mp.com:/usr/users

hp106.cal.mp.com:/usr/users

hp107.cal.mp.com:/usr/users

hp108.cal.mp.com:/usr/users

hp109.cal.mp.com:/usr/users

There are the three following options to the **showmount** command:

-a prints output in the format "name:directory" as shown above.

-d lists all of the local directories that have been remotely mounted by clients.

-e prints a list of exported file systems.

The following are examples of **showmount -d** and **showmount -e**.

```
# showmount -d
```

/applic

/usr/users

/usr/oracle

/usr/users/emp.data

/network/database

/network/users

/tmp/working

```
# showmount -e

export list for server101.cal.mp.com

/applic

/usr/users

/cdrom
```

Show Swap with swapinfo

If your system has insufficient main memory for all of the information it needs to work with, it will move pages of information to your swap area or swap entire processes to your swap area. Pages that were most recently used are kept in main memory while those not recently used will be the first moved out of main memory.

I find that many system administrators spend an inordinate amount of time trying to determine what is the right amount of swap space for their system. This is *not* a parameter you want to leave to a rule of thumb. You can get a good estimate of the amount of swap you require by considering the following three factors:

1. How much swap is recommended by the application(s) you run? Use the swap size recommended by your applications. Application vendors tend to be realistic when recommending swap space. There is sometimes competition among application vendors to claim the lowest memory and CPU requirements in order to keep the overall cost of solutions as low as possible, but swap space recommendations are usually realistic.

2. How many applications will you run simultaneously? If you are running several applications, sum the swap space recommended for

each application you plan to run simultaneously. If you have a database application that recommends 200 MBytes of swap and a development tool that recommends 100 MBytes of swap, then configure your system with 300 MBytes of swap minimum.

3. Will you be using substantial system resources on periphery functionality such as NFS? The nature of NFS is to provide access to file systems, some of which may be very large, so this may have an impact on your swap space requirements.

You can view the amount of swap being consumed on your system with **swapinfo**. The following is an example output of **swapinfo**.

```
# swapinfo

          Kb        Kb       Kb       PCT      START/   Kb
TYPE      AVAIL     USED     FREE     USED     LIMIT    RESERVE   PR    NAME
                                                                 I
dev       204505    8401     196104   4%       820534   -         1     /dev/vg00/lvol2

reserve   -         30724    -30724

memory    46344     25136    21208    54%
```

Here is a brief overview of what **swapinfo** gives you.

In the previous example the "TYPE" field indicated whether the swap was "dev" for device, "reserve" for paging space on reserve, or "memory" which is RAM that can be used to hold pages if all of the paging areas are in use.

"Kb AVAIL" is the total swap space available in 1024 byte blocks. This includes both used and unused swap. The previous example shows roughly 204 MBytes of device swap.

"Kb USED" is the current number of 1024 byte blocks in use. The previous example shows only about 8.4 MBytes of swap in use.

"Kb FREE" is the difference between "Kb AVAIL" and "Kb USED". In the previous example this is 204 MBytes minus 8 MBytes or roughly 196 MBytes.

"PCT USED" is the "Kb USED" divided by "Kb AVAIL" or 4 percent in the previous example for device and 54 percent for memory.

"START/LIMIT" is the block address of the start of the swap area.

"Kb RESERVE" is "-" for device swap or the number of 1024 byte blocks for file system swap.

"PRI" is the priority of the given to this swap area.

"NAME" is the device name for the swap device.

You can also issue the **swapinfo** command with a series of options. Here are some of the options you can include:

-m to display output of **swapinfo** in MBytes rather than 1024 byte blocks.

-d prints information related to device swap areas only.

-f prints information about file system swap areas only.

sar: The System Activity Reporter

sar is another HP-UX command for gathering information about activities on your system. There are many useful options to **sar**. I'll briefly describe the three that are most often used.

sar -u	Report CPU utilization with headings %usr, %sys, %wio idle with some processes waiting for block I/O, %idle. This is similar to the **iostat** and **vmstat** CPU reports.
sar -b	Report buffer cache activity. A database application such as Oracle would recommend you use this option to see the effectiveness of buffer cache use.
sar -w	Report system swapping activity.

timex to Analyze a Command

If you have a specific command you want to find out more about you can use **timex**. **timex** reports the elapsed time, user time, and system time spent in the execution of a command you specify.

HP GlancePlus/UX

Using HP-UX commands to get a better understanding of what your system is doing requires you to do a lot of work. In the first case (issuing HP-UX commands) you get the advantage of obtaining data about what is taking place on your system that very second. Unfortunately you can't always issue additional commands to probe deeper into an area, such as a process, that you want to know more about.

Now I'll describe another technique - a tool that can help get useful data in real time, allow you to investigate a specific process, and not bury you in reports. This tool is HP GlancePlus/UX (GlancePlus).

Figure 10-2 shows one of several interactive screens of GlancePlus. There is also a Motif version of GlancePlus. I chose to use the character-based version of GlancePlus because this will run on any display, either graphics or character based, and the many colors used by the Motif version of GlancePlus do not show up well in a book.

Two features of this screen are worth noticing immediately:

1. Four histograms at the top of the screen give you a graphical representation of your CPU, Disk, Memory, and Swap Utilization in a format much easier to assimilate than a column of numbers.

2. The "Process Summary" has columns similar to **ps -ef** which many system administrators are familiar and comfortable with. Glance-Plus, however, gives you the additional capability of filtering out processes that are using very few system resources by specifying thresholds.

Using GlancePlus you can take a close look at your system in many areas including the following:

- Global Summary of your system (shown in the example)
- CPU
- Memory
- Swap Space
- Disk
- LAN Detail
- NFS by System
- PRM Summary (Process Resource Manager)
- I/O by File System
- I/O by Device
- I/O by Logical Volume
- System Tables

Figure 10-2 is a GlancePlus screen shot.

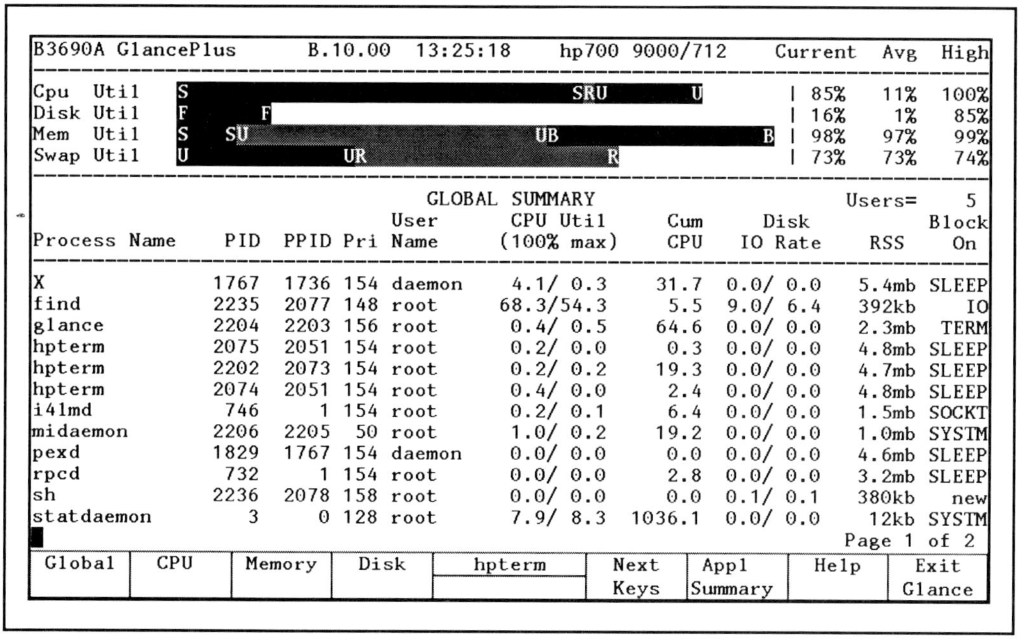

```
B3690A GlancePlus       B.10.00   13:25:18    hp700 9000/712    Current  Avg   High
─────────────────────────────────────────────────────────────────────────────────
Cpu  Util  S                            SRU              U    | 85%    11%   100%
Disk Util  F     F                                           | 16%     1%    85%
Mem  Util  S   SU                        UB               B  | 98%    97%    99%
Swap Util  U            UR                       R          | 73%    73%    74%
─────────────────────────────────────────────────────────────────────────────────
                              GLOBAL SUMMARY                       Users=    5
                            User    CPU Util      Cum      Disk           Block
Process Name    PID  PPID Pri Name  (100% max)    CPU    IO Rate    RSS      On
─────────────────────────────────────────────────────────────────────────────────
X              1767  1736 154 daemon  4.1/ 0.3    31.7   0.0/ 0.0  5.4mb  SLEEP
find           2235  2077 148 root   68.3/54.3     5.5   9.0/ 6.4  392kb     IO
glance         2204  2203 156 root    0.4/ 0.5    64.6   0.0/ 0.0  2.3mb   TERM
hpterm         2075  2051 154 root    0.2/ 0.0     0.3   0.0/ 0.0  4.8mb  SLEEP
hpterm         2202  2073 154 root    0.2/ 0.2    19.3   0.0/ 0.0  4.7mb  SLEEP
hpterm         2074  2051 154 root    0.4/ 0.0     2.4   0.0/ 0.0  4.8mb  SLEEP
i41md           746     1 154 root    0.2/ 0.1     6.4   0.0/ 0.0  1.5mb  SOCKT
midaemon       2206  2205  50 root    1.0/ 0.2    19.2   0.0/ 0.0  1.0mb  SYSTM
pexd           1829  1767 154 daemon  0.0/ 0.0     0.0   0.0/ 0.0  4.6mb  SLEEP
rpcd            732     1 154 root    0.0/ 0.0     2.8   0.0/ 0.0  3.2mb  SLEEP
sh             2236  2078 158 root    0.0/ 0.0     0.0   0.1/ 0.1  380kb    new
statdaemon        3     0 128 root    7.9/ 8.3  1036.1   0.0/ 0.0   12kb  SYSTM
                                                              Page 1 of 2
─────────────────────────────────────────────────────────────────────────────────
 Global   CPU   Memory   Disk     hpterm     Next    Appl     Help    Exit
                                             Keys  Summary            Glance
```

Figure 10-2   HP GlancePlus/UX Global Screen Shot

Since the Global Summary shown in the example tells you where your system resources are going at the highest level, I'll start my description here. Keep in mind that the information shown on this screen can be updated at any interval you choose. If your system is running in a steady-state mode, you may want to have a long interval as you don't expect things to much change. On the other hand, you may have a dynamic environment and want to see the histograms and other information updated every few seconds. In either case, you can change the update interval to suit your needs.

Global Screen Description

The Global screen provides an overview of the state of system resources and active processes.

The top section of the screen (the histogram section) is common to the many screens of GlancePlus. The bottom section of the screen displays a summary of active processes.

Line 1 provides the product and version number of GlancePlus, the time, name of your system, and system type.

Line 3 provides information about the overall state of the CPU. This tends to be the single most important piece of information administrators want to know about their system - Is my CPU overworked?

The CPU Utilization bar is divided into four parts:

1. "S" indicates the amount of time spent on "system" activities such as context switching and system calls.

2. "N" indicates the amount of time spent running "nice" user processes (those run at a low priority).

3. "U" indicates the amount of time spent running user processes.

4. "R" indicates real-time processes.

The far right of line 3 shows the percentage of CPU utilization. If your system is "CPU-Bound," you will consistently see this number near 100 percent. You get statistics for Current, Average (since analysis was begun), and High.

Line 4 shows Disk Utilization for the busiest mounted disk. This bar indicates the percentage of File System and Virtual Memory disk I/O over the update interval. This bar is divided into two parts:

1. "F" indicates the amount of file system activity of user reads and writes and other non-paging activities.

2. "V" indicates the percentage of disk I/O devoted to paging virtual memory.

The Current, Avg, and High statistics have the same meaning as in the CPU Utilization description.

Line 5 shows the system memory utilization. This bar is divided into three parts:

1. "S" indicates the amount of memory devoted to system use.

2. "U" indicates the amount of memory devoted to user programs and data.

3. "B" indicates the amount of memory devoted to buffer cache.

The Current, Avg, and High statistics have the same meaning as in the CPU Utilization description.

Line 6 shows swap space information, which is divided into two parts:

1. "R" indicates reserved but not in use.

2. "U" indicates swap space in use.

All three of these areas (CPU, Memory, and Disk) may be further analyzed by using the F2, F3, and F4 function keys, respectively. When you select one of these keys, you move from the "Global Summary" screen to a screen that provides more in-depth functions in the selected area. In addition, more detailed screens are available for LAN, NFS, Diskless Server, Swap, and System Table. Since most investigation beyond the Global screen takes place on the CPU, Memory, and Disk screens, I'll describe these in more detail shortly.

The bottom of the Global screen shows the active processes running on your system. Because there are typically many processes running on an HP-UX system, you may want to consider using the "o" command to set a threshold for CPU utilization. If you set a threshold of 5 percent, for instance, then only processes that exceed average CPU utilization over the interval will be displayed. There are other types of thresholds that can be specified such as the amount of RAM used (Resident Size). If you specify thresholds, you see only the processes you're most interested in, that is, those consuming the greatest system resources.

There is a line for each active process that meets the threshold requirements you defined. There may be more than one page of processes to display. The message in the bottom-right corner of the screen indicates which page you are on. You can scroll forward to view the next page with "f" and backwards with "b." Usually only a few processes consume most of your system resources, so I recommend setting the thresholds so that only one page of processes is displayed.

Here is a brief summary of the process headings.

Process Name The name or abbreviation used to load the executable program.

PID   The process identification number.

PPID   The PID of the parent process.

Pri   The priority of the process. The lower the number, the higher the priority. System-level processes usually run between 0 and 127. Other processes usually run between 128 and 255. "Nice" processes are those with the lowest priority and will have the largest number.

User Name   Name of the user who started the process.

CPU Util   The first number is the percentage of CPU utilization this process consumed over the update interval. The second number is the percentage of CPU utilization this process consumed since GlancePlus was invoked. I'm skeptical of using GlancePlus, or any other HP-UX command, to get data over an extended period. I rarely use the second number under this heading. If you have been using GlancePlus for some time but only recently started a process that consumes a great deal of CPU, you may find that the second number is very low. This is because the process you are analyzing has indeed consumed very little of the CPU since GlancePlus was invoked despite being a highly CPU-intensive process.

Cum CPU   The total CPU time used by the process. GlancePlus uses the "midaemon" to gather information. If the **midaemon** started before the process, you will get an accurate measure of cumulative CPU time used by the process. To use this column, start the **midaemon** in the **/etc/rc** script so that you start gathering information on all processes as soon as the system is booted.

Disk IO Rate   The first number is the average disk I/O rate per second over the last update interval. The second number is the average disk I/O rate since GlancePlus was started or the process was started. Disk I/O can mean a lot of different things. Disk I/O could mean taking blocks of data off the disk for the first time and putting them in RAM, or it could be entirely paging and swapping. Some processes will simply require a lot more Disk I/

O than others. When this number is very high, however, take a close look at whether or not you have enough RAM.

RSS Size   The amount of RAM in KBytes that is consumed by the process. This is called the Resident Size. Everything related to the process that is in RAM is included in this column, such as the process's data, stack, text, and shared memory segments. This is a good column to take a look at. Since slow systems are often erroneously assumed to be CPU-bound, I always make a point of looking at this column to identify the amount of RAM that the primary applications are using. This is often revealing. Some applications use a small amount of RAM but use large data sets, a point often overlooked when RAM calculations are made. This column shows all of the RAM your process is currently using.

Block On   The reason the process was blocked (unable to run). If the process is currently blocked, you will see why. If the process is running, you will see why it was last blocked. There are many reasons a process could be blocked. Here is a list of the most common reasons for the process being blocked.

Abbreviation	Reason for the Blocked Process
CACHE	Waiting for a cache buffer to become available
DISK	Waiting for a disk operation to complete
DUX	Waiting for a diskless transfer to complete
INODE	Waiting for an inode operation to complete
IO	Waiting for a non-disk I/O to complete
IPC	Waiting for shared memory operation to complete
LAN	Waiting for a LAN operation to complete
MBUF	Waiting for a memory buffer
MESG	Waiting for message queue operation to complete

NFS	Waiting for a NFS request to complete
PIPE	Waiting for data from a pipe
PRI	Waiting because a higher-priority process is running
RFA	Waiting for a Remote File Access to complete
SEM	Waiting for a semaphore to become available
SLEEP	Waiting because the process called **sleep** or **wait**
SOCKT	Waiting for a socket operation to complete
SYS	Waiting for system resources
TERM	Waiting for a terminal transfer
VM	Waiting for a virtual memory operation to complete
OTHER	Waiting for a reason GlancePlus can't determine

CPU Detail Screen Description

If the Global screen indicates that the CPU is overworked, you'll want to refer to the CPU detail screen shown in Figure 10-3. It can provide useful information about the seven types of states that GlancePlus reports.

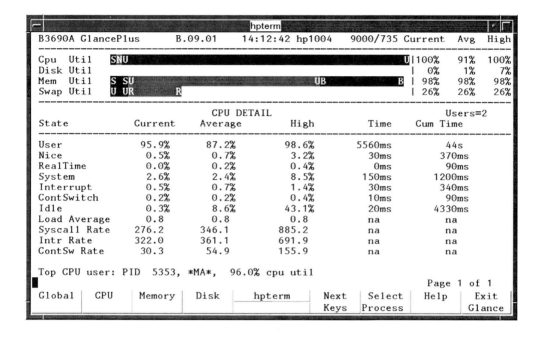

Figure 10-3 HP GlancePlus/UX CPU Detail Screen Shot

For each of the seven types of states there are columns that provide additional information. Here is a description of the columns.

Current	Displays the percentage of CPU time devoted to this state over the last time interval.
Average	Displays the average percentage of CPU time spent in this state since GlancePlus was started.
High	Displays the highest percentage of CPU time devoted to this state since GlancePlus was started.
Time	Displays the CPU time spent in this state over the last interval.

Cum Time   Displays the total amount of CPU time spent in this state since GlancePlus was started.

Here is a description of the seven states.

User   CPU time spent executing user activities under normal priority.

Nice   CPU time spent running user code in nice mode.

Realtime   CPU time spent executing real-time processes which run at a high priority.

System   CPU time executing system calls and programs.

Interrupt   CPU time spent executing system interrupts. A high value here may indicate of a lot of I/O, such as paging and swapping.

ContSwitch   CPU time spent context switching between processes.

Idle   CPU time spent idle.

The CPU screen also shows your system's run queue length or load average. The current, average, and high values for the number of runnable processes waiting for the CPU are shown. You may want to get a gauge of your system's run queue length when the system is mostly idle and compare these numbers to those you see when your system is in normal use.

The final area reported on the CPU screen is load average, system calls, interrupts, and context switches. I don't inspect these too closely because if one of these is high, it is normally the symptom of a problem and not the cause of a problem. If you correct a problem, you will see these numbers reduced.

You can use GlancePlus to view all of the CPU's in your system as shown in Figure 10-4.

```
B3692A GlancePlus       B.10.00  14:23:59    hp800 9000/829   Current  Avg  High
--------------------------------------------------------------------------------
Cpu  Util   S SUU                                          |  10%    5%   27%
Disk Util   F                                    F        |  55%   12%   58%
Mem  Util   SSU  UB        B                               |  25%   21%   25%
Swap Util   U  UR  R                                       |  10%    8%   10%
--------------------------------------------------------------------------------
                                 ALL CPUs DETAIL                Users=    3
CPU    Util   LoadAvg(1/5/15 min)   ContSw    Last Pid
--------------------------------------------------------------------------------
  0     6.0     0.2/  0.1/  0.0       193       6831
  1    13.0     0.1/  0.0/  0.0       354         17
  2     5.6     0.0/  0.0/  0.0       195         18
  3    16.0     0.1/  0.1/  0.0       329       6831



                                                              Page 1 of 2
--------------------------------------------------------------------------------
| Global  | All    | Global | NFS by |  d441522  | Next  | Select | Help | Exit   |
| Syscalls| CPUs   | NFS    | System |           | Keys  |        |      | Glance |
```

Figure 10-4 *All CPUs* Screen in GlancePlus HP-UX 10.x

Memory Detail Screen Description

The Memory Detail Screen shown in Figure 10-5 provides information on several types of memory management events. The statistics shown are in the form of counts, not percentages. You may want to look at these counts for a mostly idle system and then observe what takes place as the load on the system is incrementally increased. My experience has been that there are many more memory bottlenecks than CPU bottlenecks, so you may find this screen revealing.

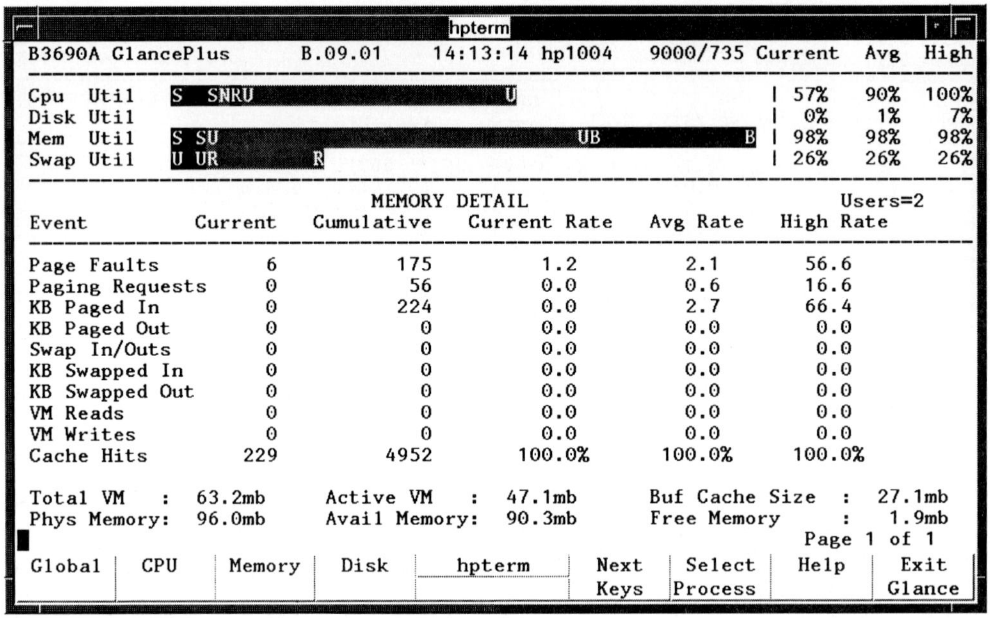

```
┌─────────────────────────────────────hpterm─────────────────────────────┐
│ B3690A GlancePlus        B.09.01     14:13:14 hp1004    9000/735 Current   Avg  High │
│─────────────────────────────────────────────────────────────────────────│
│ Cpu  Util  S  SNRU                        U                 |  57%   90%  100% │
│ Disk Util                                                   |   0%    1%    7% │
│ Mem  Util  S SU                         UB               B  |  98%   98%   98% │
│ Swap Util  U UR           R                                 |  26%   26%   26% │
│─────────────────────────────────────────────────────────────────────────│
│                              MEMORY DETAIL                       Users=2   │
│ Event           Current   Cumulative   Current Rate   Avg Rate   High Rate  │
│                                                                             │
│ Page Faults         6         175          1.2          2.1        56.6      │
│ Paging Requests     0          56          0.0          0.6        16.6      │
│ KB Paged In         0         224          0.0          2.7        66.4      │
│ KB Paged Out        0           0          0.0          0.0         0.0      │
│ Swap In/Outs        0           0          0.0          0.0         0.0      │
│ KB Swapped In       0           0          0.0          0.0         0.0      │
│ KB Swapped Out      0           0          0.0          0.0         0.0      │
│ VM Reads            0           0          0.0          0.0         0.0      │
│ VM Writes           0           0          0.0          0.0         0.0      │
│ Cache Hits        229        4952        100.0%       100.0%      100.0%     │
│                                                                             │
│ Total VM   :  63.2mb    Active VM   :  47.1mb    Buf Cache Size :  27.1mb    │
│ Phys Memory:  96.0mb    Avail Memory:  90.3mb    Free Memory    :   1.9mb    │
│                                                            Page 1 of 1       │
│ Global │ CPU │ Memory │ Disk │ hpterm │ Next │ Select │ Help │ Exit        │
│                                         Keys   Process          Glance      │
└─────────────────────────────────────────────────────────────────────────┘
```

Figure 10-5 HP GlancePlus/UX Memory Detail Screen Shot

The following five statistics are shown for each memory management event:

Current	The number of times an event occurred in the last interval. The count changes if you update the interval, so you may want to select an interval you are comfortable with and stick with it.
Cumulative	The sum of all counts for this event since Glance-Plus started.
Current Rate	The number of events per second.
Avg Rate	The average of all rates recorded.

High Rate   The highest rate recorded.

Here are brief descriptions of the memory management events for which the statistics are provided.

Page Faults   A fault takes place when a process tries to access a page that is not in RAM. The virtual memory of the system will handle the "page in." Keep in mind the speed of the disk is much slower than RAM, so there is a large performance penalty for the page in.

Paging Requests The sum of the number of times the routines used to page in and page out information were called.

KB Paged In   The amount of data paged in because of page faults.

KB Paged Out   The amount of data paged out to disk.

Swap In/Outs   The number of processes swapped in and swapped out of memory. A system low on RAM will spend a lot of time swapping processes in and out of RAM. If a lot of this type of swapping is taking place, such as high CPU utilization, you may see some other statistics go up as well. These may only be symptoms that a lot of swapping is taking place. You may see Reactivations and Deactivations.

KB Swapped In   The amount of information swapped into RAM as a result of processes having been swapped out earlier due to insufficient RAM. You may see KB Reactivated.

KB Swapped Out The amount of information swapped out when processes are moved to disk. You may see KB Deactivated.

VM Reads   The total count of the number of physical reads to disk. The higher this number, the more often your system is going to disk.

VM Writes   The total count of the number of physical writes
                   to disk.

Cache Hits   The percentage of hits to cache. A high hit rate
                   reduces the number of disk accesses. This is not a
                   field in HP-UX 10.x.

The following values are also on the Memory screen:

Total VM   The amount of total virtual memory used by all
                   processes.

Active VM   The amount of virtual memory used by all active
                   processes.

Buf Cache Size   The current size of buffer cache.

Phys Memory   The total RAM in your system.

Avail Memory   The amount of RAM available to all user pro-
                   cesses.

Free Memory   The amount of RAM not currently allocated for
                   use.

This screen gives you a lot of information about how your memory subsystem is being used. You may want to view some statistics when your system is mostly idle and when it is heavily used and compare the two. Some good numbers to record are "Avail Memory" (to see if you have any free RAM under either condition) and "Total VM" (to see how much virtual memory has been allocated for all your processes). A system that is RAM rich will have available memory; a system that is RAM poor will allocate a lot of virtual memory.

Disk Detail Screen Description

The disk detail screen is shown in Figure 10-6. You may see groupings of "local" and "remote" information.

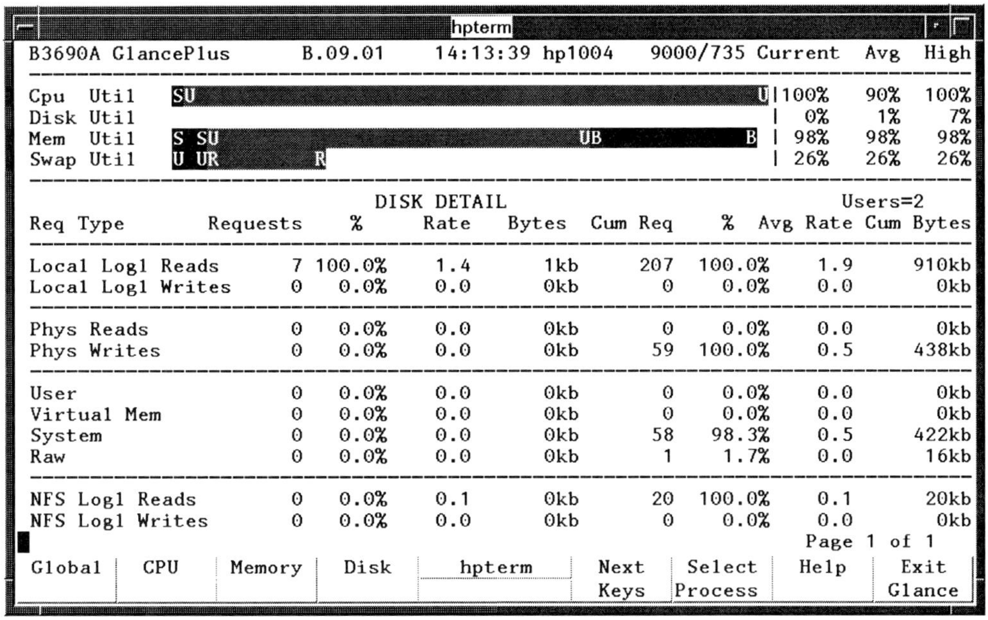

```
┌─                                              hpterm                        ·┌─
│ B3690A GlancePlus      B.09.01     14:13:39 hp1004     9000/735 Current  Avg  High │
│                                                                                    │
│ Cpu  Util  SU                                              U│100%   90%  100% │
│ Disk Util                                                   │  0%    1%    7% │
│ Mem  Util  S SU                           UB           B │  98%   98%   98% │
│ Swap Util  U UR         R                                   │ 26%   26%   26% │
│─────────────────────────────────────────────────────────────────────────────────│
│                          DISK DETAIL                            Users=2           │
│ Req Type        Requests   %    Rate   Bytes  Cum Req   %   Avg Rate Cum Bytes │
│                                                                                    │
│ Local Logl Reads      7 100.0%   1.4    1kb     207 100.0%   1.9      910kb │
│ Local Logl Writes     0   0.0%   0.0    0kb       0   0.0%   0.0        0kb │
│                                                                                    │
│ Phys Reads            0   0.0%   0.0    0kb       0   0.0%   0.0        0kb │
│ Phys Writes           0   0.0%   0.0    0kb      59 100.0%   0.5      438kb │
│                                                                                    │
│ User                  0   0.0%   0.0    0kb       0   0.0%   0.0        0kb │
│ Virtual Mem           0   0.0%   0.0    0kb       0   0.0%   0.0        0kb │
│ System                0   0.0%   0.0    0kb      58  98.3%   0.5      422kb │
│ Raw                   0   0.0%   0.0    0kb       1   1.7%   0.0       16kb │
│                                                                                    │
│ NFS Logl Reads        0   0.0%   0.1    0kb      20 100.0%   0.1       20kb │
│ NFS Logl Writes       0   0.0%   0.0    0kb       0   0.0%   0.0        0kb │
│                                                                       Page 1 of 1 │
│ Global │ CPU │ Memory │ Disk │   hpterm   │ Next │ Select │ Help │ Exit    │
│                                              │ Keys │Process │      │ Glance  │
└─                                                                               ─┘
```

Figure 10-6 HP GlancePlus/UX Disk Detail Screen Shot

There are eight disk statistics provided for eight events related to logical and physical accesses to all the disks mounted on the local system. These events represent all of the disk activity taking place on the system.

Here are descriptions of the eight disk statistics provided.

Requests	The total number of requests of that type over the last interval.
%	The percentage of this type of disk event relative to other types.
Rate	The average number of requests of this type per second.
Bytes	The total number of bytes transferred for this event over the last interval.

Cum Req	The cumulative number of requests since Glance-Plus started.
%	The relative percentage of this type of disk event since GlancePlus started.
Avg Rate	The average number of requests of this type since GlancePlus started.
Cum Bytes	The total number of bytes transferred for this type of event since GlancePlus started.

Here are descriptions of the disk events for which these statistics are provided which may be listed under "Local" on your system.

Local Logl R&W	The number of logical reads and writes to a disk. Since disks normally use memory buffer cache, a logical read may not require physical access to the disk.
Phys Reads	The number of physical reads to the disk. These physical reads may be due to either file system logical reads or to virtual memory management.
Phys Writes	The number of physical writes to the disk. This may be due to file system activity or virtual memory management.
User	The amount of physical disk I/O as a result of user file I/O operations.
Virtual Mem	The amount of physical disk I/O as a result of virtual memory management activity.
System	The amount of physical disk I/O as a result of system calls.
Raw	The amount of raw mode disk I/O.
NFS Logical R&W	The amount of NFS read and write activity.

A lot of disk activity may also take place as a result of NFS mounted disks. There are statistics provided for both "NFS Inbound" and "NFS Outbound" activity.

Disk access is required on all systems. The question to ask is: What disk activity is unnecessary and slowing down my system? A good place to start is to compare the amount of "User" disk I/O with "Virtual Mem" disk I/O. If your system is performing much more virtual memory I/O than user I/O, you may want to investigate your memory needs.

GlancePlus Summary

In addition to the Global screen and the CPU, Memory, and Disk screens described earlier, there are the following detail screens:

Swap Detail	Shows details on all swap areas.
LAN Detail	Gives details about each LAN card configured on your system.
NFS Detail	Provides details on inbound and outbound NFS mounted file systems.
Diskless Server	Provides diskless server information.
Individual Process	Allows you to select a single process to investigate.
I/O By File System	Shows details of I/O for each mounted disk partition.
Queue Lengths	Provides disk queue length details.
System Tables	Shows details on internal system tables.
Process Threshold	Defines which processes will be displayed on the Global screen.

As you can see, while I described the four most commonly used screens in detail, there are many others you can use to investigate your system further.

What Should I Look For When Using GlancePlus?

Since GlancePlus provides a graphical representation of the way in which your system resources are being used, the answer is simple: See which bars have a high "Avg" utilization. You can then probe further into the process(es) causing this high utilization. If, for instance, you find your memory is consistently 99 percent utilized, press the F3 function key and have GlancePlus walk you through an investigation of which of your applications and users are memory hogs.

Similarly, you may be surprised to find that GlancePlus shows low utilization of your CPU or other system resources. Many slow systems are assumed to be CPU bound. I have seen GlancePlus used to determine a system is in fact memory bound, resulting in a memory upgrade instead of a CPU upgrade.

The difference between using GlancePlus to determine the level of CPU resources being used and the first two approaches given in this chapter is that GlancePlus takes out a lot of the guess work involved. If you are going to justify a system upgrade of some type to management, it is easier to do this with the hard and fast data GlancePlus provides than the detective work you may need to do with HP-UX commands and HP-UX accounting. GlancePlus is useful for providing this data.

Use the GlancePlus screens I showed you to look for the following bottlenecks:

1. CPU Bottleneck
   Use the "Global Screen" and "CPU Detail Screen" to identify these common CPU bottleneck symptoms:

   - Low CPU idle time

   - High capacity in User mode

   - Many processes blocked on priority (PRI)

2. Memory Bottleneck
   Use the "Global Screen," "Memory Screen," and "Tables Screen" to identify these common Memory bottleneck symptoms:

   - High swapping activity

   - High paging activity

   - Little or no free memory available

   - High CPU usage in System mode

3. Disk Bottleneck

Use "Global Screen," "Disk I/O Screen," and others to identify these common Disk Bottleneck symptoms:

- High disk activity

- High idle CPU time waiting for I/O requests to complete

- Long disk queues

The best approach to take for understanding where your system resources are going is to become familiar with both issuing HP-UX commands and using GlancePlus/UX. You can then determine which information is most useful to you.

The most important aspect of this process is to regularly issue commands and review accounting data so that small system utilization problems don't turn into catastrophes and adversely affect all your users.

You may need to go a step further with more sophisticated performance tools. HP can help you identify more sophisticated tools based on your needs.

CHAPTER 11

Windows NT User Environment

I'll cover the most important parts of the user environment. There are books which go into excruciating detail of the Windows NT user environment. I don't believe this is necessary. Since you are a system administrator you could probably login to a Windows NT system and adapt to the user environment quickly. What I'll do in this chapter is cover some of the more important areas so before you login you have a feel for the user environment and its components.

The Environment in General

Figure 11-1 shows a Windows NT environment screen shot.

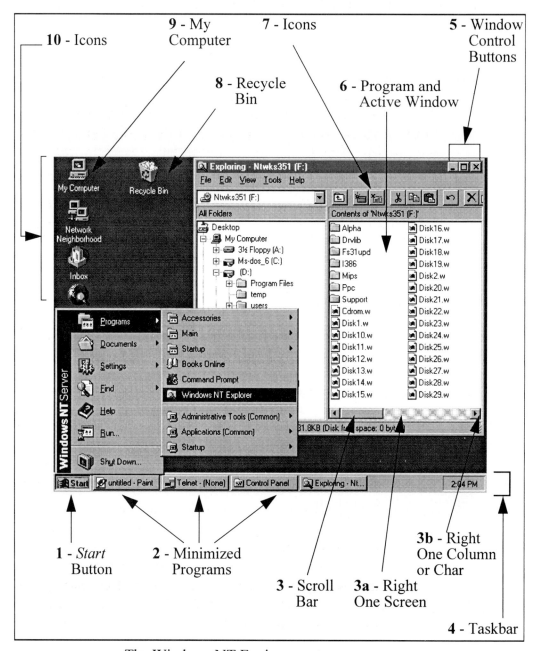

Figure 11-1   The Windows NT Environment

Let's take a look at the items shown in Figure 11-1 on a number-by-number basis:

1. *Start* - This gives you access to all of the important programs on your Windows NT system. You can see from the figure that the menus are organized in such a way that they cascade when you select one with an arrow.

2. Minimized Programs - Program windows can be minimized by selecting the minimize button of the window. When programs are minimized, you can select the icon from the taskbar to maximize the window.

3. Scroll Bar - You can use the scroll bar to move left or right as many screens as you like. You can use 3a to move right one screen at a time. You can use 3b to move one character or column at a time. 3a and 3b can also exist for moving left. There may also be scroll bars for moving up and down as well.

4. Taskbar - The taskbar has an icon for all programs you are using.

5. Window Control Buttons - These are used for quick manipulation of windows. From left to right these are suspend and send to taskbar which is also called minimize; maximize or restore to normal size depending on the current size of the window; close the application.

6. Program Window - When you start a program, you get a window in which you use that program. You can have several program windows open at the same time. In this case this is both a program window and the active window. The active window will appear on top of the other windows. Windows can be resized by placing the pointer around the perimeter and holding down the left mouse button until the window is the desired size.

7. Icons - These are used for such functions as cut, copy, paste, etc. The window in the figure is too small to show all of the icons that are part of this window.

8. *Recycle Bin* - The recycle bin is an area to place files you no longer need. You can go back and retrieve them if you later decide you need them again provided you haven't emptied the Recycle Bin which deletes the items.

9. *My Computer* - This give you a run down on your computer. Information such as printers and drives are shown here.

10. Icons - You can restart these programs by double clicking the mouse on them.

The key application in your Windows NT environment is the *Windows NT Explorer*. Let's take a look at this in more detail.

Start at the Beginning with *Start*

When you log in to a Windows NT system, you can launch applications and perform almost all of your work from the *Start* button. Figure 11-2 shows selecting the *Start* menu from the lower left hand corner of the Windows NT screen and moving the mouse to *Programs - Administrative Tools (Common)*.

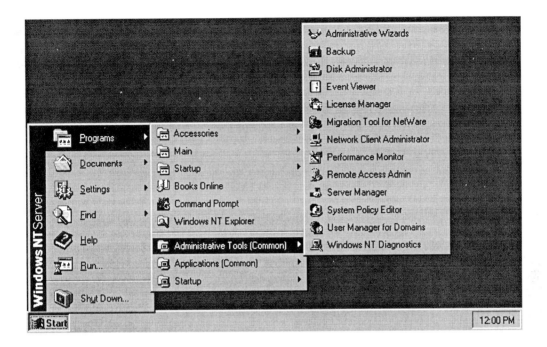

Figure 11-2   Windows NT *Start* Menu

These groups of applications are organized similarly to the old *Program Manager*. I find this organization to be superior to that of the old Program Manager. I think it is easier to find items in this cascading menu than in the old *Program Manager* technique of organization.

I would like to start going over the user interface with the *Start* menu because this is the place from which you will launch most applications.

Windows NT Explorer

You'll be spending a lot of time with *Windows NT Explorer*. You can view all of the disks on your system, other systems on the network, and perform many important functions with *Windows NT Explorer*. You invoke *Windows NT Explorer* with *Start - Programs - Windows NT Explorer*. It is shown in Figure 11-3.

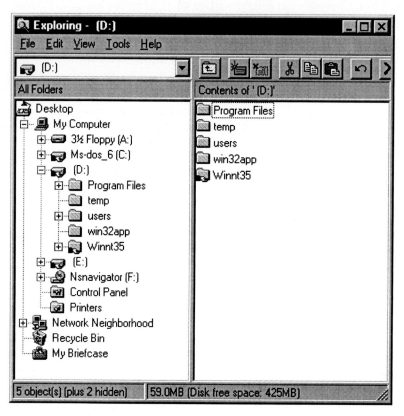

Figure 11-3 *Windows NT Explorer*

Through *Windows NT Explorer* you can view a lot of information on your system. In Figure 11-3 *My Computer* has been expanded so you can see all of the items beneath it such as *A:, C:, D:, E:, F:, Control Panel,* and *Printers*. You can determine that *My Computer* has been expanded because of the - in front of *My Computer*. Remote file systems can also be displayed in *Windows NT Explorer*. An upcoming chapter shows using *Windows NT*

Explorer to view a disk on a remote HP-UX system that is mounted to a Windows NT system using NFS. For the purposes of describing *Windows NT Explorer* features in this chapter, however, all file systems used are local to the Windows NT system.

The - or + in front of the icon on the left determines whether or not the folder is expanded. A - means it is expanded on the left side of the *Windows NT Explorer* window. A + means it is not expanded. You can, however, select the folder in which case it is expanded on the right side of the *Windows NT Explorer* window. In Figure 11-4 *Nsnavigator(F:)* is expanded on the left side because a - appears in front of *Nsnavigator(F):*.

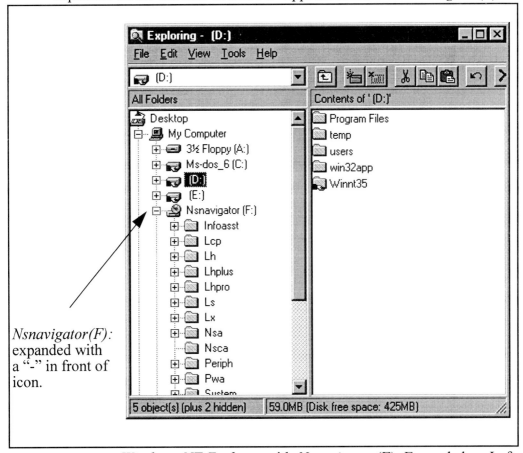

Nsnavigator(F): expanded with a "-" in front of icon.

Figure 11-4 *Windows NT Explorer* with *Nsnavigator(F):* Expanded on Left, Right Shows Contents of **D:**

In Figure 11-5 *Nsnavigator(F):* is expanded on the right side of the *Windows NT Explorer* because the icon for *Nsnavigator(F):* has been selected.

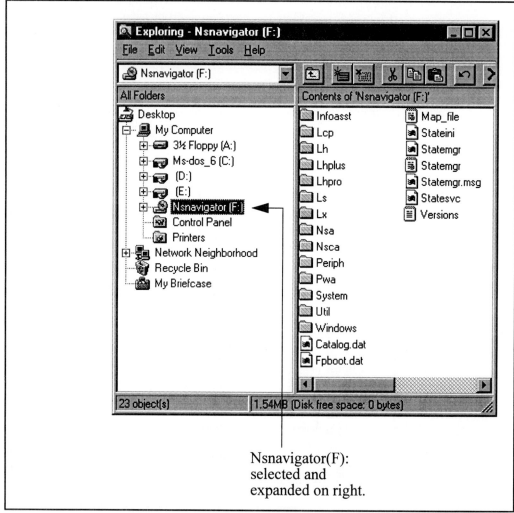

Nsnavigator(F):
selected and
expanded on right.

Figure 11-5 *Windows NT Explorer* with *Nsnavigator(F):* Selected and Expanded on Right

The icons on top of the *Windows NT Explorer* window are used as a shortcut for many functions. Figure 11-6 shows the *Windows NT Explorer* icons.

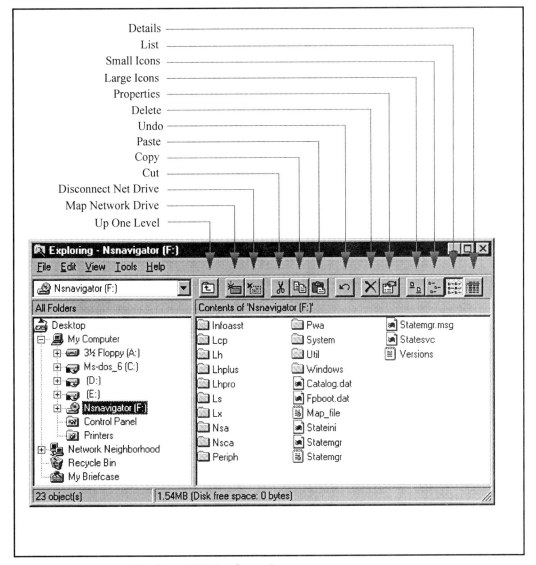

Figure 11-6 *Windows NT Explorer* Icons

The *Up One Level* icon has been used in Figure 11-7 to show how to navigate through the different levels. The diagram shows three windows, each one level above the next. The top window (Figure 11-7a) starts out at the *Nsnavigator(F):* level, then moves up to *My Computer* (Figure 11-7b), and then goes up to the *Desktop* level (Figure 11-7c). You achieve moving up these levels by clicking the *Up One Level* icon.

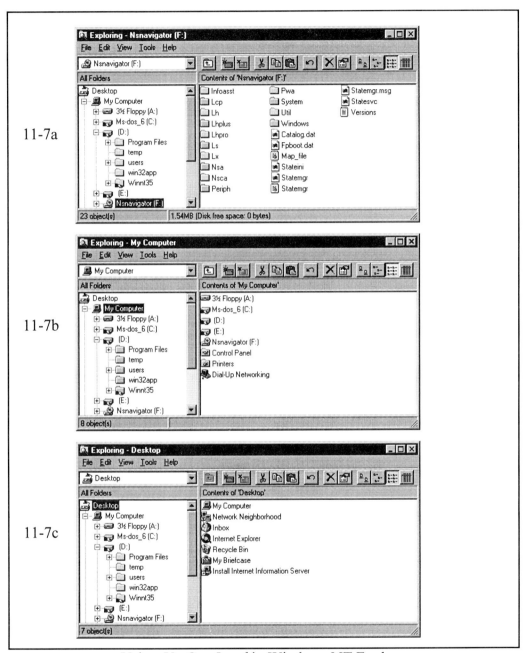

Figure 11-7 Using *Up One Level* in Windows NT Explorer

You also have control over the way in which files are displayed. We have been looking at the contents of items in "list" form in *Windows NT Explorer* figures. You can use either the icons along the top of the *Windows NT Explorer* or the *View* menu to view other forms. To view the details of files you can use either the *View - Details* menu pick or the *Details* icon. The detailed view is shown in Figure 11-8.

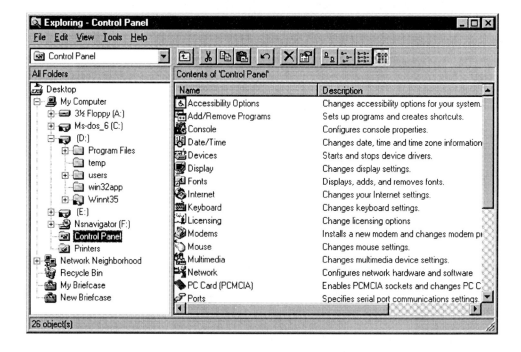

Figure 11-8 *Windows NT Explorer* Screen Using *Detail* Icon

You can see that in this figure you get a name and description for the contents of the area in which you are looking, in this case the contents of the *Control Panel*.

We have been viewing small icons throughout this chapter. There are both *Small Icons* and *Large Icons* menu picks which changes the size of the icons. Figure 11-9 shows large icons on the top and small icons on the bottom.

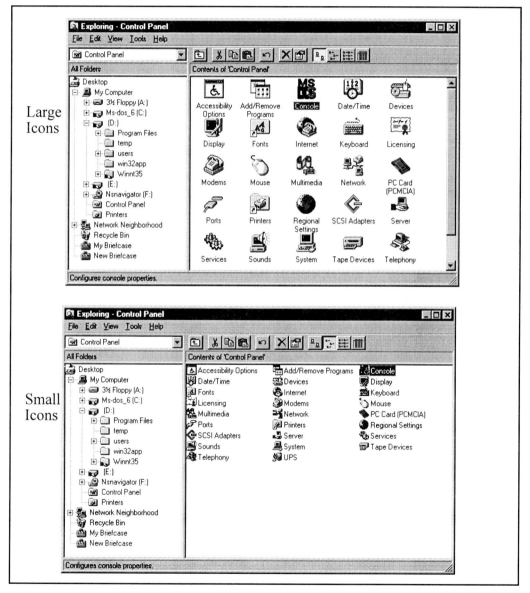

Figure 11-9 *Windows NT Explorer* Large and Small Icons

An aspect of the Windows NT Explorer that I have made good use of is the *Tools - Find - Files or Folders...* menu pick. You can select files you wish to find using this menu pick. Figure 11-10 shows a search for the field "dat" anywhere within the file name of the selected item.

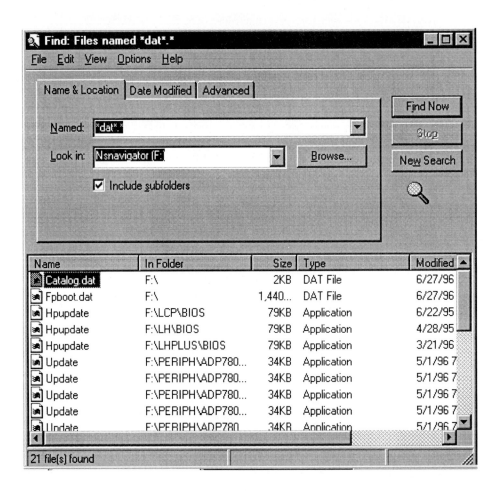

Figure 11-10 *Windows NT Explorer* Find Using *Tools - Find - Files or Folders...*

We could continue across the icons of the *Windows NT Explorer* and show all of the menu picks, but you probably have a good feel for working your way around this tool.

There are also several short cuts to using Windows NT Explorer. I find the following to be useful:

- **Ctrl - A** selects all files.

- **Crtrl - C** marks files for copying.

- **Ctrl - X** marks files for moving.

- **Ctrl - V** pastes files into their new location.

- Hitting the right mouse button while on an object will bring up a menu actions for that object.

Task Manager

Clicking the right mouse button over the Taskbar at the bottom of the Windows NT screen brings up the menu shown in Figure 11-11.

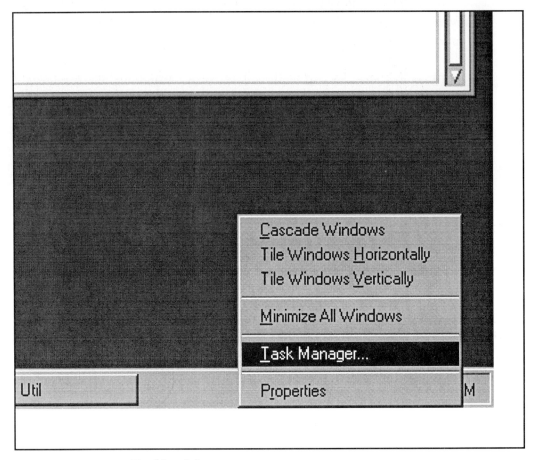

Figure 11-11 *Taskbar* Menu

This menu appears at the taskbar in the bottom right of the Windows
NT screen. From a user interface standpoint there are several options you
have related to the way windows are arranged. Most are self-explanatory,
such as cascading windows, arranging them horizontally and vertically,
and minimizing the windows. These perform all of the useful window rearranging that you would expect.

The *Properties* menu pick allows you to set *Taskbar* options as well
as add and remove items from the *Start Menu*. Adding an item to the *Start
Menu* is as easy as specifying the command you wish to run.

The most useful of these menu picks is the *Task Manager* that is high-lighted. The *Task Manager* is used for viewing the following three types of information.

Applications - There is an *Applications* tab in the *Task Manager* that is used to bring up a list of tasks that are running on the system. You see both the task name and its status in this window. You can also start, end, or switch to a task from this window. This is shown in Figure 11-12a.

Processes - There is a *Processes* tab in the *Task Manager* that provides such information as the name, ID, CPU time, and memory usage of various processes running on the system. This is shown in Figure 11-12b.

Performance - There is a *Performance* tab in the *Task Manager* that has both memory and CPU usage graphs in it. This is shown in Figure 11-12c with the pull-down menu showing the *Update Speed* options.

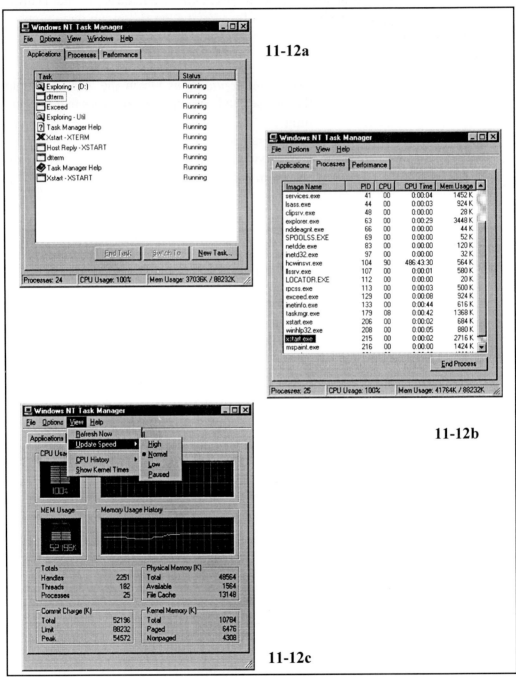

Figure 11-12 *Task Manager*

Note in these windows that the percent of CPU used and the memory consumed appears in all of the windows. These windows are useful for getting an overview of the activity on your system.

CHAPTER 12

HP-UX Common Desktop Environment

Common Desktop Environment

The Common Desktop Environment (CDE) is the direct lineal descendant of the HP Visual User Environment (HP VUE). CDE represents the effort of major UNIX vendors to unify UNIX at the desktop level. Hewlett-Packard's contribution to this effort is HP VUE, its award winning graphical user environment. HP VUE is the foundation of CDE. This chapter is an introduction to CDE. If you need to fully understand all of the nuances of CDE you'll want to buy *Configuring the Common Desktop Environment* by Charlie Fernandez, Prentice Hall, 1995.

Like HP VUE, the CDE is widely used by X terminal and workstation users. The CDE style manager, which every user has access to, makes it easy to customize CDE on an individual user basis. Sooner or later, however, you may want to provide some common denominator of VUE functionality for your users. If, for instance, you have an application that most users will run, you can set up environment variables, prepare menu picks, provide suitable fonts, etc., that will make your users more productive. Users can then perform additional customization such as defining file manager characteristics and selecting backgrounds.

To help you thoroughly understand CDE, I'll cover the following topics:

1. Why a Graphical User Interface (GUI)?

2. The Relationship among X, Motif, and CDE

3. X, Motif, and CDE Configuration Files

4. The Sequence of Events When CDE Starts

5. Customizing CDE

6. CDE and Performance

Why a Graphical User Interface (GUI)?

For computers to be used on every desktop, they had to be made easier to use. A new method of accessing computer power was required, one that avoided the command line prompt and that didn't require users to memorize complex commands, and didn't require a working knowledge of technological infrastructures like networking. Not that this information was unimportant; far from it. The information was both too important and too specialized to be of use to the average worker-bee computer user. A knowledge of their applications was all that was important for these users. After all, so the reasoning goes, to drive a car, one doesn't have to be a mechanic, so why should a computer user have to understand computer technology? The graphical user interface (GUI) makes computers accessible to the application end user.

Figure 12-1 illustrates the relationship among the computer hardware, the operating system, and the graphical user interface. The computer is the hardware platform on the bottom. The operating system, the next layer up, represents a character-based user interface. To control the computer at this level, users must type commands at the keyboard. The next several layers, beginning with the X Window System, represent the graphical user interface. To control the computer at these levels, users manipulate graphical controls with a mouse.

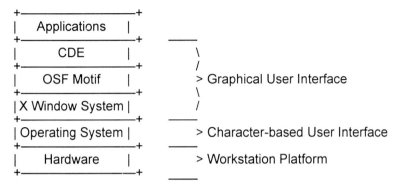

Figure 12-1   User Interface Components

GUIs replaced memorization with exploration. A user could now use pull-down menus, push buttons, sliding scroll bars, and other direct manipulation to use a computer. Typing operating system commands to perform a function is greatly reduced. With a GUI, it is both easier to learn and easier to use a computer.

While fairly inexpensive in terms of dollars (CDE is bundled "free" with the operating system), GUIs are not without cost in terms of RAM usage and performance. Despite this performance expense, GUIs have become a permanent part of the computing environment. The benefits of their utility are worth the cost.

Beyond the graphical controls that reduce training, make mundane tasks simpler to do, and generally ease the stress of using a computer, there are two other benefits of GUIs worth mentioning: multiple windows per display and client-server topology.

The benefit of multiple windows that GUIs provide is that each window (literally a rectangular area surrounded by a window frame) contains a separate application. The user can work with multiple windows open. CDE goes one step further: Its multiple workspaces allow users to separate application windows by task into specific workspaces. For instance, in a workspace named "Mail," users may have application windows showing the list of incoming electronic mail, a mail message they are currently reading, and a message they are composing for later transmission. In another workspace called "Financials," they could be working on several spread-sheets, each in its own window.

Client-server topology enables the computing resources spread around a network to be accessed efficiently to meet computing needs. In a client-server topology, powerful computers on the network are dedicated to a specific purpose (file management on a file server and running applications on an application server). Users working on less powerful client computers elsewhere on the network access the files or applications remotely. A file server reduces system administration by centralizing file back up, enabling the system administrator to backup only the file server, not each individual client computer. This setup also ensures that files will be backed up at regular intervals. An application server reduces operating costs by reducing the number and size of storage disks required and the size of RAM required on each client computer. A single version of an application resides and runs on the application server and is accessed by multiple users throughout the network.

While this sounds complicated, the CDE GUI makes it easy. To access a file, users "drag and drop" a file icon from the file manager window. To start an application, users double-click the application icon. To print a file, users drag the file to the icon of the appropriate printer in the front panel and drop it there. Users don't have to know where these files and applications are, what directories they are in, what computers they are on, or how they are accessed. It is the underlying infrastructure and control you have put in place along with the power of the GUI that allow users to concentrate on their work and not on the mechanics of their computer.

The Relationship among X, Motif, and CDE

X, OSF/Motif, and CDE are enabling framework technologies. Taken together, X, Motif, and CDE make up the three graphical layers on top of the operating system and the hardware platform.

The GUI layers provide increasingly richer ease-of-use functions in a progressive series of layers that buffer the end user from the "user hostile" character-based interface of the operating system layer.

The X Window System

The X Window System consists of the following:

- Xlib - Low-level library for programming window manipulation, graphics capabilities such as line drawing and text placement, and controlling display output, mouse and keyboard input, and application network transparency.

- Xt Intrinsics - Higher-level library for programming widgets and gadgets (graphical controls components like menus, scroll bars, and push buttons).

- Display servers - Hardware-specific programs, one per display, that manage the graphical input and output.

- Interclient communication conventions (ICCC) - A manual specifying standards for how X client programs should communicate with each other.

- Configuration files - One configuration file that specifies the default session to start (**sys.x11start**) and another specifying values for resources used to shape the X environment (**sys.Xdefaults**).

Through these mechanisms, X provides the standard upon which the graphical part of the network-oriented, client/server, distributed computing paradigm is based. A knowledge of **Xlib** and the **Xt** intrinsics is important for programming in X and for programming at the Motif level. For system administrators, however, as long as the display servers work and X client applications are ICCC compliant, you shouldn't need to delve into the X layer. CDE enables you to view X pretty much as part of "all that underlying technological infrastructure stuff" and focus on developing appropriate configurations of CDE to meet your users' work context.

Motif

Motif consists of the following:

- mwm window manager - Executable program that provides Motif-based window frames, window management, and a workspace menu in the X environment.

- Motif widget toolkit - Higher-level library of widgets and gadgets, the graphical components used to control the user environment.

- Motif style guide - A manual defining the Motif appearance and behavior for programmers.

- Configuration files - The **system.mwmrc** file containing configuration information for the workspace menu and key and button bindings. Resources for the window manager are in **mwm** in the **/usr/lib/X11/app-defaults** directory.

Motif provides the window manager for the end user, the widget toolkit for application developers, and the style guide to help developers design and build proper Motif-conformant applications. As with X, system administrators can view Motif mostly as "programmer's stuff," part of the underlying infrastructure, and focus on developing appropriate CDE configuration files.

CDE

CDE consists of the following, all of which are based on HP VUE 3.0:

- Workspace manager - Executable program that provides Motif-based window frames, window management, a workspace menu, and the front panel.

- File manager - Program that iconically manages files and directories through direct manipulation.

- Style manager - Container of dialog boxes that control elements of the CDE environment like workspace color and fonts.

- Help manager - Based on the HP Help System, this program provides context-sensitive help text on CDE components.

- Login manager - Daemon-like application that handles login and password verification.

- Session manager - Manager that handles saving and restoring user sessions.

- Application manager - Manager that registers and keeps track of applications in the CDE environment.

- Configuration files - A big bunch, most of which you can avoid dealing with (see below).

Similar to HP VUE, CDE also provides a number of basic, end-user productivity-enhancing applications. In CDE, these include things like a clock showing system time, a calendar showing system date, a datebook/scheduler program for workgroup coordination, and a MIME mailer for sending multimedia electronic mail messages.

In general, CDE provides a graphical environment into which users, or you, their system administrator, can incorporate the software tools needed to do their work.

X, Motif, and CDE Configuration Files

X, Motif, and CDE all use configuration files to shape their appearance and behavior. Elements of appearance and behavior such as foreground color, keyboard focus policy, or client decoration are resources that can be controlled by values in the appropriate configuration file. In X, Motif, and CDE the word "resource" has a special meaning. It doesn't refer to vague natural resources or generic system resources, but to specific elements of appearance and behavior. Some examples are the **foreground** resource, the **keyboardFocusPolicy** resource, and the **clientDecoration** resource. For example, foreground color could be black, keyboard focus policy could be explicit, and client decoration could be plus-title (title bar only). These would appear in some appropriate configuration file as the following:

    *foreground: black

    *keyboardFocusPolicy:explicit

    *clientDecoration: +title

Which configuration file these resources appear in depends on the scope of the effect desired (systemwide or individual user) and the graphical interface level being used (X, Motif, or CDE).

X Configuration Files

The X Window System has the following configuration files:

sys.x11start

sys.Xdefaults

system.hpwmrc

X*screens

X*devices

X*pointerkey

By convention, these files are located in the **/usr/lib/X11** directory. In addition, each X client application has its own app-defaults configuration file located, also by convention, in the **/usr/lib/X11/app-defaults** directory. Although six files are listed above, unless you're configuring a workstation for multiple - display screens (X*screens), multiple input devices (X*devices), or keyboard-only pointer navigation (X*pointerkey), you'll typically need to work with only **sys.x11start**, **sys.Xdefaults**, and **system.hpwmrc**.

The **sys.x11start** file was a script used to start X and X clients before the advent of CDE. System administrators or knowledgeable users modified **sys.x11start** so that the appropriate mix of X clients started "automatically." The **sys.Xdefaults** file was read as X started to obtain values for various appearance and behavior resources. Modifications to **sys.Xdefaults** ensured that the X environment and clients had the proper appearance and behavior. **system.hpwmrc** contained the configuration of the workspace menu and button and key bindings. **system.hpwmrc** has been replaced by the Motif version, **system.mwmrc**.

sys.x11start, **sys.Xdefaults**, and **system.hpwmrc** could be copied to a user's home directory and modified to personalize the user's X environment. These personalized versions, called **.x11start**, **.Xdefaults**, and **.hpwmrc**, overrode the systemwide versions, **sys.x11start**, **sys.Xdefaults**, and **system.hpwmrc**.

For more detailed information on X configuration files, see books such as the classic *Using the X Window System* (HP part number B1171-90067).

Motif Configuration Files

Motif added only one new configuration file to the X list: **system.mwmrc**.

By convention, this file is kept with the X configuration files in **/usr/lib/X11**. Actually, this file isn't new; it is the Motif version of **system.hpwmrc** which simply replaced **system.hpwmrc** in Motif environments.

Where X brought network and inter-client communication standards to the graphical user interface, Motif brought a standard for appearance and behavior, the standard originally defined in IBM's System Application Architecture Common User Access (SAACUA), which forms the basis of most PC-based GUIs. Thus, push buttons and scroll bars have a defined look and a defined behavior and double-clicking always causes the default action to happen.

From a programmer's point of view, the Motif widget toolkit represents quite an advance over programming in "raw" X. From a user's or system administrator's point of view, the Motif user environment is about the same as the X environment, except that the **hpwm** window manager is replaced with the Motif window manager. But, because **mwm** is itself a direct lineal descendent of **hpwm**, the way CDE is descended from HP VUE, even this difference is minimal.

CDE Configuration Files

It is possible to point to over 80 files that, in one way or another, contribute to configuring some aspect of CDE. However, if you remove from this list such files as those

- that configure CDE applications as opposed to the environment itself,

- that establish default actions and datatype definitions which, although you will create your own definitions in separate files, you will never modify,

- that are CDE working files and should not be customized,

- that are more appropriately associated with configuring the UNIX, X, and Motif environments underlying CDE, including the various shell environments,

then CDE has approximately 19 configuration files as shown in Table 12-1.

TABLE 12-1   CDE CONFIGUATION FILES

* .Xauthority	* sys.font	* Xresources
* .Xdefaults	* sys.resources	* Xservers
* .dtprofile	* sys.sessions	* Xsession
* dtwm.fp	* Xaccess	* Xsetup
* dtwmrc	* Xconfig	* Xstartup
* sys.dtprofile	* Xfailsafe	
* sys.dtwmrc	* Xreset	

Although 19 configuration files is still a lot, don't be alarmed by the number. You won't need to modify many of them, and can ignore; a couple you modify once and then forget about. You need to understand in depth for periodic modification only one or two, perhaps a systemwide ***.dt** file for custom actions and data types, or maybe **dtwm.fp** if you are required to modify the front panel on a regular basis for some reason.

Still, configuring CDE is not something you want to start hacking with without a little preparation and a good idea of what you want to accomplish. All CDE configuration files are pretty well commented, so a good first step is to print the ones you want to modify.

Table 12-2 organizes CDE configuration files according to content and the breadth of their influence.

The file **sys.dtwmrc**, like **sys.vuewmrc**, **system.hpwmrc**, and **system.mwmrc** before it, controls the configuration of the workspace manager at the system level. This includes all of the following:

Workspace Menu A menu that displays when mouse button 3 is pressed while the mouse pointer is over the workspace backdrop.

Button Bindings Definitions of what action happens when a particular mouse button is pressed or released while the mouse pointer is over a particular area (frame, icon, window, or root).

Key Bindings Definitions of what action happens when a particular key or key sequence is pressed while the mouse pointer is over a particular area (frame, icon, window, or root).

TABLE 12-2 CDE CONFIGURATION FILE INFLUENCE

Nature of Configuration File	Systemwide Influence	User Personal Influence
Environment Variables	sys.dtprofile Xconfig Xsession	.dtprofile
Appearance & Behavior Resources	sys.resources Xconfig Xresources sys.fonts	.Xdefaults
File Types & Action Definitions	misc *.dt files	user-prefs.dt
Client Startup at Login	sys.sessions Xstartup Xsession Xreset Xfailsafe	.xsession sessionetc
Workspace Manager & Front Panel	sys.dtwmrc dtwm.fp	dtwmrc user-prefs.fp
Clients/Servers & Access	Xaccess Xservers	.Xauthority

Unlike previous configuration files, **sys.dtwmrc** does not control the following configuration elements:

Front Panel   The box, usually at the bottom of the workspace, that contains commonly referenced indicators and frequently used graphical controls, including a six-button workspace switch.

Slideup Subpanels Menus that slide up from the front panel at various locations to provide more functionality without consuming more screen space.

Instead, to avoid a massively large and overly complex configuration file, these elements were separated into their own configuration file in CDE, **dtwm.fp**.

Some front panel configuration elements, like the number of workspaces and their arrangement in the workspace switch, are controlled through resources in a **sys.resources,   dt.resources**, or **.Xdefaults** file. Like other workspace manager configuration files, **sys.dtwmrc** can be copied to a user's home directory, actually to **$HOME/.dt/** as **dtwmrc** and modified to personalize the user's environment beyond the systemwide configuration of **sys.dtwmrc**.

The **sys.resources** file is one of those files you might modify once, then never again. The **dt.resources** file is one of those files you won't ever need to modify and can ignore. The **.Xdefaults** file is one you or your users may modify on occasion. The **sys.resources** file is where you put any non-default resources you want in effect when a brand new user logs into CDE for the very first time. For example, as system administrator, you may want your users to have a CDE front panel with prenamed workspaces, special colors, particular fonts, or application windows in certain locations. After the first-time login, **sys.resources** is ignored in favor of **dt.resources**. This file, **dt.resources**, resides in **$HOME/.dt/sessions/current** (or **$HOME/ .dt/sessions/home** when the home session is restored) and is created automatically by CDE. You can consider it as a CDE working file and forget about it. The **.Xdefaults** file is where you or an end user would list X resources specific to the user's personal CDE environment. **sys.resources**, **dt.resources**, and **.Xdefaults** contain a list of resources and their values.

The **sys.sessions** file controls which clients start the very first time a new user logs into CDE. The **dt.sessions** file is to **sys.sessions** as **dt.resources** is to **sys.resources**.

It may be efficient to configure CDE to start particular applications for your users. You would specify these applications in **sys.sessions**. When a new user logs in for the first time, the CDE environment includes the specified clients. At the end of this first session by logging out, the remaining clients would be recorded in **$HOME/.dt/sessions/current** for CDE (**$HOME/.dt/sessions/home** when the home session is restored).

The **sys.dtprofile** file is a template that is automatically copied at first login into each new user's home directory as **.dtprofile. sys.dtprofile** replaces **.profile** or **.login** in the CDE environment (although either **.profile** or **.login** can be sourced in **.dtprofile**). The **.dtprofile** file holds the personal environment variables that would, in a character-based environment, be found in **.profile** or **.login**. Use this separate file to avoid the interference terminal I/O commands cause to CDE's graphical environment.

The CDE login manager, **dtlogin**, presets the following environment variables to default values:

DISPLAY	The name of the local display
EDITOR	The default text editor HOME, The user's home directory as specified in **/etc/passwd**
KBD_LANG	The current language of the keyboard
LANG	The current NLS language
LC_ALL	The value of LANG
LC_MESSAGES	The value of LANG
LOGNAME	The user's login name as specified in **/etc/passwd**
MAIL	The default file for mail (usually **/usr/mail/$USER**)
PATH	The default directories to search for files and applications
USER	The user name
SHELL	The default shell as specified in **/etc/passwd**

TERM   The default terminal emulation

TZ   The time zone in effect

Variations to these default values belong in each user's **.dtprofile**. Additional environment variables can be added as needed to shape the user's environment to the needs of the work context. Just beware of using commands that cause any terminal I/O.

Like **.dtprofile**, **Xsession** is a shell script that sets user environment variables. The environment variables in **Xsession** apply systemwide. The environment variables in **.dtprofile** apply only to a user's personal environment. Furthermore, since the login manager runs **Xsession** after the X server has started, the variables in **Xsession** are not available to the X server. Variables typically set in **Xsession** include the following:

EDITOR	The default text editor.
KBD_LANG	The language of the keyboard (usually set to the value of $LANG).
TERM	The default terminal emulation.
MAIL	The default file for mail which is usually **/usr/mail/$USER**.
DTHELPSEARCHPATH	The locations to search for CDE help files.
DTAPPSEARCHPATH	The locations to search for applications registered with the CDE application manager.
DTDATABASESEARCHPATH	The locations to search for additional action and data type definitions.
XMICONSEARCHPATH	The locations to search for additional icons
XMICONBMSEARCHPATH	Same as above.

As an example, suppose you are the system administrator for several mixed workstation and X terminal clusters located at a single site. Now suppose that different users you administer have grown accustomed to certain text editors. Some like **vi**, others prefer **emacs**, and a couple wouldn't be caught dead without **dmx**. An easy way to provide each user with his or her favored text editor would be to reset their EDITOR variable to the appropriate value in the individual **.dtprofile** files.

Xconfig contains resources that control the behavior of **dtlogin** and it also provides a place to specify the locations for any other **dtlogin** configuration files you create. The **Xconfig** file works on a systemwide basis, so it's one of those files that you modify only once and then forget about. When, during login, **Xconfig** is run, several CDE configuration files get referenced: **Xaccess**, **Xservers**, **Xresources**, **Xstartup**, **Xsession**, **Xreset**, and **Xfailsafe**. Like **Xconfig** itself, most of these files are the type that you modify once when installing CDE and then, unless the network topology changes, you never deal with them again.

Xaccess, as the name implies, is a remote display access control file. **Xaccess** contains a list of the host names allowed or denied XDMCP connection access to the local computer. For example, when an X terminal requests login service, **dtlogin** consults the **Xaccess** file to determine if service should be granted.

The primary use of the **Xservers** file is to list the display screens on the local system which **dtlogin** is responsible for managing. **dtlogin** reads the **Xservers** file and starts an X server for each display listed there. It then starts a child **dtlogin** process to manage the server and display the login screen. Note that **dtlogin** works only locally; **dtlogin** can't start an X server on a remote system or X terminal. For remote display servers, some other mechanism must be used to start the server, which then uses the X Display Management Control Protocol (XDMCP) to request a login screen from **dtlogin**.

The **Xservers** file is another of those files that you may spend some time with initially and then, unless the topography of your network changes, never deal with again. When do you use **Xservers**? When a display doesn't match the default configuration. The default configuration assumes that each system has a single bitmap display and is the system console. X terminals, multiple displays (heads), multiple screens, and Starbase applications all require configuration lines in the **Xservers** file.

The **Xresources** file contains the list of resources that control the appearance and behavior of the login screen. After you substitute your company's logo for the HP logo and change the fonts and colors, you'll probably never have to deal with **Xresources** again (unless your company changes its logo).

Xstartup is a systemwide configuration file executed by the login manager from which it receives several environment variables:

DISPLAY	The name of the local display.
USER	The login name of the user.
HOME	The user's home directory.
PATH	The value of the **systemPath** resource in **Xconfig**.
SHELL	The value of the **systemShell** resource in **Xconfig**.
XAUTHORITY	The file to access for authority permissions.
TZ	The local time zone.

Because it can execute scripts and start clients on a systemwide basis, **Xstartup** is similar to **sys.sessions**. The difference is that **Xstartup** runs as root. Thus, modifications to **Xstartup** should be reserved for actions like mounting file systems.

Xreset is a systemwide companion script to **Xstartup**. It runs as root and essentially undoes what **Xstartup** put in motion.

The **Xfailsafe** file contains customizations to the standard failsafe session. The failsafe session provides a way to correct improper CDE sessions caused by errors in the login and session configuration files. As such, **Xfailsafe** is something your users are never going to use, but you can make your life a little easier with a few judicious customizations.

The **sessionetc** file resides in a user's **.dt/sessions** directory and personalizes that user's CDE session. **sessionetc** handles the starting of additional X clients like **sys.session**, but on a per-user basis, as opposed to systemwide. While **dt.session** also starts clients on a per-user basis, the clients are those of the default or current session. **dt.session** resides in **.dt/session/current**. **sessionetc**, which resides in **.dt/session**, should contain only those clients that are not automatically restored. Typically, these are clients that do not set the **WM_COMMAND** property so the session manager can't save or restore them; thus they need to be restarted in **sessionetc**.

The **sys.font** file contains the systemwide default session font configuration. These default fonts were based on usability studies, so **sys.font** is a file you may never change. However, should you encounter a situation that requires a different mix of fonts on a systemwide basis, this is where you'd change them. Note that the font resources and values mentioned in **sys.font** must match exactly the default font resources specified in the **/usr/dt/app-defaults/C/Dtstyle** file.

CDE has a bunch of files that specify CDE action and data type definitions. All these files end with the file extension ***.dt**. A ***.dt** ("dt" for "desk top") contains both data type and action definitions. The default ***.dt** files are in **/usr/dt/appconfig/types/C** and act on a systemwide basis. Similarly, **user-prefs.dt**, the master copy of which is also located in **/usr/dt/appconfig/types/C**, is used at the personal user level.

The **.Xauthority** file is a user-specific configuration file containing authorization information needed by clients that require an authorization mechanism to connect to the server.

CDE Configuration File Locations

Where CDE looks for particular configuration files depends on the nature of the configuration files, principally what the files configure and how wide their influence. Table 12-3 shows the location of system and user configuration files based on the nature of the file content:

TABLE 12-3 CDE SYSTEM AND USER CONFIGURATION FILES

Nature of Configuration File	Systemwide Influence	User Personal Influence
Environment Variables	/usr/dt/config/	$HOME/
Appearance & Behavior Resources	/usr/dt/config/C /usr/dt/app-defaults/ C	$HOME/.dt/ $HOME/.dt/sessions/current/ $HOME/.dt/sessions/home/
File Types & Action Definitions	/usr/dt/appconfig/ types/C	$HOME/.dt/types

TABLE 12-3   CDE SYSTEM AND USER CONFIGURATION FILES (Continued)

Nature of Configuration File	Systemwide Influence	User Personal Influence
Client Startup at Login	/usr/dt/config/ /usr/dt/config/C	$HOME/.dt/session/ $HOME/.dt/session/current/ $HOME/.dt/session/home/
Workspace Manager	/usr/vue/config usr/vue/config/panels	$HOME/.dt/

For each of the default systemwide file locations listed in Table 12-3, there is a corresponding location for custom systemwide configuration files. These custom files should be located in the appropriate subdirectory under **/etc/dt**. The basic procedure is to copy the file you need to customize from **/usr/dt/something** to **/etc/dt/something** and then do your modifications there. For example, to change the default logo in **Xresources**, copy **/usr/dt/config/C/Xresources** to **/etc/dt/config/C/Xresources**, open **/etc/dt/config/C/Xresources**, and make your changes.

This is an important point. Files located under **/usr/dt** are considered CDE system files and will be overwritten during updates. Thus any customizations you do there will be lost. Make all modifications to systemwide configuration files in **/etc/dt** and its subdirectories.

How Configuration Files Play Together

From the material covered so far, you've probably concluded correctly that CDE configuration files aren't something to go hacking with without a plan - a well thought out plan. You've probably figured out that the element you want to configure and the breadth of influence you want it to have determine which configuration file you modify.

For instance, if you wanted to set an environment variable, you have a choice of four configuration files: **sys.dtprofile**, **Xconfig**, **Xsession**, and **.dtprofile**. But if you want to set environment variables that affect only a particular user, your choice immediately narrows to a single file, **.dtprofile**.

Now the only remaining piece of the puzzle is to understand the order in which CDE reads its configuration files. When a configuration element (an environment variable, resource, action, or data type) is specified twice but with different values, you obviously want the correct value used and the incorrect value ignored.

The following rules apply:

- For environment variables, the last specified value is used.

- For resources, the last specified value is used. However, this is influenced by specificity. Thus **emacs*foreground** takes precedence over just ***foreground** for emacs clients regardless of the order in which the resources were encountered.

- For actions, the first specified is used.

- For data types, the first specified is used.

Table 12-4 illustrates which specification is used when CDE reads multiple specifications of configuration elements in its configuration files:.

TABLE 12-4   WHAT CDE USES FOR CONFIGURATION

Configuration Element	Element Used
resource	last encountered or most specific
environment	last encountered
action	first encountered
file type	first encountered

Put in terms of scope, a user configuration file overrides a systemwide configuration file. Looking at the order of precedence of just systemwide configuration files, the files in **/etc/dt** have precedence over those in **/usr/dt**, so custom configurations have precedence over the CDE default configuration.

For resources, the elements used to specify a GUI's appearance and behavior, CDE sets values according to the following priorities:

1. Command line -   When you start a client from the command line, options listed on the command line have top priority.

2. **Xresources, .Xdefaults, dt.resources, sys.resources,** - When CDE starts, it reads these resource configuration files to determine the value of X resources to use for the session.

3. **RESOURCE MANAGER** - Resources already in the property **RESOURCE_MANAGER** may affect an application that is just starting.

4. **app-defaults** - Specifies "default" resource values that differ from built-in resource values.

5. built-in defaults - Default resources that are "hard coded" have the lowest priority.

Specific resource specifications take precedence over general resource specifications. For example, suppose you want a certain font in your text entry areas. You could correctly specify a ***FontList** resource in your personal **.Xdefaults** file only to have it overwritten by an ***XmText*FontList** in an **app-defaults** file. Although **app-defaults** is of lower priority than **.Xdefaults**, the resource specification set there is more specific, so it takes precedence.

For environment variables, CDE sets values according to the following priorities:

1. **$HOME/.dtprofile** - User-specific variables have top priority.

2. **/etc/dt/config/C/Xsession** - Custom systemwide variables not read by X server.

3. **/etc/dt/config/C/Xconfig** - Custom systemwide variables read by X server.

4. **/usr/dt/config/C/Xsession** - Default systemwide variables not read by X server.

5. **/usr/dt/config/C/Xconfig** - Default systemwide variables read by X server.

6. **/usr/dt/bin/dtlogin** - Built-in default variables have the lowest priority.

For datatype and action definitions, CDE looks for **.dt** files according to the following priority:

1. $HOME/.dt/types

2. /etc/dt/appconfig/types/C

3. /usr/dt/appconfig/types/C

Remember, for data types or actions, the first value it finds is the one it uses. So, if you just can't get a file type or action to work, check for a duplicate entry earlier in the file or for an entry in a file with higher priority. Note also that the environment variable DTDATABASESEARCH-PATH can be set either in **/etc/dt/config/Xsession** or **$HOME/.dtprofile** to add directories where CDE can search for file type and action definition information.

Specifying Appearance and Behavior

There are only two tricks to specifying appearance and behavior resources in configuration files. The first is to specify the resource and its value correctly. The second is to specify the resource and value in the correct configuration file.

Two caveats involve colors and fonts. The CDE style manager provides a graphical interface for modifying colors and fonts. However, if you specify an application's color or font directly, this specification will override the ability of the style manager to manage that resource for the application.

Typical ways to specify a color or font directly include the following:

• Type the specification on the command line as a startup option.

• Include the specification in the application's app-defaults file.

• Use the **xrdb** utility to add resources for the application to the resource database.

The Sequence of Events When CDE Starts

The following section is a blow-by-blow account of what happens when a user logs into CDE. In this particular account, assume a distributed topology like a diskless cluster. The account begins with the boot of the hub system and nodes in step 1. By step 4, X servers are running on each node and login screens are being displayed. By step 6, the user is logged in. By step 11, the session manager is busy re-creating the user's session.

1. The **dtlogin** executable is started as part of the **init** process that occurs during the system boot sequence on the hub machine and each cluster node.

2. **dtlogin** reads **/usr/dt/config/Xconfig** to get a list of resources with which to configure the login process. This is where **dtlogin** first learns about files like **Xaccess**, **Xservers**, **Xresources**, **Xstartup**, **Xsession**, and **Xreset** and gets the values of a number of appearance and behavior resources.

3. **dtlogin** reads two files in **/usr/dt/config**:

   • **Xservers**, or the file identified by the **Dtlogin*servers** resource setting in **Xconfig**.

   • **Xresources** or the file identified by the **Dtlogin*resources** resource setting in **Xconfig**.

4. **dtlogin** starts an X server and a child **dtlogin** for each local display.

5. Each child **dtlogin** invokes **dtgreet**, the login screen.

6. When a login and password are validated, a child **dtlogin** sets certain environment variables to default values.

7. The child **dtlogin** runs **/usr/dt/config/Xstartup**.

8. The child **dtlogin** runs **/usr/dt/config/Xsession**.

9. **Xsession** runs **dthello**, the copyright screen.

10. **Xsession** reads **$HOME/.dtprofile**, setting any additional environment variables or overwriting those set previously by **dtlogin**.

11. The child **dtlogin** invokes the session manager, **dtsession**.

12.**dtsession** restores the appropriate session. For example, to restore the current session, **dtsession** reads **dt.resources**, and **dt.session** in **$HOME/.dt/sessions/current**.

At logout, the reverse happens. The session is saved and **dtlogin** runs /**usr/dt/config/Xreset**. When **Xreset** completes, **dtlogin** again displays the login screen as in step 4.

Customizing CDE

Before you modify any CDE configuration files, first develop a strategy. I know I've mentioned this before, but it's important enough to mention again.

The following questions should get you started:

1. What are your user's needs?

2. Which of those needs can be met by reconfiguring CDE?

3. At what level should these changes be made (systemwide, groups of users, individual users only)?

4. Which CDE files do you need to modify (names and locations)?

5. What are the changes and what is their order within the file?

It's also a good idea to have handy a binder containing man pages for each of the CDE components (for looking up resources and their values) and a copy of each of the CDE configuration files.

The following sections assume you're making systemwide modifications. To make modifications for individual users, follow the same procedure on the equivalent user's personal file.

Adding Objects to or Removing Objects from the Front Panel

There are two ways to add objects to the CDE front panel:

•Drag and drop them into a slideup subpanel and then make them the default for that subpanel.

•Modify the **/etc/dt/appconfig/types/C/dtwm.fp** configuration file.

To add a control button through drag and drop,

1. Drag the application icon you want as a front panel button from an application manager view and drop the icon onto the installation section (the top section) of the appropriate subpanel.

2. Place the mouse pointer over the icon and press mouse button 3 to display the subpanel menu.

3. Select Copy to Main Panel.

To add a control button by editing the dtwm.fp file,

1. If you haven't already done so, copy **dtwm.fp** from **/usr/dt/app-config/types/C** to **/etc/dt/appconfig/types/C**.

2. Add the new control definition using the format:

```
CONTROL NewControl
{
TYPE            icon
CONTAINER_NAME  Top
CONTAINER_TYPE  BOX
ICON            NewControlBitmap
PUSH_ACTION     NewControlExecutable
}
```

Note that all control definitions have the following general syntax:

```
KEYWORD value
```

To avoid a lot of typing, it's easiest just to copy an existing definition and insert it where you want your new control to be and then modify it. As you move down the list of control definitions, you're moving from left to right across the front panel (Notice the POSITION_HINTS value increases in each definition.) So, if you want your new control to be to the right of the date on the front panel, you'd insert the control on the line below "date" and add a POSITION_HINTS 3 line to your definition; if you wanted your new control to be to the left of "date," insert the control on the line above "date" with a POSITION_HINTS of 1.

The new control definition can be located anywhere in the list of control definitions. The POSITION_HINTS line keeps it from getting inadvertently bumped to a new position. It's still a good idea to copy an existing definition and avoid extra typing - it reduces the chance of typing mistakes. Don't forget to include the curly braces.

The basic control definition has six parts:

- **•CONTROL name** - The definition name. This is the only part of the definition outside the curly braces.

- **•TYPE** - The type of control. Several types exist. The most useful for customizing the front panel are probably a blank and an icon. A blank is useful as a space holder. An icon can start an action or application or be a drop zone.

- **•ICON** - The bitmap to display on the front panel. Front panel bitmaps are located in the **/usr/dt/appconfig/icons** directory.

- **•CONTAINER_NAME** - The name of the container that holds the control. This must correspond to the name of an actual container listed in **dtwm.fp**.

- **•CONTAINER_TYPE** - The type of container that holds the control. This can be **BOX**, **SWITCH**, or **SUBPANEL**, but it must agree with the type of the container name

- **•PUSH_ACTION** - This is what happens when the control button is pushed. **PUSH_ACTION** is just one of several possible actions. For more information see the dtwm man page.

To remove a control button from the front panel, type a pound sign (#) in the leftmost column of the **CONTROL** definition line. The (#) turns the control specification into a comment line.

Changing the Front Panel in Other Ways

In addition to adding or removing buttons, you can shape the front panel in other ways. These other ways use workspace manager resources to modify default values. The following resources relate to the front panel:

- **clientTimeoutInterval** - Length of time the busy light blinks and the pointer remains an hourglass when a client is started from the front panel.

- **geometry** - x and y coordinate locations of the front panel.

- **highResFontList** - Font to use on a high-resolution display.

- **lowResFontList** - Font to use on a low-resolution display.

- **mediumResFontList** - Font to use on a medium-resolution display.

- **name** - Name of the front panel to use when there are multiple front panels in **dtwm.fp**.

- **pushButtonClickTime** - Time interval distinguishing two single mouse clicks from a double-click (to avoid double launching an application accidently).

- **waitingBlinkRate** - Blink rate of the front panel busy light.

- **workspaceList** - List of workspace names.

- **title** - Title to appear on a workspace button.

Like all other workspace manager resources, these front panel resources have the following syntax:

```
Dtwm*screen*resource: value
```

For example, suppose instead of the default four workspaces, your users need a front panel with six workspaces named Mail, Reports, Travel, Financials, Projects, and Studio. Further, they prefer a large font and have decided upon New Century Schoolbook 10-point bold. As system administrator, you'd make everyone happy with the following resource specifications:

```
Dtwm*0*workspaceList: One Two Three Four Five Six
Dtwm*0*One*title: Mail
Dtwm*0*Two*title: Reports
Dtwm*0*Three*title: Travel
Dtwm*0*Four*title: Financials
Dtwm*0*Five*title: Projects
Dtwm*0*Six*title: Studio
Dtwm*0*highResFontList:
          -adobe-new century schoolbook-bold-r-normal\
          --10-100-75-75-p-66-iso8859-1
```

The screen designation is usually 0, except for displays capable of both image and overlay planes. The order of screens in the **X*screens** file is what determines the screen number; the first screen, typically the image plane, is designated as 0. Note also the inclusion of workspace names (One, Two, Three, Four, Five, and Six) in the six title resource specifications.

If none of your users have ever logged in, you're in luck. You can add the above lines to **sys.resources**. But, since you're probably not that lucky (almost no one is), the easiest way to affect the changes is to use the **EditResources** action to insert the new resource lines into each user's

RESOURCE_MANAGER property and then restart the workspace manager.

The obvious disadvantage is that you have to physically go to each user's work area and take over the machine for a few minutes. However, on the plus side, the changes are immediate and are automatically saved in the correct **dt.resources** for users who restore their current session. You also avoid having your changes overwritten, which could happen if you modify the right **dt.resources** file at the wrong time, while the user is still logged in.

Have Some Fun Yourself

It's unfortunate, but often true, that users benefit from GUIs mostly because their system administrator has slogged through a **vi** or **emacs** session editing some configuration file to get things to work as desired. However, any time you need to edit resources, you can use CDE's drag-and-drop facility to your advantage, enjoy some of the fruits of your labor, and avoid some of the drudgery.

If **dtpad** is the default editor, you can create a file with the resource modifications in it, start the **EditResources** action, and then drop the resource modifications into the resource list that appears in the **EditResources dtpad** window.

If you haven't already played around with **dtpad**, try it. In most cases, you'll probably find it suitable for your users who need a small, fast text editor they can master without learning. **dtpad** has a menu bar with pull-down menus that contain some basic functionality. More important, **dtpad** supports cut-and-paste and drag-and-drop; users don't have to memorize commands but can simply select and manipulate text directly with the mouse.

Adding Things to Slideup Subpanels

Subpanels are defined in **dtwm.fp** after the front panel and front panel control definitions. To associate a subpanel with a front panel control button, the front panel control name is listed as the container name in the subpanel definition.

To add a slideup subpanel to the front panel:

1. Copy the file **/usr/dt/appconfig/types/C/dtwm.fp** to **/etc/dt/app-config/types/Cdtwm.fp** if you haven't already done so.

2. Decide which control button the slideup is to be associated with.

3. Create the subpanel definition file in **/etc/dt/appconfig/types/C/dtwm.fp**. This will take the following form:

```
SUBPANEL    SubPanelName
{
CONTAINER_NAME  AssociatedFrontPanelControlButton
TITLE   SubPanelTitle
}
```

4. Create subpanel control definitions for the subpanel. These will take the following form:

```
CONTROL   ControlName
{
TYPE   icon
CONTAINER_NAME     SubPanelName
CONTAINER_TYPE     SUBPANEL
ICON   BitmapName
PUSH_ACTION     ActionName
}
```

As with front panel control buttons, it's easier to copy and modify an existing subpanel file than to start from scratch.

Front Panel Animation

Animation for front panel or slideup subpanel drop zones is created by displaying a progressive series of bitmaps. By convention, the bitmaps are in **/usr/dt/appconfig/icons**. The list of bitmaps to display is contained in animation definitions at the end of **dtwm.fp**.

To create an animation sequence for a drop zone:

1. Create a progressive series of bitmaps.

2. Add a list of these bitmap files to the appropriate configuration file using the following syntax:

```
ANIMATION AnimationName
{
 bitmap0
 bitmap1
 bitmap2
 bitmap3
 bitmap4
 bitmap5
}
```

3. Add a line to the appropriate control definition using the syntax:

```
DROP_ANIMATION AnimationName
```

Adding Things to the Workspace Menu

The workspace menu is defined in **sys.dtwmrc**. For one or two changes, you can modify the existing workspace menu. For major changes, it's probably easier to insert an entirely new menu definition in **sys.dtwmrc**.

A menu definition has the following syntax:

```
Menu MenuName
{
 "Menu Name"        f.title
 "Frame"            f.exec /nfs/system1/usr/frame/bin/maker
 "Second Item"      action
 "Third Item"       action
}
```

The first line specifies the menu name, following the keyword **Menu**. The lines between the curly braces list the items that appear in the menu in their order of appearance; thus the first line is the title as designated by the function **f.title**. The second line is an example of a definition that would start **FrameMaker** on a remote application server in a distributed environment. Numerous other functions exist, approximately 45 in all. For a complete list, see the **dtwmrc** (4) man page.

For users to display the menu, you need to bind the menu definition to a mouse button and a screen location using the action **f.menu MenuName**. For example, if your users want to post the menu by pressing mouse button 3 when the pointer is on the workspace background, you would insert the following line in the Mouse Button Bindings Description section at the end of **sys.dtwmrc**:

```
<Btn3Down> root f.menu MenuName
```

(Actually, it would be easier to modify the line that's already there by exchanging **MenuName** for **DtRootMenu** on the second line.)

Creating Actions and File Types

An action starts a process such as a shell script or an application. An action can be connected to a front panel button to start when the button is pushed. An action can be connected to a front panel drop zone to be performed when a data file is dropped on the drop zone. An action can be associated with an icon in a file manager window so the action can be started by double-clicking the icon. An action can be associated with a particular data type so that double-clicking the data file icon starts the action and opens the data file.

In addition to setting up a front panel and default session to meet your user's needs, the single most important thing you can do to make computing life easier for the people who depend on you is to create actions and data types.

CDE actions and data types are defined in files that end in **.dt** (for desk top). Similar to most other CDE configuration files, ***.dt** files have a systemwide version which can be copied into a user's personal directory and customized for personal use. Most systemwide ***.dt** files are found in **/usr/dt/appconfig/types/C**; personal ***.dt** files are created by copying **user-prefs.dt** from **/usr/dt/appconfig/types/C** to **$HOME/.dt/types**.

The default search path CDE uses to look for actions and file types includes the following main directories in the order listed:

- $HOME/.dt/types

- /etc/dt/appconfig/types

- /usr/dt/appconfig/types

You can add further directories to the search path using the **DTDA-TABASESEARCHPATH** environment variable. Insert this environment variable and the new search path in **/usr/dt/config/Xsession** for a systemwide influence. Insert the environment variable and search path in **$HOME/.dtprofile** for individual users.

The following are the recommended locations in which to create an action or file type definition:

- Create a completely new file in the **/etc/dt/appconfig/types** directory. This file will have a systemwide influence. Remember, the file must end with the **.dt** extension.

- Copy **user-prefs.dt** from **/usr/dt/appconfig/types** to the **/etc/dt/appconfig/types** directory and insert the definition there for systemwide use.

- Copy **user-prefs.vf** to **$HOME/.dt/types** and insert the definition there for individual users.

A typical action has the following syntax:

```
ACTION        ActionName
{
 TYPE         type
 keyword      value
 keyword      value
}
```

For example, here's a FrameMaker action:

```
ACTION       FRAME
{
   TYPE        COMMAND
   WINDOW-TYPE NO-STDIO
   EXEC-STRING /nfs/hpcvxmk6/usr/frame/bin/maker
}
```

A typical data type has the following syntax:

```
DATA_ATTRIBUTES          AttributesName
{
   keyword          value
   keyword          value
   ACTIONS          action, action
}
DATA_CRITERIA
{
 DATA_ATTRIBUTES AttributesName
```

```
keyword          value

keyword          value

}
```

Notice that a data type definition is actually in two parts, an attribute part and a criteria part. The attribute portion of the data type definition specifies the look of the datatype; the criteria portion specifies the behavior of the data type.

For example, here's a file type for FrameMaker files that uses the FRAME action:

```
DATA_ATTRIBUTES     FRAME_Docs

{
  DESCRIPTION       This file type is for frameMaker documents.
   ICON             makerIcon
   ACTIONS          FRAME
}

DATA_CRITERIA

{

DATA_ATTRIBUTES_NAME   FRAME_Docs

NAME_PATTERN   *.fm

MODE    f

}
```

You can create actions and file types from scratch using these formats. However, the easiest way to create an action is to use the **CreateAction** tool. **CreateAction** is located in the Desktop Applications folder of the Applications Manager and presents you with a fill-in-the-blank dialog box that guides you through creating an **action.dt** file containing the action definition. You can then move this file to the appropriate directory for the range of influence you want the action to have: **/etc/dt/appconfig/types** for a systemwide influence; **$HOME/.dt/types** for individual users.

Using Different Fonts

Although CDE fonts have been carefully selected for readability, you may have valid reasons to prefer other fonts. To make your fonts available systemwide throughout the CDE environment, put them in **/etc/dt/app-defaults/Dtstyle** so they will appear in the style manager's font dialog box. To make fonts available only for a particular X client application, specify the font in the **app-defaults** file for the application; by convention this file is located in **/usr/lib/X11/app-defaults**. Just remember, this overrides the fonts in the style manager.

The font dialog box can contain a maximum of seven font sizes. You can adjust this number downward by resetting the value of **Dtstyle*Num-Fonts** in **/etc/dt/app-defaults/Dtstyle**; however, you can't increase the number higher than seven.

The Font Dialog section of the **Dtstyle** configuration file has seven **SystemFont** resources and seven **UserFont** resources. Again, you can have fewer than seven system and seven user fonts, but you can't have more.

To specify fonts for a particular application, use the ***FontList** resource in the **app-defaults** file for the application.

To modify font resources on an individual-user basis, you can use the **EditResources** action as described in the section"Changing the Front Panel in Other Ways.

CDE and Performance

CDE isn't a monolithic application; it's a set of components layered on top of the operating system, the X Window System, and Motif. Each underlying layer takes its share of RAM before CDE or any other client even starts. Because of the low-level nature of these layers, the RAM they use is hardly ever regained through swapping to disk.

In some cases, operating system overhead and user application requirements restrict the amount of RAM available for a graphical user interface to little more than enough to run a window manager such as Motif. Since the CDE workspace manager and the Motif window manager take roughly the same amount of RAM, users can enjoy an enriched graphical environment with the added value of the CDE's multiple workspaces at essentially no extra RAM cost over running the Motif window manager.

Sample RAM Sizes

Table 12-5 illustrates some sample RAM sizes for HP VUE 3.0. Official numbers for CDE are not yet available, but should be similar, though a little bigger, than those contained in Table 12.5. The numbers represent working environment RAM and the RAM required after login; during login, a spike in RAM usage occurs as applications and other processes start up. This spike would include, in the case of CDE, starting **dtlogin**, **Xsession**, and **dtsession**. Immediately after login, these clients become inactive and are swapped out, so they don't appear in the working environment numbers.

A word of warning: Don't read too much into the numbers. RAM usage numbers vary with the system, the application set, and especially with how the application set is used by each user.

Additionally, kernel size, daemon size, and X server size can vary widely depending on the configuration and the user. An X server hack may be running an X server stripped down to just 1/2 MByte, the supposed X server ThrashPoint, and get excellent performance. Alternatively, a user with a penchant for large root window bitmaps can quickly swell their X server size to 12 MBytes and still not have reached the RMaxPoint.

TABLE 12-5   SAMPLE HYPOTHETICAL RAM SIZES

Process	ThrashPoint	MTRAM	RMaxPoint
misc daemons	2 MBytes	3 MBytes	5 MBytes
file buffers	1-1/2 MBytes	3-1/4 MBytes	6-1/2 MBytes
kernel	2 MBytes	3 MBytes	5 MBytes
Xserver	1/2 MBytes	2 MBytes	7 MBytes
workspace manager	3/4 MBytes	1 MBytes	1-1/4 MBytes
file manager	1/2 MBytes	3/4 MBytes	2 MBytes
help manager	1/2 MBytes	3/4 MBytes	1 MBytes
style manager	1/2 MBytes	1 MBytes	1 MBytes
hpterm console	1/2 MBytes	3/4 MBytes	1-1/4 MBytes
message server	1/4 MBytes	1/3 MBytes	1/2 MBytes
Total	9 MBytes	16+ MBytes	30-1/2MBytes

The ThrashPoint column shows the typical absolute minimum RAM required to "run" the default HP VUE components, including operating system and X server overhead, however, "run" is a misnomer. The Thrash-Point is when the system just sits there and thrashes, swapping pages in and out of RAM, unable to get enough of an application's code into RAM to execute it before having to swap it out.

The RMaxPoint column shows the other extreme, a reasonable maximum amount of RAM for running the default HP VUE including operating system and X server overhead. The RMaxPoint is when all code for every process is in RAM so nothing gets swapped out. The sizes for some items in this column can vary considerably; the kernel hack's kernel size would be smaller; the user with a penchant for big root window bitmaps would have an X server considerably larger.

The MTRAM column shows a typical amount of RAM required to run the default CDE including operating system and X server overhead. The MTRAM is when a typical user experiences acceptable performance. Acceptable means real-time response to visual controls and drag-and-drop. Again, a caveat: If the user is doing a local compile or working remotely on a heavily loaded network, performance will be worse. If the user is mostly reading Email and word processing, performance will be better.

From the table, the typical size of HP VUE (without operating system or X server overhead) is 6^+ MBytes. HP VUE includes the HP VUE managers (the Motif window manager is included in the workspace manager), a console hpterm, and the message server.

For best results with CDE, better figure a minimum of 24 Mbytes of RAM with 32 Mbytes or better being preferred.

Tactics for Better Performance

Unless all your users have RAM-loaded powerhouses for systems, you will need to spend some time developing a performance strategy. If you conceive of performance as a bell-shaped curve, satisfaction lies on the leading edge. Your performance strategy should do everything it can to keep your users on the leading edge.

Probably the most logical approach is to start small and grow. In other words, start out with minimal user environments on all the systems on your network. Gradually add software components until you or your users begin to notice performance degradation. Then back off a little. Such an approach might take several weeks or more to evaluate as you add components and as your users spend several days actually working in the environment to determine the effect of your changes on system performance and their frustration levels.

The most RAM-expensive pieces of CDE are the workspace manager, the session manager, and the file manager. The workspace manager is expensive because portions of it are always in RAM (assuming you are moving windows around and switching workspaces). The CDE workspace manager is no more expensive than the Motif window manager; if you want a GUI, it's just a price you have to pay. The session manager is expensive only during logout and login as it saves and restores sessions. The rest of the time, the session manager is dormant and gets swapped out of RAM. Saving your current work session is nice at the end of the day, but it's something to consider giving up if you want to improve your login and logout performance. The file manager is expensive because it wakes up periodically and jumps into RAM to check the status of the file system and update its file manager windows. When it jumps into RAM, it pushes something else out, for example, maybe the desktop publishing program you're using.

Here are some other ideas that you may find useful:

Terminal Emulators	**xterms** are a little less RAM-expensive than **dtterms**. Unless you need the block mode functionality of an **dtterm**, **xterm** might be a better choice for terminal emulation.
Automatic Saves	Some applications automatically save data at periodic intervals. While this feature can be beneficial, you need to evaluate its effect in light of performance. If the application is

central to your users' work, fine, but if not, it might be a good idea to disable the automatic save feature.

Scroll Buffers   Large scroll buffers in terminal emulators can be a real convenience, but they can also take up a lot of RAM. Even modestly sized scroll buffers, when multiplied by three or four terminal emulators, consume a lot of RAM.

Background Bitmaps Avoid large bitmaps; they increase the X server size. Especially avoid switching large bitmaps frequently within a session. If you are hunting for a new background, be sure to restart the X server after you've found the one you want and have included it in the proper **sessionetc** file. The most efficient bitmaps are small ones that can be repeated to tile the background.

Front Panel   Reconfigure the front panel to minimize the number of buttons. Keep just enough to meet user needs. This decreases the workspace manager size in RAM and speeds login and logout.

Pathnames   Whenever possible, use absolute pathnames for bitmap specifications. While this decreases the flexibility of the system, it speeds access time

Conclusion

Graphical User Interfaces are here to stay. While they offer users an easy-to-learn, easy-to-use computing environment, they can make life a little uneasy for system administrators. The default CDE is ready to use, but given its power and flexibility, you will inevitably want to customize the CDE environment for your users' work context and optimum performance. Take the time to develop a good idea of what changes you need to make, the order in which to make them, and exactly where to make them. In so doing, all the power and flexibility of CDE will be open to you.

CHAPTER 13

Windows NT and HP-UX Interoperability -

The X Window System

Interoperability Topics

I could spend another 500 pages covering just Windows NT and HP-UX interoperability. There are hundreds of technologies and products that enhance Windows NT and HP-UX interoperability. Since it would not be feasible for me to cover even a small fraction of these technologies and products in this book, I decided to devote five chapters to five technologies that bridge the gap between some fundamental Windows NT and HP-UX differences in operation. The following is a list of what I consider to be the top interoperability topics, which are covered in the interoperability chapters of this book.

- **HP-UX Application Server That Displays on HP-UX Using the X Window System (covered in this chapter)** - X Windows is a networked windowing environment that is the standard on HP-UX systems. If you install X Windows on your Windows NT system, you can run applications on your HP-UX system and use X Windows on your Windows NT to manage those applications. The HP-UX system is acting as the application server but the applications are controlled from X Windows running on the Windows NT system.

- **Network File System (NFS) Used to Share Data (Covered in Chapter 14)** - The next chapter covers using NFS to share data between Windows NT and HP-UX systems. NFS comes with HP-UX and by loading NFS on a Windows NT system you can freely access HP-UX file system on the Windows NT systems and vice versa. I focus only on accessing HP-UX file systems on the Windows NT systems because, as I earlier mentioned, I think it is more likely the HP-UX system will act as a data and application server and the Windows NT system will act as a client. There is, however, no reason that NFS could not be used to access Windows NT file systems while on an HP-UX system.

- **Windows NT Functionality on HP-UX (Covered in Chapter 15)** - Putting the X Window System and NFS on Windows NT brings important HP-UX functionality to the Windows NT operating system. It is equally useful to bring Windows NT functionality to HP-UX. Advanced Server 9000 is a software product that runs on HP-UX and brings important Windows NT functionality such as file and print services to HP-UX. There is a chapter devoted to Advanced Server 9000.

- **Common Set of Commands (Covered in Chapter 16)** - The Windows NT Resource Kit provides countless useful utilities including a set of POSIX commands that are familiar to HP-UX system administrators. Commands such as **chmod**, **ls**, and **mv** run on Windows NT. There is a chapter devoted to these utilities.

- **Common Software Development Environment (Covered in Chapter 17)** - With a mixed Windows NT and HP-UX based software development environment there come a lot of challenges. Any time you mix two or more operating systems in software development you end up with different development tools, compilers, and other functionality. HP SoftBench OpenStudio is a development environment that provides common development functionality in a

mixed Windows NT and HP-UX software development environment.

The previous chapters in this book cover Windows NT and HP-UX
topics separately. Although the system administration topics are pretty
much the same going from operating system to operating system, the peculiarities of each operating system define how you will perform a given
function. For this reason system administration is seldom covered as a general topic; rather, it is covered for a particular operating system. In this
book, however, the assumption is that you have both Windows NT and HP-
UX in your environment. You need to manage both and manage them separately for the most part; however, there are advantages to implementing
technology that can enhance interoperability between the two operating
systems.

What I'll cover in the interoperability chapters of this book are some
of the most basic, and at the same time some of the most useful, technologies you can put in place to help with interoperability between Windows
NT and HP-UX.

You could certainly go beyond the interoperability topics I cover to
much more advanced functionality; however, what I cover in the interoperability chapters is a big interoperability gain for very little cost and effort.

This chapter and the next work together and build on one another. In
this chapter I cover Windows NT and HP-UX interoperability by running
an X server program on a Windows NT system which provides graphical
access to an HP-UX system. Then, in Chapter 14, I use a networking product on the Windows NT system that provides transparent access to the data
on the HP-UX system using Network File System (NFS). Using the X
Window System (X Windows), you have a graphical means of connecting
a Windows NT system to an HP-UX system and using NFS you have a
way of easily sharing data between these two systems. These two technologies, X Windows and NFS, provide the foundation for a variety of other
useful interoperability between the two operating systems.

Why the X Window System?

We have covered both the Windows NT and HP-UX user environments in previous chapters. Windows NT and HP-UX have their user environments which work great in supporting their respective operating systems.

If, however, you want to go beyond logging into a Windows NT system to perform Windows NT system administration and logging into an HP-UX system to perform HP-UX system administration, then you need some way of etting access to one of these systems from the other. The X Window System is an ideal way to get remote access to an HP-UX system while sitting on your Windows NT system.

X Window System Background

X Windows is a NETWORK- based windowing environment, not a system-based windowing environment. For this reason it is ideal for giving you a window into your HP-UX system from your Windows NT system.

X Windows is an industry standard for supporting windowed user interfaces across a computer network. Because it is an industry standard, many companies offer X server products for operating systems such as Windows NT (we'll get into the "server" and "client" terminology of X Windows shortly.) X Windows is not just a windowing system on your computer but a windowing system across the network.

X Windows is independent of the hardware or operating system on which it runs. All it needs is a server and a client. The server and client may be two different systems or the same system; it doesn't matter. The server is a program which provides input devices such as your display, keyboard, and mouse. The client is the program that takes commands from the server such as an application.

The client and server roles are much different than those we normally associate with these terms. The X Windows server is on your local system; in this chapter it will be your Windows NT system, and the X Windows client is the application that responds to the server; in this chapter it will be the HP-UX system running a program such as the System Administration Manager (SAM) or HP SoftBench. We normally think of the small desktop system as the client and the larger, more powerful system as the server.

With X Windows, however, it is the system that controls X Windows that is the server and the system that responds to the commands is the client. I often refer to a powerful client as the "host" to minimize confusion over this.

Sitting on one of the Windows NT systems on a network, you could open an X Window into several HP-UX hosts. You could therefore have one window open to HP-UX_System1 and another window open to HP-UX_System2, and so on.

X Server Software

There are many fine X Server products on the market. I loaded Exceed 5 from Hummingbird Communications LTD. on my system for demonstrating how X Windows can be used in a Windows NT and HP-UX environment. Figure 13-1 shows the full menu structure from having loaded both Hummingbird's X Windows product Exceed as well as its NFS product, which I'll be using in the next chapter, called Maestro.

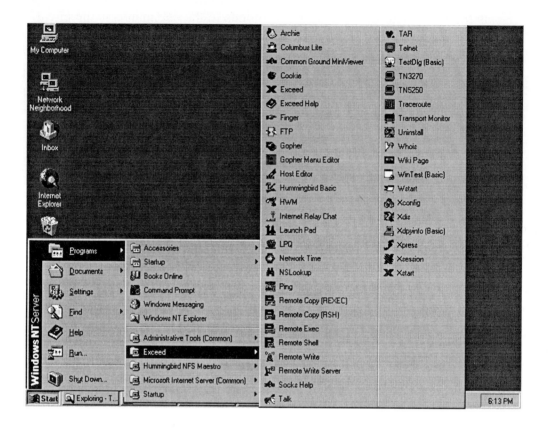

Figure 13-1 *Programs-Exceed* Menu

Not all of the items shown in the *Programs-Exceed* menu are related to X Windows. Many are for the networking products I'll get into in the next chapter.

The last menu pick under *Exceed* is *Xstart*. This menu pick allows you to establish an X Windows connection between your Windows NT system and HP-UX system. You can specify the host to which you want to connect, the HP-UX system in this case, the user you want to be connected as on the host, and the command to run on the HP-UX system. Figure 13-2 shows the *Xstart* window.

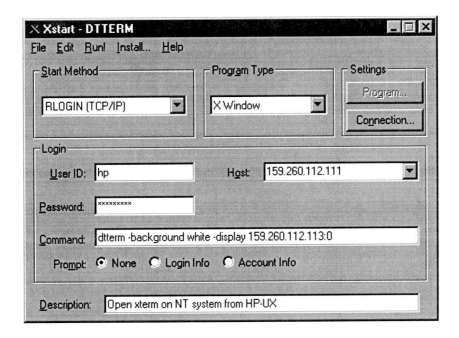

Figure 13-2 Establishing an X Windows Connection

The window in Figure 13-2 is labeled "dtterm". After you set up the *Xstart* window with the information you want you can save the configuration. In this case I am issuing the **dtterm** command so I saved the window under this name. The complete **dtterm** command is:

dtterm -background white -display 159.260.112.113:0

This command will start a **dtterm** window, which is a standard window program on HP-UX with a white background, and display the window on the system at the IP address 159.260.112.113. The IP address in this case is the Windows NT system on which you are issuing the command which is the X Windows server. The ":0" indicates that the first display on the Windows NT system will be used for **dtterm** because in the X Windows world it is possible to have several displays connected to a system.

The system on which the command runs is 159.260.112.111. This is the HP-UX system which acts as the X Windows client.

When you hit *Run!* from the pull down menu, the **dtterm** command will be run on the host you have specified in the dialog box. Although you are typing this information on your Windows NT system, this command is being transferred to the HP-UX you specified in the *Xstart* box. This will have the same result as typing the **dtterm** command shown on the HP-UX system directly.

When you hit *Run!* a **dtterm** window appears on your Windows NT system which is a window into your HP-UX system. Figure 13-3 shows the **dtterm** window open on the Windows NT system.

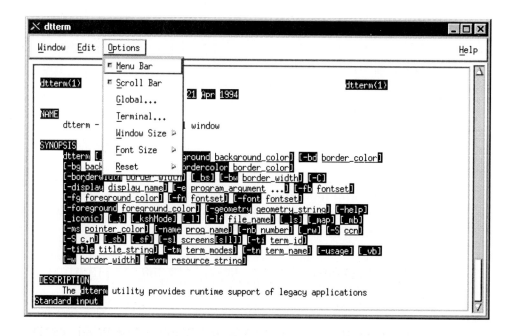

Figure 13-3 **dtterm** Running on HP-UX and Displayed on Windows NT

Figure 13-3 is a **dtterm** window displayed on the Windows NT system but running on the HP-UX system. The window has open the HP-UX manual page for **dtterm** and one of the pull down menus of **dtterm**. You could issue any commands in this **dtterm** window that you could issue if you were sitting on the HP-UX system directly. Keep in mind, though, that your access to the HP-UX system is based on the user you specified in the *Xstart* window.

You could use *Xstart* to run any program for which you have appropriate permissions on the HP-UX system. Figure 13-4 shows an **xterm** window which is displayed on the Windows NT system but is running on the HP-UX system.

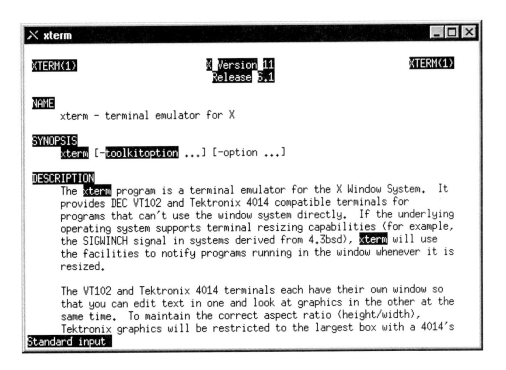

Figure 13-4 **xterm** Running on HP-UX and Displayed on Windows NT

You are by no means limited to running only terminal windows such as **dtterm** and **xterm** under X Windows in this environment. You could perform system management functions as well. Figure 13-5 shows the System Administration Manager (SAM), which was covered in an earlier chapter, running on the HP-UX system and displayed on the Windows NT system with *DCE Cell Management* selected.

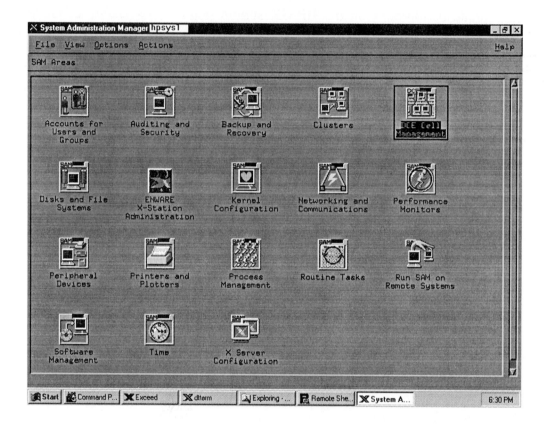

Figure 13-5 SAM Running on HP-UX and Displayed on Windows NT

In this case I have maximized the SAM window to take up the entire Windows NT environment. You still have access to the *Task Bar* at the bottom of the screen.

Another common use of X Windows software in this environment is for program development. Many users on the Windows NT system could get access to HP-UX servers using X Windows. Figure 13-6 shows the HP SoftBench development tool running on the HP-UX system and displayed on the Windows NT system. An application like SoftBench opens up many X Windows on the Windows NT system which is handled for you by the X server software.

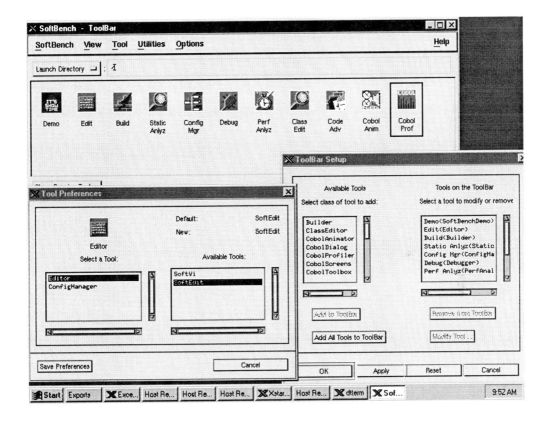

Figure 13-6 HP SoftBench Running on HP-UX and Displayed on Windows NT

This technique, using X Windows on the Windows NT system to display applications running on the HP-UX system, is powerful in this heterogenous environment. It is also inexpensive and simple to install.

We can also take this interoperability one step further by introducing data sharing into this mixed environment. This is covered in the next chapter.

CHAPTER 14

Windows NT and HP-UX Interoperability - Networking

Why Cover Interoperability?

The previous chapters in this book, except for Chapter 13, cover Windows NT and HP-UX topics separately. Although the system administration topics are pretty much the same going from operating system to operating system, the peculiarities of each operating system define how you will perform a given function. For this reason system administration is seldom covered as a general topic; rather, it is covered for a particular operating system. In this book, however, the assumption is that you have both Windows NT and HP-UX in your environment. You need to manage both and manage them separately for the most part; however, there are advantages to implementing technology that can enhance interoperability between the two operating systems.

What I'll cover in the interoperability chapters of this book are some of the most basic, and at the same time some of the most useful, technologies you can put in place to help with interoperability between Windows NT and HP-UX.

You could certainly go beyond the interoperability topics I cover to much more advanced functionality; however, what I cover in the interoperability chapters is a big interoperability gain for very little cost and effort.

This chapter and Chapter 13 combine to provide background of some useful interoperability. In this chapter I use a networking product on the Windows NT system that provides transparent access to the data on the HP-UX system using Network File System (NFS). In Chapter 13 I covered Windows NT and HP-UX interoperability by running an X server program on a Windows NT system which provides graphical access to an HP-UX system. Using the X Window System (X Windows) you have a graphical means of connecting a Windows NT system to an HP-UX system and using NFS you have a way of easily sharing data between these two systems. These two technologies, X Windows and NFS, provide the foundation for a variety of other useful interoperability between the two operating systems.

NFS Background

Chapters 1 and 7 provided TCP/IP background and TCP/IP configuration of a Windows NT system was also covered in an earlier chapter so I suggest you read those chapters if you have not done so already. I am going to jump right into NFS background in this chapter and won't go over the TCP/IP material covered in earlier chapters. I am not going to limit the discussion and examples in this chapter to NFS. There are other services used to share files that are also useful such as File Transfer Protocol (FTP) which I'll show examples of as well. Because NFS is so widely used in the HP-UX user community, it is one of my goals to expose you to how NFS can be used in a Windows NT and HP-UX environment.

NFS allows you to mount disks on remote systems so they appear as though they are local to your system. Similarly, NFS allows remote systems to mount your local disk so it looks as though it is local to the remote system.

NFS, like X Windows, has a unique set of terminology. Here are definitions of some of the more important NFS terms.

Node	A computer system that is attached to or is part of a computer network.
Client	A node that requests data or services from other nodes (servers).
Server	A node that provides data or services to other nodes (clients) on the network.
File System	A disk partition or logical volume, or in the case of a workstation, this might be the entire disk.
Export	To make a file system available for mounting on remote nodes using NFS.
Mount	To access a remote file system using NFS.
Mount Point	The name of a directory on which the NFS file system is mounted.
Import	To mount a remote file system.

Before any data can be shared using NFS, the HP-UX system must be set up with exported file systems. The **/etc/exports** file in HP-UX defines what file systems are exported.

This file has in it the directories exported and options such as "ro" for read only, and "anon" which handles requests from anonymous users. If "anon" is equal to 65535, then anonymous users are denied access.

The following is an example **/etc/exports** file in which **/opt/app1** is exported to everyone but anonymous users, and **/opt/app1** is exported only to the system named system2:

```
/opt/app1    -anon=65534
/opt/app2    -access=system2
```

You may need to run **/usr/sbin/exportfs -a** if you add a file system to export.

Although we are going to focus on exporting HP-UX file systems to be mounted by Windows NT systems in this chapter, there is no reason we could not do the converse as well. Windows NT file systems could be mounted on an HP-UX system just as HP-UX file systems are mounted in Windows NT. Remote file systems to be mounted locally on an HP-UX system are put in **/etc/fstab**. Here is an example of an entry in **/etc/fstab** of a remote file system that is mounted locally. The remote directory **/opt/app3** on system2 is mounted locally under **/opt/opt3**:

```
system2:/opt/app3   /opt/app3   nfs   rw,suid   0   0
```

You can use the **showmount** command on HP-UX systems to show all remote systems (clients) that have mounted a local file system. **showmount** is useful for determining the file systems that are most often mounted by clients with NFS. The output of **showmount** is particularly easy to read because it lists the host name and the directory which was mounted by the client. There are the three following options to the **showmount** command:

-a prints output in the format "name:directory" as shown above.

-d lists all of the local directories that have been remotely mounted by clients.

-e prints a list of exported file systems.

Using Windows NT and HP-UX Networking

I will use the NFS Maestro product from Hummingbird Communications LTD. on Windows NT to demonstrate the networking interoperability in this chapter. Figure 14-1 shows the menu for the Maestro product after I installed it.

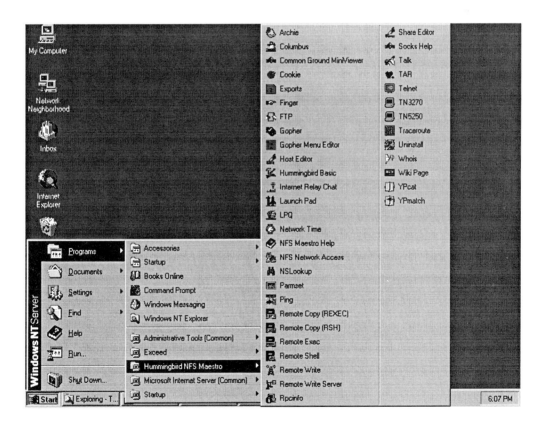

Figure 14-1 Hummingbird Maestro Menu in Windows NT

As you can see in Figure 14-1 there is much more than NFS functionality that is part of Maestro. I will cover some additional functionality later
in this chapter; however, my specific objectives are to cover the most
important Windows NT and HP-UX interoperability topics related to networking.

Before we use NFS with our Windows NT and HP-UX systems, let's
first see what file systems we have available to us.

Using the **dtterm** from the previous chapter we can sit at the Windows NT system and open a window into the HP-UX system. Figure 14-2
shows opening a **dtterm** and viewing the **/etc/exports** file.

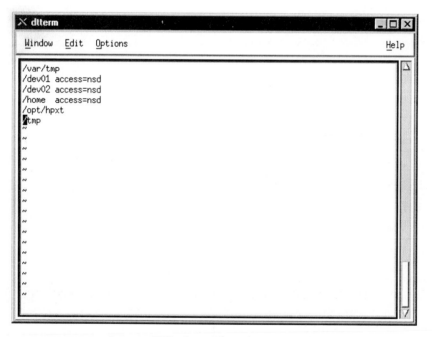

Figure 14-2 **dtterm** Window Showing **/etc/exports** on HP-UX System

There are several file systems exported on this HP-UX system. Some, such as **/opt/hpxt** and **/tmp,** have no restrictions on them; others do have restrictions. We don't, however, have to open a **dtterm** in order to see this file. We can use the Maestro menu pick *Exports* to bring up the window shown in figure 14-3.

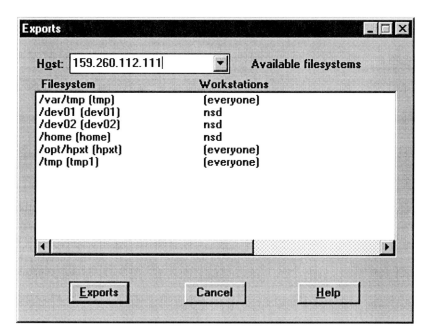

Figure 14-3 *Exports* Window Showing Exported File Systems

You can use the IP address as shown in the figure or the host name to specify the host on which you wish to view the exported file systems. You can see that this window takes the **/etc/exports** file and clarifies some of the entries. The entries for which there are no restrictions now have an "(everyone)" associated with them.

Now we can specify one or more of these exported file systems on the HP-UX system that we wish to mount on the Windows NT system. Using the *NFS Network Access* from the Maestro menu, we can specify one of these file systems to mount. Figure 14-4 shows mounting **/home** on the HP-UX system on the **G:** drive of the Windows NT system.

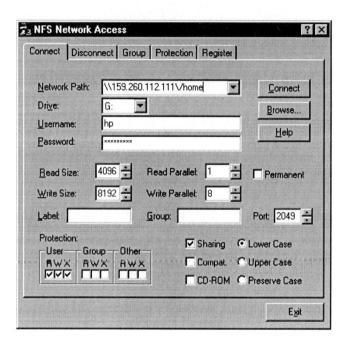

Figure 14-4 *NFS Network Access* Window Mounting **/home** as **G:**

After you hit the *Connect* button in the window, you will have **/home** mounted as **G:**. The means by which you specify the system and file system you wish to mount with Maestro is two slashes preceding the IP address or system name, another slash following the IP address or system name, and then the name of the file system you wish to mount. Note that the forward slash is part of the file system name. I used the IP address of the system. To view all of the mounted file systems on the Windows NT system you could invoke Windows NT *Explorer*. Figure 14-5 shows several file systems mounted in an *Explorer* window including **/home** on **G:**.

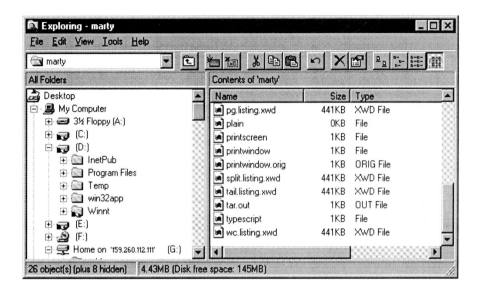

Figure 14-5 Windows NT *Explorer* Showing **/home** as **G:**

This window shows **/home** on drive **G:**. On the right side of the window is a listing of files in **/home/marty** on the HP-UX system. These files are now fully accessible on the Windows NT system (provided the appropriate access rights have been provided). You could now manipulate these HP-UX files in *Explorer* on the Windows NT system just as if they were local to the system. This is a powerful concept - to go beyond the barrier of only the Windows NT file system to freely manipulate HP-UX files.

An example of how you might go about using *Explorer* is to copy a Windows NT directory to HP-UX. Figure 14-6 shows two *Explorer* windows. The top window has an **exceed** directory on the Windows NT system which is being copied to a directory of the same name on the HP-UX system in the bottom window. As the copy from the Windows NT system to the HP-UX system takes place, a status window appears which shows the name of the file within the **exceed** directory (**exstart1.bmp**) being copied.

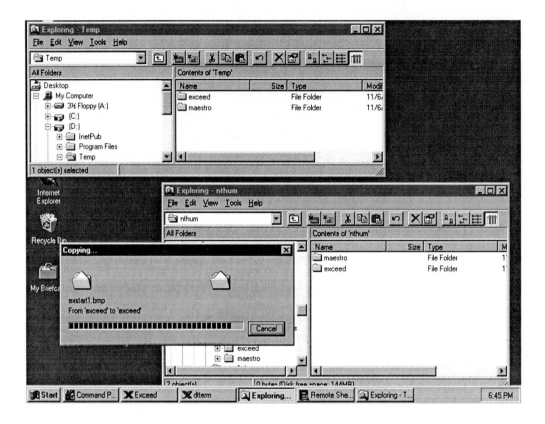

Figure 14-6   Copy a Windows NT Directory to HP-UX Using *Explorer*

This copy from Windows NT to HP-UX using *Explorer* demonstrates the ease with which files can be shared between these two operating systems.

File Transfer Protocol (FTP)

I started this chapter covering NFS on Windows NT and HP-UX for interoperability because NFS is the predominate means of sharing files in the HP-UX world. NFS is used almost universally to share data among networked HP-UX systems. NFS allows you to share data in real time, meaning that you can work on an HP-UX file while sitting at your Windows NT system. This is file sharing. You can also copy data between your Windows NT and HP-UX systems using FTP. This is not file sharing, however; the FTP functionality of Maestro makes it easy to transfer files between Windows NT and HP-UX.

Figure 14-7 shows the window that you would use to establish a connection to an HP-UX system from Windows NT.

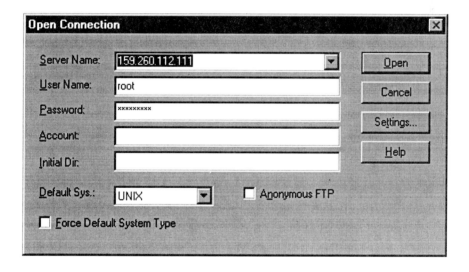

Figure 14-7   Establishing a Connection to HP-UX from Windows NT

After having established the connection, a window appears in which you can traverse the HP-UX file systems while working at your Windows NT system. Figure 14-8 shows viewing the **/opt/softbench** directory on an HP-UX system through the FTP window.

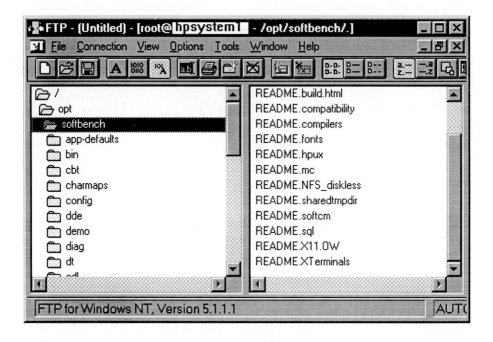

Figure 14-8 Viewing the **/opt/softbench** Directory Using *FTP* Window

You can also copy files graphically using FTP. You can open two *FTP* windows and copy files and directories from one system to the other. Figure 14-9 shows copying the directory **d:\temp\maestro** on the Windows NT system to **/home/marty/nthum/maestro** on the HP-UX system. This was performed using the icons in the two windows. The **maestro** directory did not exist on the HP-UX and was created as part of the copy.

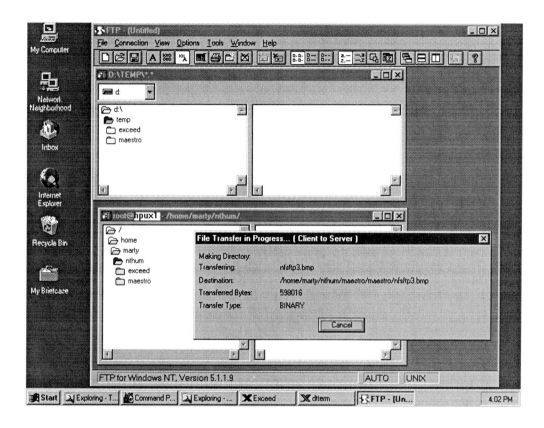

Figure 14-9 Using FTP to Copy Directory from Windows NT to HP-UX

There are a variety of options you can select when running FTP. Notice in figure 14-9 that the "Transfer Type:" is binary. This is one of the options I selected prior to initiating the transfer.

Although this functionality is not as extensive as the file sharing of NFS, it is widely used to copy files from system to system and therefore can play a role in Windows NT and HP-UX interoperability.

I used icons to specify the information to be copied in this example. You could also have used the FTP command. The following is an overview of FTP including an example of running it from the command line and a command summary.

File Transfer Protocol (FTP)   Transfer a file, or multiple files, from one system to another such as Windows NT to HP-UX. The following example shows copying the file **/tmp/krsort.c** from system2 (remote host) to the local directory on system1 (local host).

	comments
$ ftp system2	Issue ftp command
Connected to system2.	
system2 FTP server (Version 16.2) ready.	
Name (system2:root): root	Login to system2
Password required for root.	
Password:	Enter password
User root logged in.	
Remote system type is UNIX.	
Using binary mode to transfer files.	
ftp> **cd /tmp**	**cd** to **/tmp** on system2
CWD command successful	
ftp> **get krsort.c**	Get **krsort.c** file
PORT command successful	
Opening BINARY mode data connection for **krsort.c**	
Transfer complete.	
2896 bytes received in 0.08 seconds	
ftp> **bye**	Exit ftp
Goodbye.	
$	

In this example both systems are running HP-UX; however, the commands you issue through **FTP** are operating system independent. The **cd** for change directory and **get** commands used above work for any operating system on which **FTP** is running. If you become familiar with just a few **FTP** commands, you may find that transferring information in a heterogeneous networking environment is not difficult.

Since **FTP** is so widely used, I'll describe some of the more commonly used **FTP** commands.

ftp - File Transfer Program for copying files across a network.

The following list includes some commonly used **ftp** commands. This list is not complete.

ascii	Set the type of file transferred to ASCII. This means you will be transferring an ASCII file from one system to another. This is the default so you don't have to set it. Example: **ascii**
binary	Set the type of file transferred to binary. This means you'll be transferring a binary file from one system to another. If, for instance, you want to have a directory on your HP-UX system which will hold applications that you will copy to non-HP-UX systems, then you will want to use binary transfer. Example: **binary**
cd	Change to the specified directory on the remote host. Example: **cd /tmp**
dir	List the contents of a directory on the remote system to the screen or to a file on the local system if you specify a local file name.

get   Copy the specified remote file to the specified local file. If you don't specify a local file name, then the remote file name will be used.

lcd   Change to the specified directory on the local host.

Example: **lcd /tmp**

ls   List the contents of a directory on the remote system to the screen or to a file on the local system if you specify a local file name.

mget   Copy multiple files from the remote host to the local host.

Example: **mget *.c**

put   Copy the specified local file to the specified remote file. If you don't specify a remote file name, then the local file name will be used.

Example: **put test.c**

mput   Copy multiple files from the local host to the remote host.

Example: **mput *.c**

system   Show the type of operating system running on the remote host.

Example: **system**

bye/quit   Close the connection to the remote host.

Example: **bye**

There are **FTP** commands in addition to those I have covered here.

Other Connection Topics

There are other means by which you can connect to the HP-UX system. Two popular techniques for connecting to other systems are FTP, which was just covered, and TELNET. Maestro supplies the capability for both of these. I could sit on the Windows NT system using TELNET with a window open on the HP-UX system and issue commands.

Figure 14-10 shows the *Connect* window used to specify whether you want to use RLOGIN or TELNET to establish the connection.

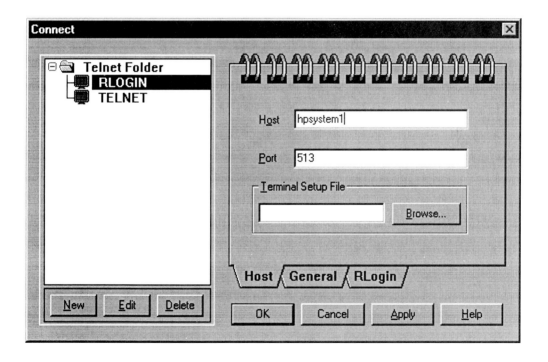

Figure 14-10 Selecting RLOGIN or TELNET

I selected TELNET in the Connect window and was able to log in to the HP-UX system as shown in Figure 14-11.

Figure 14-11 TELNET Window

In this window we could issue HP-UX commands just as if we were sitting on a terminal connected directly to the HP-UX system. I prefer the **dtterm** window used earlier with X Windows to opening a TELNET session, but TELNET is widely used in heterogenous environments. With X Windows you get graphical functionality that is not part of TELNET.

You can have as many hosts defined in Maestro as you like. Rather than type in the host you wish to connect to every time, you can manage a lists of hosts from which you select when you perform one of the functions in this chapter. In the *Xstart* and *Open Connection* windows shown earlier, for instance, there is a pull down menu that allows you to select from a list of hosts. Figure 14-12 shows the Host Name Maintenance window in

which you define the IP address and name of a system that will get added
to the file defining hosts on your system.

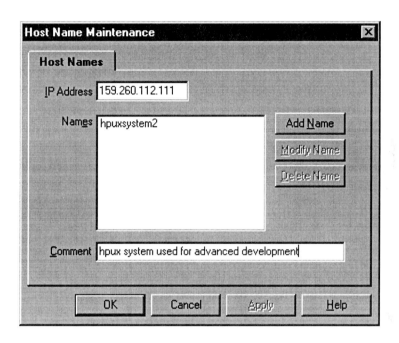

Figure 14-12 *Host Name Maintenance* Window

The host related information you specify in this window will update
the file on your Windows NT used to keep track of hosts.

Another configuration issue you have to be concerned with are the
programs running on your host, in this case the HP-UX system, that are
required to support the networking functionality such as NFS. The *Rpcinfo*
menu pick under Maestro will query the HP-UX host and list the services it
is running. Figure 14-13 shows this window.

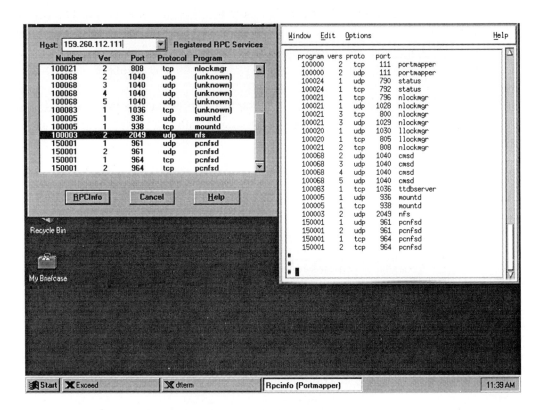

Figure 14-13 *Rpcinfo* Window (left) on Windows NT and Output of **rpcinfo** Command in HP-UX (right)

The left window is the Maestro *Rpcinfo* window. The right window is a **dtterm** window on the HP-UX system showing the result of having run the **rpcinfo** command in HP-UX.

RPC stands for Remote Procedure Call. There are a variety of programs for which there is RPC-related information. Several programs are required to achieve the Windows NT and HP-UX interoperability.

You can see that the contents of these windows are identical. The first number shown is the program number. There are widely accepted RPC numbers for various programs. For NFS the program number is 100003. The next number is the version of the protocol. In this case NFS is version 2. The next number is the port. The port number is used by both the client, which is the Windows NT system in our case, and the server, which is the HP-UX system in our case, to communicate using NFS. The next field is the protocol used which is usually UDP or TCP. The final field is the program name.

In the case of NFS I had to ensure that NFS, portmapper, mountd, and pcnfsd were running on my HP-UX system before I could use the Maestro NFS product.

Rpcinfo is a useful tool for viewing all of the information on the host to which your Windows NT system will connect.

CHAPTER 15

Windows NT and HP-UX Interoperability - Advanced Server 9000

Windows NT Functionality on HP-UX

To this point we have been discussing moving HP-UX functionality such as X Windows and NFS onto Windows NT in order to achieve interoperability. Why not do the converse? Having some Windows NT functionality on HP-UX would certainly be helpful in some cases. HP-UX resources such as printers and disks could then be shared with several Windows NT systems on the network.

HP Advanced Server 9000 is just such an HP product that runs on your HP-UX system. It provides Windows NT functionality that facilitates Windows NT and HP-UX interoperability. With Advanced Server 9000 your HP-UX system can act as a Primary or Backup Domain Controller, a file server, a print server, or other Windows NT functional component.

This chapter makes use of some of the **net** commands of Windows NT, especially the **net share** command. When I am working on the HP-UX system (*dloaner*) in this chapter I use the command line including some net commands. When I am working on the Windows NT system (*hpsystem1*) in this chapter I will use graphical Windows NT functionality which is preferable to issuing commands on the command line. I use both the command line and graphical methods so you can see the difference in the two approaches. You may want to explore some of these **net** commands using the on-line help of your Windows NT system as you progress through this chapter. Here is a list of some widely used **net** commands and a brief explanation of each:

net accounts   Used to maintain the user accounts database.

net computer   Used to add or delete computers from the domain database.

net config server

Display or change settings for a server service on which the command is executed.

net config workstation

Display or change settings for the workstation service on which the command is executed.

net continue   Reactivate a Windows NT service that has been suspended with the **net pause** command.

net file   Used for network file manipulation such as listing ID numbers, closing a shared file, removing file locks, and so on.

net group   Used to add, display, or modify global groups on servers.

net help   Display a listing of help options for any net commands.

net helpmsg	Displays explanations of Windows NT network messages such as errors, warnings, and alerts.
net localgroup	Used to modify local groups on computers.
net name	Used to add or delete a "messaging name" at a computer which is the name to which messages are sent.
net print	Used to list print jobs and shared queues.
net send	Send messages to other users, computers, and "messaging names" on the network.
net session	Used to list or disconnect sessions between the computer and other computers on the network.
net share	Share a server's resources with other computers on the network.
net start	Used to start services such as *server*.
net statistics	Displays the statistics log for the local Workstation or Server service.
net stop	Used to stop services such as *server*.

net time   Synchronize the computer's clock with another computer on the domain.

net use   Displays, connects, or disconnects a computer with shared resources.

net user   Creates or modifies user accounts.

net view   Lists resources being shared on a computer.

Let's take a closer look at how you configure and use Advanced Server 9000 in a networked environment.

Installing Advanced Server 9000 on HP-UX

It's easy to install and configure Advanced Server 9000 on your HP-UX system. Advanced Server 9000 is installed using Software Distributor on your HP-UX system just as you would load any other software. After installing Advanced Server 9000, you would run the configuration script called **asu_inst**. The following text shows running **asu_inst** to configure the HP-UX system *dloaner* to be a Backup Domain Controller (BDC) for the Windows NT system *hpsystem1*.

```
# /opt/asu/lanman/bin/asu_inst
```

This request script will prompt you for information which is necessary
to install and configure your Advanced Server for UNIX Systems.

There are two installation modes:

Express Setup - the installation scripts use default settings so
installation is quick and easy. You may change these settings
after installation completes. The server is installed as a
primary domain controller in its own domain.

Custom Setup - this mode allows you to specify the settings at the
beginning of installation. If you select this mode, you must
specify the server's name, the domain it will participate in,
and the role in that domain.

NOTE: The installation requires a password for the administrative account.
A default password of 'password' will be used, although you may elect to
be prompted for a different password at the end of the installation.

If you are installing many servers it is strongly recommended that you use
the default password for all installations. Be sure to change these
passwords after determining that your network is operating correctly.

Do you want Express Setup [y/n]? y

Advanced Server for UNIX provides a NETLOGON service which simplifies the
administration of multiple servers. A single user accounts database can be
shared by multiple servers grouped together into an administrative
collection called a domain. Within a domain, each server has a designated
role. A single server, called the primary domain controller, manages all
changes to the user accounts database and automatically distributes those
changes to other servers, called backup domain controllers, within the same
domain. You may now supply a server name (the name which this server
will be known on the network), the role that this server will perform
in that domain (primary or backup), and a domain name.

Enter the name of the server
or press Enter to select 'dloaner':

Each server must be given a role in a domain. The possible roles are:

primary domain controller:
    Administration server. Distributes user accounts information
        to backup domain controllers. Validates network logon requests.
    There can be only one primary domain controller per domain.

backup domain controller:
        Receives user account information from the primary domain
        controller. Validates network logon requests and can be promoted
    to primary if the primary domain controller is not accessible.

Enter role (primary or backup): backup

This installation will configure the server as a backup domain controller.
You will be prompted to enter the name of the primary domain controller,
and an administrative account name on the primary along with its password.
In order for this installation to complete successfully, the primary domain
controller must be running and connected to the network.

Enter the name of the primary domain controller (eg, abc_asu): hpsystem1

```
Confirm choices for server dloaner:
                        role    : backup
                        primary: hpsystem1
Is this correct [y/n]? y
_&a0y0C_J
Enter the name of an administrative account on the primary
domain controller 'hpsystem1' or press Enter to select 'administrator':

This procedure requires the password for the administrative account on
'hpsystem1'.  If the password is the default ('password') created
during installation, you will not need to be prompted for a password.
If you have changed the password, you should allow this program  to prompt
for a password after the files have been installed.

Do you want to use the default password [y/n]? y

Advanced Server/9000
Copyright (c) 1988, 1991-1996 AT&T and Microsoft
Copyright (c) 1992-1996 Hewlett-Packard
All rights reserved

Adding Advanced Server for UNIX Systems administrative users and groups
Add
Comment <Advanced Server account>
Home Dir </opt/asu/lanman>
UID <100>
GID <99>
Shell </sbin/false>
Name <lanman>
pw_name: lanman
pw_passwd: *
pw_uid: 100
pw_gid: 99
pw_age: ?
pw_comment:
pw_gecos: Advanced Server account
pw_dir: /opt/asu/lanman
pw_shell: /sbin/false
enter addusr
pw_name = lanman
pw_passwd = *
pw_uid = 100
pw_gid = 99
pw_gecos = Advanced Server account
pw_dir = /opt/asu/lanman
pw_shell = /sbin/false
enter_quiet_zone()
exit_quiet_zone()
exiting addusr, error = 0
Add
Comment <Advanced Server Administrator>
Home Dir </var/opt/asu/lanman/lmxadmin>
GID <99>
Name <lmxadmin>
pw_name: lmxadmin
pw_passwd: *
pw_uid: 0
pw_gid: 99
pw_age: ?
pw_comment:
pw_gecos: Advanced Server Administrator
pw_dir: /var/opt/asu/lanman/lmxadmin
pw_shell:
enter addusr
pw_name = lmxadmin
```

```
pw_passwd = *
pw_uid = 0
pw_gid = 99
pw_gecos = Advanced Server Administrator
pw_dir = /var/opt/asu/lanman/lmxadmin
pw_shell =
enter_quiet_zone()
exit_quiet_zone()
exiting addusr, error = 0
Add
Comment <Advanced Server GUEST Login>
Shell </sbin/false>
GID <99>
Name <lmxguest>
pw_name: lmxguest
pw_passwd: *
pw_uid: 0
pw_gid: 99
pw_age: ?
pw_comment:
pw_gecos: Advanced Server GUEST Login
pw_dir:
pw_shell: /sbin/false
enter addusr
pw_name = lmxguest
pw_passwd = *
pw_uid = 0
pw_gid = 99
pw_gecos = Advanced Server GUEST Login
pw_dir = /usr/lmxguest
pw_shell = /sbin/false
enter_quiet_zone()
exit_quiet_zone()
exiting addusr, error = 0
Add
Comment <Advanced Server World Login>
Shell </sbin/false>
GID <99>
Name <lmworld>
pw_name: lmworld
pw_passwd: *
pw_uid: 0
pw_gid: 99
pw_age: ?
pw_comment:
pw_gecos: Advanced Server World Login
pw_dir:
pw_shell: /sbin/false
enter addusr
pw_name = lmworld
pw_passwd = *
pw_uid = 0
pw_gid = 99
pw_gecos = Advanced Server World Login
pw_dir = /usr/lmworld
pw_shell = /sbin/false
enter_quiet_zone()
exit_quiet_zone()
exiting addusr, error = 0

Creating Directory: /home/lanman
Setting owner, group, and permissions for installed files....

Enter the password for administrator on hpsystem1:
Re-enter password:
```

```
Contacting the server 'hpsystem1' ... Success

Creating Advanced Server for UNIX Systems accounts database.

Starting the Advanced Server for UNIX Systems...

The Advanced Server for UNIX Systems is now operational.
#
```

After the installation and configuration is complete you have **netde-mon** running, which is an essential component of Advanced Server 9000, as shown in the following **ps** command:

```
# ps -ef | grep netdemon
    root  1100     1  0 10:18:38 ?          0:00 /opt/lmu/netbios/bin/netdemon
#
```

In addition to netdemon, NetBIOS must also be running.

Advanced Server 9000 starts several processes on your HP-UX system in addition to **netdemon**. You can also verify that the Advanced Server 9000 server is running by viewing its processes with the **ps** command.

```
# ps -ef | grep lm
    root  3285     1  0 10:37:19 ?     0:00 lmx.dmn
    root  3200     1  0 10:36:57 ?     0:00 lmx.ctrl
    root  3262  3200  0 10:37.07 ?     0:00 lmx.srv -s 1
    root  3295     1  0 10:37:20 ?     0:00 lmx.sched
    root  3289     1  0 10:37:19 ?     0:00 lmx.browser
    root  1100     1  0 10:18:38 ?     0:00 /opt/lmu/netbios/bin/netdemon
#
```

Many process are shown here such as the *lmx.dmn* which is the dae-mon, *lmx,ctrl* which is the control process, *lmx.sched* which is the sched-uler, *lmx.browser* which is the browser, and *lmx.srv* which is a client session. If Advanced Server 9000 were not running, you would use the **net start server** command to start the server. Similarly, you stop the server with **net stop server**.

In addition, you have several users and groups that have been created on your HP-UX system to facilitate using Advanced Server 9000 with your Windows NT systems. The new users are shown in the upcoming **/etc/ passwd** file and the new groups are shown in the upcoming **/etc/group** file.

```
# cat /etc/passwd
root:jThTuY9OhNxGY:0:3::/:/sbin/sh
daemon:*:1:5::/:/sbin/sh
bin:*:2:2::/usr/bin:/sbin/sh
sys:*:3:3::/:
adm:*:4:4::/var/adm:/sbin/sh
uucp:*:5:3::/var/spool/uucppublic:/usr/lbin/uucp/uucico
lp:*:9:7::/var/spool/lp:/sbin/sh
nuucp:*:11:11::/var/spool/uucppublic:/usr/lbin/uucp/uucico
hpdb:*:27:1:ALLBASE:/:/sbin/sh
nobody:*:-2:-2147483648::/:
lanman:*:100:99:Advanced Server account:/opt/asu/lanman:/sbin/false
lmxadmin:*:202:99:Advanced Server Administrator:/var/opt/asu/lanman/lmxadmin:
lmxguest:*:203:99:Advanced Server GUEST Login:/usr/lmxguest:/sbin/false
lmworld:*:204:99:Advanced Server World Login:/usr/lmworld:/sbin/false
# cat /etc/group
root::0:root
other::1:root,hpdb
bin::2:root,bin
sys::3:root,uucp
adm::4:root,adm
daemon::5:root,daemon
mail::6:root
lp::7:root,lp
tty::10:
nuucp::11:nuucp
users::20:root
nogroup:*:-2:
DOS----::99:lanman
DOS-a--::98:lanman
DOS--s-::97:lanman
DOS---h::96:lanman
DOS-as-::95:lanman
DOS-a-h::94:lanman
DOS--sh::93:lanman
DOS-ash::92:lanman
#
```

In addition to the HP-UX system modifications that have automatically taken place, the Windows NT Primary Domain Controller (PDC) now recognizes the HP-UX system as the backup domain controller. Figure 15-1 shows a screen shot from the Windows NT system *hpsystem1*, which is the primary domain controller. The screen shot shows *dloaner* acting as the backup domain controller and the default shared directories on the HP-UX system *dloaner*. The share properties for one of the shares, **C:\opt\asu\lanman** is also shown.

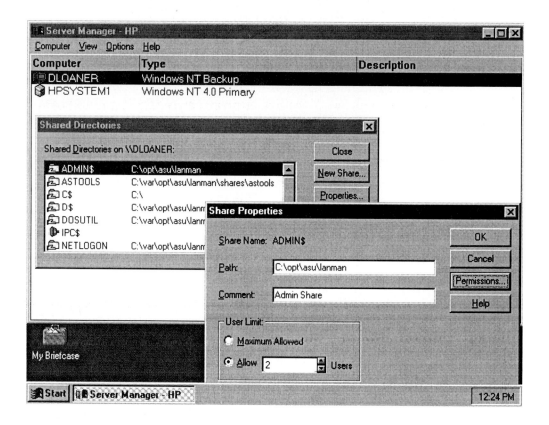

Figure 15-1   Default Shares after Loading and Configuring Advanced Server 9000

These shares can also be viewed on the command line of the HP-UX system using the net command as shown in the following output.

```
# /opt/asu/lanman/bin/net share

Sharename    Resource                         Remark
-------------------------------------------------------------------------------
ADMIN$       C:\OPT\ASU\LANMAN                 Admin Share
IPC$                                          IPC Share
C$           C:\                              Root Share
D$           C:\VAR\OPT\ASU\LANMAN\SHARES      SystemRoot Share
ASTOOLS      C:\VAR\OPT\ASU\LANMAN\SHARES...  Advanced Server Tools
```

```
DOSUTIL      C:\VAR\OPT\ASU\LANMAN\SHARES... DOS Utilities
NETLOGON     C:\VAR\OPT\ASU\LANMAN\SHARES... Logon Scripts Directory
PATCHES      C:\VAR\OPT\ASU\LANMAN\SHARES... Client Patches
PRINTLOG     C:\VAR\OPT\ASU\LANMAN\SHARES... LP printer messages
USERS        C:\HOME\LANMAN                  Users Directory
The command completed successfully.
#
```

These are the default shares that have been set up by Advanced Server 9000. Those followed by a $ are hidden shares used only for administrative purposes. When you run *Windows NT Explorer* you won't see these hidden directories.

You can set up additional shares such as the printer and disk we will set up in upcoming sections.

Sharing a Printer

In addition to the default sharing that takes place with Advanced Server 9000, there may be additional resources you want to share between Windows NT and HP-UX systems.

For example, you may have a printer used in your HP-UX environment to which you want Windows NT systems to have access. The following commands show adding a shared printer and viewing it in HP-UX.

The first command is **lpstat** on HP-UX that shows the status of the existing printer *laser*.

```
# lpstat -t
scheduler is running
system default destination: laser
device for laser: /dev/c2t0d0_lp
laser accepting requests since Feb 11 17:23
printer laser is idle.  enabled since Feb 11 17:23
fence priority : 0
no entries
#
```

Next we run the **net** command and specify the printer *laser* as a shared printer device.

```
# /opt/asu/lanman/bin/net net share laser=laser /print
laser was successfully shared
```

To see the configuration of the printer we can issue the net print command as shown below:

```
# net print laser /options
Printing options for LASER

Status              Queue Active
Remark
Print Devices       laser
Driver              HP-UX LM/X Print Manager
Separator file
Priority            5
Print after         12:00 AM
Print until         12:00 AM
Print processor
Parameters          COPIES=1 EJECT=AUTO BANNER=YES
The command completed successfully.
#
```

After printing a text file from the Windows NT system onto the device *laser* connected to the HP-UX system running Advanced Server 9000, I got a bunch of unintelligible information on the printed sheet. The Advanced Server 9000 printer was not configured raw. I issued the following command to make the printer raw:

```
# net print laser /parms:types=-oraw
The command completed successfully.
```

The new configuration, with the *TYPES=-oraw*, is shown in the following output. This device successfully printed from the Windows NT system to the HP-UX system running Advanced Server 9000 on which *laser* is connected.

```
# net print laser /options
Printing options for LASER

Status              Queue Active
Remark
Print Devices       laser
Driver              HP-UX LM/X Print Manager
Separator file
Priority            5
Print after         12:00 AM
Print until         12:00 AM
Print processor
Parameters          COPIES=1 TYPES=-oraw EJECT=AUTO BANNER=YES
The command completed successfully.
#
```

We can now view all of the shared devices with the **net** command.

```
# /opt/asu/lanman/bin/net share

Sharename    Resource                       Remark
-----------------------------------------------------------------------
ADMIN$       C:\OPT\ASU\LANMAN              Admin Share
IPC$                                        IPC Share
C$           C:\                            Root Share
D$           C:\VAR\OPT\ASU\LANMAN\SHARES   SystemRoot Share
ASTOOLS      C:\VAR\OPT\ASU\LANMAN\SHARES... Advanced Server Tools
DOSUTIL      C:\VAR\OPT\ASU\LANMAN\SHARES... DOS Utilities
NETLOGON     C:\VAR\OPT\ASU\LANMAN\SHARES... Logon Scripts Directory
PATCHES      C:\VAR\OPT\ASU\LANMAN\SHARES... Client Patches
PRINTLOG     C:\VAR\OPT\ASU\LANMAN\SHARES... LP printer messages
USERS        C:\HOME\LANMAN                 Users Directory
LASER        laser                          Spooled
The command completed successfully.

#
```

The last item in this listing is the printer *laser* that was added with the **net** command. All of the previous commands were issued on the HP-UX system running Advanced Server 9000. We can now view the shared devices of *dloaner* on the Windows NT system using *Explorer* to confirm the printer *laser* is a shared device as shown in Figure 15-2.

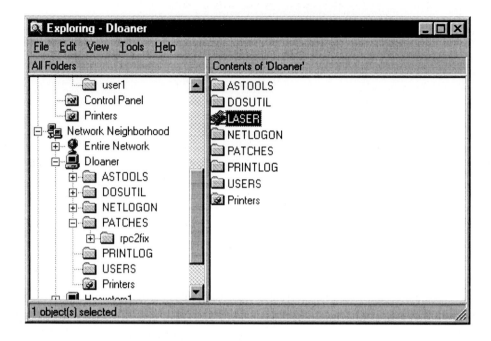

Figure 15-2   Windows NT Explorer Showing Printer *Laser*

The details of this shared printer can be viewed in *Printers* under *Control Panel*.

Sharing a File System

With the printer having been added the shares that are now set up on the HP-UX system running Advanced Server 9000 look like the following:

```
# /opt/asu/lanman/bin/net share

Sharename     Resource                          Remark
---------------------------------------------------------------------------
ADMIN$        C:\OPT\ASU\LANMAN                  Admin Share
```

```
IPC$                                                        IPC Share
C$              C:\                                         Root Share
D$              C:\VAR\OPT\ASU\LANMAN\SHARES                SystemRoot Share
ASTOOLS         C:\VAR\OPT\ASU\LANMAN\SHARES...             Advanced Server Tools
DOSUTIL         C:\VAR\OPT\ASU\LANMAN\SHARES...             DOS Utilities
NETLOGON        C:\VAR\OPT\ASU\LANMAN\SHARES...             Logon Scripts Directory
PATCHES         C:\VAR\OPT\ASU\LANMAN\SHARES...             Client Patches
PRINTLOG        C:\VAR\OPT\ASU\LANMAN\SHARES...             LP printer messages
USERS           C:\HOME\LANMAN                              Users Directory
LASER           laser                                      Spooled
The command completed successfully.
#
```

The shares shown include the printer that was added. We could now issue the **net share** command and add an HP-UX file system to be shared. To share the **/home** directory on the HP-UX system *dloaner,* we would issue the following command:

```
# /opt/asu/lanman/bin/net share home=c:/home
home was shared successfully
```

Note that the HP-UX notation for the directory was issued with the slash (/) rather than backslash (\) as you would on a Windows NT system. We can now view the shares on *dloaner*, including the new *HOME* share, with the **net** command.

```
# /opt/asu/lanman/bin/net share

Sharename       Resource                                   Remark
-------------------------------------------------------------------------------
ADMIN$          C:\OPT\ASU\LANMAN                           Admin Share
IPC$                                                        IPC Share
C$              C:\                                         Root Share
D$              C:\VAR\OPT\ASU\LANMAN\SHARES                SystemRoot Share
ASTOOLS         C:\VAR\OPT\ASU\LANMAN\SHARES...             Advanced Server Tools
DOSUTIL         C:\VAR\OPT\ASU\LANMAN\SHARES...             DOS Utilities
HOME            C:\HOME
NETLOGON        C:\VAR\OPT\ASU\LANMAN\SHARES...             Logon Scripts Directory
PATCHES         C:\VAR\OPT\ASU\LANMAN\SHARES...             Client Patches
PRINTLOG        C:\VAR\OPT\ASU\LANMAN\SHARES...             LP printer messages
USERS           C:\HOME\LANMAN                              Users Directory
LASER           laser                                      Spooled
The command completed successfully.
#
```

You could now view this share on the Windows NT system and map it to a drive as shown in Figure 15-3.

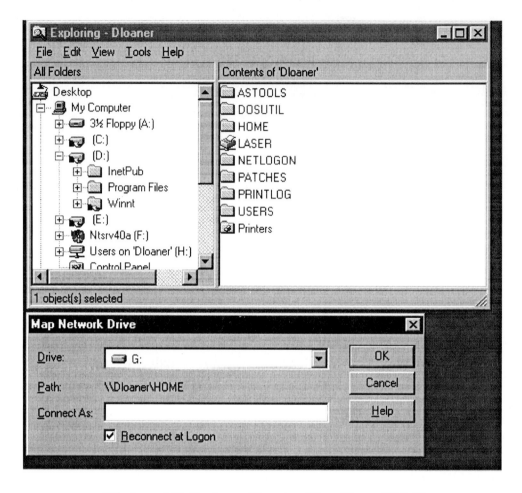

Figure 15-3 Windows NT *Explorer* Showing New Share *HOME*

Only a small subset of Advanced Server 9000 functionality was covered in this chapter. We covered using an HP-UX system running Advanced Server 9000 as a backup domain controller, sharing an HP-UX connected printer with a Windows NT network, and sharing an HP-UX connected disk with a Windows NT network. These are some of the more common uses for Advanced Server 9000. Nearly everything you can do with a Windows NT system can be done with Advanced Server 9000 so don't limit yourself to only the functionality covered in this chapter.

CHAPTER 16

Windows NT and HP-UX Interoperability - POSIX Utilities

The Microsoft Windows NT Server Resource Kit (referred to as Resource Kit throughout this chapter) has on it several POSIX utilities that HP-UX system administrators will find useful when using Windows NT. The Resource Kit in general is a fantastic system administration resource. Although I will focus on only POSIX utilities in this book, it has on it a wealth of information. The Resource Kit is available from Microsoft Press, Redmond, WA. The POSIX utilities include such useful commands as **cat, chmod, find, ls, mv,** and others. The commands that are available on the Resource Kit vary somewhat from architecture to architecture. I will focus on only the "I386" utilities and not the utilities for other architectures in this chapter.

The Resource Kit has on it the file **POSIX.WRI** that describes the POSIX utilities in detail. In this chapter I'll just provide a brief overview of the utilities and examples of using some of the utilities. Most HP-UX system administrators are familiar with these utilities in HP-UX but may find differences in the options to these utilities when using the Resource Kit version.

I have made every effort to limit the number of "add-on" products to Windows NT and HP-UX covered in this book. The Resource Kit, however, is so useful to Windows NT system administrators that not covering at least some part of it, such as the POSIX utilities, would leave a void in the discussion of Windows NT system administration. You can find out more information about the Resource Kit on the Microsoft Web site. You can buy it at many computer, electronic, and book stores. Be sure to buy the Resource Kit for the version of Windows NT you are running. There is also a Resource Kit for both the Server and Workstation versions of Windows NT. I used the Server Resource Kit for the POSIX commands covered in this chapter.

Both the source code and executables for the POSIX utilities are on the Resource Kit. The following is a listing of the POSIX executables for I386 on the Resource Kit CD-ROM. I used the POSIX utility **ls -l** to produce this listing.

```
F:\I386\GNU\POSIX> ls -l

-rwxrwxrwx   1 Everyone Everyone   101748 Sep  6 12:39 CAT.EXE
-rwxrwxrwx   1 Everyone Everyone   116188 Sep  6 12:39 CHMOD.EXE
-rwxrwxrwx   1 Everyone Everyone   110920 Sep  6 12:39 CHOWN.EXE
-rwxrwxrwx   1 Everyone Everyone   111208 Sep  6 12:39 CP.EXE
-rwxrwxrwx   1 Everyone Everyone   173580 Sep  6 12:39 FIND.EXE
-rwxrwxrwx   1 Everyone Everyone   144256 Sep  6 12:39 GREP.EXE
-rwxrwxrwx   1 Everyone Everyone    90960 Sep  6 12:39 LN.EXE
-rwxrwxrwx   1 Everyone Everyone   128532 Sep  6 12:39 LS.EXE
-rwxrwxrwx   1 Everyone Everyone    88984 Sep  6 12:39 MKDIR.EXE
-rwxrwxrwx   1 Everyone Everyone    99096 Sep  6 12:39 MV.EXE
-rwxrwxrwx   1 Everyone Everyone   114564 Sep  6 12:39 RM.EXE
-rwxrwxrwx   1 Everyone Everyone    85004 Sep  6 12:39 RMDIR.EXE
-rwxrwxrwx   1 Everyone Everyone   362528 Sep  6 12:39 SH.EXE
-rwxrwxrwx   1 Everyone Everyone    91244 Sep  6 12:39 TOUCH.EXE
-rwxrwxrwx   1 Everyone Everyone   287628 Sep  6 12:39 VI.EXE
-rwxrwxrwx   1 Everyone Everyone    95392 Sep  6 12:39 WC.EXE
```

The directory in which these utilities are located is the **F:** drive, which is my CD-ROM, in **I386\GNU\POSIX**, which is the I386 version of these utilities. The following are command summaries of the POSIX utilities. A brief description of some the utilities as well some of the more commonly used options to the utilities are included. In some cases there is also an example of having run the utility. The **POSIX.WRI** file on the Resource Kit provides an exhaustive description of each utility.

cat

cat - Display, combine, append, copy, or create files.

Some commonly used options

    -n   Line numbers are displayed along with output lines.

    -u   Output is unbuffered, which means it is handled character by character.

    -v   Print most nonprinting characters visibly.

The following example shows using the -n option with **cat**.

```
D:\WINNT\system> cat -n setup.inf

 1   [setup]
 2       help = setup.hlp
 3
 4   ;   Place any programs here that should be run at the end of setup.
 5   ;   These apps will be run in order of their appearance here.
 6   [run]
 7
 8   [dialog]
 9       caption  = "Windows Setup"
10       exit     = "Exit Windows Setup"
11       title    = "Installing Windows 3.1"
12       options  = "In addition to installing Windows 3.1, you can:"
13       printwait = "Please wait while Setup configures your printer(s)..."

                              .
                              .
                              o

20   [data]
```

```
21  ; Disk space required
22  ; <type of setup>= <Full install space>, <Min install space>
23
24       upd2x386full = 10000000,6144000 ; 10.0 Mb, 6.144 Mb
25       upd2x286full = 9000000,6144000  ;  9.0 Mb, 6.144 Mb
26       upd3x386full = 5500000,5000000  ;  5.5 Mb, 5.0 Mb
27       upd3x286full = 5500000,5000000  ;  5.5 Mb, 5.0 Mb
28
29       new386full   = 10000000,6144000 ; 10.0 Mb, 6.144 Mb
30       new286full   = 9000000,6144000  ;  9.0 Mb, 6.144 Mb
31
32       netadmin     = 16000000         ; 16.0 Mb
33       netadminupd  = 16000000         ; 16.0 Mb
34       upd2x386net  = 300000           ;    .3 Mb
35       upd3x386net  = 300000           ;    .3 Mb
36       upd2x286net  = 300000           ;    .3 Mb
37       upd3x286net  = 300000           ;    .3 Mb
38       new386net    = 300000,300000    ;    .3 Mb,   .3 Mb
39       new286net    = 300000,300000    ;    .3 Mb,   .3 Mb
40
41
42
43  ; Defaults used in setting up and names of a few files
44       startup   = WIN.COM
```

chmod

chmod - Change permissions of specified files using symbolic or absolute (sometimes called numeric) modes. Symbolic mode is described below.

Symbol of whom is affected:

u	User is affected.
g	Group is affected.
o	Other is affected.
a	All users are affected.

Operation to perform:

+	Add permission.
-	Remove permission.
=	Replace permission.

Permission specified:

r	Read permission.
w	Write permission.
x	Execute permission.
u	Copy user permissions.
g	Copy group permissions.
o	Copy other permissions.

The following example uses both modes. Using absolute or numeric mode, the permissions on the file **cat1.exe** are changed from 666 to 777. Using symbolic mode, the execute permissions are then removed for all users.

```
D:\> ls -l cat1.exe

-rw-rw-rw-    1 Administ Administ     71323 Feb 20 11:34 cat1.exe
D:\> chmod 777 cat1.exe
D:\> ls -l cat1.exe

-rwxrwxrwx    1 Administ Administ     71323 Feb 20 11:34 cat1.exe
D:\> chmod a-x cat1.exe
D:\> ls -l cat1.exe
-rw-rw-rw-    1 Administ Administ     71323 Feb 20 11:34 cat1.exe
```

cp

cp - Copy files and directories.

Some commonly used options

-i Interactive copy whereby you are prompted to confirm
wether or not you wish to overwrite an existing file.

-f Force existing files to be overwritten by files being copied if there is a conflict in file names.

-p Preserve permissions when copying.

-R Copy recursively which includes subtrees.

The following example shows using the **cp** command to copy
cat1.exe to **cat2.exe** and then a listing of all files beginning with **cat** is produced.

```
D:\> cp cat1.exe cat2.exe

D:\> ls -l cat*

-rw-rw-rw-    1 Administ Administ    71323 Feb 20 11:34 cat1.exe
-rw-rw-rw-    1 Administ Administ    71323 Feb 20 11:47 cat2.exe
```

find

find - Recursively descend a directory structure looking for the file(s) listed.

Some commonly used options

-f	Specify a file hierarchy for **find** to traverse.
-s	When symbolic links are encountered, the file referenced by the link and not the link itself will be used.
-x	Don't decend into directories that have a device number different than that of the file from which the decent began.
-print	Prints pathname to standard output.
-size n	True if the file's size is n.

grep

grep - Searches for text and displays result.

The following example shows using grep to find the expression "shell" everywhere it appears inside the file **setup.inf**.

```
D:\> grep shell setup.inf

[shell]
00000000="shell versions below 3.01",,unsupported_net
00030100="shell versions below 3.21",,novell301
00032100="shell versions 3.21 and above",,novell321
00032600="shell versions 3.26 and above",,novell326
   #win.shell, 0:
   #win.shell, 0:
[win.shell]
   shell.dll
   system.ini, Boot,     "oldshell"        ,"shell"
```

ls

ls - List the contents of a directory.

Some commonly used options

-a	List all entries.
-c	Use time file was last modified for producing order in which files are listed.
-d	List only the directory name, not its contents.
-g	Include the group in the output.
-i	Print the inode number in the first column of the report.
-q	Nonprinting characters are represented by a "?".
-r	Reverse the order in which files are printed.
-s	Show the size in blocks instead of bytes.
-t	List in order of time saved with most recent first.
-u	Use time of last access instead of last modification for determining order in which files are printed.
-A	Same as -a except current and parent directories aren't listed.
-C	Multicolumn output produced.
-F	Directory followed by a "/", executable by an "*", symbolic link by an "@".
-L	List file or directory to which link points.
-R	Recursively list subdirectories.

Several examples are included.

```
D:\> ls -a

Blue Monday 16.bmp
Blue Monday.bmp
Coffee Bean 16.bmp
Coffee Bean.bmp
Config
Cursors
FORMS
FeatherTexture.bmp
Fiddle Head.bmp
Fonts
Furry Dog 16.bmp
Furry Dog.bmp
Geometrix.bmp
Gone Fishing.bmp
Greenstone.bmp
Hazy Autumn 16.bmp
Help
Hiking Boot.bmp
Leaf Fossils 16.bmp
Leather 16.bmp
Maple Trails.bmp
Media
NETLOGON.CHG
NOTEPAD.EXE
Petroglyph 16.bmp
Prairie Wind.bmp
Profiles
REGEDIT.EXE
Rhododendron.bmp
River Sumida.bmp
Santa Fe Stucco.bmp
Seaside 16.bmp
Seaside.bmp
ShellNew
Snakeskin.bmp
Soap Bubbles.bmp
Solstice.bmp
Swimming Pool.bmp
TASKMAN.EXE
TEMP
Upstream 16.bmp
WIN.INI
WINFILE.INI
WINHELP.EXE
Zapotec 16.bmp
Zapotec.bmp
_DEFAULT.PIF
black16.scr
clock.avi
control.ini
explorer.exe
inetsrv.mif
inf
lanma256.bmp
lanmannt.bmp
network.wri
poledit.exe
printer.wri
repair
setup.old
setuplog.txt
system
system.ini
system32
vmmreg32.dll
welcome.exe
winhlp32.exe
```

```
D:\ls -l

-rwxrwxrwx  1 Administ NETWORK    8310 Aug  9  1996 Blue Monday 16.bmp
-rwxrwxrwx  1 Administ NETWORK   37940 Aug  9  1996 Blue Monday.bmp
-rwxrwxrwx  1 Administ NETWORK    8312 Aug  9  1996 Coffee Bean 16.bmp
-rwxrwxrwx  1 Administ NETWORK   17062 Aug  9  1996 Coffee Bean.bmp
drwx---rwx  1 Administ Administ      0 Feb 10 10:39 Config
drwx---rwx  1 Administ Administ      0 Feb 10 16:22 Cursors
drwxrwxrwx  1 Administ NETWORK       0 Feb 10 16:23 FORMS
-rwxrwxrwx  1 Administ NETWORK   16730 Aug  9  1996 FeatherTexture.bmp
-rwxrwxrwx  1 Administ NETWORK   65922 Aug  9  1996 Fiddle Head.bmp
drwx---rwx  1 Administ Administ   8192 Feb 10 10:39 Fonts
-rwxrwxrwx  1 Administ NETWORK   18552 Aug  9  1996 Furry Dog 16.bmp
-rwxrwxrwx  1 Administ NETWORK   37940 Aug  9  1996 Furry Dog.bmp
-rwxrwxrwx  1 Administ NETWORK    4328 Aug  9  1996 Geometrix.bmp
-rwxrwxrwx  1 Administ NETWORK   17336 Aug  9  1996 Gone Fishing.bmp
-rwxrwxrwx  1 Administ NETWORK   26582 Aug  9  1996 Greenstone.bmp
-rwxrwxrwx  1 Administ NETWORK   32888 Aug  9  1996 Hazy Autumn 16.bmp
drwx---rwx  1 Administ Administ      0 Feb 19 15:10 Help
-rwxrwxrwx  1 Administ NETWORK   37854 Aug  9  1996 Hiking Boot.bmp
-rwxrwxrwx  1 Administ NETWORK   12920 Aug  9  1996 Leaf Fossils 16.bmp
-rwxrwxrwx  1 Administ NETWORK    6392 Aug  9  1996 Leather 16.bmp
-rwxrwxrwx  1 Administ NETWORK   26566 Aug  9  1996 Maple Trails.bmp
drwx---rwx  1 Administ Administ      0 Feb 10 16:23 Media
-rwxrwxrwx  1 Administ NETWORK   65536 Feb 11 10:35 NETLOGON.CHG
-rwxrwxrwx  1 Administ NETWORK   45328 Aug  8  1996 NOTEPAD.EXE
-rwxrwxrwx  1 Administ NETWORK   16504 Aug  9  1996 Petroglyph 16.bmp
-rwxrwxrwx  1 Administ NETWORK   65954 Aug  9  1996 Prairie Wind.bmp
drwxrwxrwx  1 Administ NETWORK    4096 Feb 10 16:32 Profiles
-rwxrwxr-x  1 Administ NETWORK   71952 Aug  8  1996 REGEDIT.EXE
-rwxrwxrwx  1 Administ NETWORK   17362 Aug  9  1996 Rhododendron.bmp
-rwxrwxrwx  1 Administ NETWORK   26208 Aug  9  1996 River Sumida.bmp
-rwxrwxrwx  1 Administ NETWORK   65832 Aug  9  1996 Santa Fe Stucco.bmp
-rwxrwxrwx  1 Administ NETWORK    8312 Aug  9  1996 Seaside 16.bmp
-rwxrwxr-x  1 Administ NETWORK   17334 Aug  9  1996 Seaside.bmp
drwxrwxrwx  1 Administ NETWORK       0 Feb 10 16:22 ShellNew
-rwxrwxrwx  1 Administ NETWORK   10292 Aug  9  1996 Snakeskin.bmp
-rwxrwxrwx  1 Administ NETWORK   65978 Aug  9  1996 Soap Bubbles.bmp
-rwxrwxr-x  1 Administ NETWORK   17334 Aug  9  1996 Solstice.bmp
-rwxrwxrwx  1 Administ NETWORK   26202 Aug  9  1996 Swimming Pool.bmp
-rwxrwxrwx  1 Administ NETWORK   32016 Aug  8  1996 TASKMAN.EXE
drwxrwxrwx  1 Administ NETWORK       0 Feb 20 09:59 TEMP
-rwxrwxrwx  1 Administ NETWORK   32888 Aug  9  1996 Upstream 16.bmp
-rwxrwxrwx  1 Administ NETWORK     239 Feb 10 16:23 WIN.INI
-rwxrwxr-x  1 Administ NETWORK       3 Aug  8  1996 WINFILE.INI
-rwxrwxr-x  1 Administ NETWORK  256192 Aug  8  1996 WINHELP.EXE
-rwxrwxrwx  1 Administ NETWORK    8312 Aug  9  1996 Zapotec 16.bmp
-rwxrwxr-x  1 Administ NETWORK    9522 Aug  9  1996 Zapotec.bmp
-rwxrwxr-x  1 Administ NETWORK     707 Aug  8  1996 _DEFAULT.PIF
-rwx---r-x  1 Administ Administ    5328 Aug  8  1996 black16.scr
-rwx---r-x  1 Administ Administ   82944 Aug  8  1996 clock.avi
-rwxrwxrwx  1 Administ NETWORK       0 Feb 10 11:18 control.ini
-rwx---r-x  1 Administ Administ  234256 Aug  8  1996 explorer.exe
-rwxrwxrwx  1 Administ NETWORK    1628 Feb 10 11:20 inetsrv.mif
drwx---rwx  1 Administ Administ   47104 Feb 10 10:56 inf
-rwx---r-x  1 Administ Administ  157044 Aug  8  1996 lanma256.bmp
-rwx---r-x  1 Administ Administ  157044 Aug  8  1996 lanmannt.bmp
-rwx---r-x  1 Administ Administ   67328 Aug  8  1996 network.wri
-rwx---r-x  1 Administ Administ  123152 Aug  8  1996 poledit.exe
-rwx---r-x  1 Administ Administ   34816 Aug  8  1996 printer.wri
drwx---rwx  1 Administ Administ      0 Feb 10 16:24 repair
-rwxrwxrwx  1 Administ NETWORK    2499 Feb 10 16:23 setup.old
-rwxrwxrwx  1 Administ NETWORK     138 Feb 10 16:22 setuplog.txt
drwx---rwx  1 Administ Administ   4096 Feb 20 10:07 system
-rwx---r-x  1 Administ Administ     219 Aug  8  1996 system.ini
drwx---rwx  1 Administ Administ  167936 Feb 20 09:50 system32
-rwx---r-x  1 Administ Administ   24336 Aug  8  1996 vmmreg32.dll
-rwx---r-x  1 Administ Administ   22288 Aug  8  1996 welcome.exe
-rwx---r-x  1 Administ Administ  310032 Aug  8  1996 winhlp32.exe
```

```
D:\> ls -C

Blue Monday 16.bmpGreenstone.bmpRhododendron.bmpWINFILE.INI        poledit.exe
Blue Monday.bmp Hazy Autumn 16.bmpRiver Sumida.bmpWINHELP.EXE      printer.wri
Coffee Bean 16.bmpHelp           Santa Fe Stucco.bmpZapotec 16.bmprepair
Coffee Bean.bmp Hiking Boot.bmp Seaside 16.bmp   Zapotec.bmp       setup.old
Config          Leaf Fossils 16.bmpSeaside.bmp   _DEFAULT.PIF      setuplog.txt
Cursors         Leather 16.bmp  ShellNew         black16.scr       system
FORMS           Maple Trails.bmpSnakeskin.bmp    clock.avi         system.ini
FeatherTexture.bmpMedia          Soap Bubbles.bmpcontrol.ini       system32
Fiddle Head.bmp NETLOGON.CHG    Solstice.bmp     explorer.exe      vmmreg32.dll
Fonts           NOTEPAD.EXE     Swimming Pool.bmpinetsrv.mif       welcome.exe
Furry Dog 16.bmpPetroglyph 16.bmpTASKMAN.EXE     inf               winhlp32.exe
Furry Dog.bmp   Prairie Wind.bmpTEMP             lanma256.bmp
Geometrix.bmp   Profiles        Upstream 16.bmp  lanmannt.bmp
Gone Fishing.bmpREGEDIT.EXE     WIN.INI          network.wri
```

mkdir

mkdir - Create specified directories.

A commonly used option

-p   Create intermediate directories to achieve the full path. If
            you want to create several layers of directories down,
            you would use **-p**.

mv

mv - Rename files and directories.

Some commonly used options

-i   Interactive move whereby you are prompted to confirm
          whether or not you wish to overwrite an existing file.

-f   Force existing files to be overwritten by files being moved
          if there is a conflict in file names.

rm

rm - Remove files and directories.

Some commonly used options

-d   Remove directories as well as other file types.

-i   Interactive remove whereby you are prompted to confirm
            wether or not you wish to remove an existing file.

-f   Force files to be removed.

-r (-R) Recursively remove the contents of the directory and
            then the directory itself.

touch

touch - Change the modification and or last access times of a file or create a file.

Some commonly used options

-c   Does not create a specified file if it does not exist.

-f   Force a touch of a file regardless of permissions.

The following example creates **file1** with **touch**.

```
D:\> ls -l file1
ls:file1: No such file or directory

D:\> touch file1

D:\> ls -l file1

-rw-rw-rw-    1 Administ Administ        0 Feb 20 11:45 file1
```

WC

wc - Produce a count of words, lines, and characters.

Options

        -l   Print the number of lines in a file.

        -w   Print the number of words in a file.

        -c   Print the number of characters in a file.

The first example lists the contents of a directory and pipes the output to wc. The second example provides wc information about the file system.ini.

```
D:\> ls

CAT.EXE
CHMOD.EXE
CHOWN.EXE
CP.EXE
FIND.EXE
GREP.EXE
LN.EXE
LS.EXE
MKDIR.EXE
MV.EXE
RM.EXE
RMDIR.EXE
SH.EXE
TOUCH.EXE
VI.EXE
WC.EXE

D:\> ls | wc -wlc

      16      16      132

D:\> wc -wlc system.ini

      13      17      219 system.ini
```

CHAPTER 17

Windows NT and HP-UX Interoperability -

Software Development with SoftBench OpenStudio

HP SoftBench Openstudio -

Client / Server Comes to the Development Environment

SoftBench OpenStudio is a product designed to empower C++ developers writing distributed applications for a mixed Windows and HP-UX environment. It combines Microsoft's Developer Studio (Visual C++) with state-of-the-art distributed computing technology to provide a single environment from which to develop applications for Windows NT, Windows 95, and HP-UX.

SoftBench Openstudio provides these capabilities through a unique client / server architecture. Hewlett Packard has taken the critical components of C++ application development - the C++ compiler, the linker, and the debugger - and transformed them into CORBA object servers. In addition, HP has taken these servers and integrated them into Microsoft's Developer Studio. This means that a programmer can use Developer Studio to manipulate C++ source code on a PC and compile and debug this code on an HP-UX system using the same Developer Studio front end.

Four Key Features of OpenStudio

There are four key features of SoftBench Openstudio:

1) The remote build capability allows HP-UX object code and executables to be generated from source created on the Windows Platform.

2) The remote debug capability enables the developer to debug HP-UX executables from a Windows GUI.

3) An extended project mechanism allows the developer to easily change HP-UX specific compile and link options. This mechanism is similar to the existing project mechanism available in Developer Studio.

SoftBench Openstudio is tightly integrated into Microsoft's Developer Studio, so in order to understand the capabilities of Openstudio, one must have some familiarity with Developer Studio. Developer Studio's mechanism for managing collections of files and compiler settings is particularly relevant. In general, when Developer Studio starts up, it starts up on a workspace. A workspace consists of a collection of projects. A project consists of a single set of files and a set of one or more project configurations. Users can easily add or remove files from a project using the GUI features of Developer Studio. A configuration specifies the settings for the compiler, linker, and debugger which determine the final output for a project build. These settings include the optimization or debug level for the compiler, libraries to be searched by the linker, startup options for the program when it is debugged, and many others. The user must specify a single configuration for any particular build. Changing a configuration is a simple matter of selecting a new configuration from a pull-down list of available configurations, and creating a new configuration is similarly easy.

Manipulating HP-UX Source Code

SoftBench Openstudio was designed to enable the developer to have four main ways to manipulate HP-UX source code. These are called use cases, and they are:

1) Legacy HP-UX Code. This use case allows a developer who has code in an existing HP-UX build mechanism to manipulate the code via Visual C++. This will allow initiation of a build, browsing error messages, and debugging of the code. This use case, however, will not allow for the use of the extended project mechanism.

2) New HP-UX Code. This use case allows a developer to generate a project for an HP-UX application or library from scratch. Compiles and links can be initiated from Developer Studio, any errors browsed, and the target debugged. In addition, the extended project options allow the developer to set the HP-UX specific compile and link options from a single interface.

3) Portable code. This use case allows the developer to quickly and easily compile, link, and debug code on both HP-UX and Windows plat-

forms. Specifically, the target platform is specified using the Developer Studio configuration mechanism. When the source is to be compiled on HP-UX, the developer chooses an HP-UX specific configuration. For Windows, a Windows specific configuration is used. Switching between the two is as easy as switching between any other configurations.

4) Client / Server code. The final use case is for a developer who needs a single workspace to manage separate subprojects which correspond to code which needs to be compiled on both HP-UX and Windows. This use case is valuable when, for instance, a developer is writing the client side of an application for Windows and the server side of the same application for HP-UX. In this case, each subproject has its own configuration. Switching between the two allows the developer to "focus" on the particular component using Developer Studio.

Careful selection of class libraries can greatly improve the productivity of developers in a heterogeneous environment. A primary selection criterion should be whether the library exists on both Windows and HP-UX. Good examples of such libraries are the iostream library and the Standard Template Library available as standard C++ libraries. In addition, there are many third party software vendors who supply multiplatform libraries. One in particular is Rogue Wave Software, who supplies class libraries for basic data structures, GUI development, networking, and more.

Using such a class library is complementary to Openstudio because it provides a portable API which the developer can count on to be available on both HP-UX and Windows. The code written to this portable API can be compiled and debugged on the desired platform using the Openstudio cross development capabilities.

SoftBench OpenStudio Control Panel

The SoftBench OpenStudio Control Panel is the primary point of control for OpenStudio. It serves the following purposes:

Main integration point into SoftBench OpenStudio

Allows you to maintain Default Settings

Allows you to setup Settings for the current configuration

Allows you to set Network Drive Mappings

Gives user help with setting build options

Access to on-line help

The SoftBench OpenStudio Control Panel is shown in Figure 17-1.

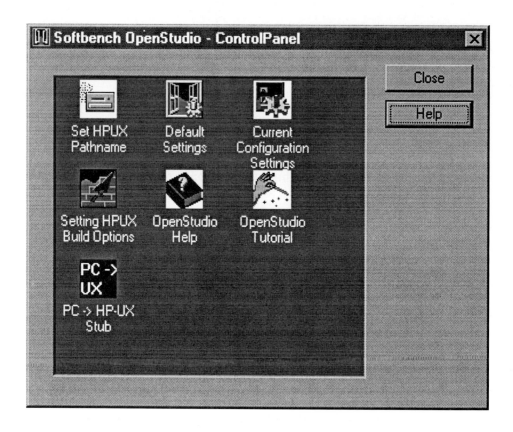

Figure 17-1 SoftBench OpenStudio Control Panel

The SoftBench OpenStudio Control Panel is a modal dialog box. When you select a particular icon in the Control Panel, the new dialog box comes up and the Control Panel removes itself. If you want the Control Panel back up, you must restart it from the *Tools* menu, by choosing *SoftBench OpenStudio*. The only exception pertains to the SoftBench OpenStudio Tutorial and Help files, which once launched are independent of the Control Panel and remain active until they are directly closed.

The following are descriptions of the functionality provided by some of the SoftBench OpenStudio Control Panel icons.

Set HP-UX Pathname: Selecting this icon brings up the Set HP-UX Pathname dialog box indicating the HP-UX machine name and path for network drive mappings.

Default Settings: Selecting this icon brings up the *Property Pages* for setting your global settings for environment variables and servers.

Current Configuration: Selecting this icon brings up the *Property Pages* for setting your current settings based upon your configuration.

Setting HP-UX Build Options: The Setting HP-UX Build Options dialog box gives assistance with setting build options. It must be used in conjunction with the Microsoft Developer Studio Build Settings dialog box. Your actual input for the HP-UX build settings takes place in the Microsoft Developer Studio Build Settings dialog box, but the convention and syntax are based upon the Setting HP-UX Build Options dialog box. Without this assistance it might be difficult entering the correct data into the Microsoft Developer Studio Build Settings dialog box.

SoftBench OpenStudio Tutorial and Help: The Tutorial gets you started using SoftBench OpenStudio based upon tasks provided with sample code. The SoftBench OpenStudio Help is the general reference and user's guide that covers all the topics involved in using SoftBench Open-Studio.

Conclusion

SoftBench Openstudio is a powerful tool for any organization involved in developing software in a mixed NT / HP-UX environment. It provides integration into Microsoft's Developer Studio, the most widely used C++ Development Environment available on the Windows platform. Using state-of-the-art distributed computing technologies, it makes HP-UX compiler, link, and debug servers available to Developer Studio. Finally, HP and its partners offer a suite of complimentary products and services, including class libraries and consulting, which make a complete development environment for software development in a heterogeneous installation.

Openstudio addresses the key issue of increased cost associated with development in a complex, heterogeneous environment.

Openstudio reduces hardware costs because developers can use a single desktop machine for both software development tasks and office automation tasks.

Openstudio decreases overall support costs because it reduces the total number of different types of machines an organization must support.

Openstudio reduces training costs because developers need only to be trained in a single development environment -- Microsoft Developer Studio -- with which they may already have some experience.

INDEX

A

Advanced Server 9000, 527-543
   net commands, 528-530
   installing, 530-537
   netdemon, 534
   default shares, 536-537
   sharing a printer, 537-540
   sharing a file system, 540-542
Accessibility options, 24
Accessories, 23
Administrative Tools (Common), 198
   Backup, 223-236
   Restore, 237-242
   Disk Administrator, 242
   Event Viewer, 243-248
   Performance Monitor, 248
   User Manager for Domains, 248-261
      Creating new users, 253-255
      Groups, 255-256
Administrative Wizards, 221-222
Audio server, 102
audevent, 293
audisp, 293
audomon, 293
audsys, 293
audusr, 293

B

Backup domain controller, 23, 24
bdf, 177, 187
   example, 188
   File system, 187
   KBytes, 187
   used, 187
   avail, 187
   %used, 187
   Mounted on, 187
   iused, 187
   ifree, 187
   %iuse, 187
/bin/find, 274

C

cacls, 124-125
CD-ROM
   during Windows NT setup, 14
   Windows NT 10 digit key, 23
checklist, 191-192
Class A address, 32
Class B address, 33
Class C address, 33
Common Desktop Environment (CDE), 455-492
   configuration files, 461-471
   file locations, 471-475
   appearance and behavior, 475
   sequence of events, 476-477
   customizing, 477-481
   slideup subpanels, 482
   animation, 482-484
   actions, 484-486
   fonts, 486-487
   performance, 487-492

Communications, 23
Control Panel, 200
    MS DOS Console, 202-204
    Devices, 204-205
    Network, 205-208
    Services, 212-214
    Printers, 214-217
    Tape Devices, 215-220
crontab, 300-303, 355-357

D

/dev, 91, 147
Device files, 90-98
DHCP, 26, 27
diskinfo, 95
DISPLAY variable, 269

E

/etc, 42, 147
/etc/group, 282, 285
/etc/lib/lp/model, 343
/etc/lp/interface, 343
/etc/passwd, 277, 285, 286, 290
export, 147

F

FAT, 18-21, 109, 112-114
    characteristics, 20-21, 114
FDDI, 326
file, 140-143
File names,
    FAT, 18, 112
    NTFS,16, 110
File size
    FAT, 20, 113
    NTFS, 18, 111
File system layout (HP-UX), 143-153
    CDFS, 143
    HFS, 143
    LOFS, 144

NFS
    VxFS, 144
Floppies with FAT, 20
freedisk, 359
fsck, 188-192

G

Games, 23
GlancePlus/UX, 415-435
    global, 417-422
    cpu, 422-424
    memory, 425-428
    disk, 428-431
    summary, 431
Graphical portion of setup, 22-35

H

Hummingbird Communications
    Maestro, 36, 37, 38
home, 147, 361
HP-UX file types, 133
    Data files, 133, 135
    Device files, 134
    Executable files, 134, 137-138
    Links, 134, 139
    Shell programs, 134, 138139
    Source code files, 133, 135137
    Text files, 133-135
HP-UX system setup, 41-107

I

init.d, 99
initd.conf, 323-325
inittab, 102-104
    action, 103
    id, 103
    process, 103
    run state, 103
Install HP-UX, 48-49
ioscan 85, 86, 92, 95, 308-309
iostat, 348-349, 397-399

IP addressing, 31-34, 47-48
  Class A, see Class A address
  Class B, see Class B address
  Class C, see Class C address

J

join, 132

K

kernel
  building, 84
  process for building, 89
  /stand, 87
  vmunix, 87, 88
  vmunix, 87, 318, 319
kill, 354, 355

L

landiag and lanadmin, 406-407
Logical volume manager, 53, 63, 171
  Logical extent, 173-174
  Logical volume, 173
  Mirroring, 174
  Physical extent, 173
  Physical volume, 172
  Volume, 172
  Volume group, 172-173
Logical volume manager commands
  lvcreate, 178
  lvchange, 178
  lvdisplay, 178-180
  lvextend, 180
  lvlnboot, 180
  lvsplit & lvmerge, 180
  lvmmigrate, 181
  lvreduce, 181
  lvremove, 181
  lvsync, 181
lost+found, 43, 147
lp related commands
  lpstat, 344-345
  accept, 345

cancel 345
disable, 345
enable, 345
lpfence, 345
lp, 345
lpadmin, 345
lpmove, 345
lpsched, 345
lpshut, 345
lpstat, 345
reject, 345
lsdev, 92-94

M

Mass storage during setup, 13
MAU, 47
mediainit, 192
mk_kernel, 87
mksf, 97-98
mnt, 148
Motif, 459-460
mount, 368
Multimedia, 23

N

Names of system, 47
net, 148
NetBIOS, 26
netstat, 401-406
Networking in Windows NT, 25-27
  interoperability, 505-525
  NFS, 506-508
  Maestro, 509-514
  ftp, 514-520
  rlogin and telnet, 521-525
Networking commands, 208
  arp, 209
  ipconfig, 209-210
  netstat, 210-212
  ping, 212
newfs, 192-193
nice, 352-353

NTFS, 16-18, 110-112
  characteristics, 20-21, 114

O

opt, 42, 43, 44, 148, 312

P

Partition capacity
  NTFS, 17
Partition during Windows NT setup, 15
Partition size
  FAT, 19
  NTFS, 17
Performance Monitor (Windows NT),
    377-388
  Charting 377-384
  Alerts, 384-385
  Logging, 386-388
Peripherals, 90
POSIX Utilities, 545-
  cat, 547-548
  chmod, 549-550
  cp, 551
  find, 552
  grep, 553
  ls, 554-557
  mkdir, 558
  mv, 559
  rm, 560
  touch, 561
  wc, 562
Physical volume commands,
  pvchange, 181-182
  pvcreate, 182
  pvdisplay, 182-184
  pvmove, 184
Primary domain controller, 23, 24
ps, 352, 407-409

R

RAS, 25
rc0.d, 100
rc1.d, 100
rc.config.d, 99
rcp, 148
regedit, 125-126
Registry, 261-266
rmt, 92
Root (/), 146-147

S

sar, 414-415
sbin, 99, 101, 148
SCSI, 52
Security
  FAT, 19
  NTFS, 17
Series 700, 49-59
  booting, 50, 51, 56
Series 800, 59-69
  booting, 60, 61, 66
set_parms, 57, 58, 67, 68
Setup boot disk, 7
Setup flowchart
  HP-UX, 43
  Windows NT, 2-4
Setup floppies, 5-6
Setup options, 11
showmount, 410
shutdown, 105-107
Software distributor, 69-84
stand, 149, 318
Standalone Windows NT, 23
Startup and shutdown (HPUX), 99-107
swapinfo, 412-414
swinstall, 55, 65
sysdef, 85
System Administration Manager (SAM)
  Running, 269-275
    Accounts for Users and Groups, 277-
      289
    Auditing and Security, 289-296

Backup and Recovery, 296-306
Disks and File Systems, 306-313
Kernel Configuration, 313-320
Networking and Communications, 321-332
Peripheral Devices, 332-340
Printers and Plotters, 341-346
Process Management, 346-357
Routine Tasks, 357-365
Run SAM on Remote Systems, 365-366
Software Management, 366-372
NFS Diskless Concepts, 372-374
Enware X-station Admin, 374-375
system_prep, 87

T

TCP/IP, 26
background, 27-34
Text-based portion of setup, 9-22
tmp, 149

U

usr, 41, 44, 149, 312
/usr/bin, 149
/usr/ccs, 149
/usr/conf, 149
/usr/contrib, 149
/usr/include, 149
/usr/lib, 149
/usr/newconfig, 150
/usr/old, 150
/usr/sbin, 150
/usr/share, 150
/usr/share/man, 150

V

var, 45, 150, 312
/var/adm, 150
/var/adm/crash, 150
/var/adm/sw, 150
/var/mail, 151
/var/opt, 151
/var/spool, 151
vmstat, 350-352, 399-401
vmunix - see kernel
Volume group commands
vgcfgbackup, 184
vgcfgrestore, 184-185
vgchange, 185
vgcreate, 185
vgdisplay, 185-186
vgexport, 186
vgextend, 186
vgimport, 186
vgreduce, 186
vgremove, 186
vgscan, 186
vgsync, 186

W

Windows messaging, 23
Windows NT disk administrator, 158-170
Creating a partition, 163-168
Repair disk, 169-170
Volume properties, 161-163
Windows NT disk management, 156
Physical drive, 156
Partitions, 156
Primary partition, 156-157
Extended partition, 157
Logical drive, 157
Volume set, 157
Mirror set, 157
Stripe set, 158
Windows NT Explorer, 115-131
Attributes, 120
Permissions, 123
Change, 124
Full control, 124
No access, 124
Read, 124

Properties, 117
Security, 121-122
Auditing, 127-131
Windows NT Resource Kit, 195
Windows NT User Environment, 435-454
Start, 439
Explorer, 440-450
Task Manager, 450-454
winnt32, 5-7

X

X client, 4
X Windows, 459
interoperability, 493-504
dtterm, 499-501
xterm, 501-502